THE HEROIN SOLUTION

THE
HEROIN
SOLUTION

ARNOLD S. TREBACH

YALE UNIVERSITY PRESS
NEW HAVEN AND LONDON

Published with assistance from the Kingsley Trust Association
Publication Fund established by the Scroll and Key Society
of Yale College.

Designed by Sally Harris
and set in Galliard type by
Graphic Composition, Inc., Athens, Georgia.
Printed in the United States of America by
Vail-Ballou Press, Binghamton, N.Y.

Library of Congress Cataloging in Publication Data

Trebach, Arnold S.
    The heroin solution.

    Includes bibliographical references and index.
    1. Heroin habit—Government policy—United
States. 2. Heroin habit—Government policy—
Great Britain. 3. Heroin—Therapeutic use.
I. Title. [DNLM: 1. Diacetylmorphine—Therapeutic
use. 2. Heroin dependence—Prevention and control.
QV 92 T784h]
HV5822.H4T73   362.2'93561'0973   81–15993
ISBN 0–300–02773–7   AACR2
ISBN 0–300–02781–8 (pbk.)

10 9 8 7 6 5 4 3 2 1

FOR SHIRLEY

CONTENTS

Preface and Acknowledgments   ix

1. *The Enigmatic Epidemic*   1
2. *Living until Death*   22
3. *Advent, Canonization, Demonization*   37
4. *Medical Value: The Modern Evidence*   59
5. *The Rolleston Era in Britain*   85
6. *The Harrison–Anslinger Era in America*   118
7. *Doubt and Uncertainty: Britain Today*   171
8. *Modern America: Something Is Wrong*   226
9. *A Practical Vision for the Future*   267

Notes   297
Index   321

PREFACE AND ACKNOWLEDGMENTS

Heroin is an enigma because this relatively simple chemical seems to produce so much harm and yet is capable of doing so much good. The solution to that enigma must start with the realization that there can be no total, unconditional old-fashioned American-style victory in a War on Heroin. Nor, on the other hand, need we conclude that no solution is possible.

We must fashion middle-level solutions aimed at creating a social balance between complete repression of this drug and allowance of its use in certain circumstances. That balance in the ultimate sense is impossible because the factors affecting it keep shifting—*but the rational and humane pursuit of that impossible balance is what constitutes the main element of the heroin solution*. The balance cannot be achieved in a mechanistic manner, like building a bridge, or in a purely scientific fashion, like creating a new drug. It can be pursued only by using human relations skills in combination with a knowledge of history, medicine, and law.

The purpose of this book is to explain the factors that must go into the pursuit of that impossible balance. Once they are understood, each community—indeed, each country—now afflicted with widespread heroin abuse might be better able to fashion its *own* solution. But once a community or a whole country has come up with new medical, legal, and social arrangements regarding heroin—and perhaps, in the process, other drugs—it must understand that it has not effected a complete solution. And never will.

It is like a marriage. Medical science may pronounce the parties healthy; the law may pronounce them united; the clergy may declare their union sanctified in the eyes of God. But that marriage can survive only if the couple maintains the human balance in their relationship, a balance that is scientifically unexplainable, never stable, always unattainable, but vital to pursue. That is the essence of social policy toward all addicting drugs, but in particular, heroin, perhaps the most troublesome drug in the world.

As a medicine, heroin* deserves another chance. But this does not mean that we should give it to anyone who wants it. Total decriminalization of heroin use

---

* The substance is referred to by three names throughout this book: "heroin" and the more scientific "diacetylmorphine" and "diamorphine." In part this was due to considerations of style—I simply did not want to keep writing the same word in sentence after sentence. But the periodic rotation in names is also part of my campaign to start treating the chemical not simply as an evil drug but also as a medicine. The scientific names are helpful symbols in that effort.

would be as destructive as the present condition of almost total prohibition. Like all medicines, heroin has positive purposes only for some people, at some times, under some conditions.

My main message is overwhelmingly hopeful for those suffering from pain, for those addicted to heroin and other opiates,* such as morphine and methadone, and for a world suddenly confronted with a virulent epidemic of heroin abuse. The problem of heroin addiction seems one of the most eminently solvable of all those I have studied. But we must look back at history and across the oceans for the beginning of new solutions, which have their roots in the old.

The issues raised by contemplation of heroin's appropriate place in society go far beyond medicine or pharmacy or law. They reach into many of the fundamental problems of morals, of ethics, and of the manner in which we nurture our civilization.

The proper study of drugs and social policy operates like the drill of the exploring geologist. By thrusting deeply at one rather narrow spot, the drill brings up samples of the various strata of rock that allow for intelligent projections about the conditions of the earth for miles around. A society's drug policy provides telling clues about how that society is coping, not simply with drug issues but also with such problems as poverty, race relations, and political conflicts.

My perspective and my undertaking to write this book have been influenced by the fact that my first wife, Shirley, died of cancer. She entered the hospital of the National Cancer Institute, a part of the National Institutes of Health in Bethesda, Maryland, in late August, 1976. On October 7, 1976, she died there. Her last seven weeks taught me many things. One of the most important was that people who are dying are still alive and in certain fundamental ways are very much like the rest of us, for we will be dying at some point and are now still alive. This may sound simpleminded, but it helped me to understand the process in which I and my two teenaged sons, Paul and David, were participating. Shirley needed what she *always* had needed from us: our love, our care, and

---

* The word *opiates* is used here to refer to the family of drugs related to, or bearing some similarity to, the natural substance opium. Opium is the dried juice of the unripe capsule of the opium poppy, *Papaver somniferum*. Morphine is the chief active ingredient in opium; codeine is another natural, but weaker, derivative. Heroin is considered a semisynthetic member of the family, being produced by heating morphine with acetic anhydride. Wholly synthetic members of the family include methadone (Dolophine) and meperidine (Demerol). In this book the term *narcotics* is usually interchangeable with *opiates*. These terminological ground rules are necessary because neither medical nor legal science is consistent or logical in its use of the terms.

our time; that is what we all need from one another. But then Shirley needed it in more concentrated doses and in a form suitable to her condition and stage in life.

Logically, I should now continue with a horror story about Shirley's treatment at the hands of the bureaucratic doctors in that big red building in Bethesda. But, save for some temporary annoyances, there is no such story to tell. The doctors and nurses at NCI were kind and compassionate. They cared. They seemed to welcome my form of caring, my advocacy, my persistent questions.

Heroin would not have made the slightest bit of difference to Shirley as far as I could tell. Conventional drugs seemed to control most of her pain. Even if heroin had been legal, I do not believe she would have agreed to take it, had the choice been put to her. She had told me months earlier that she feared its addictive potential. The point is not the need for heroin in Shirley's case but that she had loving care appropriate to her needs.

The message I wish to convey, then, in regard to all those who face the anguish of a painful terminal illness is the need for loving and humane care, not for a particular superdrug. But in some cases that care *must* involve resort to that medicine—and in those cases I submit that we must be prepared to do legal and ethical battle with the law preventing any doctor or patient from choosing it.

It is not my intention to exalt heroin into some kind of chemical superstar. However, if we can better understand how society has reacted to this drug, we may be able to evolve more rational responses to all psychoactive substances, those affecting both body and mind, and to the people who use them. As Edward Brecher wrote in 1972, "The relentless campaign to suppress heroin . . . has been more prolonged and more intensive than the campaign waged against any other drug. That campaign has failed. Until society recognizes and accepts the reasons for that failure, it can hardly formulate sound laws and policies with respect to any drug. Further, attitudes toward heroin, the most hated and most dreaded drug of all, subtly tinge popular attitudes toward other illicit drugs."[1]

While this book seeks, among other things, to rehabilitate a powerful drug, in broad philosophical terms my ideal is a drug-free society. I am a disciple of Dr. Andrew Weil, who believes that human beings seek altered states of consciousness through every conceivable means.[2] Drugs are only one way of attaining that altered state of consciousness, and a relatively inferior one. It would be infinitely better for human beings if they could reach into their own souls— through meditation or prayer—for strength, joy, comfort, for coping with the disappointments and frustrations of human existence. But for many people this does not seem to be possible. Indeed, in statistical terms, the non-drug-takers are the deviants. Most people take some type of drug fairly regularly.

In the category of "drugs" I include all mind-altering substances whether legal or not—alcohol, tobacco, and coffee together with Valium, Librium, and barbiturates, and all of these with marijuana and heroin. I would argue that no one who uses any of the legal drugs regularly has the right to feel significantly superior to someone dependent on illegal drugs. I do not see in any drug, legal or illegal, the salvation of human beings on this planet. At the same time, I am not a critic of those who do because I believe that the decision to use drugs or abstain from them is personal, like the choice of religion or atheism.

My own study of heroin started with no particular ideology about drugs. In the early 1970s I was looking into national crime-control strategies by comparing the rhetoric of the politicians with national budget reports. My theory was that although high-ranking officials of the Nixon administration were then *talking* about a "war on crime," the budget would tell if they were, in street terms, putting their money where their mouth was. To my surprise, I found that they were. To my even greater surprise, most of the drug abuse money was devoted to treatment and prevention, not to law enforcement.[3]

Heroin figured prominently not only in the public pronouncements of the Nixon strategists but also in their monetary commitments. This discovery piqued my interest. I soon realized that a better understanding of heroin, and of the myths and distortions and facts and realities about it, was essential to anyone concerned about public peace and individual security in America. I also found out that not only America was directly involved.

Heroin is a prohibited medicine in virtually the entire world. This situation came about primarily because in the 1920s the American medical and law-enforcement professions became convinced that the drug was simply too addicting to be used in medical practice. But the prohibitory laws did not make heroin abuse disappear in America; in fact, it has increased continuously since the manufacture of heroin was virtually banned in 1924. Heroin dependence soon came to be known as the "American disease." By the 1970s the American disease had taken on the dimensions of a worldwide epidemic. Heroin is still prohibited in legitimate medical practice in almost every country; yet the illegitimate use of the drug may well be at its zenith throughout the world.

Why? What should we do about it? What is the solution to this hurtful problem? To attempt to answer these questions is to confront the enigma of heroin. In this book I attempt to explain, as best I can, the many threads which are woven into the multicolored fabric of this enigma and to suggest options for unraveling some of them.

The development of a heroin solution is a humbling and complex task. Simplistic analyses and remedies often are espoused when "experts" review the histories of the United States and Britain, the two countries with the longest and most sophisticated experience with the heroin problem. This is particularly common when scholars and officials look at the legitimate use of heroin in England, where doctors have always been allowed to prescribe it for the organically ill as well as for the addicted. England also has comparatively few heroin addicts.

Adopt the English system, some therefore argue, and the world can solve the heroin enigma and stop the epidemic in its tracks. This may or may not be true. However, the more closely one looks at the English experience, the more difficult it is to discover what the British system is—or whether there is a system at all. Even more difficult to find is an English expert prepared to recommend that any feature of the British approach to narcotic control be exported to any other country, particularly the United States.

My discussions since 1974 with some of the leading British figures in addiction treatment and control have demonstrated to me how troubled and divided *they* are about what is happening in their own country regarding heroin use and abuse. It seems that the enigma presented by heroin to modern societies is fully present, with all its confusing convolutions of fact and myth, in England as in other countries.

Within the past two decades, several significant books have been based in part or in whole on an examination of the British experience with hard drug abuse and its implications for America: Edwin M. Schur's *Narcotic Addiction in Britain and America* (1962); Alfred R. Lindesmith's *The Addict and the Law* (1965); Rufus King's *The Drug Hang-up* (1972); Edward Brecher's *Licit and Illicit Drugs* (1972); and Horace Freeland Judson's *Heroin Addiction in Britain* (1974).[4] The subtitle of the Judson book is "What Americans Can Learn from the English Experience." I have been educated by Mr. Judson (as well as by the other writers) and impelled by my own experiences in both countries to broaden my focus and to inquire what Britons and Americans can learn from one another—and what the rest of the world can learn from them both.

This is, I believe, the first modern book which attempts to combine the story of heroin in ordinary medicine—that is, in the treatment of the organically ill or the injured—with the related and more familiar story of its use in the addiction arena, whether by addicts or by the doctors treating them. It provides, moreover, a fairly comprehensive comparative account of the heroin experiences of both Britain and America, a task others have performed but usually with the emphasis on one country or the other. I have attempted to pay roughly equal attention to the facts on both countries. Finally, this is not a standard libertarian tract that points to the British system, unvarnished and unchanged, as *the* heroin solution. It extols the great strengths and relative superiority of English approaches but also criticizes the current operation of British drug-dependence clinics and suggests reforms that apply not only to America but also to Britain and to many other countries.

The book brings the situation in England and America up to August 1981. Unless otherwise noted, I have not dealt with events after that time.

The idea for the book grew out of my work as director of the Institute on Drugs, Crime, and Justice in England, which I founded in 1974. This institute, now offered every other summer through the School of Justice of the American University, provides an opportunity for professionals and students to observe British approaches to narcotics and justice at first hand. Most participants have been Americans, although some have come from other countries.

I am most indebted to the participants and faculty of the institute. The participants provided fine company and searching questions. The faculty, for its part, responded to the demands of the participants with an immense display of knowledge and good humor. For their assistance in setting up the first institute and for their guidance in the intervening years, I am particularly indebted to His Honour Judge Eric Stockdale, Circuit Judge, London, and to his wife, Joan, both of whom have functioned as guardian angels for institute staff and participants; to Dr. Martin Mitcheson, director of the Drug Dependence Clinic, University College Hospital, London; and to J. E. Hall Williams, London School of Economics and Political Science. My colleague Nicholas N. Kittrie both inspired me to start the London institute—primarily by way of example, since he had set up an earlier one in Jerusalem through the American University Law School—and advised me on the organization of the initial session in 1974.

Gil Martin provided sensitive assistance for many visiting Americans over a period of years in his capacity as the resident coordinator of the institute. His wife, Dean Rhea Martin, of the Division of Social Science, the Hatfield Polytechnic, Welwyn Garden City, not only provided the same kind of gracious assistance but has also appeared as a guest lecturer every year. The "dean" of official English drug-abuse experts, H. B. Spear, Chief Inspector, Drugs Branch, Home Office, has demonstrated his grasp of the big picture as well as of minute details during his annual appearances before the institute and in responding to requests for information. Drs. Terence and Penelope Morris provided the expert advice English criminologists often give visiting colleagues, and also gave, in gracious good measure, personal support for the institute director. Dr. Allison Morris, of Cambridge's Institute of Criminology, demonstrated that enviable British-Scottish talent of knowing much about America and the United Kingdom in all their divisible parts, especially comparative crime statistics.

Sincere thanks are also due those who read portions of this manuscript and offered encouragement, including particularly Professor Edward Sagarin, of the City University of New York; Nicholas Kittrie; Professor Alfred R. Lindesmith, of the University of Indiana; Dean Richard A. Myren, of the American University School of Justice; H. B. Spear; Sir Leon Radzinowicz, of Cambridge University; Dr. Dale Beckett, of the Cane Hill Hospital, Coulsdon, Surrey; Dr. Robert Twycross, of the Churchill Hospital, Oxford; Solicitor Bernard Simons, of the London firm of Simons, Muirhead, and Allen; and Randy Cox, of the Metropolitan Clinic of Counseling, Minneapolis.

Thomas W. Fogle, my former graduate assistant at the School of Justice, provided extensive research and editorial support, as did graduate assistants Randolph Wallace, James Gagel, Ellen Mowbray, Michael Elsner, Suzanne Agness, Kim Fischer, and Michael Bryant. Myra C. Weinstein, a graduate student and the 1977–78 coordinator of the Institute on Drugs, Crime, and Justice in England, shared with me the insights of her research. Jane F. Huntington and Lyn Richmond provided helpful editorial assistance. Cathy Sacks, Mary J. Mols, Ann Critzer, and Joanne Flynn, of the School of Justice, gave much-needed clerical and secretarial support during various stages of the writing. Mort Goren, Edith Crutchfield, and Lavonne Wienke responded graciously to numerous requests for obscure items lodged in the Drug Enforcement Administration library, where they work. The College of Public and International Affairs of the American University, through its deans, Lee Fritschler, Robert Boynton, Robert Cleary, and Assistant Dean Richard L. Apperson, assisted me with grants to partially defray clerical expenses.

Gladys Topkis, my editor at the Yale University Press, and Sharon Slodki, the copyeditor, helped me at every step of the publishing effort to turn a manuscript into a book. Their patience and attendance to detail were remarkable, and their advice, wise and supportive.

My wife, Marjorie A. Rosner, read every word of this manuscript, criticized many, typed all of them, some two or three times, and through it all maintained her good humor. Her support gave me the determination to go on during critical stages of this project; only she can know how vital that encouragement was at the time.

Arnold S. Trebach
August 1981

1: THE ENIGMATIC EPIDEMIC

"What was once the 'American Disease' has become a worldwide affliction. Heroin addiction has become a major problem in a dozen new countries, with the number of addicts continuing to increase by several thousand every month. Not only are those who are becoming addicted for the most part the children of the social and intellectual elite of these countries, but the massive amounts of money now involved in trafficking have corrupted many high level officials and undermined already unstable economies."—Peter G. Bourne, 1976[1]

I

When candidate Jimmy Carter's chief advisor on health and drug policy wrote those words in the midst of the 1976 presidential campaign, one might have been forgiven for thinking that they contained a bit of political hyperbole. The years that have passed since that time have shown, sadly enough, that Dr. Bourne's remarks understated the dimensions of the problem. The number of new addicts in the world every month is becoming enormous, unknown to be sure, but certainly more than "several thousand." In any event, there is no doubt that heroin addiction has become, as Dr. Bourne said, a worldwide affliction.

No one knows why the recreational use of hard drugs, especially heroin, is spreading so rapidly. One factor, however, must be the development of efficient jet-age travel. The globe has shrunk; no country is truly far away from any other. A small fortune in heroin can fit in a space the size of a pack of cigarettes, which any one of a million airplane travelers might be carrying past customs through any international airport.

Apart from technology there is the irrational fact that the habits and styles of America, however hostile other countries might be to its governmental policies or leaders, are imitated throughout the world. Blue jeans and rock music and Coca-Cola are to be found everywhere. It is possible that the American heroin habit found in so many countries is part of this same mysterious phenomenon of imitation.

The formulation of solutions to the heroin problem is confounded by the fact that some leading American thinkers have gone to great pains to document that the heroin problem in America really does not exist, at least not in dimensions worth getting bothered about, and that the very emphasis on heroin in enforcement and treatment programs arises either from ignorance or from a shoddy desire to manipulate the public for purely political ends. Grave doubts about the war on drugs of the Nixon administration were expressed, for example, in "A Statement of Concerns" by the 1972–73 fellows of the Drug Abuse Council, a prestigious private study group then operating in Washington. That statement objected to the simplification of the drug problem in America by its portrayal as "essentially a *heroin* problem." The fellows went on to point out that many other drugs are more commonly used and abused, that the impact of heroin on crime is often hysterically overstated, and that there may be greater danger to American society and human rights from anti-heroin programs spawned by the government than from heroin addiction itself.[2]

These themes have been developed and magnified by political scientist and investigative reporter Edward Jay Epstein, who has also been a fellow of the Drug Abuse Council. In his book *Agency of Fear: Opiates and Political Power in America* (1977), Mr. Epstein attempted to make the case that the American heroin epidemic of the early 1970s simply did not exist but was manufactured by the Nixon administration. The purpose of this manufactured epidemic was not simply to win reelection for President Nixon but, according to the dust jacket blurb, to "attempt to subvert the American system through a kind of *coup d'état.*"[3] It is difficult to determine the exact nature of that *coup d'état*. However, it is clear that the evil strategy, whatever it was, rested on the creation of a heroin epidemic.

Some highly respected voices have expressed agreement with the major thrust of the Epstein thesis. Charles E. Silberman, for example, in his widely acclaimed book *Criminal Violence, Criminal Justice* (1978), made it clear that he accepted the manufactured-epidemic theory: the tenfold growth in addiction from the late 1960s to the early 1970s was a statistical artifact purposely created by the Bureau of Narcotics and Dangerous Drugs (BNDD), the immediate bureaucratic ancestor of the Drug Enforcement Administration (DEA). Silberman wrote: "What happened, as discovered by Edward Jay Epstein, a political scientist-turned-investigative reporter, was that the BNDD applied a new formula to the old 1969 data. . . . From beginning to end, as Epstein has documented in great detail, the crusade against heroin was nothing but a cynical public relations device to create the illusion that the Nixon administration was cracking down on crime."[4]

Many criminologists concentrate their critical fire not so much on the "questionable" recent growth of the heroin addict population but rather on the commonly accepted idea that the onset of heroin addiction results in a sudden increase in related crime. No, they argue, more often there is preaddictive criminality; the abuse of heroin does not cause crime but rather is part of an overall pattern of deviance. Thus, the experts differ not only as to whether a serious heroin problem really exists in America but also as to whether increasing numbers of heroin addicts may create significantly more criminal behavior.

If I had agreed with these arguments, I would not have written this book. After reviewing all the available facts, I have concluded that (1) there has been a major increase in the level of heroin addiction in America starting in the 1960s; (2) there has been a corresponding and perhaps more recent rise in heroin addiction in many other countries; and (3) these rapid increases in addiction almost always seem to be accompanied by major increases in crime, often of a violent nature, committed by addicts. The support for these threshold assumptions is to be found throughout this book.

It is impossible to determine the exact number of addicts or the exact amount of crime they commit. Yet, I have seen enough information from a wide variety of sources to believe that the rises in addiction and crime have been extremely serious. For my purposes, I am not terribly concerned with determining the precise number of addicts or the precise number of crimes they commit. My approach would not change even if it turned out that there were approximately the same number of heroin addicts in the 1960s as in the 1970s —so long as it was also accepted that the number was large and that many of the addicts constituted a major social threat. I do not seek, moreover, to defend the Nixon administration against the charge that it used the heroin issue for political ends; it apparently did do so. But all this does not change the underlying reality of the persistent, serious, and spreading problem of heroin abuse.[5]

II

I will not argue the contrary proposition to the Epstein-Silberman line: that heroin presents *the most* serious drug-crime problem in the world. It may, but no one can prove it. Indeed, it is my conviction that the most serious American drug-crime problem is due to alcohol abuse. There may be 10 million alcoholics in America alone. It has been estimated that there are now approximately five hundred thousand heroin addicts or regular users, plus as many as 3.5 million "chippers," or occasional users, in this country. The criminogenic impact of alcohol in America is stunning, since the presence of an alcohol factor—addiction or significant abuse—has been found in many serious crimes. The number of people killed in alcohol-related traffic accidents each year usually exceeds by far the number of homicides (most of which are probably alcohol-related themselves) listed in the FBI Uniform Crime Reports. In 1978 there were 19,555 homicides—but an estimated 25,000 alcohol-related traffic deaths.[6]

People under the influence of alcohol tend to commit crimes, often of a violent nature, at a much higher rate than those who are sober. People who have recently ingested heroin are usually among our meekest, most civilized citizens; lambs, even pussycats. This contrast in behavior has been noted by observers who have seen firsthand the actions of both types of consumers, those who drink alcohol and those who take opiates. In 1889, for example, Dr. J. R. Black wrote in the *Cincinnati Lancet-Clinic* that morphine "is less inimical to healthy life than alcohol" because it "calms in place of exciting the baser passions, and hence is less productive of acts of violence and crime; in short . . . the use of morphine in place of alcohol is but a choice of evils, and by far the lesser."[7] Heroin-influenced people who are affluent often are not a social problem because the presence of the chemical in the body usually does not cause excitement of the "baser passions." Such people are generally invisible and unseen, in contrast to *poor* heroin addicts, who commit crimes to obtain funds so that they may buy drugs denied them by the law. People under the influence of alcohol, of any class or social standing, are frequently a serious threat to those they love and to those they hate, especially when they are behind the wheel of a car or under the lash of the tongue of a critical relative or friend. In such circumstances, the meek may turn into murderers.

In light of these facts about alcohol—as well as real concerns about other drugs, especially cocaine, the barbiturates, and marijuana—why devote a whole book to heroin? There are a number of reasons. If I had some sensible suggestions about national alcohol policy, this book would deal with that drug, but I do not. Nor am I prepared to recommend, as I am in the case of heroin, that where no other alternative presents itself "maintenance" doses of alcohol be prescribed for addicts. Alcohol destroys human organs; heroin does not, whatever its other doleful effects are.

In my eyes, the alcohol problem appears infinitely less tractable than the heroin problem, since rivers of alcohol are consumed legally and illegally by all classes of people in America, Britain, and elsewhere every day. But by making some changes in policy and treatment strategies it is possible to anticipate major advances in the control of heroin abuse and related crime within the foreseeable future—to devise a rational heroin solution. Nothing I have read or seen about alcohol policy or treatment leads me to believe that such gains are likely in the case of alcohol, which most Americans do not even consider a drug.

My review of alcohol policy in America and elsewhere reveals no laboratory-like comparisons in which one country may be shown to be doing remarkably better than another. All Western countries seem to be failing to control the ravages of this widely available drug. The same appears to be true of Communist-bloc nations. Thus, I cannot suggest that we learn from, for example, the British alcohol policy. However, a comparison of Britain and America regarding narcotic policy does produce some revealing contrasts between two countries so much alike in so many respects. As Judson observed in *Heroin Addiction in Britain*, "Social policies find few laboratories, even metaphorically, to test them: when a major social problem has been attacked in two countries from two almost opposite approaches—as the problem of narcotics addiction has been attacked in Great Britain and the United States—a comparison of the results ought to be instructive."[8]

The social costs—deaths, stolen goods, law-enforcement and treatment expenses—of all drug abuse are huge. In 1975 a White House task force came up with a conservative annual figure of $10–17 billion.[9] During the next year, Dr. Robert L. DuPont, then director of the National Institute on Drug Abuse (NIDA), explained why his agency had just put out a study that amassed all available trend data on only one drug: "We have focused initially on heroin use rates because heroin use appears to be responsible for over 70 percent of the identified social cost of all illicit drug use in the United States today."[10] One might calculate from these two reports that the cost of heroin abuse to American society in the mid-1970s ranged from $7 to $11.9 billion every year. But like the census of addicts, the precise dollar amounts are impossible to know and truly not necessary, as long as it is acknowledged that the dimensions are huge and unacceptable. Such costs should spur both analysis and action toward solutions.

Finally, heroin has been so vastly misunderstood in America and elsewhere that the drug itself deserves searching, rational attention. During the past seventy years the official American view of heroin (and to a lesser extent, of opium) has been that it is evil incarnate. American officials, clergymen, and prominent private citizens have led the international campaign for treaties and conventions to control narcotic drugs, especially heroin and opium. They have succeeded all too well. It is time for America and the world to rediscover heroin the medicine, to acknowledge that heroin, like all medicines, is capable of abuse and, like most narcotics, may be addicting. But once we have acknowledged its abuse potential, a more positive mind-set would allow us to acknowledge how heroin might benefit many patients—those suffering from such ailments as cancer, heart disease, shingles, burns, and even from addiction itself. If at least one aspect of heroin were thus to be considered a helper, a medicine, then the discussion of new policies might proceed along more rational lines. Unless we exorcise the devil in heroin, however, neither the dialogue nor the resultant policies can be fully rational—for one does not deal with a devil in rational ways.

III

While, as we have seen, some commentators have doubted the very existence of a major heroin-addiction problem, the more common assumptions in recent decades have been that the United States is the world's center of heroin abuse, that various countries of the Far and Middle East produce the raw material, and that manufacturing and trafficking often go on under various European auspices. For some reason, heroin did not seem to be used to any great extent in those countries involved in production, manufacturing, and trafficking. If there was widespread use of opiates in any of those countries, it was usually opium smoking, which often was neither illegal nor considered a problem. It was, rather, ingrained in the culture and accepted as an integral part of life from generation to generation. But in recent years great changes have begun to be discerned in these international patterns.

Unfortunately, there are no reliable official international compilations on the extent of drug abuse. However, a unique international survey was published in 1977 by three experts who had obtained information, based on a uniform design reflecting the situation in 1975, from research scientists and physicians in twenty-five countries.[11] As is usually the case, there was a variance between the reports provided by local experts for this survey and estimates by still other experts regarding such facts as the precise number of opiate addicts in each country; however, nothing in the report was inconsistent, *in terms of broad trends*, with other reports I have reviewed.

As of 1975, the country with the largest estimated number of opiate addicts in the general population was the United States with 620,000, followed by Iran with 400,000, Thailand with 350,000, Hong Kong with 80,000, Canada with 18,000, Singapore with 13,000, Australia with 12,500, Italy with 10,000, and the United Kingdom with 6,000. The principal opiate of abuse in Iran and Singapore was listed as opium itself, but in the seven other leading countries it was heroin. The remaining countries in the sample of twenty-five reported minor opiate-abuse problems at the time.

The directors of the survey—Drs. John C. Ball and Harold Graff, of the Department of Psychiatry, Temple University, and Jean Paul Smith of NIDA—concluded, "One of the major findings to emerge from the present study is the contemporary increase and spread of heroin dependency throughout most of the nations surveyed. . . . The predominance of heroin abuse is even more marked than this tabulation indicates, as traditional patterns of morphine and opium use are shifting to heroin; this shift is especially notable in Europe and Asia for morphine and opium respectively." Even on the basis of this valuable survey, however, it is impossible to determine with any degree of certainty the number of heroin addicts in the world, or even in the twenty-five countries covered. However, the observations of the drug-abuse specialists who designed the study and wrote the individual reports provide more evidence that the number of heroin addicts is increasing dramatically throughout the world. My estimate for the world—and it is only a guess based on scattered pieces of data—is that there are at least two million heroin addicts and perhaps as many as four million.

Because America has been viewed for so many years as the nation with the answers to modern problems, many countries are looking to the United States for answers on how to cope with the heroin epidemic. Sadly, many countries seem to be learning only the harsh aspects of American drug-abuse history—prohibition, law enforcement, punishment—and ignoring the more humane features of the history of the treatment of drug addicts in this country. Even more distressing to me, the lessons to be learned from the other major model of drug-abuse control—Great Britain, with its generally more caring society—are almost totally ignored elsewhere. Thus, much of the world seems intent on repeating those chapters of American drug-abuse history that deserve only to be quickly learned, then just as quickly rejected.

We can appreciate this phenomenon by looking more closely at the spread of heroin addiction and its attendant agonies into even the most remote corners of this small planet. To most Occidentals, Borneo is a mysterious, faraway tropical island that would seem to have nothing to do with a discourse on heroin and crime. But such is not the case. Located in the northern part of the island is the state of Sarawak, which in turn is part of a relatively new country, the Federation of Malaysia. The capital city of Sarawak is Kuching.

The *Borneo Bulletin* of April 29, 1978, carried a story in which Mr. Vincent Kho, First Division police chief in Kuching, reported that heroin addiction among the youth of the city had grown considerably in the last three years.

"Addicts short of money have been resorting to stealing, extortion, and other crimes to find the cash needed to buy their 'fixes,'" the *Bulletin* reported. The police chief stated that he wanted a rehabilitation center, which Sarawak lacked; moreover, "As with other senior lawmen, Mr. Kho says he is also anxiously awaiting the extension of the amended Dangerous Drugs Ordinance to Sarawak—which will mean the death sentence can be applied for drugs possession, as is the case in Peninsular Malaysia."[12]

That ordinance was applied in the prosecution of convicted heroin trafficker Hong Hoo Chong, 40, in Peninsular Malaysia in early December, 1979. Chong had been arrested by the police in 1978 with 1,550.1 grams of heroin in his possession. The Penang High Court, equivalent to the supreme court of a state or province, had imposed the penalty of life imprisonment as well as fourteen strokes of the *rotan*. In the first appeal ever brought by the government against a life sentence in a drugs case, the director of public prosecutions, Encik Mohamed Noor bin Haji Ahmad, pointed out to the federal court of appeals that the defendant was a convicted armed robber and burglar who had gone on to trafficking; the DPP then observed, "We should regard him as public enemy No. 1 who is a danger and menace to society and, therefore, the death sentence should be the only way to exterminate him from society." In rendering his decision, Chief Justice Raja Azlan Shah of the court of appeals lectured the trial judges of the country, telling them that they should not develop a phobia about inflicting the death penalty, because "the time has now come for some more vigorous element of deterrence to be brought upon those trafficking in drugs." Finding "no redeeming features" in Mr. Chong's case, the chief justice took the extraordinary step, supported by his colleagues on the court of appeals, of overturning the life term and imposing a sentence of death.[13]

Similar approaches have been used in neighboring Singapore, which also emerged from colonial status to independence in the 1960s. Singapore seems to have learned little from its former British rulers. As in England, there is a law labeled the Misuse of Drugs Act, but the resemblance seems to end there. In 1975 the Singapore law was amended to place the death penalty on the illicit manufacture of morphine or heroin and on trafficking half an ounce or more of these drugs. Corporal punishment in the form of whipping was brought back in 1973 as a mandatory sentence in several dozen crimes. In a supportive story on the new harsh discipline of the law, *Wall Street Journal* reporter Barry Newman wrote on July 6, 1977, "While some people here oppose beating and say it doesn't reduce crime, they are a definite minority and have little influence. So Singapore is flexing its 'rotan'—a thin rod of rattan that, when brought down hard against the buttocks, splits the skin, draws blood and scars for life." But a leading police official said he doubted that these new harsh measures had much effect on controlling heroin traffic or use. The director of the Central Narcotics Bureau in Singapore, John Hanam, observed, "On the contrary, heroin seems to be more widely used than ever before." Moreover, the treatment of known heroin addicts seems, in some cases, to be rather abrupt. Addicts are withdrawn "cold turkey" as a first step in treatment at the Telok Paku rehabilitation center. Home Affairs Minister Chua Sian said that the "suffering experienced by the addict in 'cold turkey' will long be remembered by that person. We hope it will deter him or her from ever going back to drugs." But while heroin abuse was virtually unknown in Singapore ten years ago, the worldwide heroin epidemic of recent history has reached there also. As late as 1973, only ten arrests in Singapore involved heroin; by 1975, 2,263. As of 1975 in Singapore there were an estimated 2,000 heroin addicts, 3,000–4,000 morphine addicts, and 7,000–8,000 opium smokers out of a population of 2,249,900. By March 1977 the number of heroin addicts was estimated at 13,000. Singapore has invoked the death penalty for drug trafficking five times between 1976 and early 1980. Three Malaysians and two Singaporeans have been hanged under this statute. One official described the generally harsh government response in this way: "The message to the heroin user was either opt out of drugs or opt out of society." By July 1979 there was some evidence that the epidemic was slowing down, but the problem of heroin addiction had not disappeared from the small city-nation.[14]

The pattern is similar throughout a large part of the world: increasing heroin addiction, destructive crime by addicts, and a social response that is dominated by the criminal sanction even though some treatment facilities are to be found in virtually every country affected by the epidemic. The capital of heroin addiction may no longer be New York but Bangkok. It has been estimated that 6 to 8 percent of that city's 6 million inhabitants are addicted to hard drugs. According to a Reuters story of August 23, 1978, Dr. Khachit Chupanya, director of drug rehabilitation in the city, estimated that there were 300,000–400,000 addicts there. "Most of them were addicted to heroin number four, the purest grade sold on the street," the report said. The story went on to explain that Dr. Khachit had earlier published a report saying that there were about half a million drug addicts in Thailand. If these estimates are anywhere near the truth, it is quite conceivable that Thailand, with its 41 million people (approximately 1 percent addicted), has a much worse heroin problem than the United States, which may have half a million heroin addicts and regular users out of a population of approximately 220 million (.23 percent addicted). The spectacle, moreover, of an opium-producing country with a major heroin-addiction problem is also part of the new reality in the world.[15]

The situation in the British Crown Colony of Hong Kong would seem to rival that in Thailand. By some standards, it is worse. In 1975 an estimated 80,000 to 100,000 addicts inhabited the crowded colony, whose total population is 4.3 million; thus, approximately 2 percent of the entire population were dependent on narcotics, perhaps the highest rate for any country in the world. Most of these addicts were smoking or sniffing the fumes of heroin-tipped cigarettes. However, data for 1978 generated by a new computerized Central Registry of Drug Addicts, established with help from NIDA, made Hong Kong officials a bit more optimistic. It appeared that the number of addicts might be in the range of 35,000–50,000. Even these lower figures caused Hong Kong officials deep concern.[16] Many more cities in the Far East have raging heroin-abuse problems. Moreover, U.S. territory in the region has not been immune. The island of Guam, a remote corner of this planet if there ever was one, has its own Drug Enforcement Administration post staffed by five special agents. The surprising nature of a major heroin-addiction problem in this bucolic and idyllic setting was described by Peter Rieff, the resident agent-in-charge of the DEA office there, in testimony before the Select Committee on Narcotics Abuse and Control, U.S. House of Representatives, which held a hearing in Guam on July 4, 1978.

Mr. Rieff explained that Guam, an unincorporated U.S. territory in the Mariana Islands, is 30 miles long and 4 to 8 miles wide with a total area of 209 square miles. As the crow flies, Guam is 3,700 miles west of Honolulu and 1,800 miles east of Hong Kong. There are approximately 110,000 people, of whom 22,000 are U.S. military personnel and their dependents.

"As late as 1968, even experienced police officers were unaware of the presence of drugs on Guam; it was not until 1970 that police became aware of the presence of hard drugs. Felony crimes during the 1968 to 1970 period were low and increased only minimally. During the early months of 1973, the drug abuse problem on Guam reached alarming proportions. The rise in crime from the two preceding years was unprecedented (up 34 per cent). Unfortunately, the Guamanian community at large was unaware of this burgeoning interrelated problem of crime and drugs." In 1977 it dawned on the community that Guam had an estimated 782 heroin addicts.

The DEA official then did some calculations: "If one were to consider the dollar amount each addict needed to maintain his habit, the daily market transaction would amount to $15,640 or $5,708,600 per year (782 × $20 × 365

= $5,708,600). Money spent to purchase heroin during 1977 represents an expenditure of $5,115 for each resident of the territory or 5.2 per cent of the total Government budget. It is estimated that there is one addict for every 143 people on Guam."

The heroin-addiction problem caused major public concern on this little Pacific island, with barely a mention in mainland newspapers. Nevertheless, as reported by the Select Committee on Narcotics Abuse and Control of the U.S. House of Representatives, "In April 1978, the governor found it necessary to declare a state of emergency on the Island. All departments and agencies were ordered to assist in the establishment and implementation of 'Operation Save a Life.' . . . The program was designed to meet the crisis needs of heroin abusers."[17]

Almost no part of the Pacific region seemed immune from the rapid increase in heroin abuse and its attendant problems. On July 13, 1979, Detective Chief Superintendent Mal Churches reported that the amount of heroin seized in New Zealand as well as the number of criminal charges made relating to heroin could double the 1978 figures. In the first six months of 1979, Mr. Churches stated, there had been 302 criminal charges involving heroin, compared to 303 for all of 1978. In the first six months of 1979, 1,752 grams had been seized by police and customs officers compared to 1,945 grams for all of 1978—insignificant by American standards but alarming to New Zealanders.[18]

Reports from neighboring Australia told a familiar story: major increases in heroin trafficking and abuse, related increases in the marijuana arena, allegations of police corruption, and recommendations by many officials, including the police, to get tough in the fight against drugs. A rare, frank glimpse into the mind of one Australian drug-enforcement official was provided in 1979 when the retired commander of the southern region of the Australian Bureau of Narcotics, Bernard Delaney, wrote a book about his experiences. Mr. Delaney claimed that drug law enforcement in Australia had been a miserable failure; that corruption in police forces, especially in New South Wales, was making it impossible to catch the "Mr. Bigs" of the illegal trade; that civil libertarians and "other do-gooders" were hindering the battle against drugs; and that politicians must approve the greater use of wiretapping and electronic surveillance in order to catch the pushers and the dealers. Mr. Delaney openly told how he had illegally tapped telephones in order to carry out drug investigations and criticized officials in the Posts and Telegraphs Department for attempting to stop him. He justified his actions by stating, "The only way Narcotics Bureau officers could succeed in their difficult area was by cheating the system."[19]

Typical of the new and difficult problems faced by the Australians—but almost traditional for Americans and becoming so for the people of many other countries—was a report in August 1979 by Melbourne police Detective Chief Inspector Paul Delianis, head of the homicide squad. He stated that two New Zealanders had recently been executed by a New Zealand-based syndicate that had just smuggled nearly a ton of 90-percent pure heroin into Australia. The value of the drugs was estimated at more than $45 million; once the heroin was cut and adulterated, the street value would, of course, increase many times beyond that figure. Thus, Australia is afflicted not only with increased heroin abuse and trafficking but also with the usual attendant violent criminal activity.[20]

Another familiar aspect of the Australian scene was a call to consider new approaches to treating drug addiction. Speaking in the Senate on August 28, 1979, the leader of the Australian Democratic Party, Senator Donald L. Chipp, asked for the "legalization" of heroin on a limited basis to help in the campaign against heroin abuse. He stated that he did not want to make the drug available for anyone to try. "But if there is a person who has been diagnosed as a heroin addict, why can't a medical practitioner prescribe heroin on a limited basis?" he asked.[21]

Western Europe is also experiencing a massive increase in heroin addiction. On January 9, 1977, the *Sunday Times* of London estimated that in 1971 there had been no more than 11,549 heroin addicts in Western Europe, including England; by 1976 the number might have reached as high as 108,000. By late 1978 the American DEA placed the number of heroin addicts in Western Europe at 200,000, with seizures by European police in 1976 and 1977 exceeding those in the United States. Heroin-related deaths reached 1,000 in Western Europe during 1978. If these figures are correct, and I must emphasize that they are only intelligent guesses from secondary data, then the rate of growth of heroin addiction in Western Europe has far outpaced that in the United States during the 1970s.

Health authorities in West Berlin estimated that the number of addicts rose from 2,000 in 1972 to approximately 20,000 in 1977, with 84 heroin overdose deaths in the city for that year. The number of heroin overdose deaths in West Germany reached 334 in 1976, and then increased to over 380 in 1977, during which years the United States recorded respectively 1,597 and 596 such fatalities. By 1978 the two countries were drawing even closer together on this unhappy statistic—430 heroin overdose deaths in West Germany and 471 in the United States.[22]

Reports from West Germany in 1979 indicated that the trends were worsening. Journalist Hartmut Palmer wrote on May 4, 1979, in the *Sueddeutsche*

Zeitung of Munich, that only "bad news" was to be found in the latest reports from the "drug commissioners" of the Laender—German states or provinces—because these reports revealed "that the efforts made until now by state and private institutions have not succeeded in banishing the danger, in stopping the trend, and much less in reversing it. In the past 6 months, especially for young people, susceptibility to the so-called 'hard drugs' seems to have increased alarmingly. According to the estimates of the drug commissioners, the 'hard core' of chronic users has increased from 40,000 to between 44,000 and 46,000." The West Germans also were facing familiar conflicts over philosophy and policy. Palmer wrote: "In all Laender—no matter of what political color its government—there exists an almost traditional conflict of objectives between local authorities in charge of police and crime control on the one hand, and health and welfare authorities on the other hand. The first see repressive control of drug abuse as the most pressing task; for the others, therapeutic, preventive measures are the most pressing. Both claims are [well] founded, but they are difficult to reconcile."[23] There is some evidence, however, that the tilt in Germany, as in so many other countries, is in the direction of "repressive control."

The West German minister of the interior, Gerhart Baum, stated, according to a report in the September 1, 1979, issue of *Die Welt* of Bonn: "As far as I am concerned, the fight against the international narcotic trade has the same priority as the fight against terrorism. We are therefore intent on exhausting every possibility in the police sector. . . ." Baum went on to explain that a new national system of narcotic information, in cooperation with Laender narcotic offices, would be created; new techniques of police surveillance and investigation would be inaugurated; and, he hoped, the legislature would follow his request for harsher criminal penalties for narcotic trafficking. While thus emphasizing the typical law-enforcement approach to the narcotic problem, Interior Minister Baum also stated that he placed a high priority on the demand side of the equation—on the treatment of drug abusers. At the same time, he said that treatment facilities seemed inadequate to meet the increasingly heavy need. Of particular concern to Baum was the possibility that an American-style drug scene was growing on West German soil, for not only was heroin abuse increasing rapidly but also South American cocaine was starting to appear.[24]

Preliminary reports for 1979 show that the heroin overdose deaths in Germany, approximately 611, might have exceeded those in the United States, approximately 566.* Germany, moreover, with 61 million people, has only one quarter the population of the United States. If these figures are accurate, they

* By this point it should be clear that I am unable to use most statistics in the drug-abuse field with any degree of confidence. I believe they can be used only to show broad trends, not precise comparisons. See chap. 1, n. 25, below.

are of stunning historical significance because this would represent the first time that any country had recorded more heroin overdose deaths than the United States. But a host of qualifications are necessary: (1) it is difficult for any pathologist to tell precisely what drug killed a person; (2) not all drug deaths are reported; and (3) it is not known if the methods of collecting data in the two countries are precisely comparable. These are statistical qualifications, however, which apply to all such drug-abuse statistics. No one can doubt the truth of my main point here: the American disease has spread, in epidemic proportions, to the Federal Republic of Germany.[25]

The disease has also appeared in neighboring France. Increased and alarming heroin use was described by Monique Pelletier, who was appointed by the president of the French Republic to monitor the development of the drug phenomenon in the country. She estimated the drug-dependent population of the country at 30,000 to 50,000, according to a story in *Le Figaro* in January 1980, with clear indications of an upward trend. Five drug overdose deaths were counted for the entire country in 1970, 37 in 1975, and 117 in 1979.[26]

The smaller European countries, including those with reputations for peaceful life-styles and low levels of social disruption, have not been immune. Large quantities of illicit heroin and morphine are now being imported into Denmark, for example. A Copenhagen newspaper reported in January 1980 that the number of narcotic-related deaths had risen from three in 1960 to over 100 in 1979.[27]

In early 1980 it was reported, in a story all too familiar to Americans, that one heroin addict had resorted to six bank robberies in Copenhagen within a month in order to purchase his daily fix. The 27-year-old man had obtained a total of 125,000 kroner from the banks, all of which went toward the purchase of the drug on the black market. The robber-addict claimed that he had never actually used a weapon, although he held his hand in his pocket as if he had one.[28]

Many of the other familiar "side-effects" of large-scale narcotic abuse, such as official corruption, are beginning to appear in countries unaccustomed to their presence and deeply disturbed by their discovery. In late January 1980 Belgium was shocked by the arrest of Major Léon François, head of the National Narcotics Bureau, the equivalent of the American DEA, on charges that he had cooperated in a narcotics-smuggling conspiracy that moved some mysterious suitcases through Brussels National Airport. The case was shrouded in mystery and confusion, although it appears that heroin was involved, and it is certain that M. François and other Belgian drug officials were incarcerated for some time, although they were later released, again under rather mysterious circumstances.[29]

Tiny, mountain-fast Switzerland, which has not seen an enemy soldier on its soil in recent history, is not secure from its own narcotic addicts. In 1978 the number of heroin abusers in the country was reported by authorities to have been 10,000, of whom only 300 were in treatment. In February 1980 the *Neue Zuercher Zeitung* commented that "despite intensive education, Switzerland's drug scene is becoming increasingly brutal." Heroin, the story noted, was being widely traded in the country. It was also the major cause of narcotic overdose deaths. In 1974 there were 13 drug-related deaths; by 1977, there were 78. In 1979 the number reached 102. Other indicators of drug abuse and related crime were equally depressing: reports to the police of violations of the controlled-substances law rose from 6,299 in 1978 to 7,045 in 1979; the number of convictions rose from 4,465 to 5,466. Large quantities of heroin, hashish, and amphetamines were also seized by the police.[30]

The use of heroin has also risen greatly among United States troops stationed in Western Europe. Accounts vary as to the exact amount, but on April 27, 1978, Dr. Peter Bourne, then President Carter's chief advisor on drugs, stated that 8 percent of the U.S. Army's Berlin Brigade admitted to the current use of heroin, and four soldiers of the brigade had died of overdoses the previous year. In 1977, moreover, there had been 30 heroin overdose deaths among the 225,000 soldiers stationed in West Germany—up from 20 in 1976.[31]

In the midst of the worldwide spread of heroin abuse in the late 1970s came the Iranian revolution, known for its fanatical rejection of all things American. That upheaval destroyed the limited control the Shah's police had had on the export of heroin and thus allowed a vast increase in the international market. But there was an ironic twist to the story. In the land that led the retreat to Muslim fundamentalism and the rejection of the vices of the modern world, heroin use suddenly became so widespread and open that in early 1980 American television audiences were introduced to Iranian heroin smokers by name and saw them in their homes, with their friends and families. Iranian heroin thus seemed to be replacing the more traditional Persian opium, bringing with it a host of modern problems.

By the summer of 1980 reports on the Iranian heroin situation, like so much else in that tortured country, took on frightening proportions. The official government statistics indicated that there were 3 million heroin addicts, nearly one for every twelve Iranians. It appears that a large number of opium addicts were included in that seemingly improbable figure. A high school teacher in Tehran, dismayed over the widespread addiction among his students, observed, "Heroin and opium were the only commodities that became inexpensive and plentiful after the revolution." The cheap, high-potency heroin of Iran's clandestine laboratories was flooding into many other countries, including the United States and those in Western Europe. Although at first slow to respond, officials of the revolutionary government finally intervened with what may be, if the stories can be believed, the harshest response to drug selling in the annals of modern history. The roving executioner of the revolution, Ayatollah Sadegh Khalkhali, held brief trials of alleged drug traffickers, shouted "I shall exterminate you vermin!" and ordered summary executions, which were carried out within minutes. During a seven-week period, the *Washington Post* Foreign Service reported, 176 people had been executed for heroin and opium offenses. On July 8, all the while licking an ice cream cone, the revolutionary executioner held a press conference in a deserted mosque where he displayed goods confiscated primarily from the condemned, including approximately 100 kilo bags (220 pounds) of heroin.

Even though he seemed ruthlessly efficient in his chosen field, the Ayatollah Khalkhali was stung by criticism that he had not acted swiftly or harshly enough to curb rising drug traffic and addiction. Defensively, he explained that there were practical limits even to his direct method of controlling drug abuse: "If we wanted to kill everybody who had five grams of heroin, we'd have to kill 5,000 people, and this would be difficult."[32]

Barely noticed behind the headlines of war and peace in another part of the Middle East have been stories of major increases in drug use and trafficking. Egypt has even reported a recent growth in the illicit cultivation of opium poppies on hidden tracts of land in the vast country. Moreover, Egyptian newspapers told of at least two heroin seizures in February 1980. Customs officials discovered 250 grams of heroin at Cairo International Airport in the luggage of a passenger from Beirut, according to a story in the *Al-Jumhuriah* of Cairo. One week later *Al-Ahram* reported the seizure of another large quantity, at least 300 grams, at a luxury apartment in Cairo. Until those seizures, heroin trafficking during recent years had been virtually unknown in the country. In both cases the traffickers were Arabs from nearby nations.[33]

Later in the month, Israeli police, acting on a tip from Amsterdam authorities, arrested two young Tel Aviv men as they debarked from a KLM plane at Ben-Gurion Airport. The police seized 400 grams of heroin contained in a false-bottomed suitcase and another 20 grams, wrapped in plastic, hidden in the anus of one of the men. A story in the *Jerusalem Post* commented, "The country's drug addicts have apparently fallen victim to gang warfare between rival drug dealers. There is a shortage of hard drugs and prices have recently been driven up steeply."[34]

IV

The American disease is thus not only spreading throughout the world, it is taking some bizarre and circuitous routes in the journey: to the Middle and Far East, where natural opium grows, to Europe, and to American troops stationed there, who find the relatively cheap prices attractive in their attempts to deal with the sometime miseries of the soldier's life in a foreign land. And the American presence is widespread in other ways. Whatever hesitance may have developed in the aftermath of the Vietnam debacle regarding foreign adventures, one still finds officials and agents of the Drug Enforcement Administration, the Department of State, and the Central Intelligence Agency, among others, continuing the venerable American worldwide battle against drugs.

But the American international effort involves not only attempts to control the supply of heroin through intelligence and law enforcement. There are also major technical-assistance efforts to export American treatment techniques, efforts spearheaded by NIDA. Thus, such American approaches as methadone maintenance and the diversion of arrested addicts into treatment are beginning to appear in other countries, as a partial result of American help.

But if Americans are sending technical-assistance missions around the world, as well as receiving visits from foreign drug-abuse officials, some interest remains in the British experience. For most of this century that interest came primarily from Americans, as evidenced by the drug institute I established there, mainly for American experts, starting in 1974. But interest in the British drug-control system is starting to broaden considerably. As one senior Home Office* drugs official told me recently, "It used to be that we were always trying to explain 'the British system' to Americans; now the visitors are coming from everywhere."

The reactions of foreign visitors to the explanations of British officials are often a combination of puzzlement and frustration. The visitors are saying, by implication if not expressly, "Tell us how to solve the heroin puzzle by giving addicts heroin." The typical British response is never to claim that the British system is a success, to cast doubt on the notion that there is a system at all, and to be almost horrified at the thought that someone from another country might think that they were trying to export any phase of their approach, whatever it may be. Many foreign visitors wonder why they spent the money for the trip.

American officials, quite to the contrary, seem to go through cycles in which

---

* The Home Office is a national department or ministry of the British government that oversees a wide variety of matters, including police, corrections, animal mistreatment, and drug abuse, among others.

they first claim victory in the war on heroin, then quietly admit that there has been a recurrence; then some official somewhere declares another war on heroin. Edward Jay Epstein, Charles Silberman, and the fellows of the Drug Abuse Council, among others, were highly critical of the Republican heroin crusade and the statement in 1973 by President Nixon that "we have turned the corner on drug addiction."[35]

There was indeed an apparent dip in heroin abuse and trafficking, especially from Turkey, in 1973.[36] But by 1974 Mexican heroin started to fill the gap and use once again rose. The classic cycle persisted.

Strenuous anti-heroin effort, accompanied by slightly more modest rhetoric, continued into subsequent administrations. So did claims of major advances in American battles against heroin. Some of these claims were made by leading drug officials in the Democratic Carter administration. Dr. Bourne testified before a Senate committee in early 1978 that heroin-related deaths—a prime indicator of the extent of heroin addiction—had dropped roughly 40 percent during 1977. He gave much of the credit to the American-assisted Mexican program to eliminate illicit opium poppy cultivation. He also estimated that the importation of heroin into America was at its lowest point in seven years. Similarly optimistic testimony was given by Peter B. Bensinger, administrator of the Drug Enforcement Administration, and also by Mathea Falco, the State Department's director for international narcotics control. Mr. Bensinger reported that heroin-related deaths were going down dramatically.

Other such data were reported by Bensinger in statements contained in *Drug Enforcement*, the official magazine of his agency. In the December 1977 issue he declared, "A great deal of progress has been made in 1977. The price of heroin has risen from $1.26 to $1.65 a milligram and is now the highest on record; the purity level is 5 percent, the lowest in the last seven years." In the July 1978 issue he continued in the same optimistic vein: "Heroin availability continues to shrink in the United States and purity has dropped to a record new low of 4.9 percent as of the end of March, 1978. Heroin overdose deaths and injuries continue to decrease. . . ."[37]

All these data may have been correct, but the implication that the efforts of the Carter administration were making major inroads into the problem of American heroin abuse was somewhat misleading. These claims went virtually unchallenged during the first few years of the new Democratic regime. Then the cycle started to enter its next traditional phase.

Linwood Thompson operated a business at 1321 Riggs Street N.W., Washington, D.C., which is approximately one mile from the headquarters of the DEA on I Street and 1.3 miles from the White House. A resourceful reporter managed to get Thompson to pose for photographs in his place of business and to give a full and frank account of his professional activities, all of which appeared on the front page of the *Washington Post* on June 24, 1979. It seemed that Linwood Thompson, a heroin addict, was operating a "shooting gallery" in a row house that happened to be owned by the District of Columbia government. There was a basic charge of one dollar for the use of the house and five dollars to have Mr. Thompson inject the heroin, an optional but sometimes much appreciated service, especially for novices or for more experienced addicts whose veins were collapsing. Thompson said he had lived and worked in the gallery for two years, earning approximately $350 per week. He estimated that there were 100 such establishments in Northwest Washington, the section of the nation's capital also inhabited by much of the federal establishment. (Shortly after the story appeared, authorities closed the house, as they had done in the past on several occasions.)[38]

An accompanying story in the *Post* commenced, "After a sharp decline in recent years, the quality and availability of heroin appears to be on the rise in the streets of Washington, according to D.C. police." Police sources "said they believe that more than $120,000 worth of drugs are sold each day on 14th Street between T and Q streets N.W. The quality of the heroin sold is improving: the price for it is declining." A week before, D.C. Mayor Marion Barry had directed police to wage "all-out war" on drug traffic along 14th street, which was in the third police district. The story concluded, "The 3rd District's new deputy chief, William Dixon, said he was optimistic that the new offensive would rid the area of the drug problem 'once and for all.'" Thus the American heroin cycle continued.

In London too I found deep concern about recent rises in heroin addiction. In July 1979 several newspapers carried grim warnings of a coming "heroin epidemic." The major factual basis was the release of the Home Office statistical bulletin for calendar year 1978, showing that the number of known addicts had risen to a historical high, 4,122, most of them dependent on heroin. This was a 20 percent rise over 1977. The number receiving drugs in treatment as of December 31, 1978, was 2,406, also up approximately 20 percent over the previous year. Estimates of all such addicts, including those not officially known, were in the 12,000–15,000 range. The prestigious Standing Conference on Drug Abuse declared that the British clinic treatment system had failed in its original objective of controlling the spread of addiction and called for a new royal commission to review the entire British approach to the problem.[39]

The "epidemic" stories took note of the fact that in recent years clinic doctors had reduced prescriptions for heroin in favor of methadone, a practice learned from the Americans. This new approach was reflected in the Home Office statistics, which indicated that 70 percent of the addicts in treatment during 1978 were being prescribed methadone only. Some of the crucial questions raised, therefore, were whether or not the reduction in the prescribing of legal heroin had contributed to the alleged rise in addiction, to an apparent increase in the black market, and to a supposed increase in related crime by addicts turned off and turned away by the new clinical practices.

Some perspective on the heroin epidemic stories in England may be obtained by a rough comparison with the United States, which has, as we have seen, approximately 220 million people and perhaps 500,000 addicts. Britain has approximately 55 million people and an estimated 15,000 addicts. On this basis, America has an addiction rate eight times greater than England's. Some would argue that this is not only a rough comparison but also an unfair one, because the figures on addict prevalence are simply so much guesswork. I admit this defect; it is impossible to know how many addicts there are in the population of any country who have not come, somehow, to the attention of authorities. But if we look at the number of addicts in each country who *have* come into treatment, approximately 2,400 in Britain and 213,000 in the United States, then the disparities are even greater. Again imperfect figures—because addicts come in and out of treatment, because not only heroin addicts are listed in the compilations although they predominate, and because the figures are not compiled in the same way or for the same time periods—but nevertheless the ratio here would indicate a problem 89 times as great in the United States. I would settle for a statement that the problem of addiction to opiates, especially heroin, is vastly larger in America than in the United Kingdom.

A headline in the *Washington Post* in August 1979 declared, "Glut of Heroin Triggers Surge in Drug Activity in City," and commenced, "Like an invisible cloud, a phenomenal increase in heroin has enveloped Washington's inner city, supercharging street drug life with new activity, taxing police containment efforts to the limit and jamming addiction treatment centers with a new generation of junkies." The number of addicts in city treatment facilities had risen to approximately 2,000, an increase of more than 700 over the previous year.[40] Since these data covered only District government facilities and not private clinics, it is reasonable to estimate that the number in treatment in Washington alone approximated the number in treatment in all of Britain.

How can anyone make sense of these sets of facts? Do they not show that neither Britain nor America has anything to teach the other? And would it not be the height of conceit for either to attempt to teach anything to other countries? My answer to these questions is negative. All these recent stories demonstrate is the persistence of the heroin problem, its cyclical, enigmatic, even bizarre nature, and its continuing spread around the world.

Throughout that world, my colleagues in the American drug-abuse field—their hearts filled with a combination of the old missionary zeal and the even more venerable entrepreneurial spirit—are being called upon to set up a U.S.-style computer registry in Hong Kong, an Odyssey House in Australia, and a methadone-treatment program in a dozen countries. Those countries will get expert advice, but their own experts had better do their own homework. They should recall the apocryphal story about the boatload of polyglot survivors of a World War II sea battle who were cast upon a deserted island. Within a few weeks the Dutch had set up a dairy, the Germans were drilling the natives in military formations, the French had opened a restaurant, the Americans had established a management system to control all operations—and the two Britons were still sitting quietly on the beach, waiting to be introduced.

Every country now afflicted with heroin addiction must be aware that we Americans know a great deal about the heroin addiction problem, especially about managerial methods, research techniques, and computer applications. In typical fashion, we are not shy about sharing our knowledge. But despite whatever optimistic reports one may have heard, from American or foreign sources, America now has no operational solution to that problem. No country, the United States included, should be deluded into thinking that it can curb heroin addiction by better computers, more efficient management systems, harsher criminal laws, or gallons of methadone—however helpful such American artifacts might be under some circumstances. England does not have a complete solution either, but it is infinitely closer to achieving that impossible balance than we Americans are. The British, however, are sitting quietly on the beach waiting to be introduced. I shall, with their indulgence, do so.

2: LIVING UNTIL DEATH

"The care of the dying demands all that we can do to enable patients to live *until they die*."—Cicely M. Saunders, 1965[1]

"It's mediocre, pathetic medicine, this worshipping technology but not paying attention to the true needs of dying patients. I have been disgusted seeing people who are going to be dead within a few hours or days being hooked up to all this blasphemous plumbing when all they really need is a friendly word, a nice cup of coffee and some heroin."—Eric Wilkes, 1977[2]

I

It is a common mistake, I submit, to focus an investigation of the heroin enigma only on addiction, disruption, and crime. Most drug studies do so, however, ignoring the original purpose of the medicine diacetylmorphine and one of the major positive uses of the drug, the treatment of the organically ill.

Jane Zorza was one such person; she died on a June day in England several years ago with her parents at her bedside, holding her hands. She had just turned twenty-five, and cancer was the disease that killed her, as it does multitudes of people every year. There were, however, several unique features about Jane's situation: she passed away in an English hospice—a special institution for the terminally ill—and was treated with a complete range of pain-control techniques and drugs, including heroin. Her parents, both writers, penned a poignant story about the caring, professional treatment she received. That story first appeared in the *Washington Post* in January 1978, and helped spur the American hospice movement, as Victor and Rosemary Zorza intended; they had promised Jane to spread the good word about hospices.[3]

The Zorzas wrote of how Jane had become isolated in the standard English hospitals, as her illness and pain progressed. The doctors there seemed unable to face the truth, that Jane was dying and that there was no cure—or at least they refused to tell this to Jane or her parents. Jane received a painkiller every three hours even though she usually cried for a pill long before relief came.

When Jane finally was taken from a London hospital to a hospice, she was in even greater agony, a state in which many cancer patients endure, not really live, until they die. But her situation and that of her parents began to change. "What happened next was not a miracle, but the slow and thoughtful application of medical knowledge and of loving care by the nurses to yet another cancer patient—and the patient's family," the Zorzas wrote. "What did Jane want, the doctors asked her. She wanted one of us, her father or mother, to be with her—always, until she died. That was easy. The nurses wheeled another bed into Jane's room, and from then on one of us was with her day and night—except once or twice, when we were talking to the doctor. Then a nurse—or once, when the nurses were too busy, the hospice porter—came to hold her hand and talk to her."

When Victor believed the end was near, he told Jane he would stop writing his newspaper column so that he could be with her constantly. "Jane's reply was to cry out in mock horror. 'Help!' she exclaimed—and she made me promise that I would keep up the column whatever happened. She did not, she said with a smile, want me to devote myself 'completely' to her—or there might be trouble. Now, at the hospice, they gave me the other empty room which they kept for visitors, and I used it as a study."

Thus, the entire family was, to a degree, comforted and kept together. For Jane, however, there was the more specific need for pain control, which came not only from drugs although drugs *were* essential. "A girl of about the same age as Jane who remained in the London hospital after Jane left died in torment and in misery, in great pain and in anguish of mind, without being told that she was dying, though no doubt suspecting it and fearing it. She needn't have—if only she had been moved to the hospice. They gave the other girl all the conventional pain killers, but still it did not help. At the hospital, Jane had to beg for pain killers, but she would be given pills only as prescribed by the doctors, at regular intervals."

At the hospice, however, the doctors had made detailed studies of pain, in all its variations, and treated each separately. As the Zorzas explained, "They didn't wait the regulation two hours, until the effect of the pain killer had worn off. They made sure that the drugs would be administered to Jane before the pain had a chance to start clawing at her again. They didn't make her into a zombie filled with drugs. During the first couple of days the drugs—some of which would be forbidden in the United States as habit-forming—did bring on hallucinations from time to time, but these eased off later."

Then Jane's parents pondered a question which seemed unanswerable.

When we ask ourselves what it was that made it possible for Jane to say again and again at that time that she was happy to be dying, we can think of no single answer. The only satisfactory answer would be made up of the hundreds of little incidents of life at the hospice during her last days. Like the time when she said, "I would like to touch a piece of velvet before I die"—and soon a piece of velvet was brought to her. She touched it, and a nurse then put it on her bare shoulder, where it remained—forever. Or the time when a friend brought a bunch of roses, put it by her bed, extracted one flower, and held it out to Jane. "Would you like one?" the friend asked. "I have always wanted to wear a rose in my hair," Jane said, "but never dared." The nurse put the red flower in her hair, and there it stayed—forever.

Jane died happy, in large part because she received the loving care appropriate to her condition and stage in life.

It is significant, I believe, that although the doctors thought it necessary to prescribe injected heroin for Jane, her parents felt inhibited from mentioning it in the article, even though they alluded to "drugs . . . forbidden in the United States." This omission is not unusual. In both America and Britain a conscious effort is being made to prevent the American fear of heroin from curbing the development of hospices.

Could Jane have been cared for without heroin? We shall never know, but we can assume that this was highly unlikely, for her doctor is known as one who does not turn to heroin first but utilizes a whole range of pain-control methods, many not involving any drugs whatsoever. Jane's message, however, is not that heroin is *the* answer to cancer pain. Remember that the doctors in the English hospitals where she was originally treated and where she suffered so much had exactly the same legal power to prescribe drugs as did the hospice doctors. Jane's message and that of multitudes of people like her—is that total, honest, and loving care should be the overarching theme for anyone in need.

One of my major concerns is that this loving care sometimes seems to be provided by the helping professions and sometimes doesn't. It is all terribly unpredictable. One cannot even make the generalization that cancer pain-control care is better, on the whole, in England than in America, although I suspect that may well be true. Leading medical experts see the need to treat pain and to reduce the vast medical ignorance concerning it as a major health problem. Indeed, a worldwide pain-control movement is beginning within the medical profession. Whether the pain is due to cancer or to some other condition, those who study the subject are coming to realize that the failures of pain control are due in part to the improper use of available drugs and in part to the failure to use other, nonchemical remedies. The latter approaches recognize the psychological, spiritual, and personal dimensions of pain control. Almost no kind act, however simple or seemingly insignificant, is considered beyond the realm of treatment, as we saw in Jane's situation.

When I visited St. Joseph's Hospice in London during July 1979, the medical director, Dr. Joseph Hanratty, explained that the institution uses the full range of narcotic drugs, including heroin, but emphasized that treatment went far beyond drugs. In one case a cancer patient had been simply lying in bed receiving 50 milligrams of morphine every four hours and doing very little else. When Dr. Hanratty found that she had experience as a flower arranger, he enlisted her services for the hospice. Soon her bed was surrounded with her work. Her attention was diverted from exclusive concentration on her condition, her pain threshold was apparently raised, and the drug dosage went down to less than 20 milligrams every four hours. Similarly beneficial results were obtained by moving another patient's bed so that, instead of staring at the wall, she was looking out the window at the life outside, at the people walking and the cars moving in traffic. The failure to appreciate these simple human dimensions of pain control is widespread.[4]

The failures in the medical arena go beyond the choice or legality of certain drugs and into the inappropriate use of the drugs available. Two American psychiatrists, Drs. Richard M. Marks and Edward J. Sachar, encountered this problem in the prestigious Montefiore Hospital and Medical Center in New York. The doctors told of their surprise about the manner in which they first learned of this "type of drug misuse," in their words. The medical and nursing staff of the 770-bed hospital periodically called them in to deal with patients who were having severe emotional problems in coping with pain despite treatment with narcotics. Even though one patient had terminal cancer, the hospital medical staff had been reluctant to increase his narcotic dosage because of their fear that he would become addicted. The psychiatrists reported that this patient needed not psychiatric counseling but rather more pain-killing medicine. When this was administered, it "markedly relieved the patient's condition." Another patient complained of severe pain in the stump of his amputated leg and was causing a disturbance in the hospital. Again the psychiatrists were called in, and again the remedy was more narcotic treatment. The reason the medical staff had not given him adequate dosages in the first place was that he was thought to have an "addictive personality," a syndrome of dubious validity. The psychiatrists were called in to see yet another patient, "in sickle-cell crisis" because she had threatened suicide. Drs. Marks and Sachar reported, "It turned out that threatening suicide was her desperate attempt to get more medication for her severe pain."

As a result of these incidents the two psychiatrists conducted an intensive study of thirty-seven patients in pain to determine whether or not these cases were part of a pattern. They reported in a 1973 issue of the *Annals of Internal Medicine* that 32 percent remained in severe pain and 42 percent in moderate pain, even after being treated with the prescribed narcotic painkillers.[5] "There was clearly a general pattern of undertreatment of pain with narcotic analgesics, leading to widespread and significant patient distress." Why? The question and the answers, as I have indicated, had nothing to do directly with heroin or the choice of one drug over another. (In fact, the drug used in almost all the cases was a relatively low-potency narcotic, meperidine or Demerol, a synthetic opiate considered by some pharmacologists to be one-third to one-half as powerful as morphine.)

On the basis of a questionnaire answered by 102 medical residents and interns at Montefiore and at St. Luke's hospitals in New York City, Drs. Marks and Sachar suggested two broad categories of reasons for the undertreatment. First were those relating to lack of knowledge about the drug and its effects. A significant number of doctors at two of the best teaching hospitals in the country simply did not know the results of pharmacological studies showing the standard therapeutic doses of Demerol for treating severe pain, or the holding power of such doses in terms of hours. The second category of reasons involved factors beyond chemistry and pharmacology. Approximately one in five of these doctors thought that a good deal of American drug addiction had been created by excessive hospital prescribing, and it was these doctors who tended to underprescribe Demerol, even for terminal cancer patients and for those suffering the severe pain of some forms of heart disease. Also in this second category were other factors: "There is also some indication that prescribing a drug that might induce euphoria may even evoke puritanical counter-reactions in some medical and nursing personnel."

Moreover, these aberrations are not restricted to any one country. Dr. Henry G. Miller, vice-chancellor of the University of Newcastle upon Tyne, observed in 1973 that "an unholy combination of neurotic fear of addiction with the traditional Christian glorification of suffering leads a minority of physicians to practice unjustifiable parsimony in the dispensation of pain-relieving drugs (just to be on the safe side, most doctor-patients take their favorite analgesics into hospital in their sponge-bags, together with their favorite sleeping tablets)."[6]

A famous patient wrote about that unjustifiable parsimony in an American research hospital several years ago. Stewart Alsop, the distinguished American journalist, died at the NIH Clinical Center in Bethesda, Maryland, relatively without pain, on May 26, 1974, but not before he had plied his trade in regard to the other patients; he wrote of a "terrible thought" that had occurred to him during the third night of his stay there. His roommate, Jack,

> had a melanoma in his belly, a malignant solid tumor that the doctors guessed was about the size of a softball. The cancer had started a few months before with a small tumor in his left shoulder, and there had been several operations since. The doctors planned to remove the softball-sized tumor, but they knew Jack would soon die. The cancer had metastasized— it had spread beyond control. Jack was good-looking, about 28, and brave. He was in constant pain, and his doctor had prescribed an intravenous shot of a synthetic opiate—a pain-killer, or analgesic—every four hours. His wife spent many of the daylight hours with him, and she would sit or lie on his bed and pat him all over, as one pats a child, only more methodically, and this seemed to help control the pain. But at night, when his pretty wife had left (wives cannot stay overnight at the NIH clinic) and darkness fell, the pain would attack without pity.

Then Alsop explained the methods of pain control:

> At the prescribed hour a nurse would give Jack a shot of the synthetic analgesic, and this would control the pain for perhaps two hours or a bit more. Then he would begin to moan, or whimper, very low, as though he didn't want to wake me. Then he would begin to howl, like a dog. When this happened, either he or I would ring for a nurse, and ask for a pain-killer. She would give him some codeine or the like by mouth, but it never did any real good—it affected him no more than half an aspirin might affect a man who had just broken his arm. Always the nurse would explain as encouragingly as she could that there was not long to go before the intravenous shot—"Only about 50 more minutes now." And always poor Jack's whimpers and howls would become more loud and frequent until at last the blessed relief came.

On the third night of this scenario the terrible thought emerged: " 'If Jack were a dog . . . what would be done with him?' The answer was obvious: the pound, and chloroform. No human being with a spark of pity could let a living thing suffer so, to no good end."

But Stewart Alsop's observation of a terminal-cancer patient in excruciating agony led him to ask why such patients "should not experience the pleasure of heroin, the most powerful of pain-killers and probably also the most powerful of pleasure-inducers." He answered his own question: "To believe otherwise is to accept the ancient, irrational principle that suffering is good and pleasure is bad."[7] It is important to recognize that when he wrote those words Alsop had gone beyond virtually all acceptable bounds of discussion in Britain and America, even among those who advocate the innovative use of all modalities and drugs, including heroin, to control pain in cancer patients. The boundary he crossed was the ethical-religious-moral imperative: thou shalt not use chemicals to give patients pleasure. I am aware of only a few English cancer doctors and one priest (all mentioned later) who speak positively of the euphoric advantages of heroin for organically ill patients.

When an American doctor has the courage to take the reformist position on heroin, he normally refers to other qualities of the drug, even though in fact they may be closely related to euphoria. Cancer specialist John H. Glick, one of Alsop's doctors at NIH, publicly advocated the use of heroin not long after Alsop's death. Dr. Glick wrote in 1975 that he believed American doctors should use heroin in appropriate cases. One example he had recently encountered was Rita,

> a thin, wasted woman in her mid-fifties who looked 70 and was desperately short of breath. Three years earlier her cancerous right breast had been removed. Although initially she did quite well, her tumor recurred. Both hormonal therapy and chemotherapy were used with brief success, but soon she was beyond their help. By the time I was asked to see her, the breast cancer had spread throughout both lungs and was causing severe air hunger, which in turn led to extreme anxiety. In a state of near panic, Rita would struggle and gasp for breath, but instead of satisfying her air hunger, her effort simply made it worse. Her tumor also involved her spine and she was in unremitting pain, which increased every time she changed position in bed. Even during her final days the nurses were reluctant to give her frequent morphine injections because morphine can hamper breathing. She died a week after I first saw her, frightened, anxious and in pain to the end.[8]

Dr. Glick saw a clear medical need and stated it: "If heroin were legal in this country, I would have prescribed it for Rita. It would have had no effect on her tumor (heroin is not a 'cancer drug'), but it would have vastly improved the quality of her last weeks of life by reducing her pain, blunting the panic brought on by her inability to breathe, and relieving much of the tension associated with impending death."

II

Because many American medical experts and laymen alike share such senti-ments, periodically the movement for exorcism of the devil in heroin re-emerges. This occurred in 1977, when I led the formation of a national orga-nization that had the initial goal of legalizing the use of heroin for the organical-ly ill.

"Any interested party" may petition the federal government to reschedule a drug under the Comprehensive Drug Abuse Prevention and Control Act of 1970, the dominant American drug law. In effect, this means that any person with an interest may ask the federal government to move any drug from Sched-ule I, which prohibits its use in the usual practice of American medicine, to Schedule II, which would allow its use but under severe controls. Morphine, for example, is a Schedule II drug; so is cocaine.[9] In my capacity as the director of the new Committee on the Treatment of Intractable Pain, I composed a letter-petition in April 1977 to Attorney General Griffin Bell asking that heroin be rescheduled. I did so because, as far as I could tell, such a request in the language of the law had not been made in recent history. I did not expect that the Carter administration would do exactly as I requested, but I thought that such a simple and direct petition should exist on the record in Washington, where the power for change resides. Among other things I stated: "The avail-able evidence is overwhelming that the original placement of heroin in Sched-ule I was a mistake in medical, scientific, and ethical terms." I argued that it had all the characteristics of a Schedule II drug—a high potential for abuse and thus a need for severe restrictions on its use—but that it should be used legitimately in the treatment of the organically ill and the addicted. Then I made the follow-ing observation: "Clearly, there are distinctions between the two categories of people. It might be prudent for you to consider setting up separate regulations for dispensing heroin to each group. Priority should, I would suggest, be placed on releasing heroin for use with the first group, those organically ill or severely injured. However, it must be remembered that both groups should be considered patients in need of medical care and treatment. Only the medical Calvinism that sometimes seems to dominate the American medical profession would cast addicts into a treatment limbo because 'they brought it on them-selves.' If that be the test, then how do we approach the person suffering from lung cancer who had been a heavy smoker?"[10]

There was no direct response from the attorney general, nor was the petition supported by further legal action at that time. But the movement to legalize the medical use of heroin found in the White House a sympathetic ear, that of Dr.

Bourne. Typical of his position on the matter was an extraordinary letter to a congressman in June 1977, in which the presidential assistant declared: "The evidence is rather overwhelming that heroin can be an extremely useful form of medication in specific medical conditions. It has been used widely in Britain for terminal cancer, and apparently is substantially superior to any other form of treatment. In addition, I understand that it is particularly good for short term treatment of pain in children, particularly those who have had plastic surgery of the face, or have had severe burns."

If the medical evidence is so clear, why isn't it available to American doctors? Dr. Bourne explained: "The problem in this country has always been one of the overwhelming stigma associated with the drug and that it has always been politically inconceivable to even consider allowing it to be used for medical purposes. I am not sure that from a medical standpoint this makes a great deal of sense, because obviously if a drug, even heroin, is used under careful clinical conditions in the hands of responsible physicians, the risk of abuse is minimal. However, I feel it is going to take a great deal of public education before we could even consider allowing it in this country for even the most specific indications and under the most carefully controlled medical conditions."[11]

It would appear that those who feel that heroin prohibition is not based on legal logic or medical science have strong support. Later in 1977 Dr. Bourne ordered the National Institutes of Health to begin a program of research into the potential uses of such prohibited drugs as heroin and marijuana in the treatment of the organically ill (but not in the treatment of addicts).[12] Even the act of simply ordering research about the possible medical use of these drugs represented a rare demonstration of political courage. In the 1978 *Annual Report* of the White House Office of Drug Abuse Policy, which he directed, Dr. Bourne pointed to the historic significance of the decision, which reversed "a sixty-year Federal policy." The new White House position was that "to the fullest extent possible, research into the potential therapeutic usefulness of marijuana, heroin, and other drugs with an abuse potential should be dealt with exclusively as a medical issue. The available scientific data should be assessed objectively, without bias for historical precedent, legal status of the drug, or public misperceptions."[13]

Another hopeful recent sign for a more rational approach to drug policy, particularly toward heroin, was seen in the resolution passed in May 1978 by the House of Delegates of the prestigious 15,000-member American Society of Internal Medicine. The resolution endorsed "the medically supervised use of heroin for the treatment of the suffering and intractable pain of terminally ill patients." The society urged the American Medical Association to adopt the same stance.[14] To my knowledge, this was the first such vote taken by a major national organization of the American medical establishment in modern history.

But when the House of Delegates of the dominant AMA considered the subject during the next month, the vote came out the opposite way. The voting physicians adopted the recommendations of the AMA's Council on Scientific Affairs, which stated in part "that the claims that heroin has certain advantages over morphine are based on impressions and anecdotal reports rather than scientific data. The data, in fact, indicate that the effects of heroin and morphine are similar and that morphine is a satisfactory substitute for heroin in the combination of drugs commonly called Brompton's Mixture.* There is no reason to believe that the NIDA study now underway will show different results." Accordingly, the council was of the opinion that "reclassifying heroin as a Schedule II drug under the Controlled Substances Act would not provide physicians with a more effective analgesic but would increase the problems of heroin control." The group believed that overall patient care "could be improved by expanding the training of physicians in the management of chronic pain, and that this can be accomplished through special centers or through continuing medical education courses on the subject." In maintaining the position that the dangers of illegal use of heroin ("the problems of heroin control") outweigh any medical advantages for the ill, the ruling body of the American medical profession thus has kept its policy moored to a questionable sixty-year-old standard. However, its expressed concern for better control of pain and more research into the more effective use of existing drugs represents the emerging concerns of modern medicine and humane ethics.[15]

Similarly mixed signs of hopeful progress and dogged resistance were seen in the first convention of the National Hospice Organization, held in Washington, D.C., in October 1978. Pledges of future support came from speakers who ranged across the political spectrum and represented both the executive and legislative branches: Senators Edward Kennedy (D-Mass.) and Robert Dole (R-Kans.), as well as Secretary of Health, Education, and Welfare Joseph A. Califano, Jr. The possibility of legalizing heroin for medical uses, however, did not play a prominent role in the deliberations.[16]

The message from the Carter White House was not at all clear on the issue of heroin for the terminally ill. For example, a June 1978 issue of *Health Care Week* related that Monsignor William O'Brien, president of Therapeutic Com-

---

* The proper designation for this solution of narcotics and other drugs, according to the British *Pharmacopoeia*, or encyclopedia of standard drug mixtures and formulas, is the Brompton Cocktail. Nevertheless, many medical scientists use literary license when referring to the mixture.

munities of America, criticized proposals to make heroin available for the terminally ill because they would open the door to leakage to street addicts and to the use of heroin in the treatment of addicts. "The man behind this strategy, says Msgr. O'Brien, is Dr. Arnold Trebach of American University," the article stated. The story also mentioned that Dr. Bourne had called for the evaluation of heroin for possible treatment of the terminally ill.

> Reached at the White House, Charles O'Keefe, a spokesman for Dr. Bourne, replied to Msgr. O'Brien's charges with this statement: "To say that there is some conspiracy or some scheme or some program to remove heroin from Schedule I is nonsense."
>
> Mr. O'Keefe denied that Dr. Bourne recommends the use of heroin among the terminally ill. He said, "We are advocating that if the medical profession determines that that sort of research is necessary, then the response of the government should be based on the medical requirement and not on the emotional issue."
>
> However, Mr. O'Keefe acknowledged that in order to use heroin medically it would have to be moved from its present place on Schedule I. He added that structures for such moves already exist. "But that's a long way down the road, as far as I can tell," he said.[17]

Dr. Bourne left the White House under a cloud approximately six weeks after this story appeared (see chap. 8, below). His departure considerably muted top-level support for a new federal policy regarding heroin in medicine. The message from Washington on the subject remains both muted and confused.

III

The most recent messages from Britain also are not entirely clear. During the early 1970s American journalist Horace Freeland Judson (among many others) saw a rather more consistent position among English physicians. He wrote in 1974, "Of the many contrasts between British and American handling of addiction, heroin's place in ordinary British medical practice is perhaps the most arresting." In other words, while it was significant that addicts could get legal heroin from doctors under some circumstances, what was more startling to Judson was to see the relatively matter-of-fact use of diacetylmorphine by British doctors for a wide variety of common human ailments. The fear of addiction, and addicts, had not driven heroin out of ordinary British medical practice. It still has not, but that fact is not always recognized in other countries. Judson noted that English doctors used the medicine in a number of medical situations, including heart attacks, postoperative pain, shingles, severe burns, sometimes even for coughs, and most prominently in cancer cases. He wrote of meeting "a magnificent English woman, Cicely Saunders, whose vocation is care of the dying." Many people, including this writer, have a similar impression of Dr. Saunders.

Often Dr. Saunders has stated simple truths in a manner that brings about calm understanding where before there was only agony and fear. Recently she wrote, "There is no longer any excuse for unrelieved terminal physical distress." This thought is simple but stunning. Virtually everyone I know has a heartrending story about a relative who has died or is in the process of dying in the searing agony of cancer pain.[18]

The effect of this simple thought could have a liberating impact on the lives of millions throughout the world, because while many people fear death, the thought of living their last days in uncontrollable pain and stripped of dignity is their ultimate fear, acquired by having witnessed such an uncivilized death of a loved one.

At the same time it is important to recognize what the pioneers of civilized terminal care are claiming and the limitations on those claims. While all types of medical assistance fit into a continuum of overall professional care, these pioneers distinguish between attempts to control and cure cancer, on the one hand, and care aimed primarily at providing comfort once attempts to cure have been virtually halted, on the other. Nothing in my research or in my personal experience leads me to believe that current cancer-control techniques involving surgery and chemotherapy are painless. While some may be less painful than others, for many cancer patients the pain and discomfort are extreme.

Once it is accepted that a person's cancer probably will not be controlled, then the dominant theme of treatment should become comfort, not cure. This is not so much accepting defeat—although many doctors and nurses think of it in those terms—as it is accepting the reality of the patient's stage in life and the challenge of making that life meaningful and dignified up to the very end. That is where the hospice and the proper use of analgesic drugs should come into the discussion.

Once again, we must return to the work of Dr. Saunders. She symbolizes the British hospice movement, and St. Christopher's Hospice, of which she is medical director, is considered the prototype for the world, the Mother Church, as it were. Until recently, a noteworthy symbol of her work was her advocacy of the dispensation of heroin as an essential part of the hospice movement's accepted doctrine. Judson wrote of Dr. Saunders in 1973:

> She said, and most of her English colleagues agree, that heroin is often the best drug for terminal cancer patients, though she sometimes supplements

it with gin. Like morphine, heroin not only blunts the panic of air hunger but can even lessen the fact of it, reducing acute pulmonary edema. Heroin is less likely than morphine to induce nausea. It relieves pain, but more than that, it is uniquely powerful in distancing the patient from what pain he still feels, and from his anxieties. For such patients, addiction is almost inevitable, and almost irrelevant. Yet, Dr. Saunders said that their heroin dosages can be well controlled for many months; she will wake patients in the middle of the night to give them heroin so that the pain, and the necessary dose, never get out of control.[19]

Not all American journalists have been quite as supportive as Mr. Judson. A story in the *Washington Star* in June 1976 was headlined, "The Dying Is Eased by Heroin." Reporter David Braaten gave his story an archetypical American twist when he wrote, "The scene was both bizarre and ironic: Here was a distinguished British doctor, Cicely Saunders, lecturing to a distinguished audience of experts at the National Cancer Institute on her technique for treating terminal cancer patients, and the technique turns out to be shooting them up with heroin. The fact that Dr. Saunders looks more like a granny or a nanny than a pusher didn't detract one bit from the eeriness of the program."[20] The Braaten view may well be the typical American gut-level response. Perhaps such reactions convinced Dr. Saunders and her British colleagues not to mention heroin when they crossed the ocean.

In any event, many enlightened Americans do see Dr. Saunders's work primarily in terms of heroin. She must, and does, accept a good part of the "blame" for this reputation. Yet she is now taking steps to correct the impression she gave that heroin was a central part of the hospice treatment philosophy.

In October 1977 yet another American reporter, Michael Satchell, wrote an article in *Parade*, the Sunday supplement read by forty million people, which supported both the hospice movement and the prominence of heroin in treatment. The article again catapulted the issue of medicinal heroin into the national limelight. I was mentioned and quoted in my capacity as president of the Committee on the Treatment of Intractable Pain, and an outpouring of supportive letters followed.[21]

But not all the letters I received were supportive. As it happened, each of the hundreds of communications I received from the United States *was* favorable. Somewhat paradoxically, the communications from England were different. Dr. Saunders wrote to me, in part, "I am really very sad that there should be this emphasis on legalising Heroin. I am well aware that much of this is as a result of my own work and writings. . . . [A]ccording to our own [new] work, my clinical impression was wrong. Even when I still believed in my clinical impression I have had to make it plain to many audiences to whom I have spoken that the important thing is not 'what you use as the way that you use it.' Your drug addiction problem is such that the very word Heroin arouses an understandably emotional reaction. It would be most unfortunate if the pressure to do further trials with Heroin and to have it legalised were to give the impression that this was the only adequate drug in this field." Clearly, Dr. Saunders had changed her mind about the unique advantages of heroin.[22]

However, even in English cancer care there is a huge world beyond Dr. Saunders and St. Christopher's. A number of English doctors still consider heroin a wonderful drug and have pronounced views on its unique value.

Dr. Eric Wilkes is the medical director of a hospice, St. Luke's Nursing Home, in Sheffield. His drug of first choice is heroin, which is given in relatively small doses to approximately 75 percent of the patients. Most of the other patients are given no opiates at all because they do not have a severe pain problem. In 1977 Dr. Wilkes declared emphatically to Michael Satchell, of *Parade*, "I have been disgusted seeing people who are going to be dead within a few hours or days being hooked up to all this blasphemous plumbing when all they really need is a friendly word, a nice cup of coffee and some heroin." Mr. Satchell's story continued:

At St. Luke's, about three-fourths of Dr. Wilkes' patients every four hours swallow a Brompton Cocktail, named for the hospital that invented it many years ago. Although individual doses are tailored to a patient's pain and anxiety, the typical Brompton contains heroin, cocaine, gin and phenothiazine, a tranquilizer, all mixed in with a chloroform-water base. The combination has been found to keep patients totally free of pain. And the hospice wards are not full of drugged zombies sprawled out in a narcotic stupor. "To say that heroin produces stupor is a myth," stressed Dr. Wilkes. "I've had patients on 60 milligrams of heroin every four hours and they've been doing *The Times* crossword puzzle. Heroin is an excellent pain killer. It makes patients calmer and causes less nausea and vomiting than morphine. For lung cancer patients, it has an excellent anti-cough action."[23]

Many cancer patients in England, moreover, start and end their treatment not in a hospice but in a more traditional hospital, where the concern may first be "cure" and then, much later, the palliative "care" more characteristic of a hospice. One of the leading cancer hospitals in England is the Royal Marsden in London, where Dr. Eve Wiltshaw often sees patients for years of treatment and care, rather than the average few weeks of a hospice like St. Christopher's or St. Luke's. Like all English doctors, she has the legal power to use heroin as she sees fit, and she does, because she believes it to be, as she stated in July 1977, "a marvelous compound." It is one of the first, not the last, drugs she prescribes in treating a cancer patient, one who may well have years rather than days to live—quite different, the doctor noted, from the usual situation at St. Christopher's.

While many British physicians regard the medicine as the most powerful painkiller available, Dr. Wiltshaw explained that she did not view it as a "brilliant analgesic" but as a drug really no better than other drugs available. Rather, she used heroin for its euphoric effect. Patients not only get pain relief but "generally feel good, smile and laugh." At this point we have left the arena of scientific medicine and pharmacology and entered the realm of ethics, moral philosophy, and the chameleonlike dynamics of psychoactive drugs, which is where part of the discussion belongs. Dr. Wiltshaw's assessment of heroin reveals that the impact of psychoactive drugs varies not only from patient to patient but also from one clinical opinion to another. The medical Calvinists of America, Britain, and other countries must find her philosophy positively repulsive.

Few doctors ever admit that they seek to promote a feeling of euphoria in their patients by the administration of drugs. But, reflecting on the goals of cancer treatment, Dr. Wiltshaw observed, "I don't want my patients to be like zombies, but rather pain free, talking and enjoying life. Also, I would prefer that they experience a bit of clouding of realities, so they won't feel desperate. . . . Patients' relatives ask, 'They won't suffer, will they, doctor?' and in England the doctor can answer, 'No'. . . . I would not be without heroin for the world." Many patients wish their doctors felt the same way.[24]

3: ADVENT, CANONIZATION, DEMONIZATION

"Heroin proved to be an extremely useful, prompt acting and reliable drug in treating persistent coughs as well as chest pains which resulted from inflammation of both the upper and lower respiratory tract. . . . I also had an opportunity to test the surprisingly fast and reliable effect of heroin on myself. A persistent hacking cough . . . was . . . immediately arrested by a single dose of 5 milligrams."— Dr. Floret, Elberfeld, Germany, 1898[1]

"The heroin question is not a medical one, as heroin addicts spring from sin and crime. It is a social problem where the medical and pharmaceutical and allied professions can do much to aid in solving this serious problem. Society in general must protect itself from . . . evil, and there is no greater peril than that of heroin."—S. Dana Hubbard, New York City, 1923[2]

Heroin was discovered in 1874, christened and popularized as a medicine in 1898, canonized by the end of the first decade of this century, demonized in the second decade, and by the middle of the third was virtually prohibited by law from medical practice in the United States. Eventually, the United States persuaded almost the entire world to follow its repressive lead. In the next two chapters I relate the medical history of this compound, bringing in the crime and deviance dimensions when they intrude, as they often do.

I

Opium has been used to make human beings happy and to relieve their pain since the beginning of recorded history. The plant from which it is obtained, the oriental poppy, or *Papaver somniferum*, grows in a wide variety of climates and conditions. The name apparently comes from the Greek word *opion*, meaning "poppy juice," although there are other explanations for it. It is, of course, the dried juice of the poppy pod. By all accounts, the Greeks used the drug. In the *Odyssey* Homer said: "A new thought came to Zeus-born Helen; into the bowl that their wine was drawn from she threw a drug that dispelled all grief and anger and banished remembrance of every trouble. Once it was mingled in the wine-bowl, any man who drank it down would never on that same day let a tear fall down his cheeks, no, not if his father and mother died, or if his brother or his own son were slain with the sword before his eyes." Helen had obtained the drug from a woman of Egypt, Homer explained, where the "bounteous earth yields a wealth of drugs, healthful and baneful side by side."[3] References to such wondrous drugs appear frequently in the literature of Egypt as well as of Mesopotamia, China, and Persia, and of many other countries, ancient and modern.

Opium provided the most potent ingredient for a wide variety of folk mixtures and medically dispensed drugs in early England and later in America. Britons and Americans, like Helen of Troy, often combined their opium with alcohol, calling it laudanum. There are reports that the Pilgrims brought laudanum aboard the *Mayflower*, as well as paregoric, a compound of opium, camphor, and alcohol. In 1680 Thomas Sydenham was moved to rhapsodize: "Among the remedies which it has pleased almighty God to give to man to relieve his sufferings, none is so universal and so efficacious as opium."

In 1803 a young German pharmacist, F. W. Serturner, isolated the chief alkaloid, or active ingredient, of opium. In effect, it was the essence of the mother drug and was named morphine by its discoverer, after Morpheus, the Greek god of dreams. It was estimated at the time that this new substance was ten times more powerful than opium. The potency factor was heightened when the hypodermic needle came into use in the 1850s. This meant that a concentrated dose of the most powerful painkiller known to medical science could be placed directly into the bloodstream.

In America and Britain all forms of the opiates continued to be used and were dispensed directly by physicians, sold over the counter in stores, and posted through the mails. At a time when the medical profession could offer little but palliation and sympathy, it was no wonder that the opiates were referred to by some physicians as G.O.M.—God's Own Medicine. Opiates were liberally used during the American Civil War to relieve the pain and suffering of combatants and civilians alike.

But no matter how the opiates were obtained—all means were completely legal at the time—the devilish side of the drug began to make itself known. The large number of morphine addicts who appeared among Civil War veterans led some to label that type of dependence the "soldier's disease." The period after the Civil War saw a vast amount of both medical and nonmedical use of opiates in a wide variety of forms in America as well as in Britain. All forms of opiate addiction were rampant: people were addicted to opium, morphine, laudanum, as well as to any of a thousand patent medicines bearing such names as Mrs.

Winslow's Soothing Syrup, Darby's Carminative, and Godfrey's Cordial, which usually offered no indication that they contained an addicting drug.[4]

In a report in the coldly scientific pages of the *Journal of the Chemical Society*, published in 1874 by Harrison and Sons, Printers in Ordinary to Her Majesty, St. Martin's Lane, London, chemist C. R. Alder Wright described a series of experiments he had conducted to determine the effect of combining various acids with morphine. History has not provided us with a clue as to why he did so or what he was looking for. In any event, during the process of experimentation he boiled a sample of morphine with acetic anhydride, a chemical related to ordinary table vinegar, and produced a long list of compounds, including, among others, one that later became known as heroin or, more scientifically, as diacetylmorphine or diamorphine.[5]

At the time the world did not beat a path to chemist Wright's door. Indeed, he did not seem to believe that his discovery was of any major significance, and most accounts today (with few notable exceptions—Judson, for example) do not even give him credit for it. That glory has usually been reserved for the man who both named this relatively new medicine (from the German *heroisch*—strong, powerful, or heroic) and popularized it, some twenty-four years after Wright's article appeared. German pharmacologist Heinrich Dreser reported on his experiments at the Elberfeld facility of Friedrich Bayer and Co. in a paper he read in 1898 to the seventieth congress of German naturalists and physicians. By modern standards the report was an eloquent, even highly personal, endorsement of a then relatively unknown drug for the treatment of coughs, chest pains, and the discomfort of pneumonia and tuberculosis. (This was of more than academic medical interest in the late nineteenth century, since antibiotics were not yet known. As Dr. Musto has observed, "In the United States . . . tuberculosis and pneumonia were the two leading causes of death. Understandably, pharmaceutical research concentrated on treatment of respiratory diseases and their symptoms.") Dr. Dreser told his scientific and medical colleagues in Dusseldorf, "This diacetylester of morphine, called 'heroin' showed a . . . strong . . . sedative effect on respiration when compared with morphine." Moreover, Dr. Dreser claimed, heroin was much safer to use than other drugs, such as codeine, because "for heroin the lethal dose is a hundredfold higher than its effective dose, while for codeine the lethal dose is only tenfold higher than its effective dose." In other words, Dreser believed, it was difficult for a doctor to prescribe a fatal overdose because a small dose of heroin provided therapeutic relief so rapidly.

The accompanying report by a Dr. Floret provided even more revealing insights into how the drug was used during the last century in actual clinical experiments with human beings, including, in this case, the physician himself. Dr. Floret wrote:

> For six months I have been prescribing heroin . . . to patients of the walk in clinic of the Farbenfabriken of Elberfeld. Heroin proved to be an extremely useful, prompt acting and reliable drug in treating persistent coughs as well as chest pains which resulted from inflammation of both the upper and lower respiratory tract. . . . Approximately 60 patients have been treated by me with this drug so far. They all agreed that they noticed an immediate improvement and relief from the persistent cough immediately after taking the powder. . . . They also observed that the pains associated with the cough were reduced: "Doctor, the powder that you prescribed was indeed very good. Immediately after taking the powder I felt relief, I had to cough a lot less and in general the cough improved a great deal after taking the powder. . . ." I also had an opportunity to test the surprisingly fast and reliable effect of heroin on myself. A persistent hacking cough which was associated with an inflammation of the upper respiratory tract hindered my clinical activity considerably. Particularly the requirement for speaking resulted frequently in severe coughing attacks, which were immediately arrested by a single dose of 5 milligrams of heroin so that I could pursue my activities for many hours without being affected by coughs.[6]

Thus we have the first widely known open endorsement of heroin, the miracle medicine. Some of the myths about it concern the work of Dreser and Floret. Even the authoritative tome *The Opium Problem*, published in 1928 by Dr. Charles Terry and Mildred Pellens, dealt with the discovery of heroin as a "most unfortunate influence" and observed, in a misleading passage, "Dreser in Germany in 1898 produced heroin . . . which was put out as a safe preparation free from addiction-forming properties, possessing many of the virtues and none of the dangers of morphin and codein, and recommended even as an agent of value in the treatment of chronic intoxication to these drugs." Such half-truths were repeated and increasingly distorted over the years; a typical version presented in 1974 in an otherwise sound book by John B. Williams, *Narcotics and Drug Dependence*, claimed: "Heroin was first produced commercially in Germany in 1898 by Dreser as a cure for morphinism."[7]

But as we have seen, Dreser and Floret viewed heroin as cough, chest, and lung medicine. While they believed it to be nonaddictive, in this report neither doctor advocated the use of heroin in the treatment of morphine addiction. Nevertheless, the mythological explanation of heroin's birth is widely accepted even today by leading academicians and drug-abuse officials. Dr. John C. Kramer, of the Department of Medical Pharmacology and Therapeutics, University of California at Irvine, was sufficiently intrigued by the persistence of this myth to conduct an investigation of it. He reported in 1977 that "between 1899 and 1902, four physicians, a German [not Dreser], two Frenchmen, and an American, wrote papers advocating the use of heroin as an aid in withdrawal from morphine addiction." But even these four physicians were quite cautious about the use of heroin in addiction treatment and generally did not advocate long-term maintenance with the drug. Dr. Kramer wondered, as have I, about how the myth started. His answer:

> In the years following 1910, Hamilton Wright [a prominent physician, antinarcotic crusader, and statesman] and others sought to push the nation and Congress to support narcotic control legislation. In part they did this by exaggerating certain data and distorting reports regarding addiction. Among the myths they created was the depiction of all opiates as the "Demon Flower." . . . In particular, heroin was painted as a special evil. The frequency of its use as a substitute in withdrawal was exaggerated far out of proportion to the facts and the statement that it had been first introduced for this purpose was totally false. Not only was the tale used as a means to demonize heroin but it also offered an opportunity to unfairly depict physicians as important contributors to the drug problem. Evidently, the story was not contradicted at the time and thus became part of popular belief. Repeated in print over the years, even authorities in the field have come to accept it as valid. The bad press that heroin received during the late teens and the twenties was unjustified.

Kramer emphasized that the story that heroin was "introduced . . . as a substitute in the treatment of morphine addiction" was a "totally erroneous belief."[8]

It would seem, nevertheless, that the medical world must have been waiting for a new narcotic drug for the treatment of organic illnesses—one that might be nonaddictive. Dreser's report was published in the Berlin *Therapeutic Monthly* in September 1898. His speech was mentioned in the November issue of the *Journal of the American Medical Association*. The December 3, 1898, edition of the *Lancet*, the leading medical journal in England, told of a new preparation: "It is said to be a favorable substitute for morphine by not altering the blood-pressure and thus to be well borne by persons of a weak heart and feeble arterial system. Heroin is also said to be free from other disagreeable secondary effects of morphine, so that it may be administered in respiratory diseases . . . in comparatively large doses with no effect but that of a sedative upon the air passages. These statements are so promising as to render desirable a careful clinical trial of this new derivative in this country."[9]

I have encountered no evidence of such *careful* clinical trials in England or elsewhere. But there is evidence that heroin spread rapidly throughout the medical establishments of many countries within the first few years after Dreser's speech. The Bayer company advertised the new drug in a number of languages—German, Italian, Russian, and English, among others. The ads for heroin often included another famous compound from the Bayer laboratories, named by Dreser in the year after his heroin speech—aspirin.[10] But most of the medical interest remained in the more powerful narcotic drugs. As the turn of the century approached, a wide range of such opiates became available: the venerable opium itself, codeine (the other principal active ingredient in opium, although much weaker than its more powerful relatives), morphine (the more powerful essence of opium), and heroin (which in layman's terms we might call the essence of morphine). While all these opiates had general painkilling qualities for such conditions as terminal cancer, the medical reports at the time seemed to emphasize the original purpose set out by Dreser and Floret—control of the discomfort of the then-widespread scourge of tuberculosis and related conditions.

The reports on heroin in the treatment of such conditions were often enthusiastic. For example, another German physician, H. Leo, related the case of a 71-year-old man suffering from severe coughs and shortness of breath. He was hospitalized, then sent to a special sanitarium and given a standard array of drugs. Even so, his condition deteriorated, respiration became more labored, and his heart action was poor. By February 1899 the man was in agony, in a constant state of fear, and unable to sleep at night. Then, on the evening of February 3, 1899, heroin was given to him. Dr. Leo wrote: "February 4. . . . After he had taken the drug he felt very comfortable and stated he no longer felt sick. The action of the heart was somewhat more regular. The appetite was better. February 5. . . . The sensation of fear that was always with him was gone. . . . The cough was without difficulty. February 6. . . . The action of the heart was regular. The heroin was then withdrawn for eight days. The ailments he had suffered before gradually returned. Heroin was again administered and had the same beneficial action as before."[11]

But other doctors soon gave evidence of the sad fact that, alas, there is no Garden of Eden on this earth, at least not one without serpents and prices to

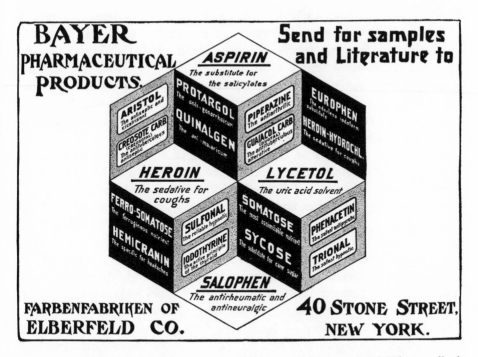

pay for the pleasures, or even simple human comforts, gained. The medical literature began to contain reports of the addictive danger of this new drug, which many had hoped would have the relief-giving powers of the other opiates but without the constant danger of addiction. (No such narcotic drug has ever been found.) In 1902 Dr. Morel-Lavallé, who advocated the use of heroin in treating morphinism and considered heroin generally safer to use than morphine, still felt compelled to warn his colleagues about the habit-forming potential of heroin. And Dr. G. E. Pettey was moved to write an article for the *Alabama Medical Journal* in 1903 entitled "The Heroin Habit Another Curse," in which he declared that of the last 150 people he had treated for drug addiction, eight were dependent on heroin, and three of these had started their habit on that drug. In Dr. Pettey's experience, heroin dependence was just as difficult to cure as the more common addiction to morphine.

Despite many such cautionary reports, the clinical popularity of heroin was widespread during the first decade of this century. In 1911 Dr. J. D. Trawick wrote in the *Kentucky Medical Journal*: "I feel that bringing charges against heroin is almost like questioning the fidelity of a good friend. I have used it with good results, and I have gotten some bad results, such as a peculiar band-like feeling around the head, dizziness, etc., but in some cases referred to, it has been almost uniformly satisfactory." However, Dr. Trawick's balanced approval of the medicine, and that of many other of his colleagues, was not to prevail.

There is evidence that during the same year in which Dr. Trawick's article appeared heroin abuse started to increase rapidly in New York City. Heroin soon replaced morphine as the drug of choice among the youthful recreational users on the streets of several large Eastern cities. Reports on annual admissions for heroin and morphine addiction to Bellevue Hospital during this period, assembled by Dr. W. A. Bloedorn and brought to recent attention by David Musto, reveal that the first admission for heroin addiction was made in 1910, that one being the total for the year, compared with 25 for morphine addiction. By 1914 it was 149 heroin to 398 morphine. By 1915 the balance had swung to 425 admissions for heroin addiction compared with 265 for morphine.[12]

By 1917, for reasons not completely clear, the movement had begun in earnest to transform heroin abuse from a troubling personal vice into a major national problem. During the rapid enlargement of the armed forces in 1917, rumors began to spread about the huge number of addicts in the service. Representative Henry Rainey declared that 80,000 draftees had been found unfit for service because they were addicted to drugs. In 1918 Dr. Royal S. Copeland, health commissioner of New York City, estimated that there were 150,000 to 200,000 addicts in the metropolis, most of whom were dependent on heroin, and many of whom were "recently discharged soldiers" under twenty-five. Clearly there were large numbers of heroin addicts at the time, but there also seems no doubt that, then as now, estimates of the size and growth of the problem varied widely.

The reasons for the public attention to heroin are equally hard to divine. One plausible explanation is that America's entry into World War I signaled the start of a period of agonizing social stresses and tensions. It was, in a way, the end of a period of isolation and innocence and the beginning of an era of fears about foreign involvement, German atrocities, Communist conspiracies, and crime and violence in the city streets. As Dr. Musto observed in 1974, "The crucial factor in heroin's transformation does not seem to have been the incidence or character of heroin use in 1917, but rather the context in which the phenomenon was interpreted. In 1917, the United States harbored a climate of ambiguous fears, which coexisted with the nation's desire to react unanimously in order to preserve the world's freedom. The battle was not against an enemy of the United States, but the enemy of mankind." In this context it might have seemed acceptable to some officials, Musto reasoned, to deliberately exaggerate the number of heroin addicts and the danger they presented to society—so long as the result was greater unity among the citizenry in order to save America from a whole catalog of new threats. "The drug was one more convenient object on which to place the blame for social disorder."[13]

II

Legal regulation of drugs had started at the state and federal level years before. Opium had already been singled out for special federal attention for reasons based apparently not on its chemical character but on that of the people who generally used it for so-called nonmedical purposes. On February 9, 1909, Congress passed a law providing that "opium . . . may be imported for medical purposes only." This was expressly intended to mean that opium could no longer be imported for the purpose of smoking, a practice then largely restricted to the Chinese inhabitants of these shores.[14]

The law was only one small part of a worldwide crusade led by American reformers to create legal controls on the use of psychoactive substances. American clergymen, statesmen, politicians—zealots and relatively sensible types together—saw the evils wrought by the uncontrolled use of drink and drugs and took direct action against the sources of evil, the substances themselves. They could not have won the legislative, judicial, and constitutional victories they did in the United States unless a significant part of the country's leadership supported them. The names of those involved fill our history books—Theodore Roosevelt, William Jennings Bryan, Woodrow Wilson, as well as many others not so well known.

By today's standards some of the legislative enactments were rational and much-needed efforts to improve the health and welfare of society. The Pure Food and Drug Act of 1906, for example, imposed the first national requirements on the labeling of drugs so that consumers might know that they contained addicting substances. Other actions seem less rational. In any event, they continued in overlapping waves of powerful protest at existing national and international conditions.

The United States saw much of its own drug problem as rooted in unrestrained international traffic. Various international conferences took place, largely at the urging of the United States, to create an international framework of control, primarily of the opiates: particularly the Shanghai Opium Commission meetings of 1909 and the Hague International Conference on Opium of 1911–1912. Out of these meetings came the Hague Opium Convention of 1912, whereby each of the thirty-four signatory nations agreed to tighten domestic controls on the manufacture and distribution of the opiates, cocaine, and other drugs, with the object of restricting their uses to medical and scientific purposes.

The American Harrison Narcotic Act of December 17, 1914 (discussed in detail in chap. 6), was regarded by many of its proponents as vital to our efforts to create an international fabric of control. If the United States could not put its own house in order, it would be in no position to attempt to convince other nations to ratify the Hague Convention. The basic themes of this scenario have changed precious little to the present day. The major thrust of the Harrison Act (at least according to some of its supporters) was to take the sale of narcotics away from grocery stores, mail-order houses, and other commercial peddlers, to place it in the hands of the medical and pharmaceutical professions, and to provide open and orderly records for virtually all drug transactions. The future key to the use of narcotics was to be a physician's prescription. And when could a physician, in conformity with the law, issue a prescription? After having registered with the district collector of Internal Revenue and after having paid his one dollar per year license or registration fee, a doctor could prescribe the controlled drugs when acting "in good faith" or "in the legitimate practice of his profession."

The initial and continuing challenge was to define the limits of good faith in the legitimate practice of medicine. Federal Treasury agents (the Harrison law was on its face a revenue measure), supported eventually by Supreme Court rulings and a cooperative medical establishment, took the lead in fleshing out that definition in regard to one vital professional activity: the use of narcotic drugs. The intrusion of the flinty eyed policeman, bearing not only the warrant of the law but also the Calvinist moral writ, had, and continues to have, two effects. The first is relatively well known—American doctors were forbidden to treat addicts by maintaining them on any of the controlled drugs. The second is less well known, indeed often ignored in almost all accounts of the period— many American doctors were frightened away from any prolonged use of these drugs in the treatment of organic illness.

It was at about this time, in the second decade of the century, that the rather special campaign against heroin began. The movement was to restrict most other drugs to medical uses and then to inhibit practitioners from using them too freely or regularly. One of the distinctive features of the developing attack on heroin, however, was a battle to prohibit its use altogether in the practice of medicine, to eliminate not only the abuse of the medicine but the very substance itself; in short, this was the beginning of the ritual of demonization.

By 1916 a massive change had occurred in the thinking of many leading American physicians. There was a growing conviction that addiction to heroin was increasing so rapidly that it should be banned despite whatever therapeutic powers it might have. One of the first steps in this direction was an order to the Public Health Service by the U.S. Surgeon General, Rupert Blue, on December 2, 1916:

> In view of the fact that the great increase in the usage of heroin at present constitutes a considerable menace to public health in the United States, it is desired to set an example and to signalize to the general public the danger which may accrue from its use. Heroin as a palliative in certain respiratory affections serves no purpose which cannot be accomplished by other agents fully as effectively and without the attendant possibility of grave disaster.
>
> You are therefore directed to discontinue dispensing heroin and its salts at relief stations of the service and to send all the stock of these drugs now on hand to the Purveying Depot, 14 Pennsylvania Avenue, N.W., Washington, D.C., either by parcel post or by freight on Government bill of lading.

The months and years that followed saw successive and similar condemnations of the medicine. In June 1919 a committee of experts appointed by the secretary of the Treasury stated that "the medical need for heroin . . . is negligible compared with the evil effects . . . of this alkaloid, and . . . it can easily be replaced by one of the other alkaloids of opium with the same therapeutic results, and with less danger of creating habituation." On May 8, 1920, the House of Delegates of the American Medical Association adopted a resolution: "That heroin be eliminated from all medicinal preparations and that it should not be administered, prescribed, nor dispensed; and that the importation, manufacture, and sale of heroin be prohibited in the United States." On December 29, 1923, the surgeon general of the U.S. Army prohibited the use of heroin in that service and ordered all existing stocks destroyed. On February 2, 1924, the surgeon general of the navy wrote to all those in his command: "I have the honor to inform you that further issues of heroin to the U.S. naval service have been prohibited."[15]

But the demonization ritual was not restricted to the medical profession. The movement against heroin took on the nature of a popular crusade which at the time attracted the energy and support of some of America's leading citizens of all professions. The Foreign Policy Association, for example, was formed in 1918 to support the creation and the principles of the League of Nations. Over the years its membership has included some of the leading intellectual and establishment figures of America as well as of other countries. It has not been unusual to find names like Felix Frankfurter or Winston Churchill among its members or to find letters of endorsement from presidents and prime ministers among its literature. During the association's early years it enlisted in the war against heroin. Its efforts included a pamphlet released in 1924 that laid out what must be considered the dominant enlightened thinking of the time.

Prepared by the association's Committee on Traffic in Opium, the pamphlet is entitled *The Case against Heroin*. On the front page is this summary of its position:

1. Heroin is unnecessary in the practice of medicine.
2. Heroin destroys all sense of moral responsibility.
3. Heroin is the drug of the criminal.
4. Heroin recruits its army from youth.
5. *Heroin can be eliminated only by international action.*

The pamphlet then went on to cite leading judicial and medical authorities on the subject of "Heroin and Crime." Dr. Alexander Lambert, an attending physician at Bellevue Hospital in New York, declared, "Heroin cuts off the sense of responsibility, in the moral sense, much quicker than morphine. It destroys the sense of responsibility to the herd. Heroin addicts will more quickly commit crime and with no sense of regret or responsibility for it. The herd instinct is obliterated by heroin, and the herd instincts are the ones which control the moral sense, in the sense of responsibility toward others and the environment in general. Heroin obliterates responsibility the same as cocaine, and it makes much quicker the muscular reaction, and therefore is used by criminals to inflate them because they are not only more daring, but their muscular reflexes are quicker." In the same vein, Dr. S. Dana Hubbard of the New York City health department warned, "Heroin used by a human being produces an unmoral savage. The boy or girl, man or woman, driven by heroin's influence becomes cold-blooded, the personality is inflated to a state of paranoic [*sic*] egoism, and the individual is capable of committing any crime."

The pamphlet also contained a restatement of the official international view regarding the drug, as expressed in 1923 by the Subcommittee on Health and Opium of the League of Nations: "In view of the fact that a question is being raised as to the possibility of prohibiting the manufacture of heroin . . . the Mixed Sub-Committee, composed of technical experts, agrees, having regard to the small therapeutic value and the harmful effects of diacetyl-morphine (heroin), to advocate the prohibition of its manufacture." [16]

Not surprisingly, such widespread fears and beliefs among leading citizens in the United States and in international organizations soon resulted in congressional action. On April 3, 1924, the Ways and Means Committee of the House of Representatives met to consider a resolution put forward by the Honorable Stephen G. Porter of Pennsylvania, who had a long history of leadership in the worldwide struggle to control narcotics. The resolution proposed that the law restricting the importation of opium to medicinal purposes—by then titled The Narcotic Drugs Import and Export Act of 1922—be amended by adding this phrase: "*Provided*, That no crude opium may be imported for the purpose of manufacturing heroin." The hearings held on that simple phrase, not even a full sentence, were to prove both important at the time and prophetic of things to come in America and much of the world.[17]

Five witnesses appeared in support of the resolution. None opposed it. Congressman Porter, the first witness, laid out a summary of the medical opinions favoring prohibition and the actions taken by various medical agencies, starting with the Public Health Service, to ban the use of the drug in their respective jurisdictions. He introduced into the record many of the statements contained in the Foreign Policy Association pamphlet. Porter made it clear, however, that he sympathized with the unfortunate plight of narcotic drug addicts and did not believe they should be called "dope fiends." Relying on a Treasury Department report, he set their number in this country at "approximately 1,000,000." Under cross-examination, Porter pointed out that to help reduce the number of future addicts, he would have preferred to prohibit the manufacture of heroin directly but doubted the power of Congress at that time to do so; thus, he chose an indirect route to accomplish the ban on manufacture which he avowed was the purpose of the proposed law.[18]

Appearing on behalf of the American Medical Association, Dr. Charles Richardson told of the 1920 resolution of the AMA approving the banning of heroin. During further questioning this leading Washington physician gave expert testimony in support of the then-accepted medical belief that "heroin contains, physiologically, the double action of cocaine and morphia. It produces the excitation of cocaine, with the sedative action of morphia." Congressman Henry W. Watson, of Pennsylvania, told Dr. Richardson that despite the seeming unity of the medical profession in support of prohibition, he had received a number of protests from physicians in his state. He mentioned as an example a letter of April 1, 1924, from Dr. H. A. Hare, professor of therapeutics at Jefferson Medical College in Philadelphia. The letter stated: "In my opinion this drug is an exceedingly useful one, performing a function that no other drug will perform under certain circumstances. The Harrison narcotic act, if properly enforced, is entirely adequate to prevent the abuse of heroin, and the mere fact that heroin is used as a habit-producing drug does not justify its entire prohibition anymore than would entire prohibition of cocaine or morphine be justified. May I add, that to absolutely prohibit the existence of this drug is a very sweeping piece of legislation, which, while protecting persons who are more or less degenerate, would deprive a multitude of worthy people of an efficient pain-relieving remedy." This seemingly sensible position was virtually laughed away when Dr. Richardson explained, in response to the Philadelphia medical professor's letter, that "three of the largest drug firms in America are located in Philadelphia."[19]

Several of the expert medical witnesses declared flatly that heroin caused insanity. For example, at one stage of the hearing Congressman Hawley asked, "Does this drug produce insanity?" Congressman Porter interjected, "Undoubtedly." And the witness testifying at the time, Surgeon General Rupert Blue, concurred, "Oh, yes."[20]

Dr. Richardson was asked whether other drugs could take the place of heroin in ordinary medical practice. "Absolutely," he replied. "Sometimes they produce headache and nausea, but they have the physiological effect. The only thing about heroin is that it is more pleasant to take." Dr. Richardson then went on to explain that although morphine did produce headache and nausea, codeine, another derivative of opium, was "nearly as good as morphia." He assured the committee that codeine could replace heroin in American medical practice.

Written testimony from a Viennese doctor, Knaffl-Lenz, was introduced by Surgeon General Blue to the effect that "heroin is incomparably more poisonous than morphine, and the therapeutic dose is not appreciably smaller than the toxic dose." Dr. Blue was asked his own opinion of the impact on a user's life expectancy. He replied that, "the drug being more poisonous," he believed it could shorten the life of an addict more quickly than morphine. No clinical studies were offered to support this assertion or any other such testimony throughout the hearing.[21]

Some witnesses claimed that heroin addicts committed crimes not only to obtain funds to buy the drug but also because the drug had the effect of propelling its users toward violent and senseless acts. Mr. Porter asked one witness if the purpose of the confirmed criminal in taking heroin before perpetrating a crime of violence was to relieve himself of moral restraint. The witness—Sidney W. Brewster, assistant superintendent and deputy warden of Hart's Island Reformatory Prison, in New York City—responded, "That is my opinion; and that is also true of cocaine. I would say this, that users of morphine, while they do commit crimes, they are not usually crimes of violence. . . . The man who uses heroin is a potential murderer, the same as the cocaine user; he loses all consciousness of moral responsibility, also fear of consequences."[22]

How did addiction originate in most cases—from medical treatment or from so-called evil association? The medical and criminological experts seemed united in their replies. A memorandum from the New York City Department of Health, introduced into the record by Porter, mentioned a three-year study by a deputy police commissioner of arrestees who also were drug addicts. The memorandum stated that "only 2 per cent of those arrested can trace their addiction to medical treatment. . . . Hence, we may conclude that 98 per cent of nearly 10,000 drug addicts acquired their vice through curiosity, morbidity, and criminal association." This was consistent with other estimates by the New York City Police Department in 1924 to the effect that a minimum of 76,000 ounces of heroin had been sold to addicts by street vendors in that city alone during the course of a year, while all 14,715 physicians in the state legitimately prescribed only 58 ounces.[23]

The diverse threads of testimony were neatly woven together in the written statement of Dr. S. Dana Hubbard, of New York City: "Heroin is the drug used by addicts of over 95 percent of New York's underworld . . . , according to . . . the police and prison statistics, and the unfortunate part of the situation is that less than 1 percent of these miserable creatures acquire the habit through illnesses. . . . The heroin question is not a medical one, as heroin addicts spring from sin and crime. It is a social problem where the medical and pharmaceutical and allied professions can do much to aid in solving this serious problem. Society in general must protect itself from the influence of evil, and there is no greater peril than that of heroin."[24] Such misinterpretations of medical and legal data at the time were referred to by Dr. David Musto, who wrote in 1974 that the American medical and legal professions in the past revealed "themselves as closely in step with . . . prevailing current national fear and quite capable of reinforcing . . . what, in hindsight, may appear as a distortion of reality."[25]

Virtually every "fact" testified to under oath by the medical and criminological experts in 1924—including claims that heroin was no better than codeine in the treatment of the organically ill; that it produced insanity; that it was more poisonous than morphine or that its therapeutic dose was not much smaller than its toxic dose; that it propelled its users toward violent criminal activity; and that it destroyed the morals of its users—was unsupported by any sound evidence. To say that some heroin addicts *who have been denied the drug* perform outrageous acts is one thing, but to claim that the drug itself produces the behavior or that it is organically harmful is a totally different and misleading argument. But at the time of this hearing, such misinterpretations went unchallenged. Nothing seemed to deter Representative Porter from carrying forward his humanitarian purpose of virtually prohibiting the manufacture and thus the use of heroin in the United States and of attempting to support international action in the hope of creating a worldwide prohibition on all manufacture and use of heroin.

The power of the emotions, forces, and people arrayed against heroin is reflected in the fact that the Ways and Means Committee *unanimously* supported the legislation, and on June 7, 1924, it became law when both houses of Congress passed it, in each case *unanimously*![26]

Since no opium was then grown in America, this action has been interpreted by some observers as the complete prohibition by Congress of the use of heroin in American medicine. That, indeed, was the purpose of the law as seen by Congressman Porter, and the result was soon close to total abolition, but not quite. Looking back on that time from the perspective of September 1936, Commissioner Harry J. Anslinger, of the Federal Bureau of Narcotics, wrote in an internal memorandum for the secretary of the Treasury: "In practice, all manufacture of heroin in the United States was discontinued shortly after June 7, 1924, although there was some supply of crude opium still remaining on hand which, having been imported prior to that date, was legally available for the continued manufacture of heroin. Stocks of finished heroin then in the hands of manufacturers and wholesale dealers have naturally decreased until, on December 31, 1935, they amounted only to 201 ounces."[27]

A significant minority of American physicians opposed the ban on heroin and continued to speak out against it. For example, a resolution appeared in a 1940 issue of the *Journal of the American Medical Association* written by Dr. A. A. Herold, of the Louisiana State Medical Society, for presentation to the AMA House of Delegates at its upcoming session.[28] The resolution said, in part, regarding the 1924 ban:

WHEREAS, Said prohibition has been in effect for a sufficiently long time to show that it does not prohibit the drug addicts from obtaining heroin by illegal means but does prohibit the medical profession from being able to utilize this valuable remedy in the treatment of diseases. . . .

RESOLVED . . . we petition Congress to rescind this amendment . . . thereby permitting the medical profession to enjoy the benefits of this very useful opium derivative.

The resolution was referred to the AMA Council on Pharmacy and Chemistry. Apparently it died there, but not before the council reiterated, as reflected in a later issue of the journal, the basic position of organized medicine in America "to the effect that heroin is not considered to be therapeutically indispensable and that the Council on Pharmacy and Chemistry renews its approval of the provisions of the law prohibiting the importation of opium for the manufacture of heroin."[29]

Many lay organizations and individuals took more extreme positions than did the AMA and its members. Countless campaigns against narcotics, especially heroin, were launched in the years between the two world wars. One of the most prominent of the anti-heroin crusaders was Richard P. Hobson, a Spanish-American War hero and prohibitionist who formed a number of organizations to combat the narcotic menace. Some notion of the difficulties faced by those who sought a rational approach to narcotics may be gleaned from Hobson's remarks in a national radio broadcast in 1928:

> To get this heroin supply the addict will not only advocate public policies against the public welfare, but will lie, steal, rob, and if necessary, commit murder. Heroin addiction can be likened to a contagion. Suppose it were announced that there were more than a million lepers among our people. Think what a shock the announcement would produce! Yet drug addiction is far more incurable than leprosy, far more tragic to its victims, and is spreading like a moral and physical scourge. . . . Drug addiction is more communicable and less curable than leprosy. Drug addicts are the principal carriers of vice diseases, and with their lowered resistance are incubators and carriers of the strepticoccus, pneumococcus, the germ of flu, of tuberculosis, and other diseases. Upon the issue hangs the perpetuation of civilization, the destiny of the world and the future of the human race.

These hysterical myths were considered so sound and noncontroversial at the time that the facilities for the broadcast were donated by the National Broadcasting Company.[30]

On July 18, 1956, Congress took the final step in the process of criminalizing this medicine that had begun thirty-two years before: it directly declared all heroin to be contraband, a non-medicine. Even under the restrictive fabric of American laws and regulations, until this final act it had been conceivable for hospitals or physicians to legally possess diacetylmorphine and to use it appropriately in professional practice. But 120 days after the effective date of the 1956 act the medicine became illegal and subject to seizure by the police without compensation. Thus, starting on November 18, 1956, no American physician could lawfully dispense diacetylmorphine to a patient for any purpose in the ordinary practice of medicine. The medicine was transformed into contraband. It was demonized by the law.[31]

On October 27, 1970, Congress enacted a broad recodification and clarification of existing drug laws. In the Federal Comprehensive Drug Abuse Prevention and Control Act of 1970, heroin was, as we have seen, placed in Schedule I, indicating again that it had "no currently accepted medical use in treatment in the United States." That is its official legal and medical status today in America and virtually every country in the world.

For years after the American opium-for-heroin import ban of 1924, many countries continued to manufacture and use licit heroin in huge quantities. The League of Nations estimated that in 1925, the year after the Porter amendment aimed at creating the groundwork for an international prohibition on heroin, world legal manufacture was 4,600 kilograms. By 1926 it was 9,000 kilograms, or approximately 20,000 pounds. But soon U.S.-backed international controls began to have an impact. By 1929 world licit production of diacetylmorphine had dropped again to under 4,000 kilograms, and by 1935 it was down to well under 1,000.[32] In recent years reports to the United Nations on legal use indicate that worldwide figures are a tiny fraction of what they once were: 101 kilograms were consumed in 1979—96 of these in the United Kingdom (see table 2).[33]

III

Thus, the American crusade against the legitimate medical use of heroin has been victorious almost everywhere. But what has been the impact of that campaign on the treatment of the organically ill in America and elsewhere?

Starting with the 1916 prohibition on use by the U.S. Public Health Service, it seemed as though the national leadership was engaged in an attack on the devil in the form of a drug. But there never has been any convincing evidence that heroin caused organic damage, produced significantly harmful side effects, or was an ineffective painkiller. The question usually raised by physicians, lawyers, and social leaders went beyond analgesia into the realm of euphoria—*was it too good?*

In the answer to that question, I submit, may be found many of our greatest problems in regard to heroin (and other psychoactive drugs). Clearly, the answer required an appreciation not simply of medicine but also of theology, moral philosophy, and human rights, among other factors. There was also some need to understand the nature and dynamics of addiction. Within the first few years of heroin's widespread use, much of the discussion by medical and legal experts concerned its addictive potential. This leap was one of faith, not science. Even though the mysteries of addiction are still far from solved today, even though no recognized expert can yet produce documented explanations why heroin epidemics, for example, come and go, the leaders of the medical profession, with the support of other powerful figures, concluded in the early part of this century that heroin was too addicting to be used in the practice of medicine. There was, and continues to be, however, no adequate medical explanation of the process by which nonaddicted patients are converted into addicts; of the reason why countless nonaddict patients have been treated with narcotic drugs, including heroin, over a period of time and have *not* become addicts; and of the reason why many patients simply ceased using the drug as soon as their discomfort disappeared. In the 1920s, it will be recalled, Dr. Hubbard testified that less than 1 percent of all addicts had originally started taking heroin because a doctor had prescribed it to treat an illness; the others presumably had become addicted through evil association—that is, through nonmedical sources. Thus the logical course of action, based on these two propositions, was to ban the use of heroin in legitimate medical practice!

Had the charges against heroin been brought only against the dangers of doctors' creating addicts out of patients whom they were treating for other illnesses—in more modern terms, "therapeutic addicts"—the course of history might have been different. But in public discussions about the emotional issues of narcotic drugs, about obtaining godly pleasures without incurring worldly debts, there has always been a good deal of confusion about the relationship between the medical dispensation of these compounds by a physician, on the one hand, and the creation of narcotic addicts, on the other.

The confusion has been over both cause and effect. It is not at all clear whether the major *cause* of addiction, in terms of the source of drugs, during the early years of this century was:

1. the dispensation of narcotic drugs by physicians to the organically ill; or
2. the dispensation of narcotic drugs by physicians to the addicted in order to prevent the discomfort of withdrawal; or
3. the dispensation of narcotic drugs by pharmacists; or
4. the sale of narcotic drugs by commercial outlets, such as grocery stores and mail-order houses; or
5. the sale of drugs on the streets; or, finally,
6. all the above.

The confusion over *effect* related to the nature of the evils that had been created. Were the American reformers in the 1910s and the 1920s concerned about the creation of:

1. addicts being treated for painful illnesses which confined them to hospitals or homes? or

2. relatively stable addicts who regularly took drugs which they purchased from their own earnings or capital, and who constituted no social problem? or

3. addicts who were criminals and constituted a threat to the persons and property of other citizens? or

4. all the above, since all forms of addiction were morally reprehensible and all would eventually cause social harm?

The confusion persists to this day. Of course, when doctors prescribe narcotic drugs to organically ill patients, there is always the danger that the patients will become addicted, especially if the medicine is continued over time. In many cases morphine and heroin addicts have been created by doctors who were treating them for such medical problems as tuberculosis, heart disease, cancer, and painful injuries. But a realistic assessment of medical experience in America demonstrates that while some criminal addicts started their deviant careers because a doctor prescribed a narcotic to relieve the pain of an organic illness, their number has never been large and as a group they have never constituted a major threat to society in any country. Thus, no reliable evidence has appeared, as yet, documenting a relationship between (1) the medical dispensation of drugs to the organically ill and (2) the creation of a significant group of criminal addicts constituting a major social problem.

It is quite rational, however, to look to other possible sources of drugs for the apparently large number of opiate addicts in early twentieth-century America. Some doctors took advantage of a potentially lucrative situation and sold great quantities of drugs to addicts without attempting to wean them from their habits. Other physicians made efforts to reduce the supply but kept prescribing when their efforts seemed to fail, as they often did. But doctors, after all, were limited in number and did charge a fee for their services. The source of addiction for many, perhaps most, people might thus have been nonmedical. What was that source? For at least the first sixteen years after Dreser popularized heroin in his Dusseldorf speech, the drug was as easy to purchase over the counter, except in those states that had laws restricting nonmedical use, as was the Bayer aspirin he popularized during the next year. Bayer heroin or Bayer aspirin: take your pick from one of many legitimate drugstores, grocery shops, or mail-order houses. It appears that heroin soon became one of the favorite drugs of the so-called criminal classes, who had no need to inconvenience themselves by paying a doctor to prescribe it for them. After the passage of the Harrison Act, a major black market developed which supplied addicts with a variety of drugs, particularly the increasingly popular heroin.

The federal campaign against addicts and the doctors who supplied them had a powerful impact on the entire practice of medicine, not simply in the arena of addiction treatment but also in that involving organic illness. Of course, after a given time a cancer sufferer regularly taking morphine might become addicted. But this was not necessarily so; modern research has shown that some cancer patients on high doses of narcotics stop taking the drug during periods of remission. Nevertheless, over the years many American doctors actually have turned away from the appropriate use of narcotic drugs in the treatment of the pain and anxiety of organic illness because of fear of arrest and prosecution by law-enforcement authorities.

The clinical impact of this widespread fear seems to be one of the least understood aspects of American medicine, but glimpses of it appear in numerous accounts, often almost as relatively unimportant sidelights. For example, when the renowned clinic in Shreveport (discussed in detail in chapter 6) was set up in 1919, its purpose was to treat addiction, not organic diseases. But, it turned out, Treasury agents scared virtually every doctor in the area away from the practice of prescribing opiates to any person not actually hospitalized who took them regularly, even if the repeated use had a clear and compelling organic basis. A recent account reveals: "The clinic treated a number of patients with chronic and terminal illness. . . . Because of the continuing threats of arrest by narcotics agents, many doctors were quite willing to give up the responsibility of prescribing narcotics to the clinic. Patients usually continued treatment with the doctor, but went to the clinic for the needed opiate."[34]

While the authors of this study did not seem overly critical of this situation (they were mainly concerned with the treatment of addiction, not organic illness), we must realize the extent of the intrusion of American criminal law and law enforcement into the practice of medicine. The police were telling the doctors, in effect, how to treat cancer, tuberculosis, and gonorrhea, among other diseases.

Such intrusions have been virtually unknown in Britain. There is no way of knowing their extent in America, then or now, but I have seen evidence that some doctors, even today, still fear the knock at the door by the narcotics agent if they resort to the regular use of heavy doses of narcotics in the treatment of patients suffering from organic disease. Witness a letter I received in late 1977: "I have lost six of my immediate family from cancer, and, for the past two years, have been fighting my own battle. . . . I guess the final pain is unbearable, as I have heard unusually strong people beg for relief. . . . I asked if my stepfather could have something to ease the pain . . . was told that he would have to wait two more hours, as state law wouldn't allow him any more morphine in less than four hours . . . and was told that it was to keep the patient from becoming addicted! Hard to accept, when I had already been told that his death was near!" The recent study at Montefiore and St. Luke's hospitals shows, moreover, that the related exaggerated fears about addiction still significantly affect the clinical judgment of some American doctors.

In his closing comments to the Fifth Institute on Drugs, Crime, and Justice in London, on July 13, 1978, Dr. Robert Twycross told of how he was explaining his usual practice to an American doctor—oral morphine (presumably in the Brompton Cocktail) every four hours, in 5- to 100-milligram doses depending on the patient's needs—whereupon his counterpart from across the ocean exclaimed, "If I prescribed 100 milligrams of morphine, the nurse would call the police!" One would like to think that this American doctor was being facetious, but one cannot be sure.

It would be reasonable to assume that with the advances in scientific research on painkillers it would be possible, certainly by now, to sort out fact from myth and to lay to rest the distortions of the past, with which we have been dealing. We shall see how reasonable that assumption is as we turn to a review of the modern research on heroin and other analgesics in the treatment of the organically ill.

4: MEDICAL VALUE: THE MODERN EVIDENCE

"Diamorphine is the only drug in this group which . . . shows any significant difference from morphine . . . which might prove beneficial [as preoperative medication] in certain clinical circumstances."
—*A Queen's University of Belfast research team, 1969*[1]

"British physicians specializing in the care of patients with far-advanced cancer consider . . . heroin . . . an indispensable potent narcotic analgesic."—*Robert G. Twycross, 1978*[2]

"Heroin was first used . . . to withdraw patients who were addicted to morphine. The result was to make them dependent on this new drug . . .

No controlled study has indicated the superiority of heroin over other opiates for the control of chronic pain. Because of the rapidity and intensity of its euphoric action . . . heroin is the opiate with the greatest abuse potential. All of the modern research now being performed to understand and control the mechanism of pain is focusing on the study of substances that are free of the addiction potential of the opiates.

It is a cruel hoax to suggest that heroin is the best pain killing medication for the treatment of terminal illness. The justification for its being withheld from the public is based on . . . extensive clinical experience and basic scientific facts."—*Henry Brill, 1977*[3]

I

Dr. Brill is one of the leading drug-abuse-policy experts in the United States, having served in numerous important positions, including membership on the National Commission on Marihuana and Drug Abuse in the early 1970s. Yet the letter quoted here—which appeared in a 1977 issue of the *U.S. Journal of Drug and Alcohol Dependence*—misstates the facts on several important counts: he has repeated the myth that heroin was originally used to treat morphine addiction; there is no scientific proof that heroin has the greatest abuse potential of all the opiates; a number of controlled studies suggest the superiority of heroin in *some* circumstances to control chronic pain; and much of the pain research going on now deals with how best to use existing *addictive* opiates, in part because so many doctors seem uninformed about them.

It was communications from eminent medical authorities such as Dr. Brill that eventually drove me to perform my own analysis of the literature at the National Library of Medicine in Bethesda. When I started this project, I expected to find a very scant literature on heroin by American researchers because the substance had been banned from medical use in the United States for so long. Surprisingly, I found that some inquisitive American doctors had obtained special research licenses in re-

59

cent years and had conducted an extensive series of reported studies on heroin. In any event, I assumed that most American doctors would understand the basic clinical and scientific facts about the drug. Here I was mistaken. Moreover, leading American doctors and government drug officials have often displayed an ignorance of even the existence of the large body of literature by English doctors and researchers regarding the use of heroin in the treatment of the organically ill, just as I did a few years ago.

My purpose in this chapter, therefore, is to summarize samples of a mass of medical and scientific literature about heroin and related opiate medicines. The need for such an exercise is illustrated not only by Dr. Brill's remark that "extensive clinical experience and basic scientific facts" indicate a negative view of heroin—an assertion not at all supported by the reported research—but also by two recent, related events. After the Carter administration issued its historic order in 1977 to commence studies on the potential use of heroin (and marijuana) in American medicine, a White House press aide explained that there was a need "to see that we expand our research on drugs we haven't studied before."[4] On May 12, 1978, the Medical and Chirurgical Faculty of Maryland, otherwise known as the Maryland State Medical Society, rejected a recommendation from the Montgomery County delegation to support the use of heroin for pain relief in the terminally ill. According to Dr. Francis Mayle, president of the society, "They wanted to see more scientific proof." Moreover, as a story in the *Washington Star* pointed out, "A key objection to the use of heroin has been that while it is an effective pain killer, it is an addictive drug, so legalizing its use would generate more cases of drug addiction."[5] Both stories illustrate how little attitudes toward heroin have changed.

II

A convenient place to start a review of the modern medical literature is a 1975 publication by NIDA, a short pamphlet providing this view of the chemistry and pharmacology of heroin: "Heroin is a highly effective narcotic analgesic, similar in pharmacological action to morphine, although its milligram potency as a pain-killer is three to four times greater than that of morphine. Heroin produces an analgesic effect by a two-fold action on the central nervous system; the pain threshold is elevated and psychological response to pain is altered. Pain may still be recognized as being present, but the individual reacts less emotionally to it." If that is the interpretation of one of the leading government drug agencies, then how can the American government continue to prohibit this extremely valuable medicine? The answer (although the question was never posed by the publication) is a familiar one and is found in the later statement that, "of all the opiates, diacetylmorphine . . . has the greatest addiction potential." No clinical or scientific documentation is offered.[6]

Today heroin is manufactured in Britain pretty much as Wright did in 1874, by adding acetic anhydride to morphine. This is not a difficult process, especially for someone with a rudimentary knowledge of chemistry, and the resulting compound is relatively simple. As Judson says, "Given the crude morphine, to synthesize heroin takes far less apparatus, time, and chemical experience than, say, to distill a drinkable whiskey. The morphine molecule is a compact linkage of three carbon rings, crocheted together by a fourth loop containing a nitrogen atom. Even some vitamins are chemically more complex. Heroin is exactly like morphine except that from each of two of the carbon rings there dangles a short chain of atoms taken from the acetic anhydride."[7] For those who are interested, the structural formulas for the two medicines look like this:[8]

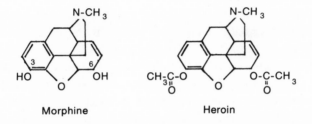

Morphine   Heroin

Of much more importance than manufacture and chemical structure is the question of how heroin works in the human body. Despite all the expert medical opinion that has been offered on what must be the most testified-about drug in the world, medical science is far from clear about the answer. Again, the redoubtable journalist Judson provides, in my opinion, the best *single* summary of the available scientific knowledge on the subject:

How heroin or any other opiate works on the central nervous system is not fully understood. Neurobiologists propose that each molecule of narcotic fits exactly, key in lock, into a receptor on the outer membrane of a nerve cell, and thus changes the nerve's response to the normal stimulating chemicals produced and transmitted by other nerve cells nearby. If the nerve, to compensate, grows more receptors, or if it varies its utilization of the normal chemicals received from its neighbors, that would explain why narcotic doses must be increased to achieve the same pain relief or the same pleasure. Pharmacologists at Johns Hopkins University demon-

strated recently that molecules of morphine or methadone do attach themselves to specific types of cells within the brain. More recently still, Avram
Goldstein and colleagues at Stanford have announced that they have extracted and partially purified, from brain cells of mice, receptor molecules
that interact specifically with opiates. The day is surely not far off when the
structure of the receptors will be known and the mechanism of their response to opiates will be worked out atom by atom; yet until then such
models remain no more than highly educated metaphors.[9]

A more charitable view of medical and biological science might allow that
only rarely is it possible to provide a complete causal explanation for any given
activity of the human body, especially in regard to the impact of a drug upon it.
More likely to be found are rigorous clinical tests observing the precise *results*
of the drug. I believe that research doctors have usually explained the results of
drug experiments accurately; for example, within two hours we observed x, y,
and z measurable or observable reactions in patients who had been given 3.2
milligrams of heroin compared to other patients who had received 10 milligrams. On the other hand, I do not believe that the scientists know *why* the
drugs produced those results.

Such scientific observations of results form the basis of all modern research
on heroin. These studies demonstrate that much of what passed for medical
science in the heroin field in the early years of this century was guesswork, some
of it probably right, much of it wrong or as yet unproven. As we have seen,
doctors charged that a major defect in the drug was that it was terribly damag-
ing to the human body, at least in comparison to the other opiates used in
medicine. Such charges have made their way into American folklore and have
been accepted at every level of American society.

Indeed, it may well be the sight of poor diseased addicts—who are indisput-
ably organically sicker as a group than the general public but for reasons other
than heroin use alone—that has distorted the view of doctors, judges, and
lawyers. Nothing in the recent medical literature reporting on scientific clinical
tests of heroin would lend support to the notion that any of the opiates—
morphine, methadone, codeine, or heroin—in and of themselves, as distinguished from impure methods of administration or adulteration, causes inordinate risks of organic damage. Indeed, what I found in the medical journals is
that medical researchers also have often been preoccupied with the impact of
heroin on the bodies of addicts rather than with the clinical value of heroin in
the practice of ordinary medicine, especially in the treatment of the organically
ill. Obviously there is a vast difference between the impact of self-medication

by an untrained individual who is not even knowledgeable about the exact mixture he is injecting and the informed prescription by a doctor of a pure, precisely measured compound, administered in hygienic fashion by a trained nurse to a patient in a normal medical setting. Fortunately, there have been studies of experiments with heroin in the latter circumstances as well.

III

Some medical authorities claim that the modern era in analgesic research commenced with a series of studies in the late 1940s by the anesthesia laboratory of the Harvard Medical School at the Massachusetts General Hospital. In a 1962 issue of the *Journal of Pharmacology and Experimental Therapeutics*, the Harvard scientists wrote that heroin had been banned in the United States because of its allegedly severe addictive potential. As a result, little information existed concerning its effect on nonaddicts. Accordingly, the doctors conducted an experiment on 522 hospital patients to see the impact of four different doses of heroin compared with a standard dose of morphine (10 milligrams per 70 kilograms, or 154 pounds, of body weight) on the relief of postoperative pain due to major surgery. The experimenters concluded, "The results of the present study showed that heroin was approximately two to four times as potent as morphine with respect to relief of moderate, severe or very severe postoperative pain during the first 150 minutes after injection. The amount of heroin needed to match the analgesic potency of morphine (10 mg) in the group comparisons ranged from 2.3 mg to 5.2 mg."[10]

But no single equation was found by the researchers to explain the relationship between the two drugs: during the first 45 minutes only 2.3 milligrams of heroin might produce the same amount of painkilling action as 10 milligrams of morphine; but by the time 150 minutes had passed, it would take about 5.2 milligrams of heroin to produce the same effects as 10 milligrams of morphine. The study did not take the next step and deal with the question: so what?

This question came up in 1977 in regard to the controversy over the use of heroin in terminal cancer cases. Dr. James H. Sammons, executive vice-president of the AMA, wrote in September 1977:

The matter of legalizing the use of heroin for administration to terminal cancer patients has been brought to our attention in the past. Our Department of Drugs has looked into this matter, and has provided us with the following analysis. It is true that heroin is more potent than morphine in relieving pain. This increased potency does not mean that the analgesic effect is enhanced; it simply means that a smaller amount of heroin is required to produce the same analgesic effect that is obtained with morphine. This property also makes heroin a more attractive drug for abuse purposes.

As for the claim that heroin would provide greater relief than other analgesics in terminal cancer patients, there is no convincing scientific evidence that it would do so. A review of this matter by Dr. Louis Lasagna of the University of Rochester published in *Pharmacological Reviews* . . . [in] 1964 notes that the results of controlled studies that have used equivalent analgesic doses have shown no significant difference between heroin and morphine. In a study by Dr. Lasagna and his colleagues, heroin caused greater euphoria than did morphine in post-addicts, but not in the chronically ill patients.

In a study reported by Dundee, Clarke and Loan in *The Lancet*, July 29, 1967 . . . heroin . . . , morphine, and methadone were compared. This study is of particular interest because it was done in the United Kingdom where the use of heroin is legal and because it was done to test the claim that heroin has certain advantages over other opiates. The results of this study did not demonstrate any clear-cut advantages of heroin over morphine. . . .

In view of the lack of evidence that heroin has a therapeutic advantage over morphine, there appears to be little or no justification for recommending its legalization in the United States for even limited clinical use, especially when its high abuse potential is taken into account.

The article by Dr. Lasagna, a preeminent American pain researcher, did indeed support the position of the AMA. It might well be rated as the scientific centerpiece of the current conventional wisdom in this country on the relative merits of heroin and morphine. Dr. Lasagna concluded his evaluation of morphine as follows: "Morphine is a good, reliable analgesic when given parenterally [by injection], but is considerably less effective when given by mouth. It can produce a variety of untoward side effects, but these are not of sufficient seriousness or frequency in most patients with severe pain to override the remarkable analgesia this drug can provide. Despite its drawbacks, and because no other established drug which can equal the analgesic performance of morphine is free of its undesirable qualities, morphine remains the standard against which all potential new morphine substitutes must be compared."

Dr. Lasagna then went on to evaluate heroin as an analgesic: "With few drugs is there a greater discrepancy between volume of published material and content of convincing and reliable information, than in the case of heroin. It was evident soon after the drug was placed on the market at the end of the 19th century that heroin possessed many, if not all, of the attributes of morphine, including the ability to relieve pain, suppress cough, depress respiration, and produce both euphoria and dysphoria." Too many research studies on heroin have been poorly conceived and executed, Dr. Lasagna observed, but others have demonstrated little significant difference between morphine and heroin regarding analgesia and addictive potential. The studies allegedly demonstrating this lack of significant difference included those by the Harvard research team mentioned above.

Nevertheless, Dr. Lasagna offered this emphatic conclusion: "In summary, heroin seems little better or worse than morphine in its capacity to produce analgesia, respiratory depression, and other side actions, or in addiction potential. To quote from the recent report of the expert Ad Hoc Panel for the White House Conference on Narcotic and Drug Abuse: 'There is a widespread misconception that heroin has effects significantly different from those of morphine. It does not, and this misconception should be dispelled permanently.' "[11]

Thus, Dr. Lasagna, Dr. Sammons, and the leaders of the American medical establishment read the reports of the Harvard researchers (and others that come to similar conclusions) about the greater potency of heroin and concluded that the difference was insignificant. But it may also be concluded, at least from the viewpoint of the patient, that a drug that is several times more powerful and also faster-acting than the currently accepted standard setter does indeed seem to have significant advantages. Moreover, later research suggests that for some patients heroin has other advantages.

Also cited by Dr. Sammons in his letter explaining the AMA's opposition to the legalization of heroin for cancer patients was a 1967 article by a group of British medical scientists. The authors, from the Queen's University of Belfast, did indeed conclude that heroin provided no clear-cut advantages over morphine as a preoperative medication given to relieve anxiety and pain and to produce drowsiness but not complete anesthesia.

Drs. Dundee, Clarke, and Loan explained that they had tested the properties of heroin, morphine, and methadone by injecting several hundred healthy female patients in random order on a double-blind basis. The patients were about to undergo minor gynecological surgery. Ninety minutes after the injection, one of the researchers subjectively assessed the degree of drowsiness, apprehension, and excitement. Here is how the Irish doctors stated the major part of their conclusions: "Our findings are disappointing with respect to the controversial diamorphine. They do not consistently demonstrate any clearcut advantages over morphine, nor do they show it to differ appreciably in toxicity from the standard drug. Increasing the number of patients might have achieved the first result, but although minor differences can be demonstrated statistically in this manner they are not likely to be of clinical importance. . . . The earlier onset of action, as compared with morphine and methadone, may be advantageous in the treatment of severe pain. In general [however] we would support the view of Lasagna (1964) . . . "[12]

Again, this research report would seem to support the current American position on heroin and morphine. It is worth noting, however, that these articles were cited by the AMA in response to an inquiry about the use of heroin in terminal cancer cases. But these subjects were not cancer patients suffering chronic intractable pain but healthy women. The authors themselves qualified their results by pointing out that they used but a single injection, "which is very different from the long-term use advocated by Saunders." (The Belfast doctors were here referring to the earlier advocacy of the use of heroin in terminal cancer treatment by Dr. Cicely Saunders.) The Irish doctors also attached "real clinical significance" to the greater amount of vomiting caused by increased doses of morphine. While they did not highlight this finding in their conclusions, it would seem to undercut the AMA's implication that all a doctor has to do in order to obtain the benefit of heroin is to increase the amount of morphine in the dose.

Another matter of even greater concern is that this team of doctors continued their clinical experiments after the research reported here, and their interpretation of the results, published in 1969, was quite different. These results are reported below, but were not by Dr. Sammons in his letter from the American Medical Association in the fall of 1977.

In 1969 the Belfast doctors reported on trials with six opiates including morphine and heroin. While they relied in part on the work already explained in the 1967 article, the interpretation was more favorable toward heroin. In the American context it is noteworthy that this report deals not with the creation of addicts, not with the treatment of addicts, and not with terminal illness. Moreover, the medical analysis does not even deal directly with the analgesic effect of the drugs but with such factors as sedation and toxicity in preoperative medication. It is not so much a question of life or death or addiction but of simple comfort. It is also noteworthy that each of the drugs studied had strong and weak points as preoperative medication. On balance, however, diamorphine had a slight overall edge. Thus, heroin was not seen as a panacea but it *was* seen as a very good medicine. According to this scientific study, "Diamorphine is the only drug in this group which, in the dose used, shows any significant differences from morphine 10 mg. which might prove beneficial in certain clinical circumstances. These include earlier onset of action, more marked sedation and relief of apprehension, coupled with fewer emetic sequelae." In other words, it seemed to act quicker, calmed the patients down more, and caused fewer of them to vomit.[13]

In 1967 a group of Scottish doctors reported on the clinical use of heroin in treating eight patients who had just undergone acute myocardial infarctions, a type of heart attack. Although the number of subjects hardly provides for a level of statistical significance, the report should not be dismissed on that ground, for it is one of a number of scientific articles suggesting that there might be unique benefits from heroin that cannot be duplicated simply by increasing the dosage of morphine. In other words, while the relief of pain may be the main function of the opiates in modern medicine, there may be other desirable qualities as well.

A team of doctors from the Royal Infirmary in Edinburgh reported that although morphine does reduce pain in patients suffering from serious heart disease, it tends to cause a drop in arterial pressure (hypotension), thus forcing a diseased heart to work even harder. The physicians found that heroin provided relief of pain and anxiety and helped patients to relax but did not cause a drop in blood pressure. Moreover, they confirmed previous findings that while morphine has a tendency to cause vomiting in heart patients, an event which for them can prove disastrous, heroin produced no such side effects among the patients in this sample. Here is the doctors' own summary of their research:

> The effective relief of pain and anxiety is an essential part of the treatment of patients with acute myocardial infarction. Morphine has long been the drug of choice for this condition in both hospital and general practice. . . .
> We have assessed the effects of intravenous heroin on the circulation as far as could be determined without added risk to patients already in jeopardy as a result of acute myocardial infarction. . . . A standard therapeutic dose (5 mg.) of heroin administered intravenously to eight patients with acute myocardial infarction caused little change in the cardiovascular system. The analgesic and sedative effects of the drug were adequate and no undesirable side-effects were observed. Heroin may be preferable to morphine in the treatment of patients with acute myocardial infarction.[14]

For most members of the public, however, the truly important questions about the use of narcotics in dealing with pain revolve not around preoperative medication or heart attacks but around relief from the agonies of cancer. It is a recurrent, widespread fear that will simply not go away. There is a sound basis for this fear in terms of the sheer number of victims. The National Cancer Institute estimates that at least 365,000 Americans will die of cancer this year, 1,000 every day. Estimates by other authorities hold that one in four living Americans, perhaps 50 million people, will eventually succumb to some form of cancer.[15]

A California man wrote me in the late 1970s: "I have watched 2 friends suffer intolerable agonies in the final stages of terminal cancer, and now I have it. I have a dreadful fear of the excruciating pain of cancer in the final stages. Has any progress been made in legalizing heroin for terminal cancer patients? My God, how can our country's leaders be so cruel and inhuman to deny the dying this relief—they can't live long enough to form drug habits."

At this point we must look at the recent studies and clinical impressions of Dr. Robert G. Twycross, of England, a research pharmacologist and now a hospice director. To show how sensitive judgments are in this arena, those studies and impressions must be viewed almost as if we were seeing two overlapping portraits. The first reveals the facts and opinions Dr. Twycross held up to the time when this book was nearly completed, which were based very much upon his scientific studies. The second portrait shows how his opinions have gradually changed, to the dismay of many American advocates of the legalized medical use of heroin, mainly on the basis of his clinical impressions. We turn first to portrait one.

However important objective scientific findings may be, it must be stated again that the major issues that arise in the care of a human being with terminal cancer do not center on the choice of the proper narcotic drug, be it heroin, morphine, methadone, Demerol, or codeine. If we think only in terms of medicines, in many cases none of the narcotics is fully adequate; the patient may be in great discomfort unless supplemental drugs such as Valium or even a simple laxative are provided. To hear Twycross talk, moreover, either at his Oxford hospice or in a London classroom, is to realize that some research pharmacologists see their function as involving far more than the analysis and use of chemicals. Robert Twycross, for one, has a heavy spiritual commitment to his work.

Of the hospice of which he is director, Dr. Twycross said, "It's not a death house, as some people thought it might be. There's a real sense of life there, of joy, which is different from happiness." On the fact that a professional hairdresser visits the hospice regularly, he stated flatly, "Women who are dying need their hair done." On pain in cancer patients, Dr. Twycross told the institute participants in London that 90 percent of the doctors in Britain and America do not know how to assess pain; that the fact of having a cancer does not necessarily mean that the malignant process is the cause of patient's pain; and that while narcotics are usually vital in the control of cancer pain, often simple diversion, such as a friend to talk with, can assume enormous importance. But, of course, the doctors must be able to discern when the time has come to turn to consideration of drugs.

It is remarkable that although heroin has been widely used for years in English cancer care, no rigorous studies or controlled experimental research on the use of the drug in such cases took place until Dr. Twycross carried out the work reported here. As we have seen, it was the use of heroin at St. Christopher's Hospice in London and missionary activity in the United States by its famous medical director, Dr. Cicely Saunders, that broadcast the word about hospices and heroin—and, indeed, seemed to equate the two. In the early 1970s Dr. Twycross joined the staff of St. Christopher's as a research pharmacologist. His main assignment was to test the assumptions then prevalent in the hospice about the value of heroin and to look into related questions regarding the overall treatment of pain and anxiety in terminal cancer.

I have chosen to focus on only a few samples of his research work which, I believe, go to the heart of the matter. The first is an article published in 1974 reporting on a rigorous and comprehensive study of the treatment accorded five hundred patients with advanced cancer admitted consecutively to St. Christopher's Hospice; 80 percent of the patients were treated with heroin. The research results raised serious questions about some common medical assumptions regarding the use of heroin in treating pain related to malignant disease. For example, despite the widely held belief in medical circles, especially in America (by Dr. Lasagna, for example), that heroin is an ineffective analgesic if taken by mouth, Dr. Twycross concluded that most patients can be maintained on orally administered heroin *or* morphine. Moreover, he found that diamorphine did not lead to the impairment of mental faculties, tolerance was not a practical problem, and addiction did not seem to occur.[16] The last point is significant not only for the treatment of organic illness but also for a better understanding of the whole field of addiction to psychoactive drugs, for there is no pharmacological explanation of why some people get addicted and others do not, despite the confident assertions about heroin's greater abuse potential by Dr. Brill quoted at the beginning of this chapter. It is also important to realize that these patients did not expect to become dependent on the drugs, their doctors and nurses did not hold such an expectation, and the assumption was that when and if the pain stopped, so would the drugs. The most dramatic example was that of a sixteen-year-old girl who received increasing doses of heroin, which plateaued at 200 milligrams daily (5 to 10 times the doses taken by many street addicts), over a period of fifteen weeks. When her bone cancer

went into remission and the pain receded, the heroin dosage was slowly reduced over a period of weeks and then eliminated completely. She showed no
signs of withdrawal or addiction and several years later was alive and well
without drugs.[17]

In regard to "impairment of mental faculties," Dr. Twycross observed,

> It has been suggested [by some medical authorities] that the prescription
> of a potent narcotic analgesic to an inoperable cancer patient "suffering
> agonies from chronic pain" was like sentencing the patient "to a kind of
> living death". . . . It is difficult to be sure exactly what was meant by a
> "kind of living death." It probably refers to the common belief that patients
> receiving narcotic analgesics are in some way "detached from reality" or
> simply lie "drugged" in bed. However, one's own experience from treating
> several hundred patients with diamorphine is that this is not so. Indeed, in
> the present series of 500 patients, 46 were discharged for varying lengths
> of time and of these 22 were on diamorphine at the time of discharge.
> These patients were alert and mobile, though one or two of the more
> elderly ones required a walking-frame. . . . It appears that 150 mg of dia-
> morphine a day by mouth is not incompatible with normal activity. I
> would suggest that "detachment from reality"—if it occurs—and drowsi-
> ness are related more to advanced physical debility than to any particular
> dose of diamorphine.

On the matter of drug addiction or dependence—which he defined in accordance with the World Health Organization as "a compulsion or overpowering drive to take the drug in order to experience its psychic effects"—Dr. Twycross stated,

> On this definition none of the patients reviewed became addicted. Occa-
> sionally a patient has been admitted to the Hospice who appears to be
> addicted. Such a patient typically has a long history of poor pain control,
> is receiving regular but inadequate injections of a narcotic analgesic and
> . . . demands an injection every two or three hours. Usually, with time and
> patience, it is possible to control the pain adequately, prevent clock-watch-
> ing and the demanding behaviour and, sometimes, even transfer patients
> on to an oral preparation. But even here, can it be said that the patient is
> truly addicted? Is he craving the narcotic in order to experience its psychic
> effects? Or, is he craving relief from his pain, in part if not in full, for at
> least an hour or two?

The 1974 article ended, nevertheless, with a plea not to overrate heroin in cancer care: "It must be clear from the summarised case histories that diamorphine cannot be regarded as a panacea for terminal cancer. . . . Unless it, or any other analgesic, is used within the context of total patient care, the results will be far from satisfactory." This article provided, therefore, perhaps the most complete report ever published on the use of heroin in terminal cancer. But the research did not *compare* heroin to morphine and did not involve a *controlled trial*.[18]

The research reported in the second article, published in 1977, did do so. The clinical research, which was *pro*spective, not *retro*spective, revealed the results of the first known controlled trial on the use of heroin as compared to morphine in the care of terminal cancer patients. This experiment was planned in advance, in contrast to the previous study, which sought to understand what had happened in the past. Over a two-year period 699 patients entered the hospice and were given either morphine or heroin orally in the Brompton Cocktail. The dose of narcotic was increased by the ward physician until the patient was free of pain. This was done on a double-blind basis; that is, neither the patient nor the attending medical staff knew which of the drugs was being used at a particular time. Other medication was also given, especially milder drugs to control vomiting. When necessary to control pain, patients were switched to injected drugs, either morphine or heroin. After studying the results Dr. Twycross summed up this seminal experiment: "It is concluded that provided allowance is made for difference in potency, morphine is a satisfactory substitute for orally administered diamorphine. However, when injections are necessary, the greater solubility . . . gives diamorphine an important practical advantage."[19]

On the basis of his written report on the controlled experiment itself and discussions with Dr. Twycross, it is clear to me that he wants neither to understate nor to overstate the value of heroin in cancer treatment but to put it in its proper place. At no point does he say that there is no difference between heroin and morphine. As a gross generalization about the 699 patients who participated in this trial he does say that morphine and heroin achieved roughly similar results when the medicine could be taken orally. But in some cases the patients were so weak or nauseated that it was impossible to get adequate doses of any drug into them by mouth. And, as Dr. Twycross explained to me when I visited him later at the hospice in Oxford, general debilitation and muscular deterioration may make it impossible to inject enough morphine in solution for the patients' worn bodies to absorb; the liquid volume of the morphine solution necessary to obtain adequate pain control in some cases is simply too large, perhaps 6−8 milliliters or more. On the other hand, only two-tenths of one milliliter (only a fraction of an inch in a small hypodermic syringe) of a heroin solution injected under the skin (subcutaneously) and not necessarily in a damaged vein (intravenously) usually contains enough painkiller to give relief in even the most distressed cases.

When one considers the actual manner in which the drug solutions are prepared by pharmaceutical companies and the realities of patient care, Dr. Twycross explained, the higher dosage levels required to relieve the pain of a particularly agonizing cancer may necessitate the injection of a volume of morphine solution orders of magnitude greater than the volume of heroin solution that would give the same amount of pain relief. Thus, a person who might require a dose of 240 milligrams of morphine would have to receive a minimum volume of 16 milliliters of commercially prepared morphine solution in order to get the same pain relief provided by 120 milligrams of heroin, which could be delivered in a volume of two-tenths of a milliliter. Since (by my calculations, not Twycross's) there are 15 to 20 drops in a milliliter and 5 milliliters in the average teaspoon, two-tenths of a milliliter of heroin solution are approximately 3 to 4 drops, barely enough to wet the bottom of that teaspoon. The equivalent dose of injected morphine solution is 80 times as great, or 16 milliliters—a volume rarely required even in cancer cases; but when circumstances do demand it, that dose would fill 3 whole teaspoons. This may not seem like much, but for someone who is ill and emaciated, an injection of that volume of liquid every three to four hours could hurt a great deal as well as cause tissue damage.[20]

When Dr. Twycross spoke before the drug institute in London, he provided a written summary of the advice he frequently gave to professional medical audiences. Included were the following items:

- Diamorphine (diacetylmorphine, heroin) is widely used in Great Britain as a potent analgesic to relieve severe acute pain (post-operative, renal colic, post-myocardial infarction) and also in advanced cancer.

- Diamorphine when given *intravenously* has an earlier onset of action, is more sedating, and causes less vomiting than morphine. These are all properties which are desirable when seeking to relieve severe acute pain.

- Because of relatively rapid in vivo deacetylation [absorption within the gastrointestinal tract] diamorphine has the same effects as morphine when given orally.

- In the vast majority of advanced cancer patients in whom regular oral medication is satisfactory, morphine and diamorphine may be regarded as interchangeable.

- However, about 10% of terminal cancer patients with pain require injected medication, either because of intractable vomiting or non-response to high doses of oral morphine.

- It is always possible to administer diamorphine in a smaller volume than morphine. . . .

- British physicians specializing in the care of patients with far-advanced cancer consider diamorphine (diacetylmorphine, heroin) an indispensable potent narcotic analgesic.[21]

That is the end of the first portrait of Dr. Twycross; now, on to portrait two. Most of the old picture stays untouched, except in one very important respect: Dr. Twycross now sees virtually no particular advantage in the use of heroin to treat cancer patients, even that small percentage who can no longer take medication by mouth. To those in America and elsewhere who cite his research as the linchpin in their argument for the legalization of heroin in medicine, his reversal comes as a stunning disappointment, at least equivalent to the earlier change of mind by Dr. Saunders. In a letter of September 16, 1980, commenting on a draft of this book, he explained his current stance, first observing that "Dr. Balfour Mount, Palliative Care Unit, Royal Victoria Hospital, Montreal, and Dr. Sylvia Lack, The Connecticut Hospice, New Haven, to name but two leading hospice figures in North America, have not . . . campaigned for the legalisation of medicinal heroin. I think you ought to include the reasons why." In his opinion, "The key to the reluctance of North American hospice doctors to campaign actively for legalisation of medicinal heroin" is that they "know that the doctors who use their present narcotics badly . . . will use heroin just as badly and, in practice, patients will be no better off. In fact, they may be worse off because the doctor will expect a magical response."

In reaction to my reminder that approximately 10 percent of terminal cancer patients cannot take oral drugs and thus have an urgent need for injected heroin (a fact I had originally learned from him at his hospice in 1977), he cautioned, "You must stop using this handy figure of '10%.' With medically available heroin, the percentage of patients in whom good pain control can be achieved will not [rise] one iota of a percent; it might, however, make the degree of pain control easier to achieve than without." But what of his research findings and public statements of just a few years earlier—which make up the major part of portrait one—indicating the indispensability of heroin in the treatment of terminal cancer patients unable to swallow or to take comparatively large doses of injected morphine? Dr. Twycross replied that since that time,

both St. Christopher's and Oxford [his current hospice] have been using,

when necessary, higher oral doses of morphine sulfate* rather than trans-
ferring to injections of heroin at an arbitrary level. This means that the
... times we convert to injections because large doses of oral morphine
sulfate appear to be relatively ineffective are extremely rare. I can remember
one incidence in the last two years [out of 500 terminal cancer cases]. I
think the incidence of conversion to heroin for pain control *per se* at St.
Christopher's is equally small. In other words, the situation has changed
since the beginning of 1978 when I was harking back to my practice up to
1976 or thereabouts. However, I think four years of experience in going
even higher (if necessary) with oral morphine sulfate is long enough for
me to say that it is extremely rare to need to convert to high dose heroin
from high dose oral morphine.

Thus, it would appear that the leading research expert in the world on the
comparative advantages of heroin and morphine in the treatment of terminal
cancer now sees little advantage in heroin. Until Dr. Twycross came to that
conclusion, I thought that his research findings, combined with those of other
medical researchers, produced an impressive scientific structure in support of
the unique value of heroin in organic medicine. Now, my opinion is that the
scientific evidence on the organic side is like that on the addiction side: equivo-
cal and conflicting. Some pieces of the scientific findings would support the
superiority of heroin; others, the similarity and equality of heroin and morphine; but none, the essential inferiority of heroin as a medicine.

However, heroin continues to be used by some British physicians for a wide
variety of organic illnesses and medical problems, most prominently in the
treatment of the painful and terror-laden ravages of advanced cancer. But it is
not a last-ditch medicine reserved for the dying in England. The drug is also
being used to treat persistent coughs; lung and respiratory diseases, as originally conceived by Dreser and Floret; the pain and discomfort following either
minor or major surgery; the discomfort and anxiety of childbirth; the pain of
shingles, a disease that affects the nerve endings; the anxiety, pain, and irregular
blood pressure following a heart attack; and the howling pain caused by burns
and other painful injuries, as opposed to illnesses. Thus, the medicine has not
one but many uses. Even in treating cancer, moreover, its success depends not
only on its greater solubility and potency, as Twycross demonstrated, but also
on the imaginative potential of physicians reaching for new techniques to provide relief from pain and anxiety. Such cancer specialists as Drs. Wilkes and

---

* In layman's terms, translate "morphine sulfate" to mean "morphine," since it denotes the usual
manner in which the drug is prepared for use in medicine.

Wiltshaw, for example, believe that many of their patients are receiving the overall therapeutic benefits of heroin in ways not possible from any other drug.

IV

Many American doctors agree with those British physicians who continue to see the advantages of heroin in treating the organically ill. So do some legislators. One of the latter acted on that belief at about the same time that Dr. Twycross was firming up his recent change of mind on the subject. In a historic action on May 13, 1980, U.S. Representative Edward Madigan (R.–Ill.) introduced a bill to amend the Controlled Substances Act so as to authorize the use of heroin for terminally ill cancer patients.[22] Cosponsored by seventeen other members of Congress, the bill met universal opposition from the federal executive branch witnesses who testified at a hearing on September 4 before the House Subcommittee on Health and the Environment. Dr. Jane E. Henney, of the National Cancer Institute, explained that the opposition of her agency was based in part on the success of its pharmaceutical research branch in pursuing an alternative approach to the problem—"that of enhancing the solubility of morphine." Dr. Henney stated that the greater solubility of heroin had concerned the American cancer experts because, as we have seen, heroin's greater dose-for-dose potency meant that less could be given. But the NCI researchers produced, according to Dr. Henney's testimony, "a very soluble and stable morphine compound. . . . The drug that these investigators developed is a freeze-dried . . . morphine acetate salt. Even if the patient requires exceedingly high doses of morphine, these can be administered in less than 1 milliliter of fluid."[23]

The development of freeze-dried morphine acetate provides a formidable obstacle to the movement supporting the legalization of medicinal heroin. Before that movement can succeed in America, and perhaps in many other countries that tend to follow its lead, it may well be necessary for *American* studies to be undertaken that would convincingly demonstrate heroin's *superiority* to morphine. The argument against the legalization of heroin is that since it is no better than morphine and the risk of addiction is greater, why not stick to morphine and continue the prohibition of heroin? Only if American, not foreign, research demonstrates its clear superiority will the government and the medical establishment have to face the political issue of actually determining the reality of the addiction risk. The answering argument might well be a simple one: the drug operates as a relatively safe medicine. End of statement. But that is a logical argument, not a political one.

The American studies whose purpose was to compare heroin with morphine in the treatment of cancer patients were undertaken in the expectation that they would help decide whether or not heroin is superior. These studies were pointed to by the AMA and by other leaders of the medical establishment as a major reason for the delay in facing the issue of freeing up heroin for medical purposes. At the same time, however, some of these same medical leaders are already expressing doubt that the research programs will come up with anything that might convince them to change their minds. According to a statement issued by the AMA Department of Drugs in October 1978, "There is no reason to expect that the results in the newer programs will differ from those reported in earlier studies."[24] This extraordinary act of prejudging the results of ongoing scientific studies was consistent with the vote in June by the House of Delegates, which, as we have seen, declared, "There is no reason to believe that the NIDA study now underway will show different results."

The NIDA study is being conducted under the direction of Dr. Raymond W. Houde at the Memorial Sloan-Kettering Cancer Center in New York. A second study, funded by the National Cancer Institute, is being directed by Dr. William T. Beaver, professor of pharmacology at the Georgetown University Medical School in Washington, D.C.[25]

The first major report of the Sloan-Kettering study was published in the June 18, 1981, issue of the *New England Journal of Medicine*.[26] Some indication that the issue of cancer pain has ceased to be an arcane professional concern is found in the media treatment of this report. On the evening of June 17 an announcer urged audiences of the NBC television network to watch the "Today" show the next morning to learn how "heroin is a bust as a painkiller." Early the next day Drs. Robert F. Kaiko and Raymond W. Houde appeared to tell the results of their study. Reporter Robert Bazell opened by observing that the doctors had just done a study of terminal cancer patients. Dr. Kaiko corrected him by remarking that the study sample was composed of 166 cancer patients with postoperative pain, "rather than terminal pain of advanced cancer."

When Bazell said that the doctors had found that heroin was no better than morphine and asked if that was correct, Dr. Kaiko, a research pharmacologist, responded, "It is *different* than morphine in some fine aspects in that its effects peak a little earlier but are less sustained. It might be better in an individual patient but overall, on the average, it does not seem to have an advantage [over] drugs that are already available." Mr. Bazell then asked Dr. Houde, "Why can't cancer patients get a drug that might even be a *little* bit better for some of them?" Dr. Houde replied, "If there were good reason to believe it were better . . . than what we already have . . . I would see no reason not to legalize it."

Both doctors made clear their conclusion that heroin had proved no better than morphine in their experiment. Neither, however, suggested that it was inferior to morphine or that it was a "bust as a painkiller."

Their report in the medical journal explained that the study had been designed "to determine the relative analgesic potency of intramuscular heroin and morphine and to compare mood and side effects" in cancer patients who had just undergone an operation. The team found there were no significant differences in pain control, mood improvement, or unwanted side effects such as dizziness, sweating, and nausea. While they did not deal directly with the solubility issue, the team did observe that Dilaudid, another high-potency narcotic which is legal in America, seemed to be even better than heroin on this score. The conclusion of the Sloan-Kettering team: "Heroin does not appear to have unique advantages or disadvantages as compared with other narcotic analgesics when used for relief of pain."[27]

The medical and political significance of the report was highlighted by the lead editorial in the issue of the journal in which it appeared. Dr. Lasagna reiterated his position of a quarter century earlier and, in the process, gave vent to some sharply worded thoughts on this chemical "source of controversy." On heroin's alleged superiority to morphine in the management of cough, childbirth, cardiac infarction, and chronic pain, the experienced pain researcher declared, "When scientifically examined," most of these claims disappear "in a dream of the shadow of smoke." So also such claims about the treatment of cancer pain as supported by the Kaiko-Houde study and a long line of previous ones. "Individual patients might be better off with heroin than morphine, and vice versa," Dr. Lasagna admitted. "Yet with so many morphine surrogates legally available and the potential problems in regard to storage, theft, and diversion, the legalization of heroin for medical use does not seem to be socially responsible."[28]

The doctors involved in the Georgetown study did not agree with the final legal and social conclusions of Drs. Kaiko, Houde, and Lasagna, although there was substantial agreement on the major medical issues. Dr. Philip Schein, chief of medical oncology at Georgetown University Hospital and Dr. Beaver's collaborator in the study of morphine and heroin in the treatment of cancer pain, stated in June 1981 that the Georgetown study also found that heroin and morphine were very similar. However, heroin had the important practical advantage that it could be injected in significantly smaller doses because of its greater potency and solubility—in line with the earlier clinical position of Dr. Twycross. When he balanced all the evidence, Dr. Schein came down on the side of legalizing the medical use of heroin, in express disagreement with the conclusion of Dr. Lasagna, which Dr. Schein said was based on "extra-medical considerations." Dr. Schein observed: "The chances of theft or diversion or addiction . . . all of these risks could be said to exist with morphine. There is no greater danger with heroin. . . . There is no reason why it should not be made legal."[29]

In light of this division of opinion by medical experts about some very sophisticated issues, it might be useful to look at this matter from another, perhaps simpler, angle. If doctors in a given country were allowed a relatively free choice by the law and medical tradition, to what extent would they decide to prescribe heroin, and to what extent, morphine? To my knowledge, the question has never been put in such a direct manner.

Britain is the only country in the world with a long tradition of the licit use of significant quantities of both drugs and a relatively calm approach to the matter—and is thus the only national laboratory in which we can pursue the inquiry. If, as one wing of this professional debate—Drs. Saunders, Twycross (now), Houde, Kaiko, and Lasagna, to name a few—argues, there is no special advantage in heroin, one might assume that doctors would rarely prescribe it for their patients. Indeed, there have been persistent reports that licit heroin use is decreasing in England. The highly reliable data from this country, however, do not support those widely credited stories. If the annual reports to the United Nations are to be believed, England stands virtually alone among the nations of the world in the regular licit use of any significant quantity of heroin—over 95 percent of all the heroin legally consumed anywhere in the world during recent years has been prescribed by English physicians.[30] In only one respect has there been a decline: the amount of heroin prescribed for addicts—23 kilograms in 1969, down to 8.5 in 1978—a subject described in detail later (see table 3).[31] But the use of heroin in the treatment of the organically ill has risen steadily; so also has the overall figure for heroin use (the organically ill plus addicts). At the same time, overall use of morphine declined. In 1971 the consumption of morphine in the United Kingdom was 364 kilograms; of heroin, 41. By 1979 overall heroin consumption had more than doubled to 96 kilograms, while morphine had dropped to 266 (see table 4).[32] These "votes" of British doctors—and, by implication, of their patients—may well be the most important pieces of scientific data in the comparative analysis of the medicines heroin and morphine. *Personal perceptions of how drugs operate in actual practice may far outweigh pharmacological findings*. It seems reasonable to project, from these significant sets of numbers, that doctors in America and in other countries might well prescribe heroin and morphine in something like this balanced manner for their patients—if the law allowed them the choice.

When I review all the available scientific evidence—official statistics, research studies, and clinical impressions—I come to the following conclusions about the value of heroin in treating the organically ill and the injured:

1. For some patients, heroin is superior to other medicines for the control of pain, anxiety, and related conditions. This is an objective scientific finding which, however, will vary with the patient's condition. As symptoms change, other drugs, such as simple aspirin, may be quite helpful—even for cancer victims.

2. For many patients with other symptoms, heroin has no special advantages. This statement also applies to a significant number of cancer sufferers.

3. There is no scientific evidence that heroin harms patients or that it is an ineffective medicine. Indeed, the scientific evidence is overwhelming that heroin provides a wide range of therapeutic benefits.

4. The weight of the scientific evidence does *not* demonstrate that heroin is *universally* superior to other medicines, such as morphine, for all patients in need of a narcotic.

5. Science cannot predict which patients will be helped by heroin. The only way in which it can be determined whether a particular patient suffering, for example, from painful cancer, a heart attack, shingles, or burns will be comforted by the drug is to administer it and observe the results. A proper assessment may require adjustment of the dosage and methods of administration over a period of days, or longer.

6. The impact of the drug on the physical and emotional condition of some patients will be influenced by what those patients expect that impact to be. In other words, chemistry and pharmacology can carry the investigation only to a certain point; beyond that point, the perceptions of the patients themselves become crucial variables.

7. No scientific justification exists for the continuing legal prohibition of the use of heroin in the treatment of the organically ill and the injured. Indeed, each patient in pain should be eligible to receive the drug in order to determine whether it provides particular benefits for him or her at that time.

These conclusions are valid, I submit, despite the change of mind of Dr. Twycross, despite the development of the more soluble morphine compound by the National Cancer Institute, and despite the findings of the 1981 Sloan-Kettering report. They are based primarily upon *medical* evidence. "There's enough convincing data in the medical literature about the efficacy of injected heroin as a potent narcotic painkiller," said Dr. Beaver in 1978. However, he added, "The hurdles to the medicinal use of heroin are legal and administrative, not medical."[33] This observation is consistent with that of many other medical experts, including, as we have seen, Dr. Bourne. It is, I believe, a fair summary of the current situation, for there are no longer any valid medical arguments left in this debate—only nonmedical issues.

V

Professor Eugene L. Shapiro addressed some of the legal issues in his seminal article, "The Right of Privacy and Heroin Use for Painkilling Purposes by the Terminally Ill Cancer Patient." His argument relies mainly on the evolving constitutional right to privacy, a concept created by the Supreme Court in a series of decisions involving important personal issues such as abortion. In *Roe* v. *Wade*, for example, the Court, in 1973, for the first time established the right of a woman to have an abortion under certain circumstances, despite contrary state law. The decision was based in large part on the right to privacy read into the Fourteenth Amendment due-process clause, which maintains that certain issues are so personal as to be beyond state power to control. At the same time the Court has refused to find "an unlimited right to do with one's body as one pleases." It is a question of a balance between the interests of the individual in maintaining personal integrity, on the one hand, and the interests of the public in maintaining "compelling state interests," on the other. The Court may, if the issue is properly presented to it, have to perform that balancing act in regard to heroin for the terminally ill cancer patient at some time in the future. In such a case the right to privacy may prevail, for, as Professor Shapiro observed, "the process of dying possesses an intimacy that is incomparable in human experience. For one dying in intractable pain, the decision to seek relief poses an impact and immediacy that is likewise without parallel." The refusal of the government to allow a person to choose medication in such a situation could be declared by the Court to be constitutionally impermissible as an invasion of the right to privacy.[34]

While this argument is important, there may be better and broader legal approaches. One argument might center on the unreasonableness of the prohibition on heroin that was created by the legislative actions of 1924, 1956, and 1970, mentioned previously. Rather than try to create a new privilege within the constitutional right to privacy, which may be a difficult chore of legal statesmanship at this time in view of the general conservatism of the Court, it may be easier to attack the laws that created the nonmedicine status of heroin head on. This direct attack would seek to have the current status of heroin declared unconstitutional because its prohibition from medicine (1) was lacking in rational support when first enacted and (2) is now even further removed from any scientific reality, in light of modern medical studies. The argument would thus have a more established legal basis than the relatively new right to privacy for it would claim that, from the very beginning, due process was violated through an arbitrary and unreasonable classification.

A related legal strategy would be to work within the framework of the federal Controlled Substances Act, part of the Comprehensive Drug Abuse Prevention and Control Act of 1970.[35] Heroin, as we have seen, is considered a prohibited medicine because it is included under Schedule I of the law, which has the following criteria:

(A) The drug or other substance has a high potential for abuse.
(B) The drug or other substance has no currently accepted medical use in treatment in the United States.
(C) There is a lack of accepted safety for use of the drug or other substance under medical supervision.

The criteria for Schedule II drugs, such as morphine, methadone, codeine, and cocaine, are as follows:

(A) The drug or other substance has a high potential for abuse.
(B) The drug or other substance has a currently accepted medical use in treatment in the United States or a currently accepted medical use with severe restrictions.
(C) Abuse of the drug or other substance may lead to severe psychological or physical dependence.

Drugs in both schedules have a high potential for abuse. The second criterion is a tautology, an absurd logical redundancy, in regard to heroin: it has no currently accepted medical use because the law makes it illegal.

The critical path of the argument runs headlong into the third criterion. What is the difference between a Schedule I classification and a Schedule II listing? Just how dangerous is the drug when it is administered "under medical supervision"? It should be possible to marshal impressive evidence, some of which appears in this book, that heroin is not significantly more dangerous, if at all, than other drugs now in Schedule II. In the case of heroin, "dangerous" would probably mean "addicting" in two senses: (1) to the people for whom it is prescribed and (2) to the general public or street addicts. When the drug was legally prescribed in America for the treatment of organic illness, it could well be argued that there was no reliable evidence of an extensive addiction problem arising out of such use under medical supervision, even in the less structured society of the early part of this century. In fact, I believe the burden of proof should be shifted to the government, and to prohibition advocates such as Dr. Lasagna, to demonstrate the dangers of using heroin "under medical supervision." Even the most ardent zealots of prohibition during the 1920s said that only 1 or 2 percent of the street addicts got started on the drug as a result of medical treatment. In the only other country that has any relevant experience, England, the problem of diversion of legal heroin from medical facilities is almost nonexistent. So, also, is any factual basis for the other brooding fear still dominating much learned discussion about heroin in America—that doctors who treat the organically ill with heroin will create hordes of addicts.

During his appearance before the Fifth Institute on Drugs, Crime, and Justice in 1978 Chief Inspector H. B. Spear, of the Drugs Branch of the Home Office, was asked about the security problem by one of the participants; upon her return, writer Helen Neal said in *New York Magazine* that Mr. Spear "told us that heroin causes no more security problems than any other narcotic. . . . Contrary to the visions some American drug-enforcement agents have about truckloads of heroin being hijacked, no such incidents occur. . . . No British hospital or hospice has been invaded by masked bandits with submachine guns."[36] The English law-enforcement officers I have met have generally agreed with this assessment.

What about the unwitting creation of therapeutic addicts by British doctors? Because of the laws and customs there, because of the legality of heroin in Britain, and also because of the close nature of English society, the country's statistics on heroin use and abuse are especially revealing and probably unmatched by any in the world for accuracy. These annual compilations contain a category labeled "origin of addiction," which provides an insight into the extent to which addiction in the society is traceable to the use of a drug in the treatment of organic illness or injury. While even the British statistics can never tell the whole story, they do cast some light on the proportion of addicts created by doctors who have treated them originally as patients for some condition other than addiction.[37]

These marvelously revealing sets of numbers show that the great majority of addicts were of therapeutic origin until the 1960s. They were generally not criminal, not deviant, not young; hardly anyone knew that they were addicts, even their spouses—except, of course, their doctors and the Home Office clerks who kept the addict index (on which more later). Moreover, only a tiny percentage were dependent on heroin, although heroin has been available in Britain since the turn of the century. For example, in 1958 there was a total of 442 known narcotic addicts; the "origin of addiction" in 349 cases was "therapeutic." The doctors "notifying" them (telling the Home Office about them) judged that their addiction arose from their treatment for some other medical condition, such as a mastectomy or a painful injury. Of these therapeutic addicts, only 19 were dependent on heroin. Most of the others were addicted to morphine, Demerol, or another opiate. Also known to the authorities were another 43 nontherapeutic heroin addicts, who probably first obtained their drugs on the small black market. Thus, only 4 percent of all the known narcotic addicts in the country during 1958 were heroin dependents who had originally become addicted under a doctor's care. These 19 people did not seem to present a threat to public order in the kingdom.

By 1968 the number of doctor-induced heroin addicts had gone down to eight; by 1972, a year during which British doctors prescribed a total of 29 kilograms of the drug to the organically ill, only three therapeutic addicts dependent on heroin were listed in the official British reports. By the 1970s, of course, these reports showed other major problems, especially the dramatic rise in nontherapeutic addicts, and it is undeniably true that the Home Office compilations must have missed some addicts hidden out there in the nooks and crannies of the British Isles. However, because the British governmental reports reflect reality better than any other set of drug statistics I have seen, it must be accepted that despite the use of heroin for decades in treating the organically ill, there is a virtual absence of addicts created by this singular medical practice. These cold facts seem to be totally ignored in most discussions of the matter.

One might argue that these facts speak to the experience of Britain, with its gentle, law-abiding society. What about the United States, with its endemic violence, frontier mentality, vast citizen armament, and hordes of criminal addicts? And what about other countries afflicted both by increasing heroin addiction and violent crime, even terrorism? It is to these points that discussion inevitably moves, away from a calm review of the available medical facts and to the enduring fears about the creation of more American-style dope fiends. I would like to think it possible to win the medical-legal argument on freeing heroin for use in the treatment of the organically ill by demonstrating its worth as a medicine, but this is not possible as long as so many opinion leaders are convinced that the addiction and crime potential is not worth the risk.

Hard as we may try, therefore, it is impossible to discuss the organically ill and the addicted in airtight chambers. For purposes of analysis I have tried to do so here. Many proponents of hospices and the legalized medical use of heroin try to do so in real life. Cancer patients are worthy, heroin addicts are not, according to some leaders in the hospice and pain-control movements. But what I have attempted to show is that the destinies of cancer sufferers and street addicts are, for perverse and irrational reasons, intertwined in America and in many parts of the world. So are the destinies and the health of many other people afflicted with a whole catalog of maladies, not even mentioned here, that require new pain-control techniques and the innovative use of all available drugs.

It becomes necessary, then, to turn our attention to the themes that have dominated our history and continue to hold present reality by the throat: control, crime, law enforcement, and above all, addiction.

5: THE ROLLESTON ERA IN BRITAIN

"When . . . every effort possible in the circumstances has been made, and made unsuccessfully, to bring the patient to a condition in which he is independent of the drug, it may . . . become justifiable in certain cases to order regularly the minimum dose which has been found necessary, either in order to avoid serious withdrawal symptoms, or to keep the patient in a condition in which he can lead a useful life."—The Rolleston Report, 1926[1]

"Over here it's beautiful. Over here I can stand up and walk around and live like a man. Over here I am a man. I can walk straight and live decently. . . . I don't have to steal, or rob anybody. I don't have to wake up sick and wonder where my next fix is coming from. In other words, I don't need to put a pistol in my hand. . . . I'm living the best life I ever lived. . . . But Jesus! The United States! . . . All those junkies . . . those poor dogs lying in the Tombs . . . throwing up over each other."—An American Addict Living in England, 1970[2]

I

For decades the primary interest of Americans in British approaches to drugs has focused not on the organically ill but rather on the addicted. Bedeviled by heroin addiction and related crime at home, hundreds of drug-abuse specialists and concerned officials have crossed the Atlantic to find out how their English counterparts have somehow managed to engineer a society not subject to the mass desecrations of heroin addicts. In particular, these transatlantic travelers wanted to see how the British contained the growth of heroin addiction by authorizing medical doctors to give addicts heroin. Once understood, such a management system might be written up into a plan of action and then, despite Calvinist opposition, implemented in American cities. A few of the more radical American observers, moreover, have viewed the English system as a shining example of the concept of government subservience to the will of the people.

But the British are neither clear nor united about what is happening on their drug scene or why. Moreover, they seem to have a revulsion toward making their approach to drugs seem radical or soft or permissive. The sense of revulsion rises almost to the level of horror at the thought of suggesting to Americans that they should import the British system. The ultimate barricade in this position is to deny that there is a British system at all.

Edwin M. Schur encountered such attitudes when he was doing the research for his book *Narcotic Addiction in Britain and America* (1962). Professor Schur quoted comments made in 1958 by M. L. Harney, superintendent of the Illinois Division of Narcotic Control: "I think we take too much time from constructive discussion of the narcotics problem for a purposeless working-over of what has been called an 'English System.' With a technique reminiscent of the Hitler 'Big-lie,' a few people assiduously have spread . . . an impression that in England there is some magic afoot which is the key to the narcotic addiction and narcotic control problem. Let us try to lay that ghost once and for all. Actually, of course, the English system of narcotic law control is not too different from our own."[3]

Then Professor Schur observed, "It is disturbing to find that British drug officials have lent some support to this contention." As an example he cited an unsigned letter from the Home Office to the Federal Bureau of Narcotics, written in 1958: "Mr. Harney's remarks seem to make a good deal of sense and I hope that the publication of the record of what he said will help to do some good in your country. As regards the visits of Americans to this country we are in this difficulty; that it is not possible for us to refuse to have a talk with visiting Americans who ask to be allowed to visit the Home Office to discuss the so-called 'British System.' However when we do see these visitors any remarks which we make are rather along the lines of what Mr. Harney has said, and *we make it clear that there is not in fact any such thing as a 'British System' which is an invention of certain Americans who wish to prove a particular point of view*."[4]

This interchange caused Professor Schur to wonder about the reasons for the British position: "Why would British officials wish to create the impression that American and British policies are essentially the same—an impression belied even by the quite explicit statements they make in frequent reports to the United Nations? The desire to avoid publicizing any startlingly different approach to addiction may stem partly from the avoidance of sensationalism which characterizes British drug policy generally. Then, too, I had the impression that British officials are eager not to be put in a position where they seem to be criticizing their law enforcement colleagues in the United States. Unfortunately these and perhaps other factors cause them implicitly to endorse an approach to addiction which they would never accept in their own country."[5]

I can testify that, on this score, not too much has changed in two decades. My British hosts were generally modest about their accomplishments, not terribly certain why, or even whether, they had been relatively successful, and not even slightly inclined to sell their approach to visitors from across the ocean.

From all this I have evolved a working philosophy of inquiry toward the British drug situation which, I submit, is necessary for any form of rational analysis. One can rely upon the English experts for a frank and full recitation of the basic facts, to the extent that they are known, but not for an interpretation of why those facts came into being—and certainly not for the even more subjective judgment of the transportability of the British system to any other country. For example, it is generally accepted that the number of heroin addicts in England is rather low, perhaps 15,000; that is a basic fact—the relatively low number, not the precise number. But why is it low? Because of the simple lack of susceptible individuals? Because of cultural forces? Because of carefully designed legal or medical policies? Can any of these factors be clearly identified and readily transplanted to another country? In order to even attempt to answer such important questions, the visitor must ultimately make independent judgments based on a review of as much of the original evidence as possible.

II

The story of English policy toward drug addiction bears remarkable similarities to its American counterpart, but, of course, the differences make the best part of the story.[6] Under the Defence of the Realm Act, emergency regulations were passed during World War I regarding the sale of the drug deemed most troublesome at the time, cocaine. Much of it was being sold to prostitutes, some of whom in turn sold it to soldiers home from the trenches on leave.[7] These regulations, later amended to include opium, accurately foretold the broad outlines of later British control schemes: possession and use of the drugs were to be restricted to medical purposes, all sales and prescriptions were to be scrupulously recorded, and such records were to be available for inspection by appropriate authorities. These principles, which reflected England's attempt to follow the Hague Convention of 1912, although it had not yet come into effect, were to reappear in the first piece of permanent drug-control legislation, the Dangerous Drugs Act of 1920. The first regulations issued under the act limited a doctor to dispensing such drugs only "so far as may be necessary for the exercise of his profession." Thus, even the language of a key section of the new English control scheme was similar to the American Harrison Act, which required a doctor to restrict the dispensation of such drugs to the "course of his professional practice only." In Britain, as in America, a conflict arose over what these legal phrases meant.[8]

At the very time that the English were starting to work out the implementation of their first drug law, they watched the spectacle of their cousins across the Atlantic mounting a series of near-hysterical public campaigns against virtually all forms of drugs, especially alcohol and heroin. Both drugs, each in its own way, were the subject of prohibition campaigns in America in the post-World War I period. Some American Treasury agents gained fame by attacking purveyors of alcohol; their brother agents in the narcotic arena, in the words of one American enforcement official, proudly sought "to trap addicts like animals."

Among the most civilized traits of English culture are a distaste of excess of any kind, on the one hand, and a vast tolerance for a rich variety of individual habits, on the other. American behavior toward drugs in the years following World War I somehow managed to offend both of these seemingly contradictory traits. In the parliamentary debate of 1920, Captain Walter Elliot, MP, attacked the United States because "they have gone in for prohibition and . . . they have developed the drug habit to an extent altogether unknown in this country." The outraged captain went on to call the Americans the "barbarians of the West" because of their "extraordinary savage idea of stamping out all people who happen to disagree . . . with their social theories" regarding narcotics, as well as alcohol—and "their recent treatment of Socialists."[9]

An article by Dr. Harry Campbell in a 1923 issue of the *British Journal of Inebriety* reported, in harsh tones unusual in British professional journals, on a trip he had made to America during the previous year:

> In the United States of America a drug addict is regarded as a malefactor even though the habit has been acquired through the medicinal use of the drug, as in the case, e.g., of American soldiers who were gassed and otherwise maimed in the Great War. The Harrison Narcotic Law was passed in 1914 by the Federal Government of the United States with general popular approval. It places severe restrictions upon the sale of narcotics and upon the medical profession, and necessitated the appointment of a whole army of officials. In consequence of this stringent law a vast clandestine commerce in narcotics has grown up in that country. The small bulk of these drugs renders the evasion of the law comparatively easy, and the country is overrun by an army of peddlers who extort exorbitant prices from their helpless victims. It appears that not only has the Harrison Law failed to diminish the number of drug takers—some contend, indeed, that it has increased their numbers—but, far from bettering the lot of the opiate addict, it has actually worsened it; for without curtailing the supply of the drug it has sent the price up tenfold, and this has had the effect of impoverishing the poorer class of addicts and reducing them to a condition of

such abject misery as to render them incapable of gaining an honest liveli-
hood.[10]

It is quite likely that sentiments like Elliot's and Campbell's had a significant
impact on the early history of British policy toward addiction control.

The Home Office, which had the responsibility for administering the new
law of 1920, soon found itself confronting one of the most important and
persistent problems in the addiction field: the need for a working delineation
of the proper boundaries of professional medical practice. Neither the law nor
the related regulations defined it. It appears, moreover, that most British doctors considered themselves relatively unaffected by the new legal strictures and
persisted in carrying on previous practices, which clearly varied considerably
from doctor to doctor. In some cases that came to the attention of the Home
Office, comparatively large supplies of narcotics—such as morphine or heroin—
had been dispensed to individuals on the basis of a doctor's prescription. Upon
looking into these cases, the Home Office often found that the drugs were
being prescribed not to treat an organic illness but, according to an article
written years later by Chief Inspector H. B. Spear, of the Drugs Branch, Home
Office, "simply to enable persons who had become addicted to satisfy their
craving." In some cases, Spear explained, British physicians had prescribed large
doses of drugs for persons they saw only rarely. At times the doctors had even
sent the prescriptions for the drugs to such patients through the mail. In still
other cases it turned out that doctors were using the drugs to feed their own
addictions. When these incidents came to the attention of the Home Office, it
found itself unable to say with certainty whether the will of Parliament was
being frustrated, for the supreme legislative body had not spelled out the meaning of medical practice. To this day that definition has never even been attempted by that august body or its counterpart in Washington. "Since it was
impossible for the Home Office to recognize cases of bona fide medical treatment," Mr. Spear wrote, "an attempt was made in 1924 to resolve this dilemma."[11]

That "attempt" turned out to be quite successful. The Health Ministry asked
the medical profession to advise the government as to what the legitimate
practice of medicine was. Minister of Health John Wheatly signed the Minute
of Appointment of the Departmental Committee on Morphine and Heroin
Addiction on September 30, 1924. (It is worth recalling that slightly more
than four months before that day the American government had prohibited
heroin entirely, even in medicine, and that the federal government's broad law-
enforcement campaign to shut off legitimate sources, from the clinics, of all

narcotics and cocaine to addicts was nearing total victory.) Mr. Wheatly appointed a group of leading physicians to the panel chaired by Sir Humphrey Rolleston, who, in addition to being a distinguished physician and a baronet, was then president of the Royal College of Physicians. The final report of the Rolleston Committee was dated January 21, 1926, but its advice is ageless.

This seminal document is one of the best pieces of social planning I have ever read and is certainly the best "government" report (it was written by private citizens at the request of officials) in the field of drug abuse. With Horace Freeland Judson I marvel at the note at the bottom of the first page: "The cost of this Inquiry (including the printing of this Report) is estimated at £65 5s. 6d." (In 1926 the pound was worth $4.86.) And with H. B. Spear I believe the British approach to drug abuse is much misunderstood, a condition that might be greatly alleviated if more people—foreigners and Britons alike—made a careful reading of key sections of the Rolleston Report.

The misunderstanding commences at the very threshold: *what did the report do?* It is commonly claimed that the report *established* the British system and clearly approved the relatively liberal dispensation of narcotics to any addict who seemed to need them. In fact, the report established nothing. It had no government authority, and the few changes in governmental policy it recommended were generally ignored at the time, with one exception. It recommended nothing that required revolutionary clinical behavior on the part of the British medical profession. The committee did seek the advice of some of the most knowledgeable members of the English medical profession regarding addiction treatment and sought to spread that knowledge to colleagues not quite so experienced in the field. In lawyer's terms the committee codified the best of the common law of medical practice. Because Dr. Rolleston's study group both analyzed existing medical practice and sought to perpetuate it for the future, its report is worth examining in some detail.

The purpose of the committee as set forth in the minister of health's minute of appointment was "to consider and advise as to the circumstances, if any, in which the supply of morphine and heroin . . . to persons suffering from addiction to those drugs may be regarded as medically advisable, and as to the precautions which it is desirable that medical practitioners should adopt for the avoidance of abuse, and to suggest any administrative measures that seem expedient for securing observance of such precautions." The very fact that the top health official in the government of a great nation would dare pose these questions so openly to the leaders of the country's medical establishment and the fact that there was no hue and cry to bring down the government or to attack the morality of the medical profession are remarkable when it is remembered that the year was 1924 and that much of the world, including the United States, viewed these substances as inherently evil and addiction to them as criminal. Britain then stood virtually alone among the nations of the world in its more reserved and civilized stance; in many respects it continues to do so, even though, as we have seen, some of its leading drug experts deny its position of uniqueness. This position of openness and balance is even more remarkable when it is realized that some powerful British figures have always opposed a policy of tolerance toward drug addiction. For example, during the early 1920s one of the highest ranking officials at the Home Office, Sir Malcolm Delevingne, repeatedly urged the Ministry of Health to issue an authoritative declaration that under the 1920 law the regular prescription of addicting drugs "without any attempt to treat the patient for the purpose of breaking off the habit, is not legitimate, and cannot be recognized as medical practice."[12] Sir Malcolm never got such a ruling from the health officials or from the medical establishment—nor has any subsequent enforcement-minded English official.

In its patient analysis the Rolleston Committee commented that in the review of the medical literature made by the Home Office when it was struggling to come up with a reasonable definition of proper medical practice in the treatment of addiction, it appeared "that some eminent physicians, especially in the United States, had expressed the opinion that persons who had become addicted to the use of the drugs could always be cured by sudden withdrawal under proper precautions." But the committee concluded that "even in the United States, where opinion is on the whole more favorable than in this country to this method of treatment, abrupt withdrawal was advocated in those cases only in which the addict could be treated in an institution and carefully nursed and looked after. No statement by any responsible medical authority had been found to suggest that such a method was practicable in the treatment of an addict under the conditions of ordinary private practice."[13]

What about the consequences of abrupt withdrawal? The committee observed, "In some cases, abrupt deprivation of morphine or heroin might cause not only intense suffering, but even fatal collapse." One must applaud the group for taking this humane position, but at the same time it should be noted that while many addicts do suffer intensely during withdrawal, the commonly accepted notion of fatal collapse seems to be unsupported by reported objective clinical evidence. These reservations are not meant to dispute the committee's conclusions on the abrupt withdrawal method, which should be criticized primarily because it does not work.

If the abrupt withdrawal method was impracticable for most addiction cases, "the question then arose whether this would justify the practice, which had in some cases been observed, of administering morphine or heroin over very long periods in non-diminishing doses." The committee carefully weighed the opposing points of view in this political-medical-legal issue that had already been faced and decided in America. The Home Office view, as we have seen, was that the object of treatment must be "cure," and that cure always involved a steady diminution of the dose and, ultimately, complete discontinuance. But some highly respected English physicians experienced in addiction treatment expressed the clinical opinion to the committee that in some cases diminishing doses were not possible—and certainly not complete discontinuance. Other physicians supported the Home Office view. Here, then, was a classic conflict involving not black and white but mixed shades of gray. At this point in its report the committee cautiously expressed the view that since some "eminent authorities" believed that long-term, even lifelong, administration was medically indicated in some cases, it could not be said that this practice "was necessarily inconsistent with *bona fide* medical treatment." In other words, they did not rule out long-term maintenance but would not yet put their final stamp of approval on it, either. It must be emphasized that these delicate judgments arose not from the expenditure of millions in public funds to execute a vast research enterprise but rather from careful, calm listening to the clinical experiences and reasoned opinions of professional colleagues—and ultimately from the application of a finely honed sense of balanced logic.[14]

The committee then noted some divergence of opinion among the witnesses as to the best definition of addiction. Therefore, the group developed its own: "the term 'addict' is used as meaning a person who, not requiring the continued use of a drug for the relief of symptoms of organic disease, has acquired, as a result of repeated administration, an overpowering desire for its continuance, and in whom withdrawal of the drug leads to definite symptoms of mental or physical distress or disorder." Many definitions of addiction have been put forth by eminent authorities since Rolleston, but none seems to have improved on this simple, sensible formulation.[15]

How many such persons were there in the country at that time? All the evidence heard by the committee tended toward the same conclusion: "In this country, addiction to morphine or heroin is rare." (The report gave no exact number, but the total in the country in 1926 was probably in the range of 100–500.) The witnesses generally concurred that addiction was declining, owing primarily to the Dangerous Drugs Act of 1920.[16] The report then went on to make a remarkable statement: "Although sources of illegitimate supply exist, it appears that those who might, in other circumstances, have obtained the drugs from non-medical sources are usually lacking in the determination and ingenuity necessary for overcoming the obstacles which the law now places in their way." H. B. Spear later characterized this conclusion as one of "astounding naivety."[17] I agree, but I must also note that *some* factors—mysterious and unknown as they might be—have worked to keep the number of drug addicts in England at very low levels throughout much of this century. While it seems highly improbable, we cannot rule out a lack of "determination and ingenuity" on the part of English addicts or would-be addicts.

The committee drew some conclusions about the latter group in relation to the new restrictions of the 1920 law. It said that some cases of addiction, but certainly not all, arose because a number of unstable people sought immediate relief from life's problems in drugs that were once easily available legitimately from a grocer or mail-order house. Now that doctors were controlling the supply, the number of new practicing addicts recruited from the large pool of "potential addicts" would therefore be diminished.[18] This may or may not be true, but many leading English drug experts seem to have forgotten that Rolleston ever made the statement, as we shall see.

The committee then came to grips with the "nature and causation" of morphine and heroin addiction: "[T]here was a general agreement that in most well-established cases the condition must be regarded as a manifestation of disease and not as a mere form of vicious indulgence. In other words, the drug is taken in such cases not for the purpose of obtaining positive pleasure, but in order to relieve a morbid and overpowering craving." The committee thus cast aside the "sin and evil" appellations often applied by their American counterparts at the time (and even to this day) and came out on the side of sickness.[19]

What did the common clinical experience of the British medical profession in the early 1920s show regarding the prognosis for this disease? "Evidence we have received from most of the witnesses forbids any sanguine estimate as to the proportion of permanent cures which may be looked for from any method of treatment, however thorough. Relapse, sooner or later, appears to be the rule, and permanent cure the exception." Although "every effort should be made by thorough and suitable treatment to free the patient from his addiction," the committee recognized that there would nevertheless be a number of people who would need drugs "for no other reason than the relief of conditions due to their addiction."[20]

This led Dr. Rolleston and his colleagues back to a definitive exploration of *the* fundamental issue: "circumstances in which it may be medically advisable to administer morphine or heroin to persons known to be suffering from addiction to these drugs." As a sort of preface to this core section, the committee dealt summarily though definitively with two types of cases. The first involved "the use of morphine or heroin for the relief of pain . . . due to organic disease, such as inoperable cancer. In such cases, the administration of the drug for prolonged periods may, no doubt, produce a craving which might persist and develop into an addiction if the disease were cured. But there can be no question of the propriety of continuing to administer the drug in quantities necessary for relief of the disease, so long as it persists, ignoring for the time being the question of possible production of addiction."

The second type of "preface" case involved the administration of drugs to addicts undergoing treatment by the "gradual reduction method." There would also be no question about the legitimacy of a physician's prescribing drugs to a patient when the dose was being slowly reduced as part of a definite plan of treatment.

The committee then defined the two classes of people for whom the indefinitely prolonged administration of morphine and heroin might be necessary. These were, first, "those in whom a complete withdrawal of morphine or heroin produces serious symptoms which cannot be treated satisfactorily under the ordinary conditions of private practice"; and, second, "those who are capable of leading a fairly normal and useful life so long as they take a certain quantity, usually small, of their drug of addiction, but not otherwise." (In its section summarizing the report, the committee restated this sentence so that it ended with the phrase "cease . . . to be able to do so when the regular allowance is withdrawn.") In effect, these were patients for whom no other course of treatment would do. Again, the committee made it clear that this conclusion was reached carefully, by assessing the weight of the medical evidence: "When, therefore, every effort possible in the circumstances has been made, and made unsuccessfully, to bring the patient to a condition in which he is independent of the drug, it may, in the opinion of the majority of the witnesses examined, become justifiable in certain cases to order regularly the minimum dose which has been found necessary, either in order to avoid serious withdrawal symptoms, or to keep the patient in a condition in which he can lead a useful life."

A reading of these last few, and often quoted, sections of the report may have led some commentators to believe that Rolleston approved of British doctors' passing out heroin tablets as if they were jelly beans. But the sentence quoted immediately above included an important caution and was followed by another: "It should not . . . be too lightly assumed in any case, however unpromising it may appear to be at first sight, that an irreducible minimum of the drug has been reached which cannot be withdrawn and which, therefore, must be continued indefinitely. Though the first attempt entirely to free a patient from his drug may be a failure, a subsequent one may be successful."[21]

The committee frowned on the idea of criminally prosecuting doctors who overprescribed before an ordinary "police court." It recommended instead the creation of a special "medical tribunal," composed primarily of doctors, to determine whether or not a physician's right to prescribe controlled drugs should be withdrawn. On December 14, 1928, a regulation provided the machinery for such tribunals for the first time in British history. This was the single important exception to the general lack of governmental action in response to the Rolleston Report. (The exception proved in the course of later events to be of little practical importance. In their first incarnation the tribunals were never used, and they were quietly dropped from the regulations in 1953, only to be reincarnated in 1973, as discussed more fully in Chapter 7.)[22] The committee also weighed the possibility of imposing a requirement that doctors treating drug addicts inform the Home Office of this fact. The advantages of such a system of official "notification" were many, including control on double prescribing. But they were outweighed, the committee felt, by the "inherent disadvantages of all forms of notification in impairing the confidential character of the relation of the doctor and patient." The government took no action on the matter of notification at the time, but the idea was to reappear later along with that of medical tribunals.[23]

Most elements of the Rolleston Report's advice are still vibrant today and would, if taken to heart by governments and by the healing professions, be a useful guide for most countries now confronted with the problems of heroin abuse and, less obviously, with the problems of controlling the pain of organic disease. In many respects Rolleston's advice is still being followed in Britain, but the addiction scene is changing, and there are strains in the venerable structure that has rested heavily on the power of the British medical profession and on the professional integrity and independence of the individual English physician. This independence and political strength meant that when there was a conflict in the borderland between law enforcement and medicine, the dominant power was that of the medical establishment. A related assumption was that the individual English physician could be counted on to provide proper overall medical treatment for addicts in addition to a properly limited supply of drugs. It was also assumed that the small number of addicts in the country would continue to be largely middle-aged or elderly, probably middle class, otherwise nondeviant, and certainly not criminal or a social problem.

In typical understated British fashion the Home Office and the Ministry of Health jointly issued a memorandum of advice to the profession in 1926 which brought the Rolleston guidelines to the attention of doctors who might encounter an addicted patient. Writing somewhat testily about that memorandum, Mr. Spear later observed that its issuance "has frequently been interpreted by North American observers [citing in this instance a 1957 report of the American Medical Association and Drs. Larimore and Brill's 1960 article, "The British Narcotic System"] as giving legal effect to the Committee's recommendations. It did not do so, and from 1920 until the present day the only limitation imposed by the law on a doctor's right to possess and supply controlled drugs has been that he should be acting 'so far as may be necessary for the exercise of his profession . . . ' "[24] In defense of my countrymen, I would point out to Mr. Spear that there is an enormous cultural divide here. Americans are used to seeing government regulations interpose themselves into all aspects of professional judgment. It is thus understandable that they would assume that an administrative memorandum from two powerful national ministries had the force of law. In many respects, even today the socialized medicine of England operates with greater respect for individual professional judgment and with less government interference than medicine in the capitalist society of America.

It is not surprising, therefore, that the British medical profession gave strong approval to the Rolleston Report. The *British Medical Journal* in 1926 urged doctors to read it, for it appeared "to have much sociological significance." The journal was particularly pleased that "no authoritative rules have been issued for guidance in the use of scheduled drugs."[25]

But if the government imposed no specific controls on the doctor's treatment of addicts, if the Rolleston Report did not have the force of law, if in the language of Rolleston "permanent cures" were not to be expected and indeed were "the exception," what *was* the dominant medical philosophy of the British approach to addiction treatment? The answer is that although they could not *cure* addicts, British doctors could *care* for them—in part by dealing with the many physical problems that often accompany the status of being an addict, in part by psychological support and counseling, and in part by prescribing opiates to some patients over a long period. This *caring* would continue until the patient developed the strength and inner resources to cure himself—a result no doctor can ever achieve—and thus to live free of drugs. But in some cases the best efforts of doctors and patients together came to naught, and those addicts received steady supplies of opiates, often heroin, until the last days of their lives. In American terms this may seem a surrender by doctors to the diseased cravings of their patients, or a failure of treatment, but from a more realistic and humane perspective it symbolizes proper medical care for a chronic, persistent illness. If American medical and legal policies during the time of Rolleston—and before and after—had been based on these ideals, we in the United States might have been spared many decades of agony that are with us still. Yet ironically, most of the affected countries of the world seem eager to follow in our footsteps.

III

The Rolleston era continued for many decades after the report was issued. British doctors continued to control the treatment of addicts, including the amount and kind of drugs they prescribed for them. The number of addicts remained small, with most being of the therapeutic variety. While Home Office officials had been given the responsibility for concern with drug problems after the enactment of the 1920 law, it was not until 1934 that a formal Drugs Branch was set up in that ministry to keep tabs on the situation and to prevent the diversion of drugs for nonmedical purposes. Its major function then (and now) was the regulation of the legal manufacture and sale of drugs; illicit use was an area of responsibility that the Drugs Branch has simply taken on, in fine British custom, because it needed to be looked after and no one else was doing so. Over the years the number of professionals in the branch has been no more than a handful—for the entire country! While it had the power to inspect the records of those involved in the legal trade of controlled drugs, such as manufacturers and pharmacists, the Drugs Branch had no direct authority to compel the disclosure of new addicts encountered by doctors. Nevertheless, Home Office officials soon developed a working list of all addicts known to be receiving prescriptions in the country—the so-called index. Operating for years without the force of a law explicitly requiring notification of addicts, the Drugs Branch has consistently produced, starting in 1936, an impressive set of addiction statistics, perhaps the best in the world, primarily because British doctors have cooperated voluntarily and notified the Home Office whenever they encountered a case of addiction. The first detailed annual compilation, that for 1936, showed a total of 616 known addicts to controlled drugs, almost evenly divided between male and female; 120 were "professional," presumably physicians and nurses. For the next twenty-five years or so, English addiction index figures were relatively stable.

But then something dramatic started to happen. First, bits and pieces of information came to the attention of the police and the Home Office—about thefts of massive quantities of drugs, including heroin, and their subsequent black market sale to musicians and hippies in London. Then, ever so slowly, the index started to reflect changes. For example, from 1959 to 1960 the total number of known drug addicts in the country dropped from 454 to 437; but the number of known *heroin* addicts rose from 68 to 94. According to Ameri-

can standards, such an increase is not worth mentioning. But this represented
an increase of almost one-third in the population of those afflicted with the
mysterious malady, and the highest total in British history up to that date. Of
perhaps even greater significance—whereas in 1959 the origin of heroin addiction was therapeutic in 21 cases, and nontherapeutic (that is, recreational or
deviant) in 47 cases, in 1960 the number of therapeutic heroin addicts was 22
and the number of nontherapeutic was 72. By 1961 the number of known
heroin addicts in England reached a total of 132, of whom 112 had become
addicted through causes unrelated to therapy. To make matters worse, the addicts were no longer middle-aged or elderly and fairly respectable; they were
younger, more deviant, more defiant: 89 of all the heroin addicts in 1961 were
thirty-four years old or younger. The "something" that happened, then, was a
change in one of the basic assumptions underlying the Rolleston Report. The
number of narcotic addicts was rising dramatically, by English standards, especially the population of young, deviant ones.

The increase in drug use was charted by Spear in an important article, "The
Growth of Heroin Addiction in the United Kingdom" (1969). Spear showed
how the recreational use of all types of controlled drugs, including cannabis,*
cocaine, and heroin, had been minimal until the 1950s. In the early part of that
decade, he states, the "first clues" for the noticeable heroin upsurge of the
1960s appeared.[26]

Those clues were that young people of native British stock were beginning
to use controlled drugs in the jazz clubs of the West End and Soho districts of
London, as well as in a few other urban areas of the country. This was a sharp
break with the traditional British pattern, which saw only residents of foreign
stock using these drugs—such as Chinese using opium and Negroes, cannabis.
When Scotland Yard raided Club Eleven in the West End on April 15, 1950,
for example, they found a racially mixed group of 200 to 250 young people, 10
of whom possessed illegal drugs, primarily cannabis; as Spear wrote, "contrary
to the normal experience in the country in cases involving Hemp, only one was
a coloured man." At about the same time clues also began to appear that native-
born English youth were interested in drugs other than marijuana. According
to several commentators on this period, one of the most important events of
the time was a burglary on the night of April 24, 1951. Kevin Patrick Saunders,
a young man known as "Mark," broke into a hospital where he had been employed and stole a large quantity of drugs, including 3,120 heroin tablets. Soon
Scotland Yard received information that Mark was trafficking in drugs in the

* Cannabis is the formal name for the plant and drug known in the United States as marijuana.
These two terms, as well as hemp, hashish, and pot, are used here interchangeably.

West End, and he was arrested in September—but not before his merchandise had reached an appreciative clientele.[27]

Spear's research later showed the links between Mark's heroin and many new addicts. That research identified two significant groups of new heroin addicts (listed in the published article, of course, by number and not name) with their date of "coming to notice"—appearing in the Home Office index through the informal system of notification. One group of 27 were part of or connected with an original cadre around Mark; the second group, of 36, were either known to have or were strongly suspected of having links with cases in the first list. Case 63, the last one, did not come to notice until September 1964. Does this impressive analysis mean that the blame for the creation of the modern British heroin problem should be laid on the slim shoulders of Mark? This might appear to be the case, but after telling his story Spear was somewhat more cautious about its implications. He saw the spread of heroin addiction among Mark's group as one of a series of clues "that were not isolated events but provided the first signs of an emerging drug sub-culture in the United Kingdom." Why did it occur? Said Spear, "We have only the evidence of the events themselves and the testimony of some of those directly involved in them, who have stated that until 'Mark' appeared on the scene there was little or no heroin circulating in the West End of London but that his appearance coincided with . . . [a] scarcity of cannabis . . . with the result that many persons who had been smoking cannabis began to use heroin and cocaine as substitutes."[28]

These clues, laid out by Spear in 1969, have stayed in that status, barely followed up by other researchers, or discounted. It is important to note, however, that if Mark's activities actually gave the initial impetus to the modern British era of heroin addiction, this provides support for the view that the very presence of heroin in hospital pharmacies—whether in London or New York—creates the danger of more addiction on the streets. Once having been uttered, and without taking a breath, that thought should be followed by another: the American heroin addiction situation was built on a grand scale in a country where heroin has been virtually illegal since 1924. But the story of Mark does show, at the very least, that there is always some risk in the presence of a highly addicting psychoactive drug anywhere in a society, even in its hospitals. The major question should be whether the medical benefits outweigh the potential for harm.

That very question came up abruptly in England during this period. Out of the blue, as it were, the home secretary on February 18, 1955, told a questioner in the House of Commons that as of the end of that year licenses to manufacture heroin in the country would not be renewed. At this point no great alarms had yet been raised about the dangers of heroin abuse, even though Mark's friends had been using heroin relatively quietly for years. But, of course, such decisions are not taken out of the blue, and indeed a great deal had led up to the formulation of this policy. For decades the League of Nations, later the United Nations, had continued its policy of discouraging the medicinal use of diacetylmorphine. The United States continued its strong stand against the nonmedical use of all narcotic drugs and maintained its prohibition of any use of heroin, even in medicine. Harry Anslinger, the zealous head of the Federal Bureau of Narcotics, was the American representative on the UN Commission on Narcotic Drugs. In 1954 that body, at Mr. Anslinger's urging, voted to ask all nations to ban the use of heroin in medicine. Thus, the venerable crusade continued unabated; even many of the arguments on both sides were unchanged.[29]

What was different in this case was the power of the English medical profession. In *The Social Control of Drugs* Philip Bean, of the University of Nottingham, cited the 1955 battle over the continued use of heroin in British medicine as one of "the best known examples of the influence of the medical profession." What was confusing about this debate, however, was that until the government actually announced the proposed ban, the British medical establishment seemed either divided, unsure, or uncaring about the matter. In 1950, for example, the minister of health, Aneurin Bevan, responding to a World Health Organization move against heroin, asked for the guidance of his medical advisory committee; its counsel was "definite and decisive that it is justifiable to ban heroin." A similar editorial position was taken by the *British Medical Journal* in 1953. The basic argument of those in favor of abolition in Britain is now familiar: the danger of addiction was great and many adequate substitutes were available. That, of course, has been the traditional posture of the American Medical Association. Indeed, during the House of Lords debate on December 13, 1955, Lord Moran, who supported prohibition, quoted a letter from a former president of the AMA to the effect that "American experience is that nobody objects to the ban on heroin except the addict. The medical substitutes are entirely satisfactory."[30]

But once the ban was actually announced—no further manufacture of diacetylmorphine after December 31, 1955—a virtually solid front of British medical support for heroin appeared. The *British Medical Journal* soon published seventeen letters on the subject, with only one supporting the government. Then the journal shifted its own editorial position and stated that it hoped the government would change its mind, since it seemed unlikely that prohibition in England could really help worldwide control. The British Medical Association sent a deputation of doctors to call upon the home secretary to tell him in person of their opposition to the ban. In June of 1955 the BMA voted in favor of a resolution protesting "the threatened withdrawal of the most excellent sedative heroin which is of estimable value in so many conditions."[31]

It is instructive to compare the deliberations in Britain in 1955 with those in America in 1924 on precisely the same subject—total prohibition of heroin from the practice of medicine. As we have seen, the Porter hearings in 1924 really considered only one side of the issue, the negative. Organized American medicine was lined up solidly on the side of prohibition. No witnesses were actually heard in opposition to prohibition, and there was no debate as such. Even more indicative of American medical, legal, and popular opinion was the unanimous vote in favor of prohibition in both houses of Congress. In Britain in 1955, on the other hand, there *was* real debate of the issues, not simply in both houses of Parliament but also in the press and among members of the public. Judson characterized the final debate in the House of Lords on December 13 as "splendid."[32] In that debate the British government indicated that it was discreetly backing away from the proposed heroin prohibition. The decision was based in part on the surprising strength of the medical opposition but also on an even more surprising attack of doubt within the government at the last moment about its legal powers to *prohibit* heroin as opposed to *controlling* it under the wording of the Dangerous Drugs Act. That doubt was settled on January 26, 1956, when the home secretary informed the House of Commons, after having consulted with legal authorities, that "the Government has been advised that it is not possible under the present law of the country to prohibit the manufacture of heroin." Since that day nothing of significance has been heard from British advocates of heroin prohibition.[33]

But much has been heard, and for good reason, from those concerned about the growth of heroin addiction. The two reports of the Brain Committee, which was originally appointed on June 3, 1958, by the minister of health, Derek Walker-Smith, have historic importance in this regard. Like the Rolleston Committee, the Brain group was composed almost entirely of doctors—seven of them, plus one pharmacist. Again, the chairman was a distinguished physician, Sir Russell Brain.[34] Why, some thirty years after the Rolleston Committee was appointed, did the British government again turn to the powerful medical profession for advice about drugs? The addiction figures for 1957 showed nothing alarming or different. Mr. Walker-Smith's minute of appointment charged the committee "to review, in the light of more recent developments, the advice given by the Departmental Committee on Morphine and Heroin Addiction in 1926; to consider whether any revised advice should also

cover other drugs liable to produce addiction or to be habit-forming"; to consider the possible need for institutional treatment for addicts; and to make
recommendations of an administrative nature where appropriate.[35]

Mr. Bean later declared, "The background to the appointment of this Committee is still something of a mystery. Neither is it clear what is meant by the
phrase 'in light of more recent developments. . . .' One possible explanation is
that from 1953 to 1959 there had been an unprecedented increase in known
addicts (from 290 to 454, i.e., about 80%) and this was almost entirely due to
the emergence of a new group of non-therapeutic, young, male heroin addicts."
Bean then went on to discount the "official view" for the creation of the committee, the appearance of new synthetic drugs.[36]

However, Bean appears to be mistaken about the number of heroin addicts
at the time: in 1959 there were only 68 in the country, representing a small rise
during the previous few years. In support of the official view, moreover, Spear
maintained in 1975, "The reason for this new enquiry was not the increasing
heroin addiction. Instead, it was felt that the time was right to review the
Rolleston principles, which had been laid down about forty years earlier, inas-
much as a large range of synthetic analgesics had been developed and the new
Single Convention on Narcotic Drugs [a major international treaty] was about
to commence."[37]

Whatever the reasons for its creation, the committee reviewed the drug addiction situation and held eleven meetings. On November 29, 1960, Sir Russell
Brain signed a typically terse English professional report of twenty-three pages,
including appendixes (Rolleston's group needed thirty-six, but they had more
groundwork to lay). The committee declared that no change in the British
approach to drug addiction, as described in the Rolleston Report, was needed
because the situation had not changed appreciably in the intervening years.

When this first Brain report was released in the spring of 1961 it was greeted
with much criticism by the press and by British drug-abuse experts.[38] Indeed,
it has almost reached the level of catechism in the British and, later, the American drug-abuse literature to say that Brain I was hopelessly naive and that the
committee needed two tries to learn the lesson—thus Brain II, released in 1965,
finally did get it "right." I have always accepted this version of The Truth, but
no longer. I am now prepared to issue my own brief revised history of this
period, so important not only to the English but to any people seeking to
understand drug dependence and to evolve a rational social response.

First things first: a more detailed but brief review of Brain I. Its initial major
conclusion was the lightning rod: "After careful examination of all the data put
before us we are of the opinion that in Great Britain the incidence of addiction

to dangerous drugs—which today comprise not only morphine and heroin but also such other substances coming within the provisions of the Dangerous Drugs Act, 1951, as pethidine, methadone, levorphanol,* etc.—is still very small. . . . There is . . . in our opinion no cause to fear that any real increase is at present occurring."[39] It is to be recalled that the report was completed in 1960, even though it was released in 1961, and that the committee did not have available to it the 1961 addiction statistics from the Home Office. Indeed, it did not even have complete 1960 figures; the data in the report showed only 68 heroin addicts for 1960, whereas the final tally shows that there were actually 68 in 1959 and a jump to 94 in 1960, mainly nontherapeutic, as we have seen. The committee, unfortunately, did not obtain better information from Home Office experts or from informal contacts on the addiction scene.

The report then reiterated some of the positions taken by Rolleston that were still valid, such as the need to treat addicts as sick rather than criminal and to provide treatment through a cooperative regimen rather than through compulsion or abrupt withdrawal, and preferably not in special institutions. Also, it made a point alluded to by Rolleston but perhaps not sufficiently understood at the time or since: "We would emphasize that there is, in Great Britain, no system of registration of addicts, nor any scheme by which the authorities allocate to them regular supplies of the drugs they are taking." I cannot count the times I have been told by respected people in positions of authority in America *and* in Britain about the registration of English addicts and how this means that they get whatever drugs they want. One American commentator, Richard Ashley, went so far as to write that in 1968 there was "compulsory registration of addicts" in England. Such a legal status as a registered addict does not exist in England and never has. When addicts are "notified" to the Home Office, this means that they have become enshrined in an official file; as a result, however, they neither gain nor lose privileges. Brain I provided a service by reexplaining the matter.[40]

The committee broke new ground when it reviewed those key sections of Rolleston defining the circumstances in which morphine or heroin could be legitimately administered to addicts. It approved of the manner in which the old committee had handled this delicate problem, accepting the concept that some addicts cannot function if their "regular allowance" is withdrawn. Brain I

* Pethidine is commonly known in America as Demerol, which has already been described. Methadone, a synthetic opiate, is considered by some clinicians to be slightly more powerful than morphine, dose for dose, in certain circumstances. Levorphanol is sold under the brand name Levo-Dromoran. It is a synthetic opiate with a degree of analgesia at least equal to that of morphine; some clinicians believe it to be twice as potent.

believed, however, that that phrase from Rolleston had given rise to the mistaken notion that this implied registration and a legally mandated level of drugs. The Brain Committee added, "We are strongly opposed to any suggestion that 'registration' would be either desirable or helpful." Thus, the 1960 report explicated what was implied in the 1926 document.

The Brain group also clarified another great contribution of the Rolleston Committee: the notion of a "stabilised addict," which is implied in that major Rolleston category of patients who might legitimately be given opiates, those who can function normally with the drug but cease to be able to do so when the "regular allowance" is withdrawn. The implications of this concept are obscene to those who believe that the narcotics are evil substances in and of themselves. The idea also runs counter to much high-level drug expertise, for it virtually destroys the venerable concept of "tolerance," which holds that some drugs, such as heroin and other powerful narcotics, are so alluring that addicts develop a virtual numbness to the relief obtained by a given dosage and are constantly asking for more, always more, never achieving satisfaction or balance. The fact that some addicts can lead fairly normal lives on level dosages of narcotics is an extremely important philosophical and clinical underpinning for the British approach to treating narcotic addiction.

Brain laid out the first extensive "official" view of the stabilized addict:

Many of those authorities and experienced persons who gave evidence to us . . . agree that this type of patient does exist. Moreover, a careful scrutiny of the histories of more than a hundred persons classified as addicts reveals that many of them who have been taking small and regular doses for years show little evidence of tolerance and are often leading reasonably satisfactory lives. . . . Consequently we see no reason to reject the idea of a "stablised addict." Indeed, to group together all "drug addicts" on the basis of a pharmacological definition may convey an over-simplified and misleading impression. There are drug addicts who have been introduced to the practice when physically healthy with drugs procured by illicit means or in the course of their professional work. This group is a very small one in Great Britain. There are those who, having been given a drug of addiction as the appropriate treatment for a painful illness, continue to be dependent on it when the original necessity for its use has disappeared. And there is a third group of those who are unable to abandon a drug rightly or wrongly prescribed for some physical or mental ailment which itself persists. Opinions may well differ as to whether those in the last group should be regarded as addicts, except in a technical sense, and where the line should be drawn between addiction to a drug and its appropriate medical use.[41]

The committee also provided revealing "Summaries of the Case Histories of Known Stabilised Addicts," including, among others:

Mrs. A., a housewife, well past middle age, had a radical amputation of the breast for carcinoma ten years ago. Severe pain at the site of the operation and elsewhere in associated areas has persisted ever since. For the greater part of this period she has been taking pethidine, prescribed by her general practitioner, at the steady rate of 3 to 4 tablets, each of 50 mg., daily. On this dosage she is relatively free from symptoms and is able to undertake her own housework. There is no indication that the dose requires to be increased, but numerous attempts at withdrawal, or substitution by codeine, aspirin preparations, etc. have met with a return of her pain and incapacity. No personality changes have been detected.

Mrs. B., also a housewife, and well past middle age, has been troubled for over ten years with very severe varicose ulceration of the leg. This has not been improved by conventional treatment. The pain has not been mitigated by antipyretic analgesics [fever-reducing painkillers, such as aspirin]. For about five years she has received 5 tablets of pethidine, each of 50 mg., daily. This enables her to carry out her duties as a housewife and to look after members of her family suffering from severe disease and psychoneuroses. There has been no need to increase the dose, but when the drug is withheld the patient pleads that she cannot carry on because of the pain.

Mrs. C., a housewife, is an old lady, and a life-long neurotic person. Suspected of a crush-fracture in the mid-thoracic [chest or breastplate] region after a fall she has complained of constant pain despite a spinal support. With four methadone tablets, each of 5 mg., per day she manages her household duties. There has been no plea to increase the dose. On the other hand withdrawals have led to such a reaction that the home and family have suffered. . . .

Mr. F. is described as a clerical worker past middle age. He suffers from a painful disease which has necessitated the amputation of limbs. For several years he has received analgesics for his pain, first pethidine and subsequently phenadoxone.* Over the last four years his dose of phena-

---

* Phenadoxone is a narcotic sold in the United States under the brand name Heptalgin. It is thought to have a potency approaching that of morphine.

doxone has been steady at the rate of twenty 10 mg. tablets daily. On this quantity he appears to have shown no mental deterioration; on the contrary he continues to work responsibly. When other, non-addictive drugs have been substituted from time to time, his pain has returned with renewed severity.[42]

Here we have the stories of four otherwise ordinary English citizens who present a rather different picture from the one we might have of drug addicts. Several, perhaps all, of these patients and their doctors would face at least the possibility of criminal prosecution in America, as well as in other countries, for the illegal dispensation or use of drugs.

It is important to note, however, that the committee was not saying that all addicts were stabilized; just the opposite. There were many categories of people dependent on addicting drugs. Each case of drug dependence required individual medical diagnosis and treatment.

In regard to the power of British physicians to determine the nature of treatment for drug addicts, the committee issued two definitive and important pronouncements. It saw no connection between the prescribing power of private doctors and the number of addicts in society: "the right of doctors in Great Britain to continue at their own professional discretion the provision of dangerous drugs to known addicts has not contributed to any increase in the total number of patients receiving regular supplies in this way." Moreover, the committee believed that British doctors rarely violated this trust by issuing drugs without adequate medical supervision, without attempting withdrawal periodically, or without a second opinion. "Only two such habitual offenders during the past twenty years have been brought to our notice," the committee revealed.

Accordingly, the first Brain report disagreed with the advice of Rolleston, and of some of the committee's own witnesses, regarding the need for special tribunals to determine whether a doctor was properly prescribing dangerous drugs in a particular case. The Brain group felt that because cases of abuse by doctors were so rare there was no need to introduce "further statutory powers to correct them." In those few cases in which a British doctor appeared to have violated his trust by prescribing drugs to addicts in an irresponsible manner, the report implied, it would be quite appropriate for officials to take action to withdraw his power to prescribe dangerous drugs or to prosecute him criminally in the ordinary courts of justice. The committee was also concerned about the great increase in the use of barbiturates and other synthetics but believed that no new statutory powers were needed to deal with the problems they presented.[43]

In summary, it can be said that the first Interdepartmental Committee on Drug Addiction took the position that no major changes were needed in the British approach to drug dependence. For that conclusion it has been severely castigated. In addition to many specific criticisms, Bean dismissed the report in general by saying that it "merely offered a bouquet to the British system and thought that everyone who was concerned with its administration was doing a grand job." Judson told of the "remembered bitterness" of one man who observed to him, "They said that everything in the garden was lovely." And Judson himself concluded, "It took two and a half years to produce a hand-wringing document that plumped for no change." Every critic of Brain I, and that means almost everyone who has commented, focuses on its failure to see the rise in heroin addiction.[44]

Others charge that the committee should have known that some doctors, certainly more than just two, were abusing their prescribing powers. One British official told me that he had personally informed the committee of several doctors who were overprescribing at that time.[45] But were the facts so alarming as to demand a change in the old British system? That is the truly important question. Perhaps, in retrospect, the fairest judgment would have been to chastise the first Brain Committee for not obtaining all the facts about the modest but definite rise in heroin addiction and about the number of overprescribing doctors—but at the same time to challenge the conventional indictment of its "no change" conclusions. I have long thought those conclusions to be erroneous. However, it may well be, in light of subsequent history, that the recommendations of Brain I were more nearly "right" than those of Brain II, despite the prevailing expert opinion in Britain.

Almost as if on signal, when the Brain Report was released in early 1961, the first big jump in nontherapeutic heroin addicts appeared in the official statistics, as we have seen, from 47 in 1959 to 72 in 1960. Then, it seemed, the sky might be the limit and the British started to worry; by 1962 the number had gone to 157; by 1963, to 222; and early returns to the Home Office in 1964 showed the upward trend continuing. Even at the time Mark was doing business in the West End, the official statistics did not reflect such recreational heroin activity. But now it showed not only in the Home Office index but also on the streets of London. Some addicts received prescriptions from their doctors only for *daily* doses of their drugs. Often, the doctors gave such prescriptions to patients who were more or less "unstabilized"—that is, those whom the physicians did not trust to use their dosages wisely. Since the numbers of these patients were growing and they were concentrated in London, they constituted an increasingly visible and deviant subculture. Some felt such an urgent need for their drugs that they started to queue up at the all-night branch of a quite respectable pharmaceutical chain, Boots the Chemist, in Piccadilly Circus—the preeminent traffic circle in the British Empire—to get the next day's supply almost at the stroke of midnight. The junkie scene in that area of London was, and remains to this day, a popular tourist attraction.

The British, however, were not amused but horrified—not only citizens who remembered the peace and dignity of the old days but also drug experts who were dismayed by Brain I and demanded that the government *do* something. In July of 1964 the minister of health did so and reconvened the Interdepartmental Committee on Drug Addiction with the following charge: "to consider whether, in the light of recent experience, the advice they . . . gave in 1961 in relation to the prescribing of addictive drugs by doctors needs revising. . . ." On July 31, 1965, Brain II responded in the affirmative.[46]

The report was the briefest of the three major British drug-addiction studies, fourteen pages of terse, direct analyses and recommendations. In part, the brevity was due to the manner in which the members read their mandate: "We interpreted our terms of reference as meaning that we were not being invited to survey the subject of drug addiction as a whole, but rather to pay particular attention to the part played by medical practitioners in the supply of these drugs." That is, the medical profession had been invited by the government to come up with some way of corralling its wayward members who were giving out narcotics too liberally.[47]

The committee described the "new situation" since its first study: the sharp increase in the number of addicts to all drugs, but particularly to heroin, with almost all the increase due to young, nontherapeutic users. The committee noted that almost all of the rise had taken place in London, which made it all the more noticeable. Of interest also was the fact that consumption of *licit* heroin in the United Kingdom had risen from 40 kilograms in 1962 to 50 in 1964, amounts that "far exceed those of any other country." The committee observed that this was no doubt due to the fact that the United Kingdom was one of the few countries legalizing the use of heroin for medical treatment, but it found the figures disturbing nevertheless.[48]

The committee then asked how the new addicts had obtained their supplies. Its answer (which the suspicious among us might say it had before it was reconvened): the supplies came not from an organized illicit traffic, not from addicts forging, altering, or obtaining double prescriptions, but rather from doctors. In the measured words of the report, "From the evidence before us we have been led to the conclusion that the major source of supply has been the activity of a very few doctors who have prescribed excessively for addicts. Thus we were informed that in 1962 one doctor alone prescribed almost 600,000 tablets of heroin (i.e. 6 kilogrammes) for addicts. . . . Two doctors each issued a single prescription for 1,000 tablets (i.e. 10 grammes). These are only the more startling examples. . . . Supplies on such a scale can easily provide a surplus that will attract new recruits to the ranks of addicts. . . . The evidence further shows that not more than six doctors have prescribed these very large amounts of dangerous drugs."[49]

Having thus, with surgical precision, identified the cause of the problem, the committee made recommendations to excise it, which it labeled "measures to curtail supplies." These measures were not directed against underworld trafficking in illegal drugs, as well they might have been in America and in other countries, but against a more limited target, licensed doctors who improperly prescribed licit drugs quite legally and who dispensed even the large doses mentioned above within the law. In a prefatory statement to its major recommendations for change, Brain II explained the balancing process so necessary to such endeavors: "We have . . . borne in mind the dilemma which faces the authorities responsible for the control of dangerous drugs in this country. If there is insufficient control it may lead to the spread of addiction—as is happening at present. If, on the other hand, the restrictions are so severe as to prevent or seriously discourage the addict from obtaining any supplies from legitimate sources it may lead to the development of an organized illicit traffic. The absence hitherto of such an organised illicit traffic has been attributed largely to the fact that an addict has been able to obtain supplies of drugs legally."[50]

Later, Dr. Griffith Edwards, director of the Addiction Research Unit, London Institute of Psychiatry (and one of the recognized sages of England's drug-abuse professional community), observed about this statement: "So far as the preventive implications of the British system at that time were concerned, this passage in the report identified the cornerstone of policy. Give an addict not too little and not too much of his drug, and the illicit market will neither be economically encouraged, nor fed by the surplus." Dr. Edwards was not sure that such a policy of "prevention by competitive prescribing" could ever be carried out in practice.[51] In 1965 the Brain Committee, however, felt it was vital to try and to seek to "prevent . . . abuse without sacrificing the basic advantages of the present arrangements"—that is, without excessive interference with the right of British doctors to prescribe for their patients. But surely compromises had to be made, and Brain II proceeded to suggest them.

The major change recommended was that, for the first time in history, the virtually unlimited power of individual English physicians to prescribe drugs was to be circumscribed, but only in regard to heroin and cocaine, and only to addicts, not to patients who were organically ill or injured. These two narcotics—which now were to be categorized as "restricted drugs"—were to be administered to addicts only by doctors specially licensed by the Home Office in new "treatment centres" for drug addicts, to be set up especially in London but also in some other areas of the country.

The second major departure recommended by Brain II was an official, mandatory system of addict notification to replace the informal system. The committee also revived the medical tribunal notion of Rolleston, but in slightly different form, in order to discipline doctors who violated the rules of the new system without having to resort to more cumbersome and formal criminal prosecutions.[52] Although the second Brain Committee report urged speed in carrying out its recommendations, they were not supported by statute until the Dangerous Drugs Act of 1967 and not actually implemented until early 1968. The first drug-dependence clinics, as the treatment centers came to be known, were opening as the year began. The regulations that mandated compulsory notification of addicts to the Home Office became operational on February 22. On April 16 regulations went into effect prohibiting medical practitioners from providing heroin or cocaine to addicts except for the purpose of relieving pain caused by organic illness or injury—or unless the practitioner was specially licensed by the Ministry of Health. In almost all cases these special licenses would be issued to doctors working in drug-dependence clinics. Tribunal machinery to discipline doctors, without resort to criminal prosecution, did not receive statutory support until the Misuse of Drugs Act of 1971 and was not implemented until 1973.[53]

In my opinion, therefore, the Rolleston era came to an end at some point in the spring of 1968. I do not mean to say that many of the principles of Rolleston are no longer applied today in addict treatment within the clinics or in the use of drugs for the organically ill. Rather, I am saying that the aura of almost complete trust and respect that Sir Humphrey's group and Brain I fairly exuded for British doctors *and* for ordinary English addicts—those gentle qualities seemed gone with the winds of a deviant heroin-addict subculture. The rules of the humane British drug-control system, nonetheless, continued to allow a wide range of medical practices in treating addiction; although English doctors were not allowed complete freedom anymore, by almost any standard they continued to be trusted. But to what extent did the new rules create unnecessary anxiety for addicts, for doctors, and for the general population? A host of important questions now have to be asked about the Rolleston era as we reflect back on it and the changes of 1968.

IV

It is paradoxical that the most outspoken supporters of British methods, however they have varied over the years, have been Americans. The most favorable single piece of commentary I have ever read about the first Brain report was written by the American lawyer-sociologist Edwin M. Schur and appeared in his 1962 book, *Narcotic Addiction in Britain and America*. Schur conducted his research in England at about the same time that the first Brain Committee was doing its work. The favorable conclusions of Schur and Brain I were quite similar, and accordingly Schur cited the report with approval as substantiating many of the points he was making. This stance alone has made Schur somewhat unpopular among British drug experts and commentators.[54]

But he compounded the felony by taking an uncompromisingly clear position on a major question. Was it the low number of addicts, or of susceptible individuals, that made it possible for the British to take a medical and rather benign approach to drug addiction? Or conversely, did the public policy of Britain function to prevent the creation of a large number of addicts in the population? After two years of intensive research on the subject, Schur was ready to answer that question: "I believe strongly that all data from diverse sources, surveyed throughout this study, point in the same direction: to the strong influence of British drug policy on the addiction situation in that country. Those who claim that the benign situation led to the non-punitive policy, rather than the other way around, do not present any real evidence to support their argument." In other words, British public policy, which at that time allowed individual physicians to treat addict-patients as their clinical discretion dictated, including the long-term prescribing of addicting drugs, not only served to allow effective medical care for specific addicts but also, and perhaps even more important, acted as a social prophylactic in preventing the spread of addiction to other susceptible individuals. Schur's conclusions in this regard, and in respect to his overall favorable impression of the British system during the Rolleston era, were echoed and even amplified by his American mentor, Professor Alfred R. Lindesmith, of the University of Indiana. These conclusions are thus often referred to as the Schur-Lindesmith thesis.[55]

The British seem to disagree strongly with this thesis, as do many Americans. For example, Dr. Thomas Bewley, of London, responded to Schur's allegation about the preventive aspects of the British approach by observing in 1966, "A series of administrative practices grew up at a time when there were very few addicts. This was described at a later stage as 'the British System.' It probably developed because there was virtually no opiate addiction in this country, and was in no way a cause of the small number of addicts." Almost every other student of the British scene seems impelled to voice similar doubts.[56]

But in 1978 Dr. Edwards took a somewhat different position when, during a most thought-provoking Cambridge University speech, he said:

> With controversies such as this which centre on the interpretation of complex historical and social processes rather than on a situation even remotely resembling a controlled experiment, a "proof" which gives victory to one camp or other may be too much to expect. . . . It cannot be doubted that the British system of response to drugs . . . in the 1920's, was founded to deal with a small problem. . . . Whether from 1926 to, say, 1960, the system contributed to the continuance of addiction at a low level is a related but different question. Given however, that social processes were such as initially (in the 1920's) to have produced a society with little addiction, it seems logically uneconomical to propose that the Rolleston policies were in addition needed to keep a situation stable which was already, of itself, seemingly rather stable. The more likely explanation is that a complex of general background social processes were responsible for the low addiction rates of 1920–1960, with a change in these background social processes being responsible for the breakdown in the equilibrium.[57]

The learned doctor did not claim to understand fully those background social processes that changed and tilted the balance in the society toward more addiction—a bit of intellectual modesty well worth imitating by the rest of us.

But intellectual modesty can never prevent students of society and its foibles from speculating about why certain events occurred. There is a crying need for scientific explanations of some important events in the addiction arena, such as the rise in heroin addiction in Britain in the early 1960s. This would seem a simple enough task; yet the analysis of English drug experts could produce no clear understanding of why this heroin upsurge took place. And if that learned and sober group could not produce a rational explanation for an occurrence of such great importance, through which many of them lived and in which some were personally involved, it seems fair to say that there does not yet exist in any of the known professional disciplines a body of knowledge that can explain, in terms of ultimate causation, the rise of drug epidemics or their demise.

Where, then, does this bring us in our reflection on the Rolleston era? I submit: to a point where we must admit our biases and shortcomings. I *want* to believe the Schur-Lindesmith thesis to the effect that a humane and benign policy of treating addicts with apparent kindness, and with licit supplies of drugs when necessary, contributes to keeping the total number of addicts in the society at a low level. But I have no objective, cause-and-effect proof for my biases—or for the contrary proposition. In the face of ambiguous information impinging on the formulation of policy, however, it would seem rational to select the course of action which is most humane and most helpful to the individuals directly affected by the policy.

That thought leads us inevitably to a consideration of how individual addicts fared during the Rolleston era and how their lives might have changed after the clinics opened in 1968. We have already seen vignettes about the situations of four "stabilised" therapeutic addicts who received large doses of synthetic narcotics, although not heroin, from individual doctors.

Even more instructive insights into the lives of addicts under the old, and the beginnings of the new, British approach may be gained from a book entitled *Drug-Trip Abroad: American Drug-Refugees in Amsterdam and London* (1972), by Walter R. Cuskey, Ph.D., Arnold William Klein, M.D., and William Krasner. Its major message was carried by the words of drug users. Collected primarily during the summer of 1970, the stories overlap into the period of the clinics but deal primarily with the years before 1968.

When Dr. Klein, who conducted most of the interviews, arrived in the summer of 1970, he proceeded along the path of many drug seekers and tourists to Piccadilly Circus. He penetrated the drug scene there and came to know a number of addicts. He said: "But this is not, as the American tourist would have you believe, the entire addict population. It is more or less the most delinquent portion—the non-working members, those most resistant to treatment, the hippie types, the lowest individuals on the drug totem pole. . . . The 'Dilly addicts are the most hopeless ones, the ones most apt to die from overdose or suicide—and deaths occur there frequently." But many drug-dependent people in England never enter the 'Dilly scene, and others somehow survive it. Those addicts who manage to live through the delinquent years of their youth, in Piccadilly or elsewhere, sometimes quit drugs on their own, "mature out," or become confirmed and rather stabilized in their life-styles and drug taking. Thus, in England Dr. Klein also met a group of nontherapeutic heroin addicts of more or less middle age pursuing more or less ordinary, nondeviant lives, although they suffered perhaps more than their share of emotional distress. And in one other way they were different: they were consuming legal opiates daily in quantities that few American or Canadian addicts even dream of.[58]

One of those Klein met was Graf, a native of western Canada who at the time of the interview was forty-five. In 1943 he was imprisoned in Canada for stealing an automobile and while in prison bought morphine which he injected. Soon after his release he was into the familiar junkie routine of stealing to buy his drugs, which cost him $20 to $30 a day, a considerable sum for those times. "It was whatever money I could come up with and whatever drugs were available at the time. By that time I was using heroin, opium, morphine. . . . It was a continuous rat-race. In and out of prison, beating, being beaten up by policemen in search of drugs, and stealing, and every way possible maintaining or accumulating the money to buy the drugs off the black market." On numerous occasions he committed himself for treatment in hospitals and on numerous other occasions he was imprisoned. When asked if Canadian officials had treated him or had merely thrown him in jail, he replied, "Just throw you in prison." He had tried withdrawing from drugs at least ten times. "About five times under medical supervision . . . and about five in prison." But to no avail.

Now that he was able to obtain fairly regular doses of legal drugs in England, he was no longer trying to quit. "I'm quite content." He had come to England in January 1962 because he had heard from a friend that conditions were much better there. "When I arrived here the friend that I had corresponded with introduced me to his doctor, a Lady Franco,* and after an interview and taking my case history, she prescribed my heroin." For eight and a half years he had been stabilized on drugs in Britain: twelve grains of heroin and eight and a half grains of seconal, a barbiturate (a grain is equivalent to approximately 65 milligrams), per day. These were pure drugs and the doses were considerably higher than he ever took in Canada; indeed, they were massive. Originally he got them from private doctors, later from a clinic.

Although he had to steal to support his habit in Canada, he did not have to in England. "I've been working ever since I arrived in this country. I've been working at the same job for eight and a half years now. I work in a taxi garage." He has a girlfriend, also an addict; because of the impact of the heavy maintenance doses of drugs, "our sex life is nil." What about other aspects of his life? "I feel here that I'm able to live like a human being. I am not in fear of being in prison for my illness or because of my addiction. . . . I am able to work and

* The correct spelling of the name of this rather well known medical doctor is Lady Isabella Frankau. However, in *Drug-Trip Abroad* the name was spelled Franco, and under this name Dr. Frankau had achieved considerable popularity among addicts. Some observers regarded her as one of the leading overprescribing doctors; others, as a helpful and caring physician living up to the oath of her profession.

have as close to a normal life as I believe I possibly can with this personality defect, I'll call it."[59]

Harold, born in Brooklyn, was thirty-seven at the time of the interview. In America he had been a persistent criminal. Unlike most of the older addicts Klein interviewed, Harold had also been in legal trouble in England, but had apparently started to settle down. His American career had included armed robbery, larceny, and burglary, among other crimes. In England his crimes had been somewhat less destructive, such as giving false information to immigration officers and an apparently minor assault and battery. He started using heroin in 1953, then cocaine in 1956; he always "mainlined" (injected them into a vein) and, after 1956, always mixed them. At the time he came to England, in 1964, his habit in the United States was costing him $250 a day—$150 for heroin, $100 for cocaine.

In the United States he had often tried to get off drugs by going into hospitals voluntarily. But the treatment was usually "cold turkey," and withdrawal never worked for him. Bitterly, he recalled his treatment by criminal justice officials when withdrawal was imposed. "When I scored drugs I was locked up in the Tombs, in Manhattan, 125th Street; when I stole, if they caught me, I was put in the Tombs. When a junky is nicked in Manhattan, he is put on the Ninth Floor in the Tombs, given thorazine, and he kicks cold-turkey. I've been on it. I've kicked that way many times. And you lay on the floor, and they throw up on each other, and you're sick as a dog. That's the treatment in America."

The authors of *Drug-Trip Abroad* wrote of Harold, "While in England, before the clinics had opened, he had been registered [yes, they used that phrase] and had received drugs from private physicians. He seems to have gone, at one time or another, to most of the half-dozen physicians criticized in the Brain Report." Harold spoke fondly of Lady Franco: "She was great. Fabulous. Wonderful woman. Good physician." After Lady Franco died, he went to another of the so-called addict physicians, who prescribed for him "60 grains of heroin and 60 grains of cocaine every other day." He denies he ever sold any of this luxurious ration: "I used it all myself." Now he is under treatment at one of the new clinics, is married to an Englishwoman, and says, "We have a wonderful life together." What of his drug intake at the time of the interview? "Every night, 12:00, I go to Bliss's Camera Store, I'm given six and two-thirds grains of heroin, 40 tablets—and six and two-thirds grains of cocaine. That's my daily dosage, which is beautiful." When he was reminded of the ever-larger amounts of drugs he used to receive, he simply said that the laws had changed.

Asked to compare the drug scenes in America and England, Harold replied:

"Over here it's beautiful. Over here I can stand up and walk around and live like a man. Over here I *am* a man. I can walk straight and live decently. . . . I don't have to steal, or rob anybody. I don't have to wake up sick and wonder where my next fix is coming from. In other words, I don't need to put a pistol in my hand. . . . I'm living the best life I ever lived. . . . But Jesus! The United States! All those junkies . . . those poor dogs lying in the Tombs . . . throwing up over each other. . . . It stinks. Let's face it: I'm a drug addict 19 years. The odds are I'll never stop. Right? So what am I gonna do? Live here or live in the United States? I'm gonna stay here."[60]

Isaac was another Canadian, born in western Ontario, and fifty years old at the time of the interview. In Canada he never held a conventional job; his occupations were gambling and stealing. Since he lived close to the United States, he often went there, sometimes stealing from hotels. Although he was never arrested in the United States for a drug offense, he had been arrested about one dozen times on drug charges in Canada. When he was seventeen he became addicted to opium, which he obtained from the Chinese living in western Canada. He became addicted to heroin during World War II and was rejected for military service because he was an addict. In Canada the cost of his habit varied from $20 to $70 per day. In 1954 he was sent to prison with a four-year sentence. "For drugs. Just possession. That's all I had ever had charged. Never trafficking or selling or anything."

He had heard that both gambling and drugs were "legal" in England and decided to emigrate with a fellow addict and gambler, Giuseppe. Both insist, however, that although they were interested in the gambling, "Drugs was the only reason we came here. All I could see was me spending the rest of my life in prison in Canada." They came to England in 1960 and, not surprisingly, found their way, after trying several other doctors, to Lady Franco. After checking with both Scotland Yard and the Home Office, Dr. Franco gave them a week's supply each. Isaac then reflected, "She was a National Health doctor, and she wouldn't accept any money. We went to the chemist and we come out of his shop and just sat in the car glassy-eyed. Here we were with bottles of hundreds of tablets they had given us for nothing. And it was perfectly legal, you know . . . and all the years we'd spent in prison fighting to survive and everything, and here. . . ." Isaac started out receiving 16 grains a day and Giuseppe 12 from Lady Franco, which soon moved up to 20 and 25. However, later, when they went to a clinic, their dosages were gradually lowered to 14 grains each daily. Isaac claimed that 14 grains did not allow him to feel "normal," which was all he wanted by that time, for he was not then so much concerned with the "buzz." He said, "Just like a diabetic, you need insulin." When the clinic-reduction regimen reached 18, they had to start buying black market heroin, and at the time of the interview were purchasing 6 to 8 grains a day in this manner.

What did Isaac think of the British approach compared with what he knew in North America?

> It's obviously superior. There's no question about it. . . . They treat addiction as it should be treated. It's a medical problem, not a police problem. And the only bad things about this system are those they copied from the Americans.
>
> Their attitude up until the changeover to the clinics [1968] was the proper attitude. A private doctor treated a patient as he saw fit. Now they blame the spread of addiction on a half a dozen doctors who were overprescribing, which in my opinion is pure nonsense. I've read the Brain Committee Report numerous times, and it's an hysterical document. It's a vindictive document, and an untrue one. . . . The papers here went stark mad. And for a year they screamed and blamed the spread of addiction on these few doctors. I think that the clinics here, the system they have here, even now, is a thousand percent better than there. Naturally. Secondly, I think that the spread of addiction here has nothing to do with the method of disposal, of distribution and so on, of the drugs. It's perhaps a little beyond me, but I think it's a worldwide thing.[61]

I agree with Isaac in questioning the conventional wisdom that the second Brain Report rescued Great Britain from the follies of the first. Of course, Brain I failed to appreciate the growth in nontherapeutic heroin addiction, which Brain II more accurately reported. But since Brain II claimed to have narrowed the problem down to only a few doctors, why did the medical profession and the government not proceed to deal with *those few*? Why was it necessary to take the jolting step of removing the power to prescribe heroin and cocaine for addicts from virtually *all* doctors except the handful who were specially licensed? Of course, it may have been that the target of the British powers-that-were at the time of Brain II was not only six doctors but most individual doctors dealing with addicts, unsupported by colleagues, by a staff, or by the very atmosphere of a psychiatric unit of a hospital. Apparently, moreover, there was a kind of compact between the government and the medical establishment that the clinic doctors, being fewer in number and specially licensed, would get the message and begin cutting all addicts down from the huge doses some of them had been receiving from individual physicians. That protocol was not explicit in Brain II, but that is what happened.

6: THE HARRISON– ANSLINGER ERA IN AMERICA

"Mere addiction alone is not recognized as an incurable disease. *It is well established that the ordinary case of addiction yields to proper treatment, and that addicts can be taken off the drug and when otherwise physically restored and strengthened in will power will remain permanently cured."*— Daniel C. Roper, 1919[1]

"Fortunately for us the head of this bureau has stood for 25 years as the greatest single bulwark against the spread of drug addiction throughout the entire world. . . . No other man, living or dead, has had a greater influence in stemming the illicit traffic in narcotic drugs than the Honorable Harry Anslinger. He has gained ground despite the pressures of international intrigue, the ruthless menace of the underworld and the conspiracy of communism to undermine the morale of its enemies with narcotic drugs."—Theodore G. Klumpp, 1954[2]

"Following the line of thinking of the 'clinic plan' advocates to a logical conclusion, there would be no objection to the state setting aside a building where on the first floor there would be a bar for alcoholics, on the second floor licensed prostitution, with the third floor set aside for sexual deviates and, crowning them all, on the top floor a drug-dispensing station for addicts."—Harry J. Anslinger, 1959[3]

I

If the key to understanding British policy toward drug addiction is to be found in the Rolleston Report and the era it symbolized, then the key to the American counterpart may well be found in the Harrison Narcotic Act and in the work of Harry Jacob Anslinger. There is more, much more, to this period, the vital half century that spanned the early 1910s to the early 1960s, but the act named after Francis Burton Harrison of New York and the work of Mr. Anslinger of Pennsylvania are the dominant symbols of the age. The reputations of both these symbols have been tarnished in recent decades. Upon a fresh review of the facts, I have come to believe that Mr. Harrison's act did not truly deserve such treatment, but that Mr. Anslinger's work richly did.

The Harrison Narcotic Act of 1914 is the cornerstone of narcotic law and policy in America. On its face, it was a tax law titled "An Act To provide for the registration of, with collectors of internal revenue, and to impose a special tax upon all persons who produce, import, manufacture, compound, deal in, dispense, sell, distribute, or give away opium or coca leaves, their salts, derivatives, or preparations, and for other purposes."[4] It was around those "other purposes" that much of the debate about the original nature of this landmark statute has revolved. In the course of that debate

118

the act has gained a reputation in some circles as a repressive piece of legislation or as one that was enacted in a spirit of fraud and deception. Some experts claim, moreover, that the public and even Congress may not have been aware that this tax law could be turned into an instrument for not merely taxing but also *controlling* the use of narcotics. They were also allegedly unaware that the statute had the potential of radically altering time-honored American habits. These arguments were put forth by the respected and courageous scholar Alfred Lindesmith, who has long claimed that the basis for the current approach to the drug problem in America is remarkable because it was established not by statute but by the arbitrary actions of Treasury Department officials. In regard to the Harrison law, he stated in 1965, "Its ostensible purpose appeared to be simply to make the entire process of drug distribution within the country a matter of record. . . . There is no indication of a legislative intention to deny addicts access to legal drugs or to interfere in any way with medical practices in this area."[5]

Edward Brecher, in the same vein, wrote in his authoritative book, *Licit and Illicit Drugs* (1972),

> The supporters of the Harrison bill said little in the Congressional debates (which lasted several days) about the evils of narcotic addiction in the United States. They talked more about the need to implement the Hague Convention of 1912. . . . Far from appearing to be a prohibition law, the Harrison Narcotic Act on its face was merely a law for the orderly marketing of opium, morphine, heroin, and other drugs—in small quantities over the counter, and in larger quantities on a physician's prescription. Indeed, the right of a physician to prescribe was spelled out in apparently unambiguous terms: "Nothing contained in this section shall apply . . . to the dispensing or distribution of any of the aforesaid drugs to a patient by a physician, dentist, or veterinary surgeon registered under this Act in the course of his professional practice only."

Accordingly, Brecher concluded, "It is unlikely that a single legislator realized in 1914 that the law Congress was passing would later be deemed a prohibition law." Writing the same year in his book *Heroin*, Richard Ashley declared that the story of the Harrison Act was similar to the events surrounding the Gulf of Tonkin Resolution during the Vietnam War era: "a classic example of an uninformed Congress and an uninformed public being manipulated by a bureaucracy for its own ends." Mr. Ashley declared flatly, "The act was passed as a revenue and record-keeping measure and nothing more." In yet another important book published in 1972, *The Drug Hang-up*, Washington attorney Rufus

King expressed a similar sentiment: "The Harrison Act was not in any sense a prohibition statute, but rather a mild regulatory measure."[6]

Carrying the tale forward to its logical next step, each of these authors concluded that federal prosecutors and narcotics policemen perverted the will of Congress and the American people when they later remade this taxing and record-keeping measure into a stratagem to restrict the use of drugs by addicts and also to control their doctors and the pharmacists who sold to them. Yet another scholarly critic, Troy Duster, wrote in *The Legislation of Morality* (1970) that "the bill was designed to place the addict completely in the hands of the medical profession." Professor Duster continued, "It is one of those ironic twists" that the provision of the law authorizing a registered physician to dispense drugs in the course of his professional practice, "intended for one purpose, was to be used in such a way as to thwart that purpose." The thwarted purpose, of course, was the legitimate prescription of drugs by doctors to addicts.[7]

These are all standard liberal interpretations of this important phase of American history. I have long subscribed to them, and they may well contain much truth.

There is no doubt that on its face the Harrison Act was a tax law, not a control scheme. At that time in history, however, the authority of the federal government to exercise so-called police powers—the control of intrastate events as opposed to interstate commerce—was very much in doubt. But since the early years of the Republic the sweep of the national taxing power into even the most remote corners of American life has never been seriously challenged. And thus it became a time-honored congressional strategy to pass taxing laws that had hidden within them schemes of social and commercial control.

It is often difficult to interpret what a law was intended to accomplish even when legislators have made honest attempts to spell out their exact intentions. But when their purpose is to conceal their ultimate purpose, the task of interpretation becomes infinitely more difficult. The Harrison Act was viewed by its proponents as an amendment to the 1909 federal law prohibiting the importation of opium except for medical purposes—the aim being to prohibit its importation for the purpose of smoking. In other words, the law indirectly used the commerce power to prohibit the recreational use of a narcotic drug and yet to preserve its medical use. On January 17, 1914, moreover, Congress enacted a related statute imposing an intentionally prohibitive tax—$300 per pound—on opium prepared for smoking *within* the United States.[8] The Harrison bill was being considered at the very time this statute was being voted on favorably—and the January antiopium law also used the taxing power to prohibit the use of a narcotic drug for nonmedical purposes. Prohibition of drugs was thus a very popular idea in the corridors of Congress at the time. I mean "prohibition" in the sense in which it has generally been used in this country—making a drug illegal for so-called recreational use but leaving open the question of medical use. Even this definition is not completely satisfactory, as we shall soon see.

The limited record of the congressional discussion of the bill makes it clear that the chief aim of its sponsors was to control narcotic addiction; despite the words of the commentators cited above, taxes and records were secondary considerations. This was not a bland revenue measure. Some sense of what the members of Congress thought at the time may be grasped by looking at the favorable report on the pending bill submitted to the House of Representatives in June 1913 by Mr. Harrison, of the Ways and Means Committee. The report spoke not of an intention to enact a taxing law but of the "real and, one might say, even desperate need of Federal legislation to control our foreign and interstate traffic in habit-forming drugs, and to aid both directly and indirectly the States more effectually to enforce their police laws designed to restrict narcotics to legitimate medical channels." Despite those liberal revisionists who look back upon the good old days before the Harrison Act, the report pointed a critical finger at the unrestricted importation, manufacture, and sale of the opiates and cocaine "in such forms as to be available to anyone who desires them or who desires to trade on the addiction of his fellow creatures to them." It also observed that Italy, Spain, Austria-Hungary, Germany, and Holland, "with a total population of 164,000,000 . . . consume less than 50,000 pounds of opium annually; while the United States, with a population of 90,000,000, imports and consumes over 400,000 pounds of opium per annum." Although most of the individual states had pharmacy laws imposing restrictions on the free sale of addicting drugs, the national pattern of control was spotty and thus ineffective. As a result, "There has been in this country an almost shameless traffic in these drugs. Criminal classes have been created, and the use of the drugs with much accompanying moral and economic degradation is widespread among the upper classes of society. We are an opium-consuming nation today." No witness, the report continued, ever suggested to the Ways and Means Committee that the free traffic in narcotics ought to continue; the only question was how best to exert controls. The consensus of expert officials was that "only by customs law and by the exertion of the Federal taxing power can the desired end be accomplished." With such documents on the public record, it is hard to see how any reviewer of the period could believe that Congress did not intend to effect comprehensive and stringent new controls on the traffic and use of narcotics.[9]

The record of debates on the bill makes it equally clear that the legislators were responding to a dire situation that, in their opinion, needed controlling and not simply taxing. For example, on June 6, 1914, Senator Harry Lane (D.-Oregon) said, almost in passing, "This bill is one, I presume, to curtail the use of drugs such as opiates and cocaine." The record is replete with references by congressmen to "dope fiends" as well as more balanced discussions of the need for a policy of moderation and cautious experimentation under the new law. On August 15, 1914, Senator Altee Pomerene (D.-Ohio) observed, "We must have a cure for the drug habitué, but we must not forget the innocent sufferer on his or her bed of sickness and pain. Let us protect the country from the physician or druggist who is encouraging the drug habit for purely commercial purposes; but let us not by too much red tape hinder the physician in the proper practice of his profession. We can prevent the abuse of the drug without unduly hampering its proper use." Later that same day Senator Lane observed that he had been superintendent of an institution that cared for a number of "opium, cocaine and other drug fiends," that few of those actually addicted recovered, but that "we are now by this legislation attempting to save those who have already contracted the habit and stop others from acquiring the habit, and that is a good motive." Such remarks suggest that many of the bill's supporters in Congress fully expected it to restrict the manner in which doctors and pharmacists practiced their professions—in particular, the dispensing of drugs in large quantities when there was no clear legitimate medical diagnosis. These legislators wanted a "cure for the drug habitué" and a stricter control on the freely prescribing doctor and on the liberally dispensing pharmacist, but they did not want the cancer sufferer or the tuberculosis patient to be denied his medicine if it came in the form of a narcotic drug.[10]

Many learned commentators, such as Britain's Dr. Harry Campbell in 1923, blame virtually all of America's drug-abuse trouble on the law itself, rather than on harsh methods of administration and enforcement. Despite its bad reputation, however, I am, on balance, prepared to ascribe "a good motive," in Senator Lane's words, to the Harrison Narcotic Act itself. Although I have long considered it a repressive piece of legislation, a fresh reading of the historical record now leads me to believe that it was, on the whole, a rather intelligent, rational, and progressive one.

Because the legislators felt constrained to use the taxing power, they had to set up their scheme of social control indirectly. The basic elements of the system were that all those who dealt in or dispensed opium, cocaine, and their derivatives, such as morphine and heroin, had to register with the district collector of internal revenue and pay a one-dollar tax annually; the sale or dispensing of the drugs had to be done pursuant to a written order on a form provided by the commissioner of internal revenue; duplicates of the orders had to be kept available for official inspection for two years; the forms could be sold only to persons who had registered under the act—and because Treasury officials would not allow unqualified persons to register, the system kept the drugs in professional channels.

If we combine an assessment of the legislative history with an analysis of the language of the law itself, the following conclusions about its intent emerge:

1. The Harrison Narcotic Act was clearly intended to prohibit the use of narcotic drugs and cocaine (not a narcotic but feared as a drug of abuse) for recreational purposes.

2. The act also was meant to remove all these drugs entirely from the ordinary nonmedical channels of commerce: from grocery stores, from mail-order houses, and from over-the-counter sales in pharmacies. The major exception to this prohibition was that preparations containing only small amounts of the drugs—not more than two grains of opium, ¼ grain of morphine, ⅛ grain of heroin, and one grain of codeine—could be sold without a prescription. But there was even a restriction on this exception—drugs in this category had to be sold as medicine and not to evade the purpose of the act, which I interpret to mean, not to recreational users.

3. There was no intent to interfere with the ordinary practice of medicine in the treatment of organic illness or injury. Indeed, the act was clearly aimed at restricting these drugs primarily to such uses.

4. The intent was to prevent doctors and pharmacists from simply selling repeated doses of these drugs to addicts when no honest attempt at medical treatment had been made. In this way there was a clear restriction on the practice of medicine, at least in some of its most callous forms.

5. The law was ambiguous on the very point that many critics claim was unambiguous. That point was the propriety of the behavior of a doctor who had registered under the act and paid his tax, who believed he was acting "in good faith" and "in the course of his professional practice only," and who was prescribing opiates or cocaine to addicts in nondiminishing doses. Most liberal critics claim that the framers of the law expressly left this area of practice free of regulation or expressly authorized such prescribing. From my reading of the record I come to neither conclusion, for I would have to guess that had all the framers been polled at the time, the vote would have been split and indecisive,

with some opposed, others supportive, and still others unsure. I challenge those who see clear support for addict maintenance in the Harrison law to produce more concrete evidence.

I think the best interpretation of the act is that while it made many important advances in improving the health of this country through better controls on drugs, it left open the issue of whether the legitimate practice of medicine included the right of a doctor to prescribe narcotics to an addict in nondiminishing doses over a long period of time. I see nothing sinister in this ambiguity; it is merely a reflection of the unsettled issues that inhabit the borderland between law and medicine. As we have seen, the legal and medical professions in Britain were still unsure of the propriety of this type of dispensing fully ten years after the Harrison law was enacted, and the Rolleston Committee was formed for the very purpose of providing advice on this troubling question. Even today disputes continue on the wisdom and propriety of such medical practices—in Britain, in America, and in much of the world.

On all the other major parts of the law, there is more agreement among those who have studied the matter: narcotic drugs should be restricted to medical purposes and available only on a doctor's prescription; they should not be freely available to anyone with the purchase price in a grocery store or pharmacy, or through the mails; all those who handle such drugs legitimately should be required to keep careful records of these transactions, which should be available for inspection by appropriate authorities; and while preparations containing only small amounts of the controlled drugs may be "exempt" from stringent controls and thus salable over the counter, even those exempt potions should be sold only for medical purposes. These points are still very much the law today. There is nothing in this scheme of legal controls that would prevent the United States from adopting the British addiction-treatment system in all its details. As I have said, these were exactly the basic features of the English Dangerous Drugs Act of 1920, and of current law in that country. The differences have been in the manner in which the two countries interpreted their respective laws and in the manner in which they approached addicts and their addictions. The differences are instructive and, for an American, discouraging and even embarrassing. But to say that one wishes the law had been used in other ways—so that, for example, willing doctors could legally have dispensed drugs to willing addict-patients whom they were personally treating—must be distinguished from admitting that at least some of the framers of the law would have vigorously opposed legal addict maintenance by doctors. In any event, they left the matter open and decidedly ambiguous.

II

Into this ambiguous gap moved the federal executive officials empowered to enforce the act. As soon as the new law came into effect, on March 1, 1915, agents of the Bureau of Internal Revenue started to investigate and then to seek prosecution of doctors who continued their old habits of prescribing for addicts. In this connection, it is to be observed that there are at least two categories of doctors who deal with addicts: first, those who seek in good faith to provide many kinds of assistance, sometimes including drugs, to comfort patients and perhaps eventually to wean them from their chemical dependency; and, second, those who in bad faith see a path to a lucrative career by providing drugs to as many customers as possible without regard for their health or well-being, hiding all the while behind their license to dispense narcotic drugs. It would seem that the more enlightened view of the hidden scheme of social control in the Harrison Act might have persuaded the Bureau of Internal Revenue to pursue the latter but not the former. There is no evidence, however, that the federal drug policemen generally distinguished between the two categories in their enforcement activities. There *is* evidence that tens of thousands of doctors and pharmacists were charged under the act and a lesser number were actually prosecuted. One report stated that between 1915 and 1938 alone, over 25,000 physicians were formally reported to federal authorities for violations of the law, approximately 5,000 of whom were convicted and either fined or imprisoned.[11] For most physicians, the fear of being charged was sufficient to scare them away from even talking to an addict, much less treating one.

Because of its importance and its legal ambiguity, it was to be expected that appeals from convictions under the Harrison Act would ultimately reach the Supreme Court. The first cases to wend their way to the high court involved unscrupulous physicians who deserved to be called dope doctors. It is possible that the government prosecutors wanted cases involving the worst type of doctors to form the basis for the original tests of the new law.

In the land that invented judicial supremacy, it would seem that the Supreme Court would, in due course, have straightened out the issue left undecided by the Harrison Act: whether or not it was legal for a duly registered physician, acting in good faith, to prescribe nondiminishing doses of drugs to an addict. The standard opinion of most legal and medical commentators is that the high tribunal has indeed performed that clarifying mission, but I submit that this view is misguided. My review of the cases to this date, more than six decades after the law was enacted, shows a confusing line of decisions providing no clear judicial guidance but ample ammunition to support either point of view, and some in between.

The first Supreme Court decision under the law was *United St ites* v. *Jin Fuey Moy*, handed down on June 5, 1916.[12] The defendant was a physician of Chinese descent from Pittsburgh who apparently had a reputation as a dope doctor. He was indicted through the efforts of Treasury agents along with Willie Martin, an addict, because he had conspired with Martin to have in the latter's possession one dram of morphine. (One dram, or drachm, is equivalent to 60 grains or 3,888 milligrams.) A prescription for the drug had been supplied by the doctor, who was registered under the Harrison law, but Martin, of course, was not registered. The prosecution argued that Martin had violated the law simply by being in possession of a controlled drug and that both doctor and addict were thus involved in the conspiracy. "The question," according to Justice Oliver Wendell Holmes, Jr., who wrote the opinion of the court, was "whether the possession conspired for is within the prohibitions of the act." Put another way, was it the intention of the framers of the law that simple possession by a citizen not registered under the law would be a violation and thus considered a federal crime (subject to a maximum $2,000 fine, five years' imprisonment, or both) without going into the issue of intent?

The answer of the court was in the negative. The justices stated their belief that section 8—which made it unlawful for "any person" not registered to have such drugs in his possession and further declared that "such possession or control shall be presumptive evidence of a violation"—was meant to apply only to persons ordinarily expected to register under the act, such as importers, manufacturers, physicians, and pharmacists. Justice Holmes declared that to give the act the literal meaning argued for by the federal prosecutors would make it criminal for any citizen to be in possession of opium or its derivatives, even though he might have acquired it legitimately, and would thus make the act a far-reaching internal police measure rather than a revenue measure. Because the justices did not believe that Congress intended to stretch the then-extant view of federal police power to the constitutional breaking point, they interpreted the statute in a restrictive fashion and thus saved its constitutionality. "Any person" in the law, the court thus told the country, did not mean "any person"; and simple possession of a controlled drug by an ordinary private citizen was not a federal crime, as yet. Thus, the Supreme Court upheld the action of the U.S. District Court in Pittsburgh, quashing the conspiracy indictment.

The result was uncertainty and confusion. Even so sound a scholar as Alfred

Lindesmith, among others, concluded from the obtuse Holmes ⟨
the convictions (which had never initially occurred) had been up⟨
possession of drugs by an addict had been ruled a violation of the ⟨a…
was even greater consternation at the time of the decision. Although they knew
the ruling had prevented prosecutions for simple possession of drugs, enforcement agents were unsure of the practical impact of the decision. It seemed to
some to destroy the law's effectiveness and to weaken the Treasury Department's
campaign against addicts and their suppliers. In an annual report shortly after
the case was decided, the commissioner of internal revenue declared, "This
decision makes it practically impossible to control the illicit traffic in narcotic
drugs by unregistered persons, as the mere possession of any quantity of the
drugs is not evidence of violation." The government was forced, the commissioner declared, to prove an actual sale in every case.[13] This issue of possession
was left in limbo at the time.* Subsequent decisions of the court, however,
proved more pleasing to federal enforcement agents.

On March 3, 1919, the high court decided two cases that dealt with two
important issues: the constitutionality of the Harrison Act and the legality of
sales to an addict by a physician under that law. Shortly after the law had gone
into effect, Dr. Charles T. Doremus, of San Antonio, Texas, a duly registered
and tax-paying physician under the act, had sold 500 one-sixth grain tablets of
heroin (a total of over 5,000 milligrams) to one Ameris, who, in the language
of the indictment, "as was well known by Doremus, . . . was addicted to the
use of the drug as a habit, being a person popularly known as a 'dope fiend.'"
The doctor was indicted through the efforts of federal prosecutors for violation
of section 2 of the law because his prescription of the drug to Ameris was not
in the course of his regular professional practice and was purely to allow Ameris
to gratify his habit. Again, a U.S. District Court quashed the indictment, this
time because it held the Harrison Act unconstitutional since it was not really a
revenue measure, and, as a police measure, it invaded the police power reserved
to the states.

In *United States* v. *Doremus* the Supreme Court flatly overruled the district
court and upheld the constitutionality of the law. Justice Day, speaking for the
majority, reviewed the long history of decisions sanctioning the use of the
taxing power to accomplish social objectives: "The act may not be declared

---

* This loophole was almost completely closed by an amendment to the act on February 24, 1919,
making possession of a package of drugs without a tax stamp prima facie evidence of a violation,
unless obtained by a physician's prescription. Revenue Act of 1918, P.L. 65–254, 40 Stat. 1057,
1919.

unconstitutional because its effect may be to accomplish another purpose as well as the raising of revenue. If the legislation is within the taxing authority of Congress—that is sufficient to sustain it." [14]

In *Doremus* the court did not deal directly with the issue of the prescribing of drugs to addicts but it did so in the other case decided that day, *Webb* v. *United States*. Both Dr. Webb and one Goldbaum, a retail pharmacist, had been convicted for regularly supplying morphine in huge quantities to known addicts in Memphis, even though both the doctor and the pharmacist had registered under the act, paid their taxes, and used appropriate prescription forms. The facts of the case revealed that "Webb regularly charged fifty cents for each so-called prescription, and within this period [eleven months] had furnished, and Goldbaum had filled, over 4,000 such prescriptions; and that one Rabens, a user of the drug, came from another state and applied to Webb for morphine and was given at one time ten so-called prescriptions for one drachm each, which prescriptions were filled at one time by Goldbaum upon Rabens' presentation, although each was made out in a separate and fictitious name." [15] These facts are important because they largely determined the outcome of the case, and well they should have. There was no evidence of medical care, merely the selling of drugs. It was precisely this kind of abuse by doctors and pharmacists that the Harrison Act was meant to prohibit. But, nevertheless, the question had to be faced whether these prescriptions were legal under the exemption provided in the act.

To clarify that issue, the circuit court of appeals posed this now-famous question to the high court: "If a practicing and registered physician issues an order for morphine to an habitual user thereof, the order not being issued by him in the course of professional treatment in the attempted cure of the habit, but being issued for the purpose of providing the user with morphine sufficient to keep him comfortable by maintaining his customary use, is such an order a physician's prescription under exception (b) of [section] 2?" The court replied tersely, "to call such an order for the use of morphine a physician's prescription would be so plain a perversion of meaning that no discussion of the subject is required. That question should be answered in the negative." That decision was widely interpreted as declaring illegal once and for all the "ambulatory method" of treating addicts, which involved giving them drugs for self-administration outside an institution. In more modern terms, the decision has been interpreted to mean that the Supreme Court considered the maintenance of addicts invalid under Harrison. In 1973, for example, David Musto wrote that the question in the Webb case had been, "Could the legitimate practice of medicine include the maintenance of addicts?" The negative answer of the court, he inferred, gave the highest legal endorsement possible to antimaintenance forces.[16]

This conventional interpretation may be correct, but others are possible. I would argue that the question as posed by the court of appeals was misleading on several counts. First, it answered itself by asking, in effect, is an illegal act (an order issued *not* in the course of professional treatment) legal (a prescription)? The answer has to be in the negative. Is a crime legal? Of course not. Second, and even more important, the facts of the case showed that the doctor involved was engaged not in a good-faith treatment program but in a peddling operation. The maintenance of addicts under a doctor's care should be distinguished from the sale of drugs to addicts by a doctor who happens to use technically legal prescription forms. It is my contention, therefore, that the Supreme Court was not here presented by the controlling facts of the case with the issue of the legality under the Harrison Act of a maintenance program carried out in good faith within the context of medical treatment. The much-quoted language from the case about keeping an addict comfortable "by maintaining his customary use" was a classic instance of *obiter dicta*, literally "words said in passing," or nonessential to the decision. There was no evidence that Dr. Webb tried to make addicts comfortable or that any were put into that state, only that he peddled large amounts of drugs without concern for the medical condition of any patient. While these differences may seem subtle, they are a vital part of the legal and medical issues involved. But the high court clarified none of them and left the legal and medical professions, and the country, with a vague and misleading decision.

On December 6, 1920, Dr. Jin Fuey Moy appeared on the title page of another Supreme Court decision. Again, and even more convincingly than four years before, the facts showed him to be an unscrupulous peddler of narcotics. The court pointed out that among other nefarious practices, "His charges were not according to the usual practice of medical men, but according to the amount of the drug prescribed, being invariably one dollar per dram." Moreover, "in some cases he made a superficial physical examination, in others none at all." This time the doctor was actually convicted of a violation of the Harrison Act and appealed his conviction to the Supreme Court, which affirmed it. Again I would argue that, despite the appearance that this decision struck down maintenance of addicts, I see it as clearly mandated by even the most restrictive view of the prevailing statute. No rational system of law or medical treatment can approve of a doctor's simply handing addicts the drugs they ask for and charging them by the dose. The decision, moreover, made it clear that the doctor had authorized sales in quantities that could well have fueled a large illicit market. The main issue was the illegal sale of morphine in large quantities according to the harmful customs that had prevailed legally before the law of 1914. However, the opinion also stated that the physician's immunity under the statute did not extend to a sale "intended to cater to the appetite or satisfy the craving of one addicted to the use of the drug," again lending support to the notion that all forms of maintenance were prohibited by the law. The *responsible* maintenance of addicts was not the issue in the case, but the court did not make that distinction—nor have most later legal and medical commentators.[17]

In the next case dealt with by the court, it appeared that a New York physician, Morris Behrman, had prescribed to Willie King, an addict, 150 grains of heroin, 360 grains of morphine, and 210 grains of cocaine, all at the same time. The doctor argued that this was a proper attempt to treat his patient and that he expected King to administer the drugs to himself over a period of several days. There was no evidence that the doctor was a simple peddler, but at the same time the amount of drugs was huge. Did the amount of drugs prescribed in itself answer the question about the doctor's good faith? In *United States* v. *Behrman*, decided on March 27, 1922, the court seemed to say that it did. And it also said that a smaller amount might have been noncriminal: "It may be admitted that to prescribe a single dose, or even a number of doses may not bring a physician within the penalties of the act; but what is here charged is that the . . . physician by means of prescriptions has enabled one, known by him to be an addict, to obtain . . . more than 3,000 ordinary doses." Although it was apparently troubled by the plea of good faith, the court reached the same result as in the previous two cases: "Such so-called prescriptions could only result in the gratification of a diseased appetite for these pernicious drugs or . . . in unlawful parting of them to others in violation of the act." But what if Dr. Behrman had honestly believed that patient Willie King was not "ordinary" and needed such huge doses in order to function? The majority seemed to say that the quantity destroyed the claim of good faith, even without evidence before the court bearing directly on the issue. And that is precisely what bothered Justice Holmes, who dissented along with McReynolds and Brandeis, declaring that in "the absence of any charge to the contrary it must be assumed that he gave them in the regular course of his practice and in good faith." Nevertheless, the majority opinion apparently provided another sturdy brick in the antimaintenance structure.[18]

But then, on April 13, 1925, the court erected a legal-medical structure of a different character. Dr. Charles O. Linder, a respected senior physician from Spokane, Washington, had been convicted because he had prescribed one tablet of morphine and three tablets of cocaine to a known addict, Ida Casey, who was also an informer for the Treasury agents. In dealing with Dr. Linder's appeal, the Supreme Court for the first time said something positive about addicts. Speaking through Justice McReynolds, it declared, "They are diseased and proper subjects for . . . treatment, and we cannot possibly conclude that a physician acted improperly or unwisely or for other than medical purposes solely because he has dispensed to one of them in the ordinary course and in good faith, four small tablets of morphine or cocaine for relief of conditions incident to addiction." The court also upheld the doctor's right to give the addict-patient such drugs for self-administration, a controversial practice then and now. The Linder decision has been viewed by some commentators, Professor Lindesmith, for example, as repudiating the earlier "antimaintenance" decisions and as casting severe doubts on the enforcement activities of the Treasury Department. There is certainly support in the decision for this point of view, since a doctor's prescription of drugs to an addict had been upheld as the good-faith practice of medicine. If addiction is actually a disease, it should be treated by doctors. But in another section of the opinion the Linder court expressed its support for a prescription given in good faith "when designed temporarily to relieve an addict's pains."[19]

It is possible, therefore, to read Linder as not repudiating the previous decisions but simply adding a compassionate note, that a doctor may prescribe small doses of drugs to help an addict *temporarily*—but not over long periods and certainly not for maintenance in nondiminishing doses, and not to allow an addict to maintain his "customary use." The Supreme Court has never clarified the issue.

Was, then, the maintenance of addicts on nondiminishing doses by a registered physician acting in good faith made illegal by the Harrison Narcotic Act? Did the Supreme Court clarify the issue in the decade after the act went into effect? No, it left the matter ambiguous. In part this was due to the nature of the facts in the cases presented to the court. Not a single one of these decisions involved a clear constitutional or legal test of a maintenance program. They involved several peddler-doctors and a one-time sale by one doctor, not the repeated prescribing of drugs to the same addicts by the same doctor within the context of a program of medical treatment. I would argue, moreover, that the legality of good-faith addiction maintenance with legal drugs, such as morphine or methadone, has *never* been directly faced or decided by the Supreme Court. That issue *was* faced and decided by a lower yet more pervasive level of authority—by the regulations and prosecutions of federal police officials.

III

The American people owe a great debt to Alfred Lindesmith and to his small band of allies, such as Rufus King, who not only wrote about the abuses of this era but also attempted, often in lonely battle, to do something about them by creating a more humane approach to addicts. Lindesmith's analysis of how the Treasury Department rushed into the opening provided by the new law and the decisions relating to it is a masterly indictment of the repressive zeal of the federal government in the narcotics arena.[20]

In the face of ambiguities in the original law and in subsequent Supreme Court decisions, it appears that two groups in America—the leaders of the medical profession and of the federal narcotics enforcement establishment—united to fashion their own interpretations of the day-to-day rules that would prevail in dealing with addicts and their status in American life. The dominant group seems to have been the enforcement officials, but while many doctors were intimidated and harassed by police agents, many were enthusiastic collaborators with their police colleagues. The contrast with the British doctors, who provided a balanced control on law-enforcement zeal, is startling.

One of the most instructive parts of the American record is found in successive versions of Treasury Department regulations and directives to subalterns throughout the revenue bureaucracy of the country. Over the years the regulations and instructions demonstrate how Internal Revenue officials took upon themselves the practice of both law and medicine. They shaped the vague and conflicting federal court decisions into definitive pronouncements reflecting their own version of proper practice; armed with those regulations, they rushed into arenas the judges might have feared to enter. And in the process they told the nation's doctors how to practice their profession. Nor were the intrepid officials of the Treasury afraid to offer ethical and moral judgments about the nature of narcotic addiction. American administrative regulations took on the force of ruling law.

The logical impossibility of this situation was revealed by a little-known incident in Helena, Montana, reported by David Musto. On May 18, 1915, a druggist of that city wrote to tell the attorney general of the United States that he had an apparently legal prescription for cocaine for six users, but "the revenue agents who are neither lawyers nor physicians tell me that these prescriptions are in excessive amounts." Because the doctor continued to insist that the doses were not excessive in the cases involved, the pharmacist was placed "in an anomalous position." He asked the chief legal officer of the country for "a straight-out, clear-cut answer and not a vague one" on what to do. The attorney general could not help him, in part because many Justice Department experts agreed with the Montana druggist that the law was ambiguous on the matter. That vagueness did not prevent the persistent pursuit by Treasury agents of doctors who prescribed for addicts.[21]

In order to deal with such complaints, the Treasury Department had already, on May 11, issued a new regulation which amounted to a medical bulletin and a legal warning to the physicians of the country. Two aspects of TD (Treasury Decision) 2200 are pertinent here. First, the regulation declared that if a doctor wished to prescribe drugs in an amount "more than is apparently necessary to meet the needs of the patient in the ordinary case," he "should indicate on the prescription the purpose for which the unusual quantity of the drugs so prescribed is to be used." To this day there is no precise definition of the drug needs of "ordinary" cases, but the practical act of defining was in reality left to revenue agents, who were "neither lawyers nor physicians," because they had the front-line responsibility for enforcement. Second, the regulation stated, "In cases of treatment of addicts these prescriptions should show the good faith of the physician in the legitimate practice of his profession by a decreasing dosage or reduction of the quantity prescribed from time to time." Thus did an agency devoted to taxes and finances tell the country, especially its doctors, that the legitimate practice of medicine could not include the prescribing of nondiminishing doses of drugs to addicts, even if the attending doctor believed it to be proper in the given case, even if the dosages were moderate, and even if the physician was acting in good faith within a regimen of medical treatment. The Supreme Court had not even issued a decision on the Harrison Act, but within a few months after it went into effect the Treasury Department had already taken a definitive position on this complex legal, medical, and ethical issue.[22]

After the Supreme Court decided the Doremus and Webb cases on March 3, 1919, the Treasury Department, on July 2, 1919, revoked TD 2200 and replaced it with TD 2879, which was even more restrictive and more intrusive into medical practice. The Doremus and Webb cases had involved doctors who were accused of prescribing large quantities of drugs in single transactions; they were not apparently involved in maintenance programs. Nevertheless, the Webb opinion contained a clause saying that a physician's prescription was illegal if it had been issued not "in the course of professional treatment in the attempted cure of the habit, but . . . for the purpose of providing the user with morphine sufficient to keep him comfortable by maintaining his customary use." From this clause the administrative officials of the revenue agency proceeded to fashion new regulations that made virtually all medical programs for the treatment of addicts illegal when they involved the use of drugs, *even when the physician attempted to show good faith, in accord with the guidance of TD 2200, by periodically reducing the dosage.* That was the import of TD 2879, which replaced TD 2200; the Treasury Department claimed the revocation was mandated by Doremus and Webb even though the facts of neither case had the vaguest connection to such a good-faith treatment program.[23]

On July 31, 1919, the new regulations and related enforcement policies were explained in a directive from Daniel C. Roper, commissioner of internal revenue, entitled "Enforcement of the Harrison Narcotic Law" and addressed "To Collectors of Internal Revenue, Revenue Agents, and Others Concerned." Roper's communication took note of the fact that there had been an "emergency already precipitated in certain districts," apparently referring to the impact of his department's enforcement activities on the lives of addicts. He then went on to offer a restrictive, even repressive interpretation of the many conflicting medical and legal opinions that were being debated at the time in America. It was, in a sense, a reverse mirror image of the Rolleston Report: unbalanced, intrusive into medical practice, inhumane for the addict, against almost all forms of drug relief for the dependent person, and all this with the force of law—for although the memorandum was merely advisory, it was treated as legal writ by revenue agents and others who feared their heavy hand.[24]

The chief taxing officer of the nation proceeded to identify three classes of medical cases and then defined the proper treatment for each. The first category was "the treatment of incurable disease, other than addiction," or organic illness, such as cancer or tuberculosis. Commissioner Roper assured the medical profession that "such bona fide cases of incurable disease should not occasion difficulty in the proper administration of the law." But a reading of the rest of that first section demonstrates graphically why American doctors became fearful of the use of narcotic drugs, not simply in the treatment of addiction but also in cases for which these drugs were primarily intended. The internal revenue commissioner cautioned doctors to be wary of giving too much of a drug to persons suffering from incurable organic disease who were also addicted to the drug. "Too much credence should not be given to the unsupported statements of the addict himself because the confirmed addict will go far beyond the truth in an attempt to secure an ample supply of narcotic drugs with which to satisfy his cravings. . . . The danger of supplying persons suffering from incurable diseases with a supply of narcotics must be borne in mind, because such patients may use the narcotics wrongfully, either by taking excessive quantities or by disposing of a portion of the drugs in their possession to other addicts or persons not lawfully entitled thereto."* Even in cases of terminal diseases, therefore, a doctor could not feel secure in using narcotic drugs to relieve the suffering of his patient. The image of a terminal cancer patient obtaining extra doses of drugs by lying about his pain and then selling off his excess supplies or using the drugs "wrongfully" might seem to be a cruel caricature, but not in the eyes of federal enforcement agents at that time.[25]

The second category of cases described by the commissioner of internal revenue was "Aged and infirm addicts." This was clearly the most compassionate chamber in the enforcement strategy set out by the Treasury Department, for it provided for the maintenance of this class of people. "Cases will come to your attention," Commissioner Roper advised his enforcement agents, "where aged and infirm addicts suffering from *senility, or the infirmities attendant upon old age,* and who are confirmed addicts of years standing will, in the opinion of a reputable physician in charge, require a *minimum amount of narcotics in order to sustain life.*" Although modern research has cast grave doubts on the belief that withdrawal from narcotics threatens the life of an addict, this clearly opened the way for humane exceptions to a harsh enforcement policy. That exception, based only on the use of discretionary power by an executive official and not on legislative action or judicial decision, was expressed as follows: "In such cases prescriptions to meet the absolute needs of the patient may be written and filled without involving a criminal intent to violate the law." As in the first category, compassion was followed by a warning about the criminal law complications that might attend upon providing drugs to even the aged and infirm addicts: "Even in these cases every reasonable precaution should be exercised to prevent the aged and infirm addict becoming the innocent means whereby unauthorized persons may engage in the illicit use and traffic in these habit forming drugs."[26]

Most attention in the directive was devoted to the third category, "The ordinary addict," one not aged, not infirm, not suffering from an incurable disease. Roper launched his discussion of this category with a far-reaching medical pronouncement: *"Mere addiction alone is not recognized as an incurable disease."* He then provided a prognosis for treatment results: "It is well established that the ordinary case of addiction yields to proper treatment, and that addicts can

---

* This language, exhibiting suspicion of both doctor and terminal patient, should be contrasted with that of the Rolleston Report: "In such cases, the administration of the drug for prolonged periods may, no doubt, produce a craving which might persist and develop into an addiction if the disease were cured. But there can be no question of the propriety of continuing to administer the drug in quantities necessary for relief of the disease, so long as it persists, ignoring for the time being the question of possible production of addiction."

be taken off the drug and when otherwise physically restored and strengthened in will power will remain permanently cured." (Such pronouncements stand in stark contrast to the experience of many addicts and the advice given by Rolleston seven years later. The contrasts on these points may well be the core of the differences between British and American approaches to drug dependence.) Anticipating the doubts and fears this posture would raise in the minds of addicts, Roper observed, "The average addict does not believe this and it is symptomatic with him to have a fear and distrust of any treatment or cure. Whenever the occasion presents itself, the hope of successful treatment should be instilled in the minds of the unfortunates addicted to this terrible habit."

Despite these reassurances, the directive recognized that the position of the Treasury Department interpreting the Doremus and Webb cases as prohibiting all drugs to an addict "for the mere purpose of satisfying his cravings" created "serious difficulties." Addicts suddenly deprived of their drugs suffer "in an extreme manner both physically and mentally." What followed in the directive was a confusing series of orders suggesting that (1) some medical help should be provided for addicts, primarily by local officials but with federal help where possible; (2) clinics supported by local funds should be encouraged, where reputable doctors could treat ordinary addicts with narcotics by reducing the dosage and eventually taking them off drugs entirely; (3) revenue agents should not harass such doctors who are working in clinics and are prescribing narcotics to ordinary addicts "*in a proper manner to meet their immediate needs to prevent collapse*"; (4) on the other hand, "so-called reductive ambulatory treatment does not meet with the approbation of the Bureau" because this gives the addict control of the drugs, which he will either use improperly himself or sell; (5) every potential violator of the law must be investigated and reported, whether he is a smuggler, manufacturer, or doctor; and finally came this peroration: "In no other way can this menace to the manhood of our country be eliminated. The commercial or so-called 'Morphine Doctor' must be kept under proper surveillance, and in every case where clear evidence of his willful intent to violate this law is procured no compromise will be made, but his vigorous prosecution will be insisted upon."[27]

This important directive from the chief narcotics enforcement officer of the nation created as many questions as it purported to answer. How could an addict fit within the category of the "aged and infirm" and thus qualify for "legal" maintenance supplies of narcotics? Was it legal for a doctor in a clinic to provide drugs to "ordinary addicts" in steady doses for a month, two months, six months? To reduce doses for six months? Two months? And so on. From a purely legal point of view, the document provided no clear guidance to those in the field of addiction control and treatment. Because the legal rules were so vague and contradictory, they gave enforcement agents the authority to take any action they pleased. When the revenue agents believed that compassion was in order, the rules provided for it; when prosecution was demanded, it was always possible to find at least one phrase in the rules that would support it, so long as even a small dose of drugs had been prescribed for an addict. Of course, one element of consistency ran throughout the common law of enforcement of these legally schizophrenic rules: the puritanical stricture that wherever possible the use of drugs should be penalized. But ambiguity and imprecision were still dominant—and where laws are insufficient, men and not laws rule. Thus, arbitrary rule by the narcotics agent came about because of events shortly after the Harrison Act went into effect, although it was the last thing its framers desired, and it continued for decades afterward.

Had I observed those events at the time, had I read Commissioner Roper's communication of 1919, and had I then been asked for legal advice by a doctor-client about the proper course of action, I believe I might have advised him, first, to refuse all treatment of narcotics addicts; second, when prescribing drugs for the organically ill, to attempt to avoid repetitive doses over long periods of time; and third, to keep all prescriptions of narcotic drugs for such organically ill patients somewhat below the absolute minimum dosage, even if some pain and discomfort resulted. Of course, this soon became the stance of much of the medical profession in America. I would not have been proud to have given that legal advice, and I do not believe doctors can be proud that their colleagues of an earlier generation, and many today, followed it.

Over the years since 1919, Treasury Department regulations have reflected the growing accumulation of enforcement activity and court decisions. However, as Professor Lindesmith has pointed out, the regulations have never reflected the doubts that should have been raised by the Linder opinion. It appears that the very existence of that case was never even mentioned in any of the Treasury Department regulations during this period. Organizational descendants of the Roper directive retained the essential features of the original. Under these regulations, any doctor who gave drugs to an addict continued to risk the possibility not only of professional censure but also of criminal conviction and imprisonment.

It is remarkable that the leaders of the American medical profession so strongly endorsed the enforcement position, which viewed addiction more as moral depravity than as disease and held that addiction could be permanently cured provided that addicts were first distanced from their drugs, usually by the rapid withdrawal method. The dominant medical theory in this country held that it was simply bad medical practice to prescribe drugs for addicts, except on an emergency basis and for a very brief time. The fact that this medical posture happened to agree with the controlling law-enforcement doctrine meant that a law enforcement–medical alliance was conveniently formed which dominated policy formulation in areas considered important to it. The process of discussion and cooperation between enforcers and healers was not remarkably different from that which was taking place in England at about the same time, although the British results were significantly different and were announced somewhat later, in 1926.The American enforcement leaders said, in effect, we interpret the law to demand that drugs be kept away from addicts, even when given by well-intentioned doctors. The doctors said, in effect, we interpret the lessons of medical experience to demand that drugs be kept from addicts, without reference to any external demands, such as those imposed by the law; but it is indeed helpful that the law supports our medical position. Thus, there was congruence on the issue of how to fill in the ambiguity of the Harrison Act regarding the definition of legitimate medical practice.

The medical arguments were usually expressed in terms opposing the ambulatory treatment method, and at times they seemed to approve of the administration of narcotics to addicts confined in hospitals or prisons. But since such institutional maintenance programs were virtually nonexistent, the practical effect was almost total prohibition of drugs for addicts. For example, in 1920 a committee of the AMA recommended that "ambulatory treatment of drug addiction, as far as it relates to prescribing and dispensing of narcotic drugs to addicts for self-administration at their convenience, be emphatically condemned." In 1921 a committee of the AMA Council on Health and Public Instruction was even more vigorous in its condemnation:

> Your Committee desires to place on record its firm conviction that any method of treatment for narcotic drug addiction, whether private, institutional, official, or governmental, which permits the addicted person to dose himself with the habit-forming narcotic drugs placed in his hands for self-administration, is an unsatisfactory treatment of addiction, begets deception, extends the abuse of habit-forming narcotic drugs, and causes an increase in crime. Therefore, your committee recommends that the American Medical Association urge both Federal and State governments to exert their full powers and authority to put an end to all manner of such so-called ambulatory methods of treatment of narcotic drug addiction, whether practiced by the private physician or by the so-called narcotic clinic or dispensary.

The statement of the medical committee included this paragraph: "In the opinion of your Committee, the only proper and scientific method of treating drug addiction is under such conditions of control of both the addict and the drug, that any administration of habit-forming narcotic drugs must be by, or under the direct personal authority of the physician, with no chance of any distribution of the drug of addiction to others, or opportunity for the same person to procure any of the drug from any source other than from the physician directly responsible for the addict's treatment." The AMA House of Delegates adopted these recommendations in 1924 and they thus became the official position of organized medicine in the United States—and remained so for many years. It is to be noted that as the police agents of the Treasury Department intruded into the practice of medicine, so also did medical doctors not fear to express an organizational opinion on the relationship between a particular form of medical treatment and the incidence of crime by addicts so treated.[28]

Successive directives of the narcotics control officials in Washington continued to combine legal analysis with directives to the physicians of the country about how to treat drug addiction. In a later version of the pamphlet issued as a guide to narcotics agents "and others concerned," dated June 23, 1928, the Treasury Department pointed out its continuing opposition to ambulatory treatment and self-administration of prescribed drugs by addicts; then the pamphlet declared, "Medical authorities agree that the treatment of addiction with a view to effecting a cure, which makes no provision for confinement while the drug is being withdrawn, is a failure, except in a relatively small number of cases where the addict is possessed of a much greater degree of will power than that of the ordinary addict." In other words, the leading narcotics police agency of the country took a position opposing the medical treatment of addicts on an outpatient basis, opposing giving them drugs which they administered themselves, but approving of the institutional treatment of addicts under a regimen in which the drugs would be withdrawn. The pamphlet contained brief descriptions of cases involving successful federal prosecutions of doctors who had given drugs to addicts in situations that did not fit these official guidelines.[29]

In September 1963, as this era drew to a close, the Treasury Department issued yet another version of its pamphlet on Harrison. By this time there had been additional lower federal court decisions and more medical studies, but the basic posture on maintenance and outpatient clinics had not changed since the 1920s. The pamphlet repeated the exact language of the 1921 AMA committee and then cited with approval yet another authoritative declaration, this one issued on May 14, 1962, by the AMA and the National Research Council. The joint statement recognized drug addiction as an "illness" but persevered in the earlier position that the approved method of treatment was institutional confinement in a drug-free environment, as well as "extensive postwithdrawal rehabilitation and other therapeutic services." The AMA–NRC statement then made clear, once again, the dominant medical–law enforcement position on the controversial core of the addiction treatment field: "The maintenance of stable dosage levels in individuals addicted to narcotics is generally inadequate and medically unsound." The joint statement, as cited in the Treasury Department pamphlet, also supported compulsory civil commitment for the treatment and withdrawal of addicts as well as the use of a relatively new substance, methadone, in such institutional withdrawal programs. However, the pamphlet continued to accept the compassionate chamber for so-called aged and infirm addicts, which was phrased even more broadly than before: "Under adequate precautions (in or out of an institution) and after proper consultation, addicted persons may be supplied with maintenance drugs if withdrawal represents a hazard to life." Reflecting the new fashion on the horizon, moreover, the pamphlet added, "Oral medication with methadone will usually suffice."[30]

The Treasury Department regulations and directives, then, generally demanded that drugs be kept away from addicts and that doctors and addicts who violated these precepts be imprisoned. There were, however, many exceptions to this generally harsh rule. The very creation of the "aged and infirm addict" category in the Treasury regulations by departmental fiat is one of the most concrete examples of this type of exception. It allowed doctors to continue to dispense drugs purely to cater to the cravings of addicts who happened to fit into the classification, which nowhere was clearly defined and which then had no statutory support. It was probably intended to apply to older addicts who were set in their ways and in their dosage—and who did not constitute a social threat. The addicts who were allowed to take advantage of this system very likely resembled the stabilized addicts described by the first Brain Report in Britain. In light of the standard interpretations of this era, a rather fascinating paradox is thus suggested. Although the British and American approaches seem, in many respects, to be starkly different, the basic characteristics of many of the addicts receiving maintenance doses of drugs through open and known doctor's prescriptions were remarkably similar.

If the qualities were similar, the quantities were not. We have seen that from the 1920s to the early 1960s the total number of all known addicts receiving drugs under medical treatment in Britain never reached 1,000 and was usually well below that figure. Dr. John A. O'Donnell, a prominent American narcotics researcher, has studied the practice of addiction maintenance by doctors in the southern states after the Harrison Act was passed. In an interview with Edward

Brecher in the early 1970s, O'Donnell reported that southern law-enforcement officers had told him that they estimated the number of such cases in each of their states "from 200 to 400 or 500 elderly addicts maintained by physicians, against whom they had no idea of taking any action." Brecher observed, "This indicates that far more addicts were being maintained on legal opiates in the Southern states than in the whole of Britain."[31]

Narcotics agents, like police officers in other areas, tended not to enforce the law against those who, in their view, seemed not to be basically bad people, for example, medical professionals. In testimony before a congressional committee in 1956 it was rather frankly admitted that eighteen doctors, nurses, and druggists in the Toledo, Ohio, area were known by a narcotics agent to be taking drugs, but neither he nor his superiors had any intention of doing anything but allowing them to continue to be thus "treated for addiction in lieu of prosecution." It is quite possible that there was a heavy element of class bias in the exemptions provided for professionals; indeed, this is Professor Lindesmith's interpretation.[32] This type of bias extended to the very top of the narcotics enforcement hierarchy, to the U.S. commissioner of narcotics, Harry Anslinger, who admitted in writing that he had helped a U.S. senator (allegedly Senator Joseph McCarthy, of Wisconsin) obtain regular supplies of morphine.[33] Anslinger also wrote that he had helped a Washington society lady obtain regular supplies of Demerol.

When would a narcotics enforcement official see an exception as justified, and when would arrest and prosecution be invoked? Even where the evidence was strong that a physician was acting in good faith, had the support of local police and correctional officials, and was a reputable doctor and not a peddler, there was always the risk that *federal* agents would move in if he attempted to provide some form of drug treatment to addicts on a regular basis. When such cases actually reached federal trial courts, there was the further risk that the judges would misinterpret the Supreme Court rulings and treat the *dicta* as the *holdings*—and would therefore act as if the Supreme Court had prohibited *all* forms of drug maintenance for addicts, including those carried out in good faith by an honest physician.

One informative example involved Dr. Thomas P. Ratigan, Jr., who, like Dr. Linder, resided and practiced in Seattle. Unlike Dr. Linder, however, he was heavily engaged in treating addicts, to whom he provided large quantities of drugs. During a two-year period Dr. Ratigan purchased a total of 54,900 half-grain tablets of morphine, which he used to treat approximately 14,000 patients. Mindful of the need to follow the regulations, and also because of the dictates of his own medical philosophy, Ratigan did not usually allow patients to take drugs home for self-administration but rather injected them in his office. The only exceptions were when the addiction was related to an organic illness. He charged one dollar per treatment, whereas other local doctors charged three dollars or five dollars for similar services. Ratigan's activities were followed closely by federal narcotics agents, who finally arrested him in May of 1934. The charge was that he gave injections of drugs to addicts only "to satisfy their cravings" and not to meet some legitimate medical need. Several doctors appeared in support of the prosecution, testifying that addiction could be cured by compulsory withdrawal and that there was no medical reason to provide drugs for addicts. At the same time the expert medical witnesses had to admit on cross-examination that there was no place in the state where addicts could receive such treatment. On October 14, 1934, apparently impressed by Ratigan's good-faith attempts to deal with a difficult medical problem and by his relatively modest fees, the jury found him not guilty.

But his troubles did not end there. He persisted in his medical practice, and the federal agents persisted in their efforts to stop him. In April 1935 Dr. Ratigan was arrested once more. He got out on bail, was rearrested, retried on new charges regarding his unconventional practices, and this time, on August 20, 1936, convicted. The terribly uncertain ground on which well-meaning doctors walked when they sought to treat addicts with drugs is illustrated by the fact that a jury of laymen had to determine whether, under the Harrison Act, the defendant physician had crossed that invisible line between good-faith medical practice and criminal activity; in Dr. Ratigan's case, one jury found good faith, the second, criminal intent—and both were looking at essentially the same facts. He received a sentence of seven years in federal prison plus a $10,000 fine for thirteen violations of the Harrison Act. While he served that sentence his license to practice medicine was revoked by the State of Washington. Even though he continued to fight for his cause from prison and after his release, the ordeal broke Ratigan. He left prison a pauper, and apparently was never able to practice medicine again. No evidence was ever presented that he had committed any "offense" save that which he openly admitted and advocated—the careful administering of drugs to addicts in a medical setting as part of a plan of treatment. Local drug-abuse officials and members of the state legislature held mass meetings after his conviction to support him and his cause. According to Rufus King, "The main theme of Ratigan's supporters was that if drug addicts could get their supply of drugs at cost there would be no illegal peddlers, and since there would then be no significant recruiting of new addicts the problem would tend to disappear in a single generation as the existing addict population died off." [34]

Whether or not these hopeful projections were accurate, they showed grass-roots support for the concept of good-faith maintenance of addicts by a responsible physician. At the higher levels of the society and the government, of course, that support did not exist. Ultimate proof was that the U.S. Supreme Court refused to review Ratigan's case, the only instance I know of where the court had a clear opportunity to deal directly with the issue. In one sense it might be argued that in refusing to review the conviction the court was putting its stamp of approval on the criminalization of good-faith maintenance under the Harrison Act. On the other hand, the high tribunal refuses to review cases on a variety of grounds, most having nothing to do with the substance of the controversy.

It will always be argued that Ratigan should have known by the early 1930s that one did not supply drugs to addicts, and certainly not on a regular basis. That was the Department of the Treasury's main message to the doctors of the country. But what if there was evidence that the patient, in addition to suffering from addiction, was also afflicted with an incurable disease? During the very time Ratigan was fighting his battles in Seattle, an Atlanta physician, David B. Hawkins, wrote this prescription:

> Rx For Mr. A. E. Holley Age 44 Address 395 Hood St., Atlanta, Ga. Exception 1. Article 85. Morphine Sulph. Grs. XV. 30 H.T. ½ Grs each. Sig. Use as directed. 3 days treatment. David B. Hawkins, M.D. Date March 12, 1935. U.S. Reg. No 6950.

Dr. Hawkins was indicted for issuing this prescription and for supplying drugs to two other addicts, Roy Nash and Ruth Spann, under roughly similar circumstances. In his defense, Hawkins argued that he was protected in large part by the Linder decision and also by the exception promulgated by the Treasury Department in its own regulations regarding patients suffering from incurable disease. In accordance with the specific instructions of those regulations, Hawkins had written "Exception 1. Article 85" on the prescription, thus indicating that he was treating a patient who, in his professional opinion, had an incurable disease. Hawkins testified that he had known Holley for a long time as a morphine addict and also as a sufferer from pulmonary tuberculosis, heart disease, and other organic illnesses. He often gave this patient prescriptions for fifteen grains of morphine, as he had in the one quoted above, for "3 days treatment." The testimony in regard to Ruth Spann and Roy Nash was roughly the same, as were the charges: that Hawkins had issued the prescription in violation of the Harrison Act because he was not acting in good faith or in the course of his professional practice but only to satisfy the cravings of addicts.

Nothing in the record of the case indicates that Dr. Hawkins was a peddler like Dr. Jin Fuey Moy or Dr. Webb or that he was engaged in a cause like Dr. Ratigan. The practical question seemed to have come down to whether he was treating the organic conditions or the addiction. The prosecution called medical witnesses who testified that they had examined Holley and found no evidence of serious organic disease, only that he was a morphine addict. Indeed, one Dr. J. C. Blalock testified that he had examined all three addicts in the case and found nothing organically wrong with any of them save for their state of addiction. Other evidence was elicited on the issue of how much morphine should have been given to someone "in a dying condition" (if it were to be admitted, as it was not, that Holley had such a condition), and expert medical testimony indicated that five grains a day would have been acceptable.

Stop and reflect for a moment on what such trials of physicians meant in legal and ethical terms. It may be that Dr. Hawkins was a charlatan and a peddler, but nothing appears in the record to this effect. Therefore, the physician was being tried for the offense of giving a patient drugs for one condition, a craving for drugs, when he claimed it was for an interrelated set of maladies, only one of which was addiction. The doctor also claimed that in his professional judgment the dominant medical problem was terminal and organic. If Hawkins was wrong, then it appears that his greatest offense was an error in professional judgment. Nowhere in the record of the case can be found the so-called guilty mind (*mens rea*) that the law, through painful centuries of experience, has required before a person can be deemed to have violated a criminal statute. But, in accordance with American practice under the Harrison Act, the trial judge felt that there was sufficient evidence of criminal intent to allow the case to go to the jury, which returned a verdict of guilty, whereupon the judge imposed a sentence of eighteen months' imprisonment.

Had this case occurred in Britain, it would not, by my reading of English law, have been considered a crime in the first instance. Had the narcotics agents believed that the case fit into the exception for terminal disease—or even that for an aged and infirm addict, which Dr. Hawkins did not claim but which conceivably might have applied—they would have maintained a discreet silence, as they did in hundreds of other cases involving addicts throughout the country. But apparently the officers of the law doubted the good faith of the doctor, as did the jury; and the law allowed imprisonment when bad faith was found.[35]

It is of some interest, as U.S. Circuit Judge Foster stated in the decision, "that on March 7, 1937, about five months after the case was tried in the lower court, Roy Nash died in the Veterans' Hospital in Atlanta, Ga., of chronic pulmonary tuberculosis." In part because Dr. Hawkins had been found guilty of ministering to the other two addicts (who apparently were still alive) the U.S. Circuit Court of Appeals refused to disturb the conviction even though Mr. Nash's demise under these circumstances would seem to have destroyed the credibility of the one expert witness, Dr. Blalock, who had examined all three addicts and found none of them suffering from organic illness. One is forced to wonder if there would have been persuasive legal evidence of "good faith" had all three addicts managed to die while the appeal was pending.[36]

This case, and hundreds more like it, very effectively conveyed the disturbing message to American doctors that the administration of opiates to patients, even those suffering from terminal illness, could be a chancy venture indeed, especially if it appeared that the patient had developed a dependence on the drug in addition to the organic illness. The federal narcotics enforcement establishment saw nothing amiss with the case and deemed it important enough to bring to the attention of field agents and doctors. Thus, the decision of *Hawkins* v. *United States* appears in several of the pamphlet descendants of the 1919 Roper directive.

IV

If the provision of stable doses of drugs for a lengthy time was discouraged by the agents of the law and the leaders of American medicine, what were the *accepted* approaches to treating addicts during this era? It is possible to discern three major types of approved treatment. The first was offered in the narcotics clinics from approximately 1919 to 1923. The second was various methods of institutional confinement without drugs. The third was individual or group mental health therapy, also without drugs.

Let us first deal with the third type since it is so often ignored. The psychoanalytic theories of Sigmund Freud underlie modern psychotherapy in all its conceptual permutations. The basic notion is to help the afflicted individual come to grips with the personal dynamics at the root of his problems—which in some cases include alcoholism or heroin addiction. The actual process is an intellectual one involving both therapist and patient. If a strictly Freudian approach is followed, the patient may come to understand the trauma of his early childhood, may undergo the cleansing experience of emotional catharsis regarding unresolved hates and loves, and may build a more integrated and coping approach to present problems. Thus, a process of healthy confrontation with oneself may develop and a subsequent growth of a new life-style that does not need the support of drugs. In this context, the notion of prescribing maintenance doses of heroin, morphine, or methadone to a heroin addict is usually seen as disruptive of the treatment process. There is much less pressure to confront painful anxieties when an injection of heroin takes the pain away and replaces it with peace, even euphoria. Freudian psychotherapy demands that a patient face emotional pain and conquer it, not that the physician remove the pain with a medicine. In more modern terms, this modality is often called detoxification and psychiatric counseling—the procedure usually being to place the patient in a hospital for a supervised and gentle period of withdrawal followed by a much longer period of outpatient psychiatric treatment to get at the root causes of the dependency. There is something bracing, even noble, I believe, about the very thought of such a course of action in the face of a serious drug dependency.

My preference for this type of treatment, however, reveals something about my class and intellectual biases. Psychotherapy is at base an intellectual and coping procedure for people who can approach emotional problems in a rational fashion, buoyed in part by a personal history of winning at least some of life's previous battles. But as Jerome J. Platt and Christina Labate pointed out in *Heroin Addiction* (1976), psychotherapy has always proved to be of limited value in the treatment of heroin addiction. "The rational approach of talking through one's problems is not meaningful to the heroin addict," they declared.[37] But while psychotherapy and related concepts of mental health treatment have been of limited value, *some* addicts have been helped by such treatment and it cannot be dismissed as entirely useless. At the same time, major attention must be paid to those approaches that might help a large number of addicts and not just the relatively few who happen to have middle-class, intellectual, coping backgrounds.

This leads us to a review of the first type of approved treatment, the narcotics clinics created as a result of the Treasury Department's tightening enforcement of the Harrison Narcotic Act in 1919. As reflected in Commissioner Roper's directive of July 31, the enforcement activities of the revenue agents, spurred on by the Doremus and Webb decisions, had created great anxiety in many communities, whereupon the commissioner suggested that local officials set up clinics to assist addicts suddenly facing strict new policies of enforcement. Some clinics had already been established by local officials, but the greatest number were organized at about this time with the encouragement of the federal government. There is no systematic evaluation of the operation or success of the clinics, but the Bureau of Narcotics made allegations years later that they had been abysmal failures.[38]

The pattern of clinic creation, according to David Musto (whose authorita-

tive account of the clinics is a seminal contribution to our knowledge of addiction treatment), was quite uneven. Many were simply extensions of such public
health ventures as facilities to treat tuberculosis, venereal disease, or mental
illness. Many large cities, including New York and New Orleans, had clinics,
while others, such as Boston, Philadelphia, and Chicago, apparently did not.
When they were created, estimates of the number of addicts in the country
ranged from 200,000 to 4,000,000. Available records suggest that no more
than 15,000 showed up for treatment at all these early narcotics clinics, of
which there were perhaps forty-four in the country, although the records to
support such statistical generalizations are not entirely clear. The clientele and
the treatment varied greatly from clinic to clinic.[39]

No one has adequately explained the reasons for the ambivalent official policy
that surrounded the clinics. It seemed as if the Bureau of Internal Revenue
urged the creation of the clinics in one breath and their closing in the next.
Some clinics had just been formed in 1919 when federal agents began making
the rounds to attempt to close them. In part, this may have been because
Commissioner Roper was a reluctant dragon; he believed that his bureau
should not have had the responsibility of narcotics enforcement but, rather,
that it fell within the scope of the U.S. Public Health Service. Also, federal
officials viewed the clinics purely as a temporary solution. Any fair evaluation
of the clinic experience in America at the time would probably conclude that
their support at the top levels of government was chaotic, that some showed
promise of worthwhile treatment approaches to addiction and others were
almost private peddling operations, that they provided treatment to only a
small fraction of the nation's addicts, and that their major worth may well be in
the lessons that a few of them provided in this form of mass assistance to
addicts. A brief review of the experiences of two important clinics, those in
New York City and in Shreveport, Louisiana, suggests the value of these lessons.

The New York City Health Department's Worth Street Clinic was in operation from April 1919 to March 1920. The Physicians' Protective Association
opposed the clinic, claiming that addicts should be treated by private doctors,
not the government. Nevertheless, the clinic was opened and soon began receiving addicts by the hundreds. Some three thousand addicts had appeared at
the clinic by July 1, of whom 80 percent were under age thirty; 69 percent were
addicted to heroin. As Musto wrote, "70 percent attributed their use of drugs
to 'bad associates' and only a few to illness or pain." The great majority were
white males, of varied origins such as American, Jewish, German, Polish,
Irish, and Russian. The experience in treatment bore some similarities to the

first days of the British clinics some decades later. Because there was no medical method for precisely calibrating an addict's needs, the claims of the patients were the initial guides for setting dosages. The drug favored by the patients was heroin, followed by morphine, and occasionally cocaine. The average dose of the opiates was 10 grains a day, with a maximum of 15. In today's terms in America, these were massive doses. But the clinic followed the reductive ambulatory system, decreasing half a grain every other day. When the addict became uncomfortable, he was offered a bed in Riverside Hospital, which had once been used for tuberculosis patients. An addict who refused hospitalization soon found his dosage reduced to zero. At Riverside the treatment consisted of laxatives, rest, and good food for five to six weeks. The relapse rate of addicts treated at the hospital was believed by its doctors to have been over 95 percent.

Many of the doctors at the clinic and the hospital soon soured on the idea of a medical approach to treating addicts that included the use of drugs, even in diminishing doses. They began to view their patients as ingrates, morally depraved individuals who could not be trusted with any type of treatment save abrupt withdrawal, abstinence, and confinement. It was also considered impossible to operate effective treatment facilities when illegal drugs were so readily available on the streets. "Conclusions drawn from the New York experience influenced the Treasury Department's attitude toward all clinics," wrote Musto. That may well have been the case, but it appears that the federal campaign against maintenance or the use of even reductive doses in treatment had begun *before* the unfavorable results from New York had been documented. In any event, the medical approach to addiction in New York City was abandoned in 1920, and for over four decades the method favored by the leading medical addiction experts in that metropolis operated virtually alone—that of strict law enforcement.[40]

Few doctors survived a direct assault by the federal narcotics agents with their reputations and practices intact. Willis P. Butler was one of the few who did, and the clinic he operated in Shreveport from 1919 to 1923 has received considerable attention. Its importance as a model of addiction control and treatment has been acclaimed by a number of drug-abuse experts. Dr. Charles E. Terry, for example, wrote Dr. Butler in 1928, "In looking back over the work that has been done here and there throughout the country, I know of no single piece that can compare with yours as a constructive experiment in the practical handling of cases. The only criticism that I would make is that you did this work probably about twenty years ahead of the time when it could be appreciated." Professor Lindesmith devoted considerable space in his 1965 book to a full description of the Shreveport system in order to demonstrate its positive features and to refute the unfavorable and misleading account propagated later by federal narcotics officials. At the conclusion of his description of Shreveport and the other clinics Dr. Lindesmith observed that "the clinic plan bears almost no relationship to British practice." It appears that Lindesmith was referring to the fact that at the time drug dependence clinics had not yet appeared on the British scene.[41]

My impression is that Dr. Butler created the best single model of community opiate control and treatment in American history. The Shreveport method contained, moreover, some of the best elements of what came to be known as the British system—and, as suggested in the previous chapter, the organizational feature of the clinic itself was not a vital element, perhaps even an undesirable one, in England. Thus, if an explorer wishes to seek out a successful model to replace the current approach in America, a trip to Britain would be most helpful but an excursion back into time but within the same country might be equally instructive.[42]

In 1919 Dr. Butler was securely established as the Caddo Parish Physician and Coroner, a position he was to hold for forty-eight years. As federal enforcement agents cut down on the availability of drugs throughout the country in 1919, crime was seen to increase in Shreveport, apparently owing to the work of addicts looking for money to buy drugs. "Thievery was bad. They were stealing stuff off front porches," Dr. Butler stated.[43] Shortly thereafter a friend came with a request: Dr. Oscar Dowling, president of the Louisiana Board of Health, asked Dr. Butler to look into the possibility of setting up some type of treatment program for addicts, patterned perhaps after the clinic recently established in New Orleans. Responding to this request, Dr. Butler visited the New Orleans clinic. He later recalled, "I saw right away that the clinic was trying to fool their patients off of drugs. They were mixing morphine in solution and reducing their dosage drastically. The addicts knew what they were doing because some of them were doubled up in pain. I knew enough about addicts, I had seen plenty of them in the county jail . . . to know that you shouldn't try to do that to them."[44] Butler thereupon determined to set up his own approach to dealing with addicts. An accomplished student of medical and law-enforcement politics, he then went to the Shreveport Medical Society, outlined his plan, and sought the society's support and active cooperation. The society passed a resolution approving the plan and agreed that in the future the 100-plus members would not treat addicts but would send them to the clinic. Dr. Butler stated that the clinic operation would not be involved in the normal medical practice of dispensing opiates to nonaddicts to treat organic illness.

On May 3, 1919, Dr. Butler opened the clinic at Schumpert Memorial Sanitarium, the largest hospital in Shreveport. Terry and Pellens stated that 1,237 patients attended the clinic during the four years of its existence, and Waldorf, Orlick, and Reinarman were able to obtain and study the records of 762 of them. Many of the patients typified the southern, rural, drug-dependent person—middle-aged or older, addicted to morphine, generally noncriminal, receiving his drugs from a doctor. At the same time other age groups and occupations were represented, and some addicts, indeed, were criminals, suggesting that the patients were not recruited from just one segment of society. The age breakdown was: 15–30 years, 39.2 percent; 31–40 years, 34.2; and 41 and over, 22.6. (At the New York City clinic, fully 68.5 percent of the addicts attending were in the 15–30 age bracket.)[45]

Most of the Shreveport addicts had severe organic problems that had to be treated by a physician. Thus, the traditional separation of patients into (1) the addicted and (2) the organically ill or nonaddicted was, for Dr. Butler, a useless and misleading dichotomy. In most cases it was almost impossible to determine if a patient was suffering from cancer or tuberculosis first and drug addiction second, or vice versa. In a practical sense, this should not have made any difference so long as a responsible doctor felt free to work out a sensible plan of treatment for each patient according to the patient's overall needs. It could well be argued that these treatment concepts are the essence of the British approach, and they were what Dr. Butler was able to implement in Shreveport for a few years.

His approach to most of his patients who exhibited organic illness along with addiction was to treat the organic illness first. Many of the patients, for example, had venereal disease—so many that the clinic soon had a second specialty. If it *was* venereal disease, or another treatable ailment, the appropriate medical treatment was given, not only at the clinic but also, where necessary, at two hospitals affiliated with it. If and when the organic illness was brought under control, attention then shifted to the addiction. Patients deemed physically healthy enough to undergo the detoxification process were pressured to do so. Drug dosages were slowly reduced for healthy patients in an ambulatory status. At the critical point the patient was placed in an isolated detoxification ward at the hospital. Staff was in constant attendance, security was tight, and every effort was made to combine humane care with firmness. Oral opiates and sedatives were used to ease the patient through the process, which initially lasted approximately one week. Once off drugs, patients often stayed in the hospital for some weeks longer, sometimes up to a month.

In retrospect, it seems that a major element in the Shreveport approach was not so much the process of detoxification, which was not particularly unusual, but the fine clinical judgment which was required to determine that a patient had truly reached the stage where he could be induced to undergo detoxification, at a time when the prognosis for success was good. Once that judgment had been made, and once the process had been started, those patients who refused to go through with it were dropped from the program. Those just described represent the first group of patients—while they were initially ill, they had treatable diseases, and, once treated, they had to undergo detoxification.

A second group were those considered "healthy" except for their addiction. In the minds of the director and the staff, these patients were ready for detoxification immediately. They might get drugs for a few days or weeks on a non-diminishing basis, but as soon as a hospital bed was available, they faced the same pressure as the first group to undergo detoxification.

Addicts in the third group were designated "incurables." Often they were people with a serious organic illness such as cancer, tuberculosis, or advanced venereal disease. Many of the doctors in the parish were afraid of prescribing repetitive dosages of opiates even to the organically ill because of the possibility of harassment and arrest by federal narcotics agents. Thus the clinic took over even in those cases where an argument might well have been made that the apparent state of addiction was in reality a continuing need for medicine to combat pain due to organic illness.[46] "The other doctors got so scared of the federal narcotic agents," Dr. Butler recalled, "that the only time they would give narcotics to patients, even if they had cancer, was when they were actually in the hospital. But if they were at home, either I or one of the seven other doctors on the clinic staff would have to go to the home to give them their drugs to control the pain."[47]

Were these patients, then, receiving the equivalent of home hospice treatment, in more modern terms? Of that we cannot be sure. At the time the issue of whether they were addicts, or simply organically ill, or both did not arise. They needed medicine and they got it from the clinic doctors. In a sense they were receiving morphine maintenance although that term would seem to have been more appropriate for the other group of "incurables"—those patients who had no apparent organic illness but who were addicts of long standing and advanced years, the "aged and infirm" in the language of the Treasury Department regulations. Thus, while the Shreveport clinic has been called a morphine maintenance program, in reality only this third group, composed of two types of patients (the terminally ill and the aged and infirm), who accounted for approximately one-third of the total case load, received that drug in nondiminishing doses for a long period of time.

The drug of choice for almost all addicts in Shreveport was morphine; 98.4

percent of the addicts who appeared during the history of the clinic reported dependence on that drug, .5 percent claimed heroin, and 1.2 percent other drugs. The drugs of choice in the New York City clinic at the time were heroin, 66.5 percent; morphine, 21.1 percent; and others, 12.1 percent. Heroin was never dispensed by the doctors of the Shreveport clinic.[48]

The amount of drugs received by addicts was large by current American standards, although comparable to those reported from England. Upon entering the clinic, addicts were asked to reveal their normal daily use; replies ranged from one-quarter grain to 30. After they entered treatment, addicts typically tried to get as large a prescription as possible. The clinic did allow ample supplies but not as much as many addicts wanted. The upper limit of morphine per day was in the range of 10 to 12 grains; the median dose for all patients was approximately 7½, or 486 milligrams. All were "vein shooters," according to Butler. During 1979 the average daily dose of oral methadone dispensed to maintenance patients by public clinics in Washington, D.C., was 25.7 milligrams. In recent years a low average dosage has come to be regarded as the mark of an efficient program. It should also be noted that methadone and morphine are roughly similar in potency, dose for dose.[49]

In other respects the Shreveport experience cast doubt on some accepted principles of the modern drug-abuse field. Dr. Butler stated that he had no difficulty in stablizing dosages. In other words, the process of tolerance did not seem to come into play. Once the initial process of negotiation had been completed, addicts placed in a maintenance modality tended to stay at the same level. (This is consistent with the significant observations about the existence of stabilized addicts made later by the first Brain Report in Britain.) There were also no problems with overdoses, and rarely were there reports of otherwise healthy addicts being unable to function because of huge daily doses from the clinic. Butler stated later, "I never found one we could give an overdose to, even if we had wanted to. I saw one man take 12 grains intravenously at one time. He stood up and said, 'There, that's just fine,' and went about his business."[50]

But while the Shreveport clinic gave out large doses of morphine, it did not operate as a hedonistic drug parlor where patients simply dropped in for their fixes; rather, the doctors cared very much about the other "business" of their patients. Requirements of responsible living were imposed at the outset on addicts who wanted to enter the program. It was expected, as a matter of primary importance, that patients who were able to work have a legitimate occupation. If a new patient did not have a job, Butler considered it his responsibility to get him one. The same was true of a decent place to live. Such job-

and home-finding activities were often carried out by the inspectors loaned to the clinic by the city government. One, Captain John Hudson, was the chief of detectives of the local police department. Thus, the police department had an investment in helping addicts function in a socially responsible fashion. At the same time the presence of the inspectors on the clinic staff added another element of control and supervision. Like other aspects of the clinic operation, there was nothing covert about the functions of the inspectors; they helped, and they controlled, and they did both openly. Just as openly, "bums" and "loafers," in Butler's words, were simply not tolerated on the rolls of the clinic.

Neither were criminals, and this fact raises some interesting issues and paradoxes. Fingerprints were usually taken from new patients, and these were sent to central federal collecting agencies in order to determine if the patients had criminal records. Reportedly, fourteen clinic candidates left town before negative reports came back. But at the same time almost one third of the patients openly admitted on intake questionnaires to having some form of criminal record, usually minor. It appears that a patient with a criminal record could obtain treatment if the doctors and the inspectors believed that he was currently leading a noncriminal life. One of the main functions of the inspectors was to keep in touch with the patients in the community so that such information could be learned by the clinic as a matter of routine and not simply when the addict got arrested as a result of concerted police action. Today such intervention by a clinic would raise issues of civil liberties and coercion; at that time and place, they seemed to be generally accepted. In any event, criminality did not appear to be a major problem among the addicts in treatment. Indeed, while the clinic was in operation there was reliable evidence of a drop in crime throughout the community, as compared with the time period just before it opened.

The almost universal support that Butler's work received from local officials was remarkable and important. Musto reported that federal agents investigating the clinic "discovered a political environment which they found unique among communities with clinics: 'There is absolute cooperation between Dr. Butler, the Police Department, the City officials, and the Federal officials.'"[51] The clinic operation was a model not simply of a particular set of medical treatments but, even more important, of a practical match between that medical model and the culture of the community, in all its permutations—political, economic, social, and ethical. Local law enforcement, for example, was content to stay at the perimeter of the problem. The leaders of the community and the people of the community were comfortable with the manner in which the doctors were dealing with the problem of narcotic addiction. The existence of that cultural match, of that state of community comfort, must be recognized as a vital part of the lessons of Shreveport. An almost impossible balance had been achieved, for a time, among all sorts of potentially conflicting forces.

The underlying medical and ethical philsophy that motivated Dr. Butler was revealed in an article he published in the March 1922 issue of *American Medicine*. On the need for flexibility in dealing with the narcotics problem he observed, "No law can possibly meet the needs of all the different parts of the country without some very liberal interpretations." Noting that morphinism was variously considered a crime, a disease, a vice, and a sociological problem, he stated: "No matter what different persons may call the condition, the patient is a sick person, and as such is entitled to and should have proper consideration, care, and treatment, either for the causes that are responsible for him being an addict, or for the addiction itself. . . . The fact that an addict cannot get his medicine in some legal way does not mean that he will not, or in many cases that he should not get it in some other way. If we fail to provide a legal way for the needy suffering to obtain relief, are we to blame them for seeking relief from some other source? They suffer with mental and physical troubles and should be given proper and humane consideration." What about the common practice then, and throughout this era, of jailing addicts as a type of cure? "I have never seen a patient who was forced into jail," cautioned the doctor, who also served as the county jail physician, "and forcefully treated (or rather mistreated) remain well when released. That method is inhuman and wrong. . . . I consider the usual 'iron bars' or 'cold steel' treatment to be as cruel and wrong as an operation with no anesthetic."[52]

Butler's philosophy was consistent with the Rolleston Report, published four years later and an ocean away. Sadly, in America Butler and Shreveport were exceptions to the dominant pattern of iron bars and cold steel.

The choice of morphine as opposed to other drugs *may* have been significant; on the other hand, it seems more reasonable to believe that the choice by doctors of any treatment drug, whether heroin or morphine or others, assumes significance only if it happens to be the choice of the local addicts in the first place, or if they can be convinced to switch to it. While I strongly advocate the medical use of heroin in part for the treatment of addicts, and while some of the cancer patients would undoubtedly have been helped by the drug, at that time in Shreveport the patients believed they wanted and needed morphine. Those beliefs were the dominant consideration in this complex equation. Heroin was still legal at the time, and Dr. Butler might have used it but never did. In choosing treatment drugs the vital factor is not so much chemistry or pharmacology as the *match* between the perceived choices of the addicts or patients and the drugs dispensed by doctors. It must be recognized also that not even the proper match is always sufficient. In New York the clinic doctors prescribed heroin and morphine for their patients but within a regimen that simply did not work for the addicts in that community, in that cultural situation, at that time.

There is no scientific evaluation of the impact of the Shreveport clinic on the relapse rate of patients, on crime in the community, or on the black market in drugs. The tests of Butler's work have been subjective. In repeated undercover operations, federal narcotics agents found it almost impossible to make illegal purchases of morphine. Crime in the community seemed to decline. And it was Butler's impression that relapse among addicts who had gone through the program was rare. But, as one report observed, "We expect that perhaps the relapse rate for Shreveport addicts was higher than Dr. Butler's impression."[53] In light of the high relapse rates of opiate addicts everywhere, this observation seems reasonable. However, it does appear that the relapse rate was not so high as to create conditions that the community felt were intolerable. In the end, the most realistic evaluation of a deviance-control program is whether it results in a level and type of deviance that the community can tolerate.

Can the lessons of the Shreveport model be applied in modern-day New York, Washington, or even London? Let us remember, again, what the key elements of the model were. Not a static mechanism but rather a process of accommodation—worked out on the spot by doctors dealing with actual addict-patients in humane ways that worked for large numbers of them at that time and place. Whether any system can work today in any city depends on whether it can come close to achieving that virtually impossible social, medical, chemical, and political balance always being sought, usually unconsciously, by those running opiate treatment and control programs. In order to deal with many of the young and deviant addicts of today's large cities, the Shreveport process, I believe, would have to be amended to include more longer-term maintenance for "healthy" addicts. But the decision whether or not such a change was necessary would have to depend on the practical diagnosis of real cases, one by one. It cannot be made in advance by the criminal law or on the spot by agents of the police—but, of course, it is now in America and in most countries of the world.

The tragedy of the Shreveport clinic operation is that even though it "worked," it was destroyed by the Department of the Treasury. While no single organizational element made it work, the dispensation of drugs by doctors to addicts was essential to its success. That essential element simply could not be accepted by the federal narcotics agents even though all the responsible officials of the community, including the local federal judge and the federal prosecutor, as well as the medical leaders, believed that Dr. Butler should continue his work.

Narcotics agents harassed the clinic to death, going back time after time, refusing to accept the favorable evidence their investigations uncovered. No reliable evidence of peddling or other criminal activity was ever found, but the Department of the Treasury could not tolerate this last clinic in the country, and it closed on February 10, 1923, although some patients were still treated in the local hospitals by Dr. Butler into 1925. Reflecting on the closing process, Butler, a soft-spoken southern gentleman, observed fifty-seven years later, "They did it deliberately and viciously."[54]

It has traditionally been stated by students of drug abuse that American law and policy made criminals out of addicts. More disturbing is the realization that agents of the United States government purposely destroyed the one American model that offered genuine hope of effective and humane community addiction treatment and control.

The annual report of the commissioner of internal revenue for 1921 hailed the closing of the clinics, albeit somewhat prematurely: "Results obtained from closing 44 narcotic clinics formerly operated in the United States have been most gratifying. The action has been endorsed by the highest medical authorities."[55]

With the last narcotics-dispensing clinic actually closed in 1923, the Treasury Department and the AMA had a clean slate on which they could etch their theories about the correct method for dealing with addicts, which brings us to the third and final type of approved treatment during this era. In one form or another, the confinement of addicts in institutions has been the predominant mode of treatment during this century.

The basic idea of treatment within confinement must have been seen as logical at the time, even humane. In simplified terms, the argument was as follows: Drugs hurt addicts. When drugs are available, addicts use them because they do not have the willpower to resist using them. If drugs are not legally available, addicts will go to almost any length to maintain their supply through illegal channels. In order to cure these unfortunate people, they must first be separated from their supply of drugs by the walls of an institution, and then, once safely ensconced behind those barriers, they can be given the best medical treatment and restored to health free of their addiction. A convenient analogy was at hand—the infectious disease model wherein quarantine and confinement were considered conventional elements of the medical regimen.

Confinement in a locked institution may have seemed harsh for narcotics addicts, but, like so much other medical treatment, some pain and anxiety were to be expected and tolerated if a greater good was to be achieved: eventual full cure.

This logic was not espoused by "bad" doctors while "good" physicians believed otherwise. Dr. Butler, for example, used confinement within a hospital as an essential phase of detoxification of healthy addicts. As we have seen, he claimed that this approach had much success in Shreveport. Of course, the commitment was voluntary and relatively brief. Moreover, the Rolleston Report of 1926 indicated that the dominant opinion of British medicine favored institutional treatment: "The best hope of cure being afforded by treatment in a suitable institution or nursing home, the patient should, if possible, be induced to enter such an institution or home."[56] Sir Humphrey's committee recognized, however, that it might not always be possible to convince an addict to enter an institution voluntarily and devoted most of its attention to treatment by what the Americans came to call the "ambulatory method" involving "self-administration." In fact, confinement of addicts for the purpose of treatment has been used for relatively few British addicts. The British, therefore, talked about institutionalizing addicts but did not back up their words with deeds.

The Americans did do so, however. While no one has comprehensive data on the matter, it appears that the institution most frequently used to confine addicts has been the conventional American prison. Indeed, some states have had laws making the status of merely being an addict a criminal offense. In 1962 the Supreme Court definitively ruled in *Robinson* v. *California* that such status laws were unconstitutional, a violation of the Eighth Amendment "cruel and unusual punishment" clause, because addiction was a disease.[57] The federal narcotics establishment has denied repeatedly that it treats addiction as a crime. But the Supreme Court decision and the official federal executive denials have had little practical effect. On one charge or another, countless American addicts have somehow ended up behind bars. Within a few years after the enforcement of the Harrison Act began, Harrison Act violators became the largest single category of inmates in the federal prison system. As Musto said, "The three federal penitentiaries . . . had a cell capacity of 3,738 while on the first of April 1928 they had a population of 7,598. Of the prisoners, about 2,300 [30 percent] were narcotic law violators, of whom 1,600 were addicted."[58] Throughout this period there continued to be many federal prisoners who were addicted and whose imprisonment could be traced primarily to that fact, although the formal charges were frequently some offense other than the unauthorized possession or sale of drugs. However, the proportion of drug law violators tended to decrease as years passed. In 1950, for example, there were 2,017 narcotic law violators in federal prisons—only 11.2 percent of all federal inmates at the time.[59]

While the proportion of drug law violators declined in federal prisons, the ratio remained high in some state and local jails and prisons. Lt. Joseph Healy, of the Chicago Police Department, boasted to a Senate subcommittee in 1955: "Now we have the house of correction loaded. I was talking to the warden today, and he said the place is loaded with addicts. The county jail is pretty well loaded. And last week at this hearing, there was a State Senator from the State of Illinois who testified as to the prisoners in Joliet; there is pretty close to a thousand addicts down there."[60] The large number of addict-prisoners was traceable in part to the increasing severity of sentences by judges, which were often produced by the establishment of mandatory minimum sentences, at both the federal and state levels, for violations of narcotics laws. These harsh laws reflected the increasing frustration, even hysteria, of the leaders of American government and society at their inability to reduce illegal narcotic use.

The frustrations over dealing with addicts extended to prison wardens and correctional staff. Their concerns about coping daily with large numbers of imprisoned addicts were shared by powerful members of Congress, including Representative Stephen G. Porter, who had spearheaded the movement to ban the importation of opium for the purpose of manufacturing heroin. During the hearings on the heroin ban he had advocated federal narcotics farms for addicts. Introduced in 1928, the Porter Narcotic Farm Act became law on January 19, 1929, but the first institution, in Lexington, Kentucky, was not opened until 1935, and the second, in Fort Worth, Texas, not until 1938. These farms, or narcotic hospitals, as they were later renamed, virtually served as separate prisons for some inmates who had been sentenced by federal courts and also as a place of voluntary commitment for other addicts who sought admission on their own initiative. Although there is some debate about the results of this experiment, the overwhelming weight of professional opinion is that the federal narcotic hospitals have not been very successful.

James V. DeLong surveyed the entire field of addiction treatment for the Ford Foundation report *Dealing with Drug Abuse* (1972) and stated: "It is generally thought that the programs started in the 1930's were almost total failures. Between 1935 and 1964, there were 87,000 admissions to the two centers, of which 63,600 were voluntary and 23,400 were federal prisoners. Of the voluntary patients, 70 percent left against medical advice. A series of studies of addicts released from the abstinence facilities found that up to 90 percent of those followed up relapsed into drug use within a few years." DeLong allowed that this conclusion was subject to later debate because "it may exaggerate the failures." This has been the argument of Dr. John O'Donnell, long associated with the Lexington center. For example, O'Donnell argues, the return of some released patients to drugs for brief periods should be expected. "The revisionist approach to the Lexington experience," DeLong observes, "has caused many observers to soften their adverse judgments somewhat."[61]

Precious little softening was observable in the adverse judgments made by Edward Brecher and his *Consumer Reports* staff when they studied the work of the federal narcotic hospitals and comparable state efforts. Brecher's review of various research follow-up reports concluded that the failures were underestimated and in some cases should have been closer to 100 percent than 90. "At any given time after being 'cured' at Lexington, from 10 to 25 percent of graduates may appear to be abstinent, nonalcoholic, employed and law abiding. But only a handful at most can maintain this level of functioning throughout the ten-year period after 'cure.' Almost all become readdicted and reimprisoned early in the decade, and for most the process is repeated over and over again. The above figures are not to the discredit of Lexington; satisfactory research of several kinds has been done there since 1935. But no cure for narcotic addiction, and no effective deterrent, was found there—or anywhere else."[62]

Lexington and Fort Worth represented the beginning of a humane and well-intentioned movement that became known as civil commitment. "In theory," wrote DeLong, "civil commitment is the nonpunitive incarceration of an addict for purposes of rehabilitation."[63] In both theory and practice, however, there proved to be serious difficulties with the idea. But for liberals and conservatives alike, civil commitment offered the hope of moving forward in the campaign against drug abuse without formally invoking the criminal sanction. Accordingly, during the 1960s, several states, most notably California and New York, attempted to improve on the federal experience with their own distinct but related versions of compulsory institutional noncriminal treatment. The federal government also came up with new approaches to therapeutic institutional treatment in the Narcotic Addict Rehabilitation Act of 1966. Labeled the "new wave" by Nicholas N. Kittrie in his landmark study of the borderland between criminal law and mental health therapy, *The Right to Be Different* (1971), these laws properly fit into the modern historical era, discussed later.[64] Suffice it to say here that Kittrie, Lindesmith, Brecher, and DeLong, among others, saw similar failures and added dangers in the new wave of civil-commitment statutes as they applied to narcotics addicts. Although these laws seemed more enlightened and humane, these authors argued, the result for addicts was still confinement without drugs for long periods of time. As in the past, revisionists have appeared with research findings suggesting that civil commitment is not only humane but effective.

On balance, I am inclined to agree with the critics, not the revisionists, in part because of their documentation of the failures of civil-commitment programs to achieve favorable results—and even more because of the logical impossibility of the core concept itself. As civilization slowly progressed to the point where it was recognized that imprisonment for civil debt was impossible in ethical and practical terms, so also it may soon be acknowledged that civil imprisonment for drug addiction is simply a contradiction in terms. *Voluntary* hospitalization is quite feasible, but not *involuntary* civil commitment—unless, of course, the issue of legal commitment for mental incompetency is raised. This is a totally different arena, one that has, up to now, directly involved relatively few narcotics addicts.

V

All this inevitably leads us to the remarkable career of Harry Jacob Anslinger. Born and raised in the Pennsylvania Dutch town of Altoona, he started his federal service during 1917 in the Ordinance Division of the War Department in Washington, D.C. Anslinger transferred to the State Department in 1918 and soon showed a high degree of initiative in obtaining the agreement of foreign governments to support America's campaign against alcohol trafficking in the Caribbean area. In 1926 this initiative was rewarded with an appointment to the position of chief of the Division of Foreign Control, Prohibition Unit, Treasury Department. He thus found himself working in an agency that sought to control not only alcohol use, through enforcing the Volstead Act, but also drug use, through the Harrison Act.

Originally, the Harrison Act had been one of the many general responsibilities of the agents of the Bureau of Internal Revenue. On January 1, 1920, a special narcotics division had been set up, headed by Levi G. Nutt during the important decade of the 1920s. A scandal removed Nutt in 1930. During that same year the Federal Bureau of Narcotics was created as a separate agency within the Treasury Department. When Nutt was removed, attention turned to the bright, aggressive Anslinger, who by then had become assistant commissioner of prohibition. He took over the new bureau as U.S. commissioner of narcotics when it came into being on July 1, 1930, and stayed in that position until his retirement in 1962 at the age of seventy. Even after retirement, he continued to represent the United States until 1969 as its delegate to the United Nations Commission on Narcotic Drugs.[65]

It would be difficult to overstate the impact Mr. Anslinger had on America and the world. Although a police leader, he was also a consummate politician, a species never too far ahead of the will of its constituency. His remarkable tenure in federal service under nine presidents—he liked to brag that this was two more than J. Edgar Hoover could claim—could not have been achieved had his actions not been in tune with major themes close to the moral heart of America. Thus, for America Harry Anslinger was both leader and follower, policeman and preacher, politician and poet, a symbol of protection from the evils of addicting drugs. Although Anslinger left the Bureau of Narcotics in 1962, the vestiges of his labors are still everywhere to be found, not only in the United States but also throughout the world.

It is equally remarkable that the core ideas Anslinger supported had already been well established before he took office—the need to separate addicts from their drugs; disapproval of clinics, ambulatory treatment, and self-administration of drugs by addicts; the necessity of compulsory institutionalization in order to cure addicts; the wide use of the criminal sanction, including severe prison sentences, to penalize violators of narcotics laws; and the supreme evil of heroin, the main drug of abuse, which deservedly was in a special status of prohibition, not allowed even in the treatment of the organically ill. His main accomplishments were in two arenas: maintaining these idealistic ramparts from the counterattacks that were sure to come and spreading this ideology throughout much of the world.

To properly understand his achievements, it is necessary to reflect on what may be called the natural balancing dynamic of American political conflicts. On most important issues, this country has gone through periods of liberal or radical action followed by periods of conservative or restrictive reaction. And almost always the genius of American politics and conflict resolution has been to move the main battle toward a centrist, compromise position—with none of the most powerful antagonists pushing for final and complete achievement of their goals for fear that complete victory might destroy the process of accommodation. Even though extreme solutions might be advocated in highly emotional terms by most of the concerned general population, American opinion leaders on any particular issue have tended to move the visible national debate away from extremes toward results that would not destroy the opposing leadership camp. The process of compromise has not always worked, of course. A war was necessary to achieve independence from England in 1776. And the issue of slavery could not be compromised peacefully.

The conflict over our national policy toward drugs has ever been one to stir the minds and emotions of the nation's people. Nineteenth-century America was, in the eyes of some observers, a dope fiend's paradise. The policy of governmental laissez-faire may be characterized as reflecting liberal, even libertine, precepts. As the forces supporting greater control gained strength, around the turn of the century, it was clear that some accommodation was going to be necessary. The movement for control culminated in the Harrison Act of 1914 and its subsequent strict enforcement by the Treasury Department. They represented conservative reactions in the natural balancing process of American politics. The rightist position evolved into prohibition of any drugs for addicts, except in rare and temporary circumstances. If the liberal or leftist position was represented by free trade in drugs before 1914 and the rightist or conservative stand by prohibition, what was the center position? It lay, I would submit, just about where the few decently run clinics were in the early 1920s. An addict could not buy narcotics as freely as aspirin or tobacco, but he could get them from a doctor who was treating him in good faith. And in those communities with well-run clinics an addict did not have to live in fear of harassment by the police, of possible arrest, or of imprisonment for the practice of what should have been viewed as a minor personal vice, not a heinous crime. But the clinics and that gentle centrist position were destroyed by the Narcotics Unit of the Treasury Department with the active support and encouragement of the AMA as well as of other leaders of American society. This position, far to the right on the ideological spectrum, was quite consistent with the country's position on alcohol during the same period.

According to the traditional rules of the balancing dynamic, however, a liberal reaction should have taken place within a reasonable period of time on both issues. The reaction and a resultant accommodation did occur regarding alcohol, and by 1933 prohibition of that drug had ended. A counterreaction in regard to narcotics also occurred, and recurred, during the 1920s, the 1930s, the 1940s, and the 1950s. No respected voice argued for a return to the free trade of the pre-1914 days, but several endorsed the medical treatment of addicts and the medical dispensation of drugs to them. Among them were some of the most respected professionals in the country: Dr. Lawrence Kolb, of the U.S. Public Health Service; Lester Volk, a physician, lawyer, and member of Congress; Congressman John Coffee; August Vollmer, who had been president of the International Association of Chiefs of Police and chief of police in Berkeley, California; and, of course, Alfred Lindesmith, of Indiana University.

Although these liberal opponents of narcotics prohibition and the FBN had their differences, most would probably have agreed with the words of Congressman Coffee in a joint resolution he introduced on April 7, 1938, which called for the medical dispensation of drugs to addicts: "Morphine which the peddler sells for a dollar a grain would be supplied, of pure quality, for 2 or 3 cents a grain. The peddler, unable to meet such a price, would go out of business. . . . Courts would cease to be crowded with delinquents who owe their downfall to the necessity of meeting the dope peddler's exorbitant demands. Jails would be emptied; Federal prisons would lose a quarter or a third of their population."[66]

This liberal activity produced no change in governmental policy—a stunning fact when viewed in the context of past American history. Heroin abuse continued unabated, as did dependence on other opiates and cocaine. By the 1950s the liberal argument had begun to rely heavily on unfavorable comparisons of American methods with the British system. Musto stated, "Faith in the 'British System' characterized the anti-FBN forces in the 1950s and 1960s. If in the United States the willing physician and addict were not kept apart by arbitrary rulings of the FBN and intimidation, America could, like Great Britain, solve the addiction problem."[67] So, as memories of the true facts about the American narcotic-dispensing clinics faded into history, advocates of a more moderate policy in dealing with addicts could look across the Atlantic for inspiration.

This liberal revisionist counteractivity reached its height during the middle and late 1950s. The prestigious New York Academy of Medicine produced a report in 1955 that called for treating addicts as sick rather than criminal, and for a medical approach to addiction, including a return to the legal dispensation of drugs to addicts under medical care.[68] In September 1955 Senator Price Daniel, of Texas, held hearings before a subcommittee of the Senate Judiciary Committee that faced squarely the issues raised by the Academy proposals. The American Bar Association and the American Medical Association in 1955 formed a joint committee on narcotic drugs that called, in its reports of 1958 and 1959, for a relaxation of the repressive criminal-law approach and a consideration of more moderate methods, including the British system. During the 1950s, moveover, numerous articles appeared in the popular press echoing what the expert reports were saying: "Make Dope Legal"; "The Dope Addict—Criminal or Patient?" and "How Much of a Menace Is the Drug Menace?"[69]

Leading members of the professions most intimately involved—medicine and law—took positions calling for a move toward the center and a retreat from narcotics prohibition. But they failed. The 1950s saw not compromise on drug-abuse policy but the most repressive federal drug laws and penalties in American history. The Boggs Act of 1951 amended the Harrison Act and imposed mandatory minimum penalties—two to five years for the first offense, five to ten for the second, and ten to twenty for the third, with no possibility for a suspended sentence or probation after the first conviction.[70] The Boggs Act of 1956 was even harsher, increasing penalties for all sorts of drug violations: any sale or smuggling conviction carried a minimum of five years and a maximum of twenty, while the second offense meant ten to forty years.[71]

Throughout this era heroin continued to be seen as the special threat to the well-being of American society, and the Daniel subcommittee referred to it as "the most deadly of all" in its report leading up to the 1956 act. The report also stated, in harmony with Mr. Anslinger's views: "Heroin smugglers and peddlers are selling murder, robbery, and rape, and should be dealt with accordingly. Their offense is human destruction as surely as that of the murderer. In truth and in fact, it is 'murder on the installment plan,' leading not only to the final loss of one's life but to others who acquire this contagious infection through association with the original victim."[72] Accordingly, penalties in the later act were much harsher when a heroin sale was involved, and there was a new twist—if an adult sold to a person under eighteen, the sentence could be death upon the recommendation of the jury. Finally, the 1956 law filled a little-noticed gap in the legal structure of the country when it demanded that all heroin legally possessed at the time of the law's passage be surrendered within 120 days; after that date all quantities not surrendered would be declared contraband.

Why did the traditional American balancing dynamic fail to work in regard to narcotics policy? Two answers seem likely. First, it may have been that the absolutist position calling for prohibition and the harshest criminal penalties was the dominant position of the general population and that no leader—whether politician or doctor or lawyer—could openly deviate from it. But the balancing dynamic assumes that leaders will do what they are supposed to do—*lead* opinion, not simply *follow* it.

A second and, in my eyes, more persuasive argument is that Harry Anslinger was such an effective politician that he was able to maintain his repressive position despite the campaign for more humanity and moderation. That may well have been his greatest accomplishment during the thirty-two years he was in power—not that he took absolutist stances but that he was able to beat the leaders of the opposition into the ground and thus preserve a repressive policy that has caused untold misery and is with us yet. Anslinger used tactics that were unethical, immoral, and sometimes, apparently, even criminal. He attempted to silence Professor Lindesmith, starting in 1939, when the Indiana academic first appeared in print opposing the repressive policies of the Bureau of Narcotics. A bureau agent warned the members of the board of the university and then the president that the young professor was dealing with a "criminal organization"—which turned out to be an innocent research and reform group, the World Narcotics Research Foundation. Such direct attacks on freedom of speech and press against Lindesmith and other critics of the bureau were common despite the protections of the First Amendment and the federal civil rights statutes making it a crime to interfere with those rights.[73]

Anslinger maintained excellent relations with Congress, and he seems to have controlled virtually every legislative inquiry in the drug-abuse field while he was in office. Sometimes he accomplished this by the behind-the-scenes politicking that is regular fare in Washington. On other occasions he would present information that was, intentionally or not, a simple distortion of the truth but tending to support his belief in the absolutist position on drugs. Time after time he repeated the critical side, and only that side, of the early clinic story in America. During the Daniel subcommittee hearings in September 1955, for example, Anslinger assailed the witnesses who had testified in support of clinics for addicts in the following somewhat convoluted testimony:

Mr. Anslinger. Mr. Chairman and honorable Senators, the proposal of the proponents is, in fact, a proposal for the United States Government to sell poison at reduced prices to its citizens. Now, that is—narcotics are labeled as poisons all over the world, by treaty. Our traditional policy since 1912 has been to oppose legalized sale of narcotics. . . .

Those clinics were closed by the action of the medical authorities, the recommendation of the medical authorities and by the State legislature. In one year of operation—now, mind you, the proponents say, "Well, we didn't have time enough." Well, that is nonsense. They were in existence for five years. In one year of operation we seized in the illicit markets 75,000 ounces of narcotic drugs. Today we will only seize about 6,000 ounces, without clinics. . . .

The Chief of Police of Shreveport said, "Well, this is very simple for me. When I have a burglary in the town, I just go down to the clinic at 4 o'clock when they get their customary supply." Most of those addicts were selling to other addicts who would not appear at the clinic.

Senator Daniel. Just a moment, Commissioner Anslinger, you say this was the Chief of Police of Shreveport?

Mr. Anslinger. Yes, sir.

Senator Daniel. Did he say these were addicts on free drugs who were committing crimes?

Mr. Anslinger. Were committing crimes. There were thieves from all over the area, and the record will show that many criminals came in from Texas to get their supply at the Shreveport clinic.

Senator Daniel. To get their supply of dope?

Mr. Anslinger. Yes, sir; and it was—the people of Shreveport demanding that those clinics be closed.[74]

Years later Dr. Butler recalled that during the first year or so of the clinic operation, the commissioner of public safety (often called the chief of police because he was the head law-enforcement officer and no other official in the city had that function) criticized the treatment center and its clients, in the presence of a few prominent businessmen, saying that if he had his way he would throw all those addicts—"bums and street characters"—into the nearby Red River. Butler was outraged and asked to speak to the commissioner alone, and then told him, "I'm going to violate the confidence of one of my patients now because I did not like what you said in front of those other gentlemen. I want you to know that your mother is one of those patients that you would like to drive into the river."

The commissioner was shocked and apologetic. "You mean to tell me that my mother gets her medicine from you? . . . I've never denied my mother anything. You know I'm a man of considerable wealth. . . . But I have wondered why she was spending so much money [in the past] and what for." Dr. Butler replied, "On peddlers . . . getting illegal drugs . . . and all she's using is two grains of codeine a day, that's all that's necessary; she has extreme cardiac asthma, and I'm going to see she gets it as long as she lives."

It is sad to think that the American system of drug-abuse control had forced a seventy-five-year-old woman to buy her medicine, one of the mildest narcotics known to medical science, from street peddlers. One wonders, even under the law-enforcement methods used then, why she was not considered organically ill rather than addicted, but we have already seen how those categories got confused when the long-range dispensation of narcotic drugs was needed.

But on one point there now seems little reason to wonder. In May of 1980 I asked Dr. Butler directly if the story testified to under oath by Anslinger was true. Butler replied, "No, sir. It's a fantasy of somebody's imagination. . . . [The commissioner of public safety] . . . praised the clinic to the highest" in letters to officials all over the country. There was nothing he would not do for the clinic after that incident, including assigning two of his top detectives to work as investigators for it. Current accounts of the clinic document the almost universal support it had from local officials. Apparently the "chief of police" had special reasons for giving his, despite the later account rendered by Mr. Anslinger in sworn testimony.[75]

Anslinger took stands of similarly doubtful veracity on the British experience with drug abuse. His attack on the early American clinics was almost always coupled with an attack on the British situation at the time. As bureau critics normally said that the British had solved the problem of narcotic addiction, Anslinger just as frequently counterclaimed that (1) the British system was no different from the American and (2) in any event, there were terrible problems of crime and addiction in England. A typical statement by Anslinger appeared in a letter published in the October 23, 1954, issue of the *Journal of the American Medical Association*. He observed: "Several years ago a professor of sociology at an American university who is a self-appointed expert on drug addiction, after interviewing a few drug addicts, wrote an article in which he advocated that the United States adopt the British system of handling drug addicts. . . . 'Adopt the British system' is now urged by all self-appointed narcotic experts who conceal their ignorance of the problem by ostentation of seeming wisdom. . . . The British system is the same as the United States system. . . . There is a black market for opium in the United Kingdom. . . . There is a very considerable black market for hashish (marijuana) in the United Kingdom. . . . There is also a black market for morphine and meperidine." It is true that there was a black market for drugs in England; no country has ever totally eliminated the illegal sale of drugs for which there was a demand. But the marked differences between the British and American situations have already been documented. In saying, moreover, that the two systems were similar, Anslinger made a mockery of the truth. Those distorted opinions are believed by many influential decision makers to be the truth even today.

To Anslinger and the agency he headed must also go a great deal of the credit for bringing the criminal sanction–absolutist drug enforcement system to much of the world. Much of this missionary activity occurred during World War II, when American power was virtually unchallenged in many parts of the world. In the Far East, for example, as Lindesmith has demonstrated, the Bureau of Narcotics was able to move in behind Allied armies and demand the elimination of culturally ingrained patterns of narcotic use, such as opium smoking; these were replaced by strict abstinence supported by the criminal sanction. In many of these areas today—Hong Kong, Thailand, Borneo, and Singapore, among others—opium smoking has been replaced by virulent epidemics of heroin smoking or injecting. Japan and Germany also adopted their own versions of the Harrison Narcotic Act and the strict enforcement ethic. As the new postwar order was being established in the late 1940s, the essential message of Commissioner Roper's memorandum to his Internal Revenue agents and to others concerned in 1919 about the troublesome domestic narcotic problem was being carried, by agents of the successor Bureau of Narcotics, to some of the remotest corners of the world, and to some of the busiest as well.[76]

The full story of Harry Jacob Anslinger's destructive contribution to American and international drug-control policies has not been written, and this account, for reasons of space, must omit much of the known detail, including his campaign that eventually led to the prohibition of marijuana in 1937 and the lumping together of that relatively mild drug with the addicting narcotics such as heroin, his linking of drugs with the international communist menace, and all the other varieties of unethical and illegal practices he used against those often highly respectable people who opposed his repressive policies.[77] Any current reform movement must deal not only with present harsh realities but also with the legacy of hysteria and irrationality so well implanted by the first commissioner of narcotics.

VI

Two eras came to an end in the 1960s, the Rolleston in Britain and the Harrison-Anslinger in America. Britain saw increased heroin addiction and the opening of clinics. America saw the departure of Anslinger and the rise of methadone-maintenance clinics. In many ways the two countries were becoming more similar, but major differences remained in the design and tone of their respective models of addiction control and treatment. That of the United States had been broadcast to much of the world; that of England had been restricted almost exclusively to that relatively small nation. The operational principles dominating each of these models were as follows.

In Britain:
- Opiate addiction, including dependence on heroin, was a disease and not a form of vicious self-indulgence.
- The disease was usually chronic, recurring, and long-term.
- Permanent cures were rare, and thus care over an extended period of time, rather than cure, was necessary for some patients.

- The nature of this care was almost exclusively a matter to be determined by the medical profession through the professional judgments of individual doctors.
- The medical care of addiction would almost never involve the abrupt withdrawal of drugs from patient-addicts, since this was considered both a cruel and an ineffective way of treating ill people. Because permanent cure was the exception, this harsh method virtually assured a relapse in many patients, who then might resort to illegal sources of supply.
- The medical care of addiction usually required doctors to seek to convince patients to reduce their intake of drugs, in part through counseling and in part through slow reduction of the dosage.
- Where the doctor's best efforts to terminate the use of drugs failed, it was legitimate medical practice to prescribe relatively stable doses of narcotic drugs to some patients over an extended period of time.
- Since heroin has always been considered part of the pharmacopoeia of English medicine—a "most excellent sedative . . . of estimable value in so many conditions," in the words of the British Medical Association—it was rather unremarkable for it to be prescribed, along with other drugs, by some doctors for some addicts under some circumstances.

In the United States:
- Opiate addiction was not a true disease although it was often formally labeled as such; rather, it reflected weakness of character and will and indicated a depraved nature.
- Dope fiends could control this vicious self-indulgence through an exercise of personal will, equivalent to "taking the pledge" in regard to alcohol.
- Permanent cures were possible, therefore, and it was simply a matter of finding the right combination of the proper medical treatment, a strong-willed doctor, and an addict who had seen the light.
- The nature of the care and cure of addicts was to be determined in part by the medical profession and in part by criminal justice authorities. Law-enforcement officials had a role in controlling the weakness of addicts as well as the weakness and avarice of doctors, pharmacists, and drug manufacturers.
- The medical care of addiction often involved the abrupt withdrawal of drugs followed by care in a "narcotics farm" or treatment within various other institutions through compulsory civil commitment. The element of compulsion was crucial in dealing with addicts, as with lepers or the

mentally ill. For many recalcitrant addicts the only appropriate institution was the ordinary prison, a resolution demanded by the simple fact that they continued to violate the narcotics laws, among others.

- As in Britain, the medical care of addiction often saw American doctors seeking, through counseling and other forms of psychological support, to convince patients to reduce their intake of drugs. But where the doctor's best efforts failed, it was considered outside the bounds of proper medical practice to prescribe narcotic drugs to any patient for an extended period of time, even if the doctor considered it medically necessary to relieve his patient's suffering. Doctors who persisted in this practice were threatened with prosecution and the loss of their right to practice medicine, and in thousands of cases they were prosecuted and convicted.
- While heroin was once part of the pharmacopoeia of American medicine for treating the organically ill, it was virtually excluded by a congressional enactment in 1924 and completely excluded in 1956. Although some doctors considered heroin a useful drug in the treatment of addiction during the early narcotic clinic era (1919–1923) and in the treatment of nonaddicts, the prohibition on heroin was widely supported by the American medical and criminal-justice professions. The drug was held to have no medical value, it could not be administered by doctors in methadone-maintenance clinics, and it could be used in relatively rare experiments only upon the securing of a special license from the federal government.

7: DOUBT AND UNCERTAINTY: BRITAIN TODAY

"There are growing feelings of doubt and uncertainty about the apparent success of the British system. . . . What the Americans have to learn from us and what we have to learn from them is probably much less than many of the international drug experts jet-setting around the world would have us believe."—Robert Searchfield, 1974[1]

"If one looks just at positive policies for the medical treatment of heroin addiction . . . then paradoxically it seems that Britain has on a very much shorter time scale adopted the same medical policies as the U.S. Rather than having anything to teach the U.S., perhaps we should be acknowledging that we have rather more slowly been learning the same lessons."—Jasper Woodcock, 1977[2]

"Those wretched doctors! . . . even though they're my friends. . . . About 1972 they started moving off heroin to physeptone. Then off i.v. to oral. The result: the addicts go back on the black market, lose their jobs, and stop paying taxes. The cost is £500 per week. All this because the clinic doctors believe the addicts shouldn't have drugs!"—Terence E. Tanner, 1979[3]

I

The three Englishmen quoted here are all experts on the drug-abuse situation in their country. They all see that situation somewhat differently, although on some points they are in substantial agreement. What is important for outsiders to realize is that the English experts have had, and continue to have, profound disagreements—not simply in intellectual terms but in emotional ones—about what happened since the clinics opened and why. It is hazardous for an outsider to venture into this controversial thicket and attempt to explain it. But that, with some trepidation, is what I intend to do in this chapter—to tell the story of modern British heroin addiction, its treatment, and its control since 1965.

Horace Freeland Judson attempted to tell part of this tale in his 1974 book. After returning from directing my first English institute that same year, I also wrote about it in a brief newspaper article. Both Judson's book and my article came to optimistic conclusions about the overall health of the British system and compared it favorably with the American. The result was predictable: while some British experts expressed quiet pleasure about these published opinions, the dominant response was one of disdain. Robert Searchfield's remark about jet-setting international drug experts was a reference to the two of us.

Alan Massam, a British reporter, who

wrote the article containing Mr. Searchfield's words, observed: "The tributes of Professor Trebach (who insisted the system works) combined with the quietly confident position of the British medical establishment that heroin addiction has at least been contained, should make this patriotic reporter glow with satisfaction. Unfortunately, however, Horace Freeland Judson, Professor Trebach, and the British medical establishment seem to have been looking at British addiction problems through the wrong end of the telescope." Mr. Massam then pointed out what our improperly focused lenses had been missing— that "the apparent containment of heroin addiction is a myth," that the clinic system does not deal with many other problems such as barbiturate and alcohol abuse, and that the British approach deals only with symptomatology and not with the causes underlying the use of drugs, especially by the new generation of abusers who partake of many psychoactive chemicals.[4]

In response, I would first observe that heroin addiction did indeed rise during this period, a subject which has been discussed and to which we shall return. There is no doubt, next, that the clinic system deals almost exclusively with opiate abuse and, within the opiate family, primarily with the most troublesome offspring, heroin. That substance is also my focus, on the theory that only by narrowing one's field of vision, akin to looking through the "other" end of the telescope, is it possible to thrust through the welter of confusing facts toward a closer approximation of the truth. For these reasons I have purposely ignored extended discussions of other drugs—marijuana, barbiturates, alcohol, and LSD, among others. All these drugs pose vital issues that must be addressed, but unlike some of my colleagues, I claim that a sensible way to do so is one at a time; in this case I mean *one drug family*, the opiates, and in particular, heroin.

As for the failing of the British system to deal with underlying causes rather than mere symptoms, I am somewhat at a loss to comment intelligently. After many years of working in the overlapping fields of civil rights, delinquency, and drug abuse, I must confess that I could not confidently recognize an "underlying cause" if it walked up and sat in my lap. Others might, but I would need an introduction. In my work, therefore, I attempt to fashion improvements on any piece of a social problem where my mind can rationally grab hold, whether that piece be root, underlying, superficial, or symptomatic. Root causists tend to be impractical utopians. While I will continue to speculate about the causes of drug abuse, therefore, I will never claim to have uncovered one that is "root" or "underlying."

Since I wrote those optimistic words in 1974, moreover, the drug-abuse situation in England has changed for the worse. My opinions have changed accordingly, but not to the extent of believing, as do many English and American commentators, that the venerable British system has been destroyed or that the differences between English and American approaches are now insignificant. Nor do I see the English addiction problem coming even close to the dimensions or character of the American. In comparative ornithological terms, I still see a gentle English addiction sparrow and, across the ocean, a predatory American heroin eagle.

II

In order to tell the story of the modern British era, it is necessary to return briefly to 1965 and to some pragmatic questions of causation and intention.

What actually moved the Brain Committee, which represented the leadership of British medicine, to recommend those drastic changes on July 31, 1965? The facts they mentioned—the drastic rise, by British standards, in the number of young, deviant heroin addicts and overprescribing by the few doctors who treated addicts—may have been the most important reasons. But there were others as well.

Some telling insights into the combination of science and opinion that moved the British medical establishment at the time of Brain II were provided by Dr. Thomas Bewley, one of the few highly respected doctors who regularly treated addicts before *and* after the inauguration of the clinic system. Dr. Bewley testified before the second Brain Committee and, while the committee was still deliberating, in April 1965, published the essence of his testimony in the *Lancet*.[5] Bewley reviewed the key facts as he saw them—that in the past most addicts were created in the course of medical treatment or because, being doctors and nurses, they had easier access to drugs; that the new addicts had become addicted by contact with other addicts and thus there was a small epidemic of new young, troublesome heroin and cocaine injectors; that while some of them may have had personality factors predisposing them toward addiction, the creation of new addicts primarily "depends on the number of vulnerable people in the community and on the number who are already addicted."

"Prevention is more important than cure," Dr. Bewley cautioned, "and, if potential addicts had less contact with addicts and less ease of access to narcotics, there would be less addiction. In view of this the practice of issuing drugs to persons already addicted may have to be reconsidered." Bewley then explained the reconsideration that he and his medical colleagues had already completed. Both Rolleston and Brain I had agreed on the circumstances in which heroin and morphine could legitimately be prescribed—first, for a patient in whom complete withdrawal produces serious symptoms that cannot be treated normally in private practice, and second, for a patient who can lead a fairly useful and normal life with regular quantities of the drug, usually small, but cannot function normally in society when the regular allowance is with-drawn. However, Dr. Bewley declared that the new addicts were social misfits, with or without drugs: "The patients described here fall outside this category, in that most of them had unsatisfactory work records, which were not im-proved by taking drugs."

Upon reading those words, I heard echoes of Shreveport forty-six years before. It seems that every person with direct involvement in the drug-abuse problem draws a line beyond which drugs for the addict shall not pass. In 1919 Dr. Willis Butler drew the line at bums and loafers, at young, healthy addicts. But aged and infirm addicts, those too old to change, those who could not work, those who were really respectable people, like doctors and policemen, and who constituted no social threat—they were on the proper side of the drug line. The British medical establishment drew its own line in 1965 at roughly the same place, but with somewhat different results. The descendants of the Rolleston committee could tolerate the idea of a general practitioner providing regular supplies of narcotics to somebody's old, gentle mother, who had be-come used to her morphine when in the hospital twenty years ago for a cancer operation, but they positively gagged at applying the Rolleston rules to that mother's mod son, with his long hair and hippie clothes, who lived on the state, never worked a day in his life and did not intend to, and now wanted his heroin free from the National Health Service. It was simply too much to take—perhaps because, as Willis Butler explained in May 1980, responsible doctors just did not give regular supplies of drugs to people who did not really need them.

In the process of choking on the prospect of treating defiant young heroin addicts the same as the deserving aged and the infirm, the British medical leadership showed its fundamental unease with the basic idea of maintenance for *anyone*. Indeed, Dr. Bewley, like Butler an enlightened and humane physi-cian, in that revealing 1965 article seemed to make a wholesale refutation of the Rolleston–Brain I concepts of the existence of stabilized addicts and the feasi-bility of maintenance; he even referred with approval to the core position of his American colleagues, the 1963 joint statement by the AMA and the National Research Council that the maintenance of stable doses for addicts was "gener-ally inadequate and medically unsound."

It is remarkable that Dr. Bewley read the history of American approaches to dealing with this new type of British addict, who was quite "common" in America, in a way that must have delighted Harry Anslinger, who always claimed that law enforcement had reduced the number of addicts in America drastically after the passage of the Harrison Act. "The continuing reduction in the number of addicts in the United States is due more to the activities of the Federal Bureau of Narcotics than to better treatment," Dr. Bewley advised his British readers. Since the English saw American-type addicts on their soil, and the possibility of an American-type heroin epidemic, a glint of legal steel was certain to appear in future British medical strategy, but no responsible person, certainly not Bewley, suggested adopting the American system. What Bewley did advise became the core of the Brain II final recommendations—compulsory notification of addicts, new restrictions on the prescribing of drugs by general practitioners to addicts on an outpatient basis, and the creation of special treatment units, preferably as parts of psychiatric hospitals. But neither Bewley nor Brain II recommended taking away the power of decision from those doctors who, under the future scheme, were to continue treating addicts—the power of deciding if, how much, and how often an addict-patient would get drugs. Thus, while the British in 1965 looked to America for lessons and flirted with American solutions, Brain II did not signal the creation of an Anslinger era in England, as is often stated or implied by American commentators.[6]

Nevertheless, the British medical leadership clearly was uncomfortable with the idea of maintaining any addict on drugs, especially the hundreds, soon to be thousands, of new young heroin users on the streets of London and other big cities. That reluctance, in the minds and hearts of British doctors, about the basic "rightness" of legal heroin for young, healthy addicts was to reemerge in the 1970s with powerful clinical impact.

It is possible to argue now—with the benefit of hindsight—that there should have been some profound discomfort about the underlying logic of the new arrangements proposed in 1965. Bewley and Brain had set up an appealingly rational argument: (1) a few irresponsible doctors are prescribing massive doses of heroin and cocaine to addicts; (2) these addicts sell off their surplus supplies in the gray market (legal drugs, illegal sales) and in the process recruit susceptible youth into the ranks of the addicted; thus (3) the overall policy solution is to take away from all doctors, with a relatively few licensed exceptions, the traditional power to prescribe heroin and cocaine to addicts. This legal action, while jolting, would stop the epidemic in its tracks by going to the very source, the overprescribing doctors. This argument has been generally accepted in Britain. But there were other possible explanations for the problem that suddenly appeared on the English drug scene of the mid-1960s, and other possible policies in response to it, some of which we have already discussed.

The 1960s in the United States saw massive youth unrest and revolt, due to a host of issues including the Vietnam War, and drug taking was a central part of that scene. As a Dutch sociologist and drug-abuse expert told me in Amsterdam in 1977, "I watch the drug trends very closely in California because they tell me what our troubles will be ten years later." While the time element may not be subject to precise measurement, the basic idea holds much truth, for the British as for the Dutch. Thus, the phenomenon of imitating American habits sheds some light on why English youth of the 1960s were suddenly using a wide variety of drugs, including heroin.

But like their American counterparts, they wanted more than drugs. The drifting, alienated youth of the West End and Soho were looking for something besides what they had in traditional English society—the established religion and accepted values—to make sense of lives that seemed to make no sense to them anymore. Into this void came new ideas, some of them containing much beauty not even remotely understood by the staid minions of English law and medicine. Some new people came also, such as the young Reverend Kenneth Leech, fresh from Trinity College, Oxford, seeking a ministry at St. Anne's Parish among the young and the distressed. Leech saw that the new drug takers were influenced by many forces besides drugs. He and they saw both beauty and meaning in the haunting words of the new rock singers, especially the American Paul Simon, who often lived and sang in the West End, and also his sometime partner, Art Garfunkel.[7] Leech saw, for example, in Simon's song *Blessed*—sung at the Open Air Mass on St. Anne's Day in 1965—an expression of the quest of the youth for new meaning in what was for them a spiritual desert. That song assigned deep spiritual values to methedrine drinkers, marijuana sellers, and those who dwelled in illusions. The heroin epidemic among the youth of the 1960s might find more understandable explanations in the lyrics of Simon and Garfunkel than in the prescriptions of Swan and Petro (two of the most notorious of the so-called overprescribing doctors).

Radical criminologists on both shores of the Atlantic, moreover, have made sport of theories of causality which blithely assume that the mere availability of a drug is the most powerful force in producing virtual epidemic use of it. This mechanistic notion denies that there is any higher meaning to the taking of a particular drug by a user or that he has any power of choice in deciding to take or not to take one drug or another. Thus, "accessibility is cast not as something chosen but as an 'epidemic' which is mysteriously 'caught' by the actor," criminologist Jock Young told the Anglo-American Conference on Drug Abuse in April 1973. "Needless to say, accessibility without motivation explains nothing. I may have plentiful access to both coal gas and milk but this does not mean I will bubble one through the other and drink it, as occurs in the Grassmarket in

Edinburgh!"[8] The very notion of choice seems out of place when applied to heroin—for it is assumed that this superdrug attracts users as a powerful magnet does metal filings. While this notion may apply to addicts in the full flush of dependence, it does not explain the choices made by new heroin users in the experimental stage, which may go on for years without actual addiction, despite widespread beliefs to the contrary.

When, therefore, one scans the full spectrum of the chaotic drug scene in England at the time, a host of unanswered questions emerge. If the taking of drugs is, by most standards, an irrational act—perhaps spiritual or metaphysical or escapist, even decisive but not wholly logical—why assume that the logical policy of reducing the power of doctors to prescribe for addicts would reduce the use of drugs? Why not assume that many young, deviant drug takers, because their very sense of being, of integrity, demanded defiance of social norms, would find it more meaningful to obtain illegal heroin on the street than legal heroin from an overprescribing doctor? If one does assume the power of that need for deviance, even defiance, then cutting off the junkie doctors might have been expected to bring in the Mafia "waiting in the wings," as some observers at the time put it. This is not to say that the government and the medical profession should have ignored irresponsible action by doctors, but those learned leaders should have been aware—through reading American history if not British—that drug policies cannot be constructed like an engineering project and that tough legal "dams" rarely stem the flow of psychoactive chemicals to those who, for whatever reasons, fervently desire them.

There were many logical policy options other than those recommended by Brain II. Major reliance could have been placed on reinstituting the administrative tribunal machinery originally created in 1928 in response to a Rolleston Committee recommendation and allowed to lapse in 1953. There is persuasive evidence that the immediate propelling energy for the reactivation of the Brain Committee was a visit to Lord Brain by Home Office officials who were concerned about the number of addicts being supplied, they believed, by a few overprescribing doctors. These Home Office officials wanted to preserve the existing system, but they also wanted the lapsed tribunal machinery to be revived. They did not recommend (they told me) either the creation of clinics or enactment of the restriction on the right of individual doctors to use heroin and cocaine in addict treatment. The Home Office, then, wanted tribunals, which Brain II supported, but the committee went a good deal further than the Home Office wanted or expected.[9]

Brain II might have supported other ingenious arrangements, such as those proposed by Charles Jeffrey and H. B. Spear (at that time the chief inspector and deputy chief inspector, Drugs Branch, Home Office) to the committee in July 1964. They proposed that in the future no general practitioner should be allowed to treat more than a specified, low number of drug addicts, that a second opinion should always be required from a consultant psychiatrist when a doctor first dealt with a drug addict, and that the dose of heroin should be set in consultation between the two doctors. This proposal was not adopted by Brain, in part because it would have left in place a large measure of the traditional wide authority of all licensed physicians to prescribe heroin and cocaine to addicts.[10]

Some of the arguments against the system proposed by Brain II were based on psychiatric concepts. "Because of his personality defects, an addict needs a strong, stable one-to-one relationship with a wise male adult who will be able to play the role of the deficient father," psychiatrist H. Dale Beckett told the Medical Society of London as the new system was being established. "This kind of one-to-one relationship I cannot see being established at what is bound to be an emotionally cold, efficient, clinical Out-Patient Department where numbers of other addicts are treated as well. As I see it, this relationship is of first importance and it would have been far better established between one addict and one general practitioner who would then have carried on maintaining his patient on a dose of heroin which had been ascertained during a brief in-patient period in a hospital." This relationship, Dr. Beckett reasoned, would have provided help to the addict up to that point when his developing maturity might have led him to discontinue the drug.[11]

The second Brain Report was signed on July 31, 1965, but over two and a half years passed before the new system was in place. Under the very noses of Members of Parliament and the government medical and drug officials, on the streets where they always walked and around the West End and Soho and Piccadilly restaurants where they often dined, the drug scene that so agitated Brain and Bewley continued, even expanded.

The index of all addicts known to the Home Office for 1965 revealed a total of 917 dependent on all drugs, of whom 509 were nontherapeutic heroin addicts—and 259 of the latter were new addicts added to the index that year. By 1967, the year before the new system went into effect, the total of known addicts had nearly doubled, to 1,729; the number of nontherapeutic heroin addicts had more than doubled, to 1,290; even more ominous for the future, the number of *new* recreational (and presumably young and deviant) heroin addicts had nearly tripled, to 745.

Some of the overprescribing doctors continued to overprescribe, but others, perhaps discouraged by the criticism of the Brain Report, began to withdraw from the junkie scene. The announcement that Dr. Geoffrey Dymond would no longer be seeing heroin addicts was front-page news in the *Sun* of November 11, 1966. He had had at least eighty addicts as patients, some of whom, in a fashion diametrically opposed to what modern American addicts might have done, appealed directly to the Home Office for help. The Home Office could not provide drugs to addicts but it did urge the Ministry of Health to move forward with the creation of clinics, as recommended by the Brain Report. Leaders of the voluntary agencies dealing directly with the expanding number of drug addicts in London's West End, such as Reverend Kenneth Leech, berated the government for its indecision and delay in setting up the clinics. While the government dawdled, the need for medical help increased. As a result, the overprescribing doctors became essential for a society in transition, not at all sure where it was going. In his book *Keep The Faith Baby* Kenneth Leech later summed up the ambivalent attitude of the authorities: "The attitude of the Ministry of Health was twofold. First, they condemned those wicked, overprescribing doctors. But, secondly, they hoped that these same doctors would continue to prop up the old system until the Ministry was ready with its new treatment centres, and would then gracefully withdraw." [12] As doctors withdrew before the new clinics were all in place, the scene became more chaotic. The death of Lady Frankau in 1967 threw even more addicts onto the few doctors willing to help them.

On July 7, 1967, the *Daily Mail* and the *Sun* both revealed the existence of a private clinic for addicts operated by Dr. John Petro in the tea buffet of the Baker Street underground station. Petro, a licensed physician, was apparently seeing large numbers of patients on a regular basis in the cafeteria of a subway station in the middle of the nation's largest city. Besides performing other medical functions, he was writing prescriptions (three pounds sterling each, please) for heroin and cocaine. Dr. Petro continued to attract attention and even appeared, on January 11, 1968, as the new clinics were slowly taking shape, on the David Frost television show in England. As he left the studio he was arrested by an officer of Scotland Yard's drug squad, not for overprescribing but for failing to keep proper records of the dangerous drugs in his possession. On February 14 Dr. Petro was fined £1,721 for seventeen offenses. Then the British government and the medical establishment took two rare actions. The home secretary took away Dr. Petro's power to prescribe dangerous drugs. The General Medical Council took the more drastic step—it ordered an "erasure," the removal of John Petro's name from the medical register, that compact red volume containing the names of all licensed English physicians. The erasure order went into effect at the end of 1968.[13]

Usually paired in the public mind with Dr. Petro was Dr. Christopher Michael Swan. But Dr. Swan's involvement with heroin was limited, for he seemed to specialize in amphetamines and barbiturates. Neither doctor, moreover, had been targeted by Brain II, since neither was known to be in the drug field until after the report had been issued. Be that as it may, Dr. Swan soon came to public notice with the opening in 1968 of the East London Addiction Centre, on Queensbridge Road, Shoreditch, a poor neighborhood in the East End of London. Addicts and drug abusers flocked to him, and within a nine-month period Swan had signed over 5,000 prescriptions, dispensing 530,000 Drinamyl (in the U.S., Dexamyl) and 41,000 Methedrine tablets, among other drugs. He soon was in serious difficulty with the law for a wide and bizarre variety of offenses, including issuing false prescriptions and soliciting to murder the bouncer he had once employed to keep order in his addiction center. He was sentenced to fifteen years' imprisonment.[14]

Reverend Leech went so far as to say that the treatment centers would not even have come into existence had it not been for a vigorous campaign by the voluntary agencies, such as the one he led, "much of it in the face of strong resistance."[15] The reasons for the resistance described by Leech are not at all clear; it appears, even by his account, to have been indecision and fear of the unknown more than resistance; the government officials seemed to be saying: we are unhappy with the growing addiction problem and we want to set up new treatment programs, but we are not sure how best to organize them and how to define their goals and methods of operation. It is quite possible that the government officials charged with implementing Brain II were also troubled by doubts about the wisdom of the new policy.

Action, however, was finally taken. Under the new system enacted into law and spelled out in administrative regulations, the power of general practitioners to dispense heroin and cocaine to addicts ceased, as we have seen, on April 16, 1968; compulsory notification of "new" addicts commenced on February 22; and around the turn of this fateful year the new treatment centers, usually called drug-dependence clinics, had started operations, although a few had actually been functioning for some time. Approximately forty clinics have been set up over the years throughout the country, fourteen of them in the London area, where most heroin addiction is found. These clinics are usually operated by regional health authorities with funds from the National Health Service and were set up originally under authority of the Dangerous Drugs Act, 1967, which was superseded by the Misuse of Drugs Act, 1971, the comprehensive law that came into effect in 1973.

That 1971 law, continuing to restrict the use of controlled drugs to medical practice, imposes criminal penalties for unauthorized use and sale. Drugs are divided into three categories depending on their supposed degree of harmfulness. Class A drugs include the opiates—morphine, heroin, methadone, and levorphanol, for example—as well as cocaine; class B, cannabis, cannabis resin, and codeine, among others; and class C, certain milder drugs such as methaqualone and amphetaminelike compounds. No mandatory minimum sentence exists in English law. Illegal possession of a class A drug carries a maximum sentence of seven years' imprisonment; class B, five years; and class C, two years. Most possession cases are tried in a magistrate's court, where the sentence is usually a fine and probation. Only after repeated convictions for possession does this court impose a sentence of imprisonment, often for only a few months; the legal limit is twelve months. Trafficking and international smuggling cases may be dealt with more severely under the 1971 enactment, however. In those cases the maximum term of imprisonment in a conviction involving a class A or B drug is fourteen years, and for a class C drug, five years.[16]

Unlike the United States, with its patchwork of overlapping federal and state laws, this legal scheme applies throughout the United Kingdom, to London, to Welsh hamlets, and to Midlands cities. These sentencing provisions, moreover, are not only uniform but also mild in comparison to those of the United States. U.S. federal drug law allows for much longer sentences, including life, in a variety of circumstances, and for mandatory minimums. So do many states. These striking differences are found in the sentencing laws as well as in the severity of the sentences actually imposed, all of which we shall later review in detail.

For mysterious reasons, the simplest operational details of the English addiction control and treatment system set up under the 1971 statute are often misstated by both British and American experts.[17] Examples of the misinterpretation of clinical practice and of the new laws are so common that it might be helpful if I selected some frequently asked questions about the system which allow responses summarizing its essential structural features.

Question: What impact were the new laws meant to have on the treatment of the organically ill? *Answer*: The changes were not directed toward the organically ill. We have already seen that heroin was used extensively to treat those suffering from cancer, heart disease, and other ailments. But some of the leading English physicians involved in treating cancer patients and the terminally ill have recently reduced their use of heroin. The reasons are not entirely clear to me, although these decisions may have been influenced by the American fear of heroin and by a desire on the part of the British hospice leaders to convince Americans that they can care humanely for terminal patients without heroin. They were not influenced by the law or by police harassment, which were factors in the United States. Moreover, the reduction in heroin use for the organically ill has been highly selective; as we have seen, the drug's overall use by English doctors between 1969 and 1978 almost tripled.

The new laws and regulations in England specifically exempt the organically ill and the injured from the key provisions dealing with the addicted. The extent of this legal exemption is not often clearly understood in America. Under the administrative rules implementing the Misuse of Drugs Act, 1971—Misuse of Drugs (Notification of and Supply to Addicts) Regulations 1973—the first situation in which an "addict" does not have to be notified to the Home Office is where the doctor is "of the opinion, formed in good faith, that the continued administration of the drug . . . is required for the purpose of treating organic disease or injury."[18] Thus, the organically ill do not even fall within the notification system. They also do not fall within the legal prohibition preventing general practitioners from prescribing heroin and cocaine to addicts, even in those cases where the patient is both addicted and organically ill or injured. In other words, any general practitioner in England may prescribe heroin and cocaine to an addict if the purpose of the prescription is, for example, to treat cancer, a heart attack, or a severe burn. The likelihood that an English doctor might be prosecuted in the criminal courts, as was Dr. David B. Hawkins, of Atlanta, for providing morphine to a patient he believed was suffering from both addiction and tuberculosis has always been remote; now, it would seem to be virtually nonexistent.

Question: What was the most important change brought about by the new system? *Answer*: The major practical change was to remove the power to prescribe heroin and cocaine for addicts from private physicians and to place it in the hands of physicians in special treatment centers.

Question: To what extent does the new system control the discretion of clinic doctors in making prescribing decisions? *Answer*: In a practical sense, hardly at all. Clinic doctors retain all the independence of any licensed practitioner as described by the Rolleston Committee Report in 1926 and which existed for all physicians before Brain II was implemented in 1968. A clinic doctor may decide to refuse to treat a patient at all, to offer psychiatric therapy but no drugs, oral methadone but nothing else, large doses of injectable heroin, any one of a dozen narcotics on a long-term maintenance basis, or any combination of these approaches.

Question: Does this mean that the power to treat addicts has been totally taken away from private physicians? *Answer*: Absolutely not. Any licensed physician in England may treat any addict in the course of his professional practice, may provide counseling and other forms of non-drug therapy, and may prescribe so-called maintenance doses of methadone, morphine, or other drugs— *with the exception of heroin and cocaine*.

Question: What new legal rights did addicts obtain? *Answer*: None. The rights of addicts remain unchanged, as far as I can tell. If anything, addicts are now somewhat more restricted because if they want heroin or cocaine they must somehow convince a clinic doctor, as opposed to a private physician, to prescribe it. As a Home Office official pointedly explained to me, "Addicts have no rights simply because they are addicts."

Question: Why weren't more of the overprescribing doctors of the 1960s prosecuted or otherwise disciplined? *Answer*: The act of prescribing large quantities of drugs for addicts on a regular basis is simply not a crime in England, as it is in America. The Brain Committee soundly criticized these doctors but observed that they were operating within the law when they provided large doses of drugs to addicts. Equally paradoxical in American eyes is the fact that the then-unofficial system of notification to the Home Office was observed by the junkie doctors "without exception," according to Mr. Spear, in regard to the large new crop of young heroin addicts. When the so-called overprescribing doctors emerged into the limelight, the official remedies were, in the main, to prosecute them for some criminal offense, such as failure to keep proper records, or to ask the private General Medical Council to have them stricken from the medical register for "infamous conduct," both of which were considered by the British to be awesome penalties, inappropriate for simple cases of giving addicts excessive supplies of drugs.

The General Medical Council, I was told by Home Office experts, simply was not in the frame of mind at the time to entertain charges of overprescribing against physicians. Prosecutions in the criminal courts for such conduct, moreover, were rare. Despite diligent searching over the years, I have yet to uncover a case of a *successful* prosecution of a British doctor simply because he gave a patient, even an addict, superabundant supplies of drugs. It is difficult to establish negative facts, and this one has been particularly difficult for me to accept because of my American preconceptions and also because the British drug-abuse specialists do not consider it terribly significant, but it is nonetheless a fact: British law does not intrude into medical judgments about the prescribing of drugs to patients. The posture of the British criminal law is reflected in a little-known case reported in the London *Daily Telegraph* of September 9, 1955. It seems that Dr. James M. Rourke, of Kensington Church Street, had been prosecuted by the police because he had given a patient, apparently an addict, heavy doses of drugs, in alleged violation of the regulations at the time. Magistrate Geoffrey Raphael dismissed the prosecution with this sweeping declaration: "There is nothing in these regulations . . . which limits the quantities of drugs which may be lawfully prescribed by a doctor. It may well be that this conduct of the defendant was gravely improper. It is not for me to decide any such issue. It may be that it is a matter which may be referred to the disciplinary board of the medical practitioners." Since, as we have seen, the GMC chose not to get involved in such cases, there have been in the past virtually no formal sanctions for overprescribing, unless the physician was guilty of other misconduct, such as failing to keep proper records (Dr. Petro) or issuing false prescriptions (Dr. Swan).

Question: Does more finely tuned machinery now exist to discipline "irresponsible" doctors? *Answer*: Yes, the tribunals recommended by Brain II. It is worth recalling that the tribunals had originally been recommended by Rolleston in 1926, implemented by regulation in 1928, never actually used in a single case, and then quietly dropped from those regulations in 1953 when they underwent a regular revision. During the days of the overprescribing doctors of the early 1960s, then, there simply were no legal provisions for tribunals. Brain II recommended a revival, which occurred in 1973.

The new provisions authorize the home secretary to call into existence tribunals, representing both the medical and legal professions, to review the facts in individual cases of alleged misuse of the power to prescribe drugs. The tribunals make recommendations to the secretary about the appropriate action to take, including withdrawal of the right to prescribe so-called dangerous drugs, those controlled by the major drug laws. Nevertheless, it must be emphasized that a clinic doctor who follows the notification requirements may provide the complete range of drugs to addicts as well as other non-drug therapies, with little to fear from the authorities. The same is true for general practitioners, as long as they do not prescribe heroin and cocaine, of course. This is in contrast with American approaches—old and new, for they have not changed significantly—under which any private doctor (one not in an approved methadone clinic) who treats an addict with drugs *for any condition* faces the risk of prosecution and does not know until after indictment if he has committed a crime or might lose his license to practice medicine. Whether or not the act of "overprescribing" is criminal is still a matter for an American jury to decide.

The first time a tribunal was actually invoked against a British doctor, as far I can determine, was in 1974 under the new regulations. Up to July 1980, according to Home Office records, nine doctors in all were proceeded against by the tribunal route for overprescribing or for some related inappropriate use of the prescribing power. Out of those nine cases, seven orders, or directions, were issued. Thus, the total of successful criminal prosecutions for overprescribing has been zero; of successful tribunal proceedings, seven. These simple numbers are powerful evidence of the majestic professional independence enjoyed by British physicians in the drug arena.[19]

Question: What are the major legal controls in England on the prescribing of drugs by doctors? *Answer*: Only a few broad legal rules apply to the treatment of addicts, again a stunning comparison with the mass of American regulations controlling drug treatment clinics. In sum, they are: only specially licensed doctors, normally found in clinics, may prescribe "restricted drugs," now heroin and cocaine, to addicts; all doctors who encounter a new addict must notify the Home Office; and a doctor who prescribes any dangerous drug must do so "acting in his capacity as such." That last phrase is elastic and means that the drug must be used in the legitimate practice of medicine, the definition of which in Britain has always included the right to prescribe drugs to addicts. The likelihood of prosecution, even for violations, is remote for almost all British doctors. For example, if an ordinary private practitioner were to prescribe heroin and cocaine to an addict purely for the purpose of maintaining him comfortably in his state of addiction, this would ordinarily not be considered a criminal offense unless it were part of much broader and more serious criminal activity. In the usual case the doctor would be quietly visited by a drug official, told that the Misuse of Drugs Act of 1971 forbids such prescribing without a license issued by the home secretary, and cautioned to desist. In the event that he did not, a tribunal could be called into existence by the home secretary, and, upon the advice of that body, the secretary might issue a formal "direction" to the doctor ordering him to cease prescribing heroin and cocaine for addicts. If he violated that direction, *at that point and only then would the physician have committed a criminal offense and be subject to prosecution*. The same procedure would apply to a violation of the requirement that new addicts to *any* dangerous drug be notified. However, no prosecution for failing to notify an addict has ever occurred. The contrast with the intrusion of American criminal law into medical practice is stark.

Question: There is strong evidence that some government officials are unhappy with the coordinated decision of the London clinic doctors in the 1970s to cut down on the prescribing of heroin. Why do they not order its increased use? *Answer*: They do not have the power. There simply is no centralized administration of the clinics, at least not in substantive detail. No British official has the power to compel any clinic doctor to provide or withhold any drug to any patient, whether cancer sufferer or heroin addict.

Question: Perhaps the greatest practical stumbling block to serious consideration of the use of heroin to treat American addicts has been the realization that the need for two to four injections per day would necessitate allowing addicts to take their heroin with them away from medical supervision. What legal restrictions have the English placed on the practice of "take-home" heroin? *Answer*: None of any controlling significance. This is viewed as a matter very much within the professional medical judgment of the clinic doctor. There is virtually a full range of practice. Some doctors have told me that they never prescribe heroin, so the issue is moot; others require heroin patients to inject at the clinics in small wooden booths—fixing rooms—demurely covered with curtains for the purpose; still others mail a packet of individual prescriptions, normally seven to fourteen, to cover a week or a fortnight, to a local pharmacist, who then fills one per day. In the last case, so-called take-home heroin is allowed. The patient receives one day's supply at a time. Since the clinics came into operation, a conscious effort has been made by physicians to spread the prescriptions around to various chemist shops, primarily near the residences of patients, in order to break up the junkie subculture that congregated near such well-known places as Boots, the all-night chemist in Piccadilly, waiting for the clock to strike midnight and the pleasure of filling the next day's prescription. The same procedures are followed for other drugs, including oral and injectable methadone.

III

When the clinics started operating in late 1967 and early 1968, it might be assumed that the new directors walked into their offices reasonably well prepared by their medical training both to diagnose addiction and to provide specific treatment. This was, after all, a medical approach to a public health problem. But the psychiatrists in charge had neither the ability to make scientific diagnoses nor a manual of treatment.

Philip H. Connell is one of the leading practicing drug-abuse physicians in Britain, recognized around the world for his work. To my knowledge, he has at his disposal the most extensive facilities of any drug dependence doctor, as the director of the outpatient clinic at the Maudsley Hospital in London and the inpatient drug ward at the Bethlem Royal Hospital, some miles away in Kent. Yet despite his knowledge and experience, Dr. Connell never fails to tell his listeners that "there is no specific treatment of drug abuse." It is not a disease for which there can be a prescribed treatment, he declares, and it is probably not a metabolic disorder, as some American drug-abuse doctors have claimed. Moreover, it is difficult to determine with certainty if a new patient is an occasional user or an addict. Once it is determined that he is an addict, "There is no laboratory method which can determine the dose taken, and patients are notoriously unreliable in their claims." In sum, Dr. Connell believes that drug addiction is a condition which may or may not be a disease, for which there is no specific treatment, no reliable diagnostic method, and no accurate testing technique to assess how much of the substance that forms a central part of that condition the patient is consuming.[20]

It is no wonder that when the addicts began descending on the clinics, many of the new doctors, as they later frankly reported, were frightened. They were determined, nevertheless, to try to clean up the mess created by the junkie doctors, for they certainly were not going to prescribe heroin irresponsibly as did Swan, Petro, Frankau, and their ilk. They might have been guided in these uncharted seas by the advice of the *British Medical Journal*, which declared, as the new centers were starting, that "the steady aim—rather than the pious hope—of the Clinics must be to get their clients off heroin. . . . If ever community psychiatry is to have meaning it is in the treatment of addiction."[21]

It is ironic that some of them also sought guidance in the experience of the American clinics of the 1920s. Dr. Connell concluded that, "quite apart from the law-enforcement attack on doctors running such clinics in the 1920s in the U.S.A. it seemed that these clinics failed because of lack of supervision, lack of definition of the goals of treatment and because of the ability of addicts to coerce doctors who were not clear what they were doing, to give excessive doses of drugs." But Dr. Connell observed that a major exception was the clinic operated by Dr. Willis Butler in Shreveport. The reasons for Butler's success, Dr. Connell said, were that he instituted controls on prescribing, insisted on responsible behavior by addicts, and maintained good relations with community leaders. Dr. Connell referred to a statement by the Shreveport director of public safety, who wrote of the community benefits of the clinic and the fact that it had practically eliminated bootleggers in narcotics.[22]

It would appear, therefore, that while there was no government-imposed regimen of treatment, and never has been, many of the new clinic directors were planning to apply concepts of community psychiatry and greater controls on prescribing in dealing with addicts. Perhaps some of the directors recognized that they were seeking to create some form of community balance, some way of making the community and the addicts more comfortable together, which would mean in large part making the addicts less deviant, less visible, more like ordinary people. For many addicts this meant psychiatric treatment, eventual conquest of the drug habit, and a drug-free life, at least for a while.

But how does a psychiatrist treat a person taking drugs who does not accept the humane definition of himself as sick? He may see himself as a normal person taking drugs; or if he sees himself as sick, he may look upon the drug as the only medicine holding his life together; or he may believe that his life-style is meaningful and exciting. Neither psychiatry nor psychiatrists had easy answers. Many, perhaps most, addicts simply wanted their drugs free of charge, regularly, and in adequate dosages. This created immediate conflicts because, as we have seen, doctors are educated to give out drugs only for a clear-cut medical reason. As Dr. Connell observed, "It is against the ethics of most doctors to prescribe narcotic drugs to people who do not need them for the relief of organically based pain."[23] But give out drugs the new clinic directors did. They did not know what else to do because they wanted to head off an illegal market and to keep their patients coming back.

Psychiatrist Margaret Tripp answered a want ad and soon found herself, in early 1968, the first director of the addiction unit of St. Clement's Hospital. For the first few months she operated in competition with a local physician, Dr. Swan, but after the new regulations went into effect prohibiting his prescribing, she was soon operating alone in London's Cockney East End. She told Judson how desperately the clinic wanted to get the addicts in off the street: "As you clearly realize, our purpose at the beginning was to *seduce* the buggers. . . . But a lot of my colleagues would cheat themselves about this. When the general practitioners were prescribing heroin—ah, that was vicious. 'But when *I* give heroin, it's medical treatment.'" This did not necessarily mean that Dr. Tripp or any clinic doctor gave out as much heroin and cocaine as addicts asked for—or sometimes demanded on threat of physical harm. Often, they used a combination of medical diagnosis, bargaining, *and* seduction.[24]

By the end of 1968 almost 1,000 new heroin addicts had been coaxed out of hiding and into the clinics; 1,299 had come to notice during 1967 and 2,240 during 1968—almost all the 2,782 known addicts to all dangerous drugs in the country. But after that initial leap the Home Office index for the early years of the clinics leveled off. The entire situation regarding addicts and their observable acts of deviance seemed to be stabilizing. The new approach, with the clinics as the balance wheel and centerpiece, seemed to be working. Judson so reported in the early 1970s, and indeed the figures for the first four full years (1969–72) of clinic operation seemed to document that the problem had been contained. The total number of addicts to all dangerous drugs who came to notice during 1969 was 2,881, while the number receiving drugs in treatment at the end of the year was 1,466. The corresponding figures for 1972 were 2,944 and 1,619.[25]

I saw the same controlled situation when I arrived for my first study trip in March of 1974. There were some rough edges but apparently no organized, criminal black market or increase in serious crime. The clinics seemed to have settled down into a routine; secure, even smug, in their new place in the sun. Although neither psychiatry nor the treatment of addicts has held a position of great prestige in British medicine, the holding of one of the 600 new licenses to treat addicts with heroin and cocaine had taken on an intriguing and rather unique status. But something was amiss, and *it*—whatever it was—was taking place in the minds and emotions of the clinic doctors and staffs.

A good part of that professional unrest revolved around the issue of treatment or control. When a doctor and the staff dealt with an addict-patient, what was their goal: to get him to change or to prevent him from becoming a further social problem? If the former, then the clinic professionals might well have to confront the addict and demand that he reduce drug usage, enter into psychotherapy, and lead a normal social life with a job, family, and all that. In a sense, this was the ultimate goal of the health care professionals and would apparently lodge neatly under the rubric of treatment. But if a patient could not or would not benefit from treatment, then the staff had to face the issue of whether or not they should provide drugs anyhow, thus controlling the deviance of the addict, since obtaining his drugs legally would make crime unnecessary to support his habit.

The type of conflict that can arise was discussed by Gerry Stimson, of the London Institute of Psychiatry, who reported on a typical action by one clinic doctor as reflected in the physician's notes in early 1975: "I made the following bargain (my offer, not his). I will supply heroin 5 × 10 mg pills daily from 14.2.75 if he can tell me of a job arranged when he comes on March 5th (with starting date) and can show me pay slips the following visit. If unemployed we shall use time for a transfer to methadone."[26] If addiction is a disease, it could be asked, and if heroin and methadone are medicines to treat the disease, why should the securing of a job by the patient affect the choice of medicines by the healer? Was this treatment a bargain? Social control? A mixture? In actual practice such questions were not easily answered and continually bedeviled clinic staffs; they still do.

I should have become aware of these problems troubling the clinic staffs (but did not) when I visited my first drug-dependence clinic, at the University College Hospital, and met its director, Martin Mitcheson. I was surprised when Dr. Mitcheson stated flatly that he was extremely uncomfortable with his power to dispense heroin to addicts. "It's like being the commander of NATO and knowing you have the nuclear bomb in your arsenal." He would rather, he said, not have that option.[27] At the time I viewed this as a philosophical exercise, but I should have seen it as part of a pattern of clues about the growing distress among the staffs of the London drug-dependence clinics.

That distress focused on the practice of prescribing injectable drugs to addicts. (Heroin is provided only in a form suitable for injection. The British say they learned about methadone from the Americans but got the directions wrong—and thus, when the clinics started, almost all the methadone was provided in ampules for injection, a practice unknown and shocking to many Americans.) During the early years of the clinics, despite the treatment-or-control conflict, it was accepted that many addicts would receive steady doses of injectable heroin or methadone; that others would move to oral methadone; and that still others would eventually, at some indefinite point in the future, come off drugs entirely, when they were ready.

By the mid-1970s the mood of the clinics was clearly changing. The clinic doctors and staffs appeared infinitely tougher, more impatient with the foibles of addicts. As evidence of this change in attitude, there was now a concerted move away from prescribing injectable drugs, especially heroin.

Critical stories about the drug situation continually appeared in the public and professional press. On January 9, 1977, for example, Danah Zohar and Peter Watson wrote in the *Sunday Times* of growing international trafficking in heroin, of its spread throughout Europe, and of the increasing violence among members of Britain's Chinese community involved in the heroin traffic. Zohar and Watson attacked the latest Home Office addiction statistics as much too low and documented their concern about the overall European heroin epidemic with the table on page 191.

On January 31 the *Times* published an article by Stewart Tendler that directly attacked the clinic system as inadequate to meet the complex new problems arising in the addiction field and asked in its headline, "What has gone wrong with the system other countries envied?" By February 19 the *Lancet* editorialized that while the clinic system did appear to be working reasonably well, "it would be oversanguine to suppose that the system of treatment and control conceived 10 years ago did not, in the light of experience and changing circumstances, require critical review and probably some revision."

Table 1. Impact of Heroin on Europe

	1971	1975	1976
Seizures of heroin	Europe: 22.2 lbs. U.K.: negligible	U.K.: 9 lbs. 14½ oz.	Europe: 1,100 lbs. U.K.: 31½ lbs.
Estimate total on market (DEA worldwide practice assumes roughly 10% of available heroin is seized)	Europe: 220 lbs. U.K.: negligible	U.K.: 106 lbs.	Europe: 11,000 lbs. U.K.: 315 lbs.
Addicts	Europe: 8–10,000 U.K.: 1,549	Europe: 86–108,000 (1975–76) U.K. (official): 1,974 U.K. (estimated): 6–8,000 Holland: 10–20,000 Sweden: 10–15,000 France: 25–30,000 Italy: 35,000	

SOURCES: U.S. Drug Enforcement Administration and London Metropolitan Police Department.

During the 1977 institute I kept asking clinic directors, researchers, and government officials why the change had occurred. I received a variety of unsatisfactory answers. When I asked Dr. Philip Connell to tell me the scientific basis for the change in the prescribing policy, for the move away from injectables and from heroin, he replied, "There is no scientific basis."[28]

By that reply I did not gather that the doctors and clinic staffs were acting frivolously. I understood, rather, that they had made decisions based on their professional judgment. But the emotional strain of dealing with addicts constantly must be appreciated as having an understandable impact on clinical judgments. Nothing in medical or nursing education can adequately prepare a professional for this draining, harsh, dirty business. I got the impression that many of the clinic psychiatrists, nurses, and social workers had simply been worn down to the point of utter annoyance by addicts who came back year after year seeking not improvement, not a better life, not rehabilitation, but drugs to stick into their veins. And I suspect also that the clinic staffs were making an ethical judgment that what they were doing year after year could not be justified by any set of social values with which they were familiar.

Many dedicated staff people were emotionally torn up after having served too long on this social front line. It has been common, over the past eight years, to hear from a social worker, "Well, you've visited us just in time, haven't you? This is my last day; I can't take it anymore." Or from a young clinic director, "I am terribly depressed. Two of my patients just died." And from that same psychiatrist, "I had a patient yesterday who went out and sat in the middle of the street because I would not give him the drugs he wanted. I did not try to stop him. My staff are more softhearted than I and they dragged him in twice. We finally worked out a compromise on the prescription he would get." Since this clinic was in a very busy part of the city, anyone who sat in the street must have been desperate and a formidable patient to deal with.

The emotional strain of continually dealing with addicts, combined, I submit, with the ingrained professional medical dislike of providing drugs for nonorganic reasons, especially to deviant youth and to unproductive adults, worked to create a more intense revulsion to the needle among the London clinic staffs. A typical regimen would call for an addict to come in for a fortnightly consultation during which the psychiatrist-in-charge would discuss his health and provide supportive therapy if it seemed indicated. There might also be individual and group therapy with the social workers. Of course, there were many unscheduled appearances of addicts who had "lost" their scrips and come in for emergency prescriptions. During those days when addicts would inject at the clinics, the waiting room was filled with people who were there in part because of a low tolerance for delayed gratification. They did not want to wait for their appointments, for their prescriptions, for anything. It was sometimes, in Dr. Mitcheson's words, "like a scene from 'The Rake's Progress.'" The situation was worse in those clinics, like St. Clement's, that maintained a dayroom where addicts congregated almost continuously, some forever whining about their stingy prescriptions and the entire group working to reinforce the image of the addict and the subculture.

All this became more than the clinic staffs could tolerate. Thus, I believe that in the end change was spurred not so much by pressure from the outside critical reports that the clinics were failing to control the spread of addiction but rather by pressure from inside. And it was not purely an emotional gut-level decision, although emotions and viscera played a part as they always must. There were rational arguments.

The best argument I have heard in support of the move away from injectable heroin and methadone in England starts with the fact that the very act of injecting is an unnatural manner of taking something into the body. Each injection causes a minute physical trauma; three to four injections per day over a period of years can cause the collapse of veins and harm to other tissue. Unsanitary injections often cause infections and the spread of disease. Second, there is some evidence that much of the junkie culture and the very habit itself are centered around the injecting ceremony—that the drug may hold less importance for some addicts than the needle itself. Injecting in psychiatric terms may be symbolic of compulsive masturbation or even self-destruction. Third, injectable heroin has to be taken three to four times per day while oral methadone may be taken only once, thus allowing the addict to live a more normal life. Fourth, the extreme highs created by huge doses of injectable drugs allow the addict to escape confrontation with the anxieties that control his life; he must confront those emotional problems if he is to conquer them. In psychiatric terms, the drugs are an emotional crutch that the addict must cast aside if he is to learn to walk on his own. These arguments may or may not be fully persuasive when all the available evidence is weighed in the balance.

I have often told clinic directors and their staffs that I still had difficulty, in view of all the facts as I saw them, with the overall wisdom of their decision. Often, in response, they point to a "scientific basis" for that decision: the highly significant study by Dr. Mitcheson and Richard Hartnoll, a research psychologist. These two men conducted the only controlled experiment (ever, anywhere in the world, to my knowledge) on the use of heroin and oral methadone in the treatment of heroin addicts. Unfortunately, the study produced no clear, unequivocal conclusions. Indeed, in discussing its implications for clinical practice in July 1978, Mitcheson observed, "I feel like I am in a balancing act, like the man who pushed a wheelbarrow over Niagara Falls. It's a question of achieving a totally illogical balance."[29] In other words, Mitcheson himself believes the results of the experiment could have conflicting policy implications. He has said publicly that he believes the coordinated London clinic decision against injectables was made primarily on the basis of clinical hunches—and that the results of his study have been used as after-the-decision confirmation.

The singular experiment, which could have taken place in no other country, was conducted between February 1972 and February 1975 at the University College Hospital Drug Dependency Clinic.[30] Out of 260 patients seeking assistance during these years, 96 confirmed young (18–35) heroin addicts were selected. After a thorough screening and medical examination, they were randomly assigned (without being told that they were taking part in a study) to one of two groups. The first was offered heroin maintenance (HM). The second was offered oral methadone (OM). Because many refused the latter offer, the trial does not provide a strict comparison between one drug and another but rather between the use of heroin plus mental health therapy, on the one hand, and a variety of alternative treatments—methadone, group therapy, psychiatric counseling, etc.—on the other. However, the designation OM was applied to the entire second group, which had been refused heroin but accepted some other form of treatment, including oral methadone. In the HM group there were 44 addicts; in OM, 52. Each was carefully studied for a twelve-month period in a variety of ways by research workers who had a nonjudgmental attitude toward drug taking and were often on friendly terms with the addicts.

This group of 96 addicts seemed to resemble the general run of British addicts today: 75 percent male; mean age of 23.9; most having started opiate use during the mid-to-late 1960s. Almost all were native Caucasian, of British of Irish stock, and of the full range of social classes.

At the end of the study period, a number of important variables were assessed and compared. On some items there were no observable differences. Fully 62 percent of the HM group and 63 percent of the OM were unemployed. It appeared that 33 percent of both groups suffered from some form of poor health during the year. Those figures include three deaths resulting from the use of illicit drugs, two in HM and one in OM.

But there were some apparent differences. During the twelfth month crime was a major source of income for 61 percent of the OM group but only 43 percent of the HM group. This would seem to be both statistically significant and important for social policy. But Mitcheson and Hartnoll caution that, at the beginning, the OM group tended to be more criminally active. "If this difference is taken into account, then the difference between the two groups at twelve months . . . does not reach significance." (It should be of interest to Americans and other foreigners that only one armed robbery was recorded for the entire group, Dr. Mitcheson told me.) Most offenses were petty, such as shoplifting and selling drugs in the gray market.

A review of arrest data suggested that the HM group might be more law-abiding; 71 percent of the OM group were arrested at least once during the year compared with only 52 percent of the injectable heroin users. Only 19 percent of HM had been arrested two or more times compared with 41 percent of OM. Here again, however, Mitcheson and Hartnoll insist that the greater initial tendency toward crime of the addicts in the oral methadone group reduced the level of statistical significance to virtually nothing.

Although the study directors thus saw conflicting implications of the most important variables, on one they themselves came to a secure conclusion. There seemed no doubt that the heroin injectors stayed in treatment longer than those in the oral methadone group; 74 percent of HM were in regular attendance at the clinic during the last three months of the test year compared with only 29 percent of OM. (When he spoke in July 1979 of that piece of data, Dr. Mitcheson observed to some visiting Americans: "If your paymasters will pay you sufficiently to keep addicts in treatment, then you had better give them heroin." When, later that year, I told the National Drug Abuse Conference in New

Orleans about the item of data and Dr. Mitcheson's remark, the response of the Americans there was, "Of course! What did you expect? If you give them whatever they want . . . ")

Reflecting on their groundbreaking experiment, Mitcheson and Hartnoll observed that providing heroin to an addict "may be seen as maintaining the status quo although ameliorating the problems of acquiring drugs. . . . By contrast, refusal to prescribe heroin (and offering oral methadone instead) may be seen as a more active policy of confrontation that is associated with greater change." This meant that some of those in the OM group faced up to their problems and sought to fashion a life less dependent on chemicals. But others dropped out of sight of the clinic entirely. "Gray" results of this nature are the reasons I insist that decisions in the drug policy arena go far beyond the bounds of any one conventional professional discipline. The following thoughts of Mitcheson and Hartnoll inhabit the same no-man's-land:

> Refusal to prescribe heroin is thus associated with a considerably higher abstinence rate, but at the expense of an increased arrest rate and a higher level of illicit drug involvement and criminal activity among those who did not become abstinent. The long-term implication of this approach is that although it is more "therapeutic" in terms of discouraging continued drug use, it also leaves a group of heavily drug-involved people outside clinical "control." This prospect might be considered undesirable to society, both because of the criminal activities of this group and because they form the basis of a potentially expanding illicit drug sub-culture. On the other hand, the implications of maintaining addicts with heroin include the prospect of a larger and steadily accumulating clinical population of chronic heroin addicts, somewhat less criminally involved and perhaps less likely as individuals to create a large demand for illicit drugs. . . . In relation to policy in the United Kingdom, the results do not provide strong evidence that entirely justifies continuing the policy of maintaining addicts with injectable drugs, nor do they show that present policies are a clear failure in terms of the British drug situation.

And what are the implications for policy in the United States and other countries? Mitcheson and Hartnoll give roughly the same response. They saw both advantages and disadvantages in the use of injectable heroin for addiction treatment. Only by careful experimentation can other countries test these murky waters, they say, and they must do the testing themselves, on their own cultural shores.

The results of this seminal study should convince any reader, if further con-

vincing were needed, that the British have no quick-fix, packaged solution to
the growing worldwide problem of heroin addiction. Making heroin available
for legal dispensation to addicts by doctors may seem to be the ultimate answer
to many liberals and the ultimate surrender to many practical conservatives, but
in reality it would be only a threshold step. Doctors would still have to make
impossible clinical judgments, and the leaders of society and government would
continue to be confronted with broad policy issues requiring a difficult social
and ethical calculus. But without the availability of legal heroin, neither a given
country nor its professional helpers can cross the threshold so they may even
start to achieve the illogical balance Dr. Mitcheson described.

While not containing final answers, this study is nevertheless replete with
lessons. Particularly impressive are several telling pieces of data. I consider
many untreated heroin addicts to be potential social disasters. I therefore find
it significant that the availability of legal heroin tended to keep addicts in
treatment while its nonavailability drastically reduced clinic attendance. Even
though there was more criminality before treatment in the OM group, I find it
persuasive that crime was a major source of income for only 43 percent of the
injectable heroin group as compared with 61 percent of the oral methadone
group. I am also impressed with the fact that 41 percent of the oral methadone
group had been arrested two or more times during the year compared with 19
percent of the injectable heroin group. This study therefore tends to confirm
my leaning, in the social balancing act, toward the continued, though not
exclusive, use of heroin in addiction treatment.

Be that as it may, the clinic directors and staffs do not agree. The move away
from injectables continues. One of the leaders of that movement is Martin
Mitcheson, who disapproved of injectable prescriptions for new patients starting in February 1975. By the beginning of 1976 that policy applied to old
patients returning to the University College Hospital Drug Dependency Clinic
after a lapse of treatment—and at that time, all patients were expected to reduce
their intake of injectable drugs. Faced with the same set of impossible choices,
most of the other London clinics came to the same practical clinical decisions.
On a tour of the United States in May 1977, Dr. Mitcheson was able to report,
"The compromise which seems to be developing in London is that only two
clinics are prepared to prescribe injectable drugs to new patients. These two
clinics are intending to pursue a strict policy of offering injectable drugs for a
limited period of time only."[31]

During a visit in July 1977 to one of those clinics, the outpatient unit at
Maudsley Hospital, I heard Dr. Connell and his staff explain the compromise
they had evolved: a new addict who claimed to be on injectables would get a

prescription made up of one half the injectable drug (heroin or methadone) and one half oral methadone. That mixed prescription would be provided for six months at the most. With the help of counseling and supportive therapy, at the end of six months the patient would switch to oral methadone, which might well be at a high dosage. But by the end of twelve months the daily dosage of oral methadone had to be down to 80 milligrams a day at the maximum, perhaps still high by American standards but not by British.

Most of the London clinics, Mitcheson explained, felt that even this type of compromise was ill-advised. A visit in July 1977 to London's East End, where Dr. Swan once ran his liberally dispensing private surgery, and to St. Clement's Clinic, where Dr. Tripp initially tried to seduce the buggers with heroin, demonstrated how strongly the staffs supported the new policy. It was not an edict passed down from on high by the government or even from the consultant psychiatrist then in charge, Dr. J. Denham. Nurse Pat Ellis explained that the laissez-faire attitude of the early days of the clinic had allowed a nucleus of chronic injectors to settle into a junkie life, often in the protected confines of the clinic dayroom. In a handbook for new staff and patients it is admitted, "We can see now that immediately [after] they were stabilized *some* pressure should have been put on them to reduce their prescription and we feel now that we have actually done some of them a great dis-service in making life so easy for them on a settled prescription." Pat Ellis observed, "We no longer see the point of putting people on everlasting prescriptions of injectable drugs." The dayroom has been closed; staff members attempt to visit established injecting addicts in their homes in order to support them and encourage them to change; and new patients are offered, "where we think necessary," a small prescription for oral methadone, tranquilizers, or vitamins, and "social help (intensive if required)."

The sincerity of Pat Ellis's support for the clinical and ethical soundness of the new approach cannot be doubted. He also believes it is working: "About 14 percent of our patients over the past 12 months have come completely off drugs voluntarily. . . . Many more are reducing their prescriptions, and I feel that the success of them is affecting others. Whereas in the early days especially when the day centre was being used extensively, the patients used to compete with each other to get their prescriptions raised. . . . They are now veering a little to thinking, 'If he can come off, so can I.' "[32]

According to staff people in several clinics, they are nicer places to work in now. In July 1978 an experienced social worker at the University College Hospital clinic explained that there is much less chaos, fewer agonized patient demands, and less emotional trauma for the staff. She was asked what she thought the clinics should do, however, if it could be demonstrated that refusal to prescribe injectables pushed addicts into the black market and thus contributed to a rise in crime, especially of a violent nature. She replied, "That would present an extremely difficult situation and something would have to be done. But I will no longer work at a clinic where injectables are dispensed."[33]

Clinics in the "provinces"—any place outside London, as city dwellers are apt to say—have also moved away from injectables and toward oral methadone, psychotherapy, or both. In any event, few provincial clinics provided heroin maintenance to many patients even in the early days. Dr. John McClure, consultant psychiatrist at the Queen Elizabeth II Hospital in Welwyn Garden City, just north of London, did prescribe some heroin in the late 1960s but soon abandoned the practice in favor of other approaches.[34] The clinic doctors at the Mapperly Hospital in Nottingham had originally prescribed injectable drugs for addict-patients, but that changed in 1975 when a new young psychiatrist took charge. After three years at Mapperly, in July 1978, Dr. Phillip McClean revealed his clinical philosophy and demonstrated just how pervasive the new approach was: "I do not feel that for the vast majority of opiate addicts the prescription of drugs is indicated. . . . I do not run a clinic. I run a unit in a psychiatric hospital, both inpatient and outpatient. For inpatient detoxification, I use oral methadone, but I cannot see giving addicts injectable drugs. The only reason I would is to lure them into treatment. [But] I've never prescribed heroin to anyone and I don't believe in maintenance. The purpose of using any drug is not to get them feeling good but to prevent withdrawal pains."[35]

With sentiments and practices such as these dominating British addiction treatment, it is understandable why such experts as Jasper Woodcock, director of the Institute for the Study of Drug Dependence in London, would tell an audience in Phoenix, Arizona, on November 11, 1977, "So long as opiate addiction was confined to those initated through medical treatment, unrestricted prescribing of addictive drugs did not lead to any major problems. As soon, however, as we began to experience addiction as a social phenomenon with its own subculture, we took fright of the consequences of unrestricted prescribability and quickly imposed controls. No sooner had we done this, than we began also to shift toward methadone maintenance which is now almost total." Accordingly, Woodcock assured the First International Conference on Substance Abuse that in the treatment of heroin addiction Britain has "adopted the same medical policies as the U.S. Rather than having anything to teach the U.S., perhaps we should be acknowledging that we have rather more slowly been learning the same lessons."

Of course, Harry Anslinger and others of his ilk said some of the same things in decades past. But there seems to be more substantial support for *this* claim of similar systems. Oral methadone is the only drug allowed for the maintenance of addicts in the United States, where the predominant medical-legal ethic is a belief in methadone maintenance plus psychiatric treatment or other forms of mental health therapy without drugs, all leading toward eventual cure. Methadone is the drug used for most British addicts in treatment now, and the move is clearly toward inducing cures through psychiatry. Not all British experts, however, have been as supportive of this method as was Woodcock. In a critical article in the *Manchester Guardian* of October 30, 1979, criminologist Cindy Fazey wrote that the British system had been destroyed by the impact of Brain II; while Rolleston had defined the problem as medical, now it was seen as "psychiatric." That definition had led to unworkable American-style policies, claimed the consultant to the United Nations Division of Narcotic Drugs.

The same sense of despair about the direction of current events in the British addiction field was expressed by Dale Beckett, consultant psychiatrist at the addiction clinic that once existed as a unit of the Cane Hill Hospital, at Coulsdon in Surrey. He wrote to me on May 20, 1980: "I myself think it is a pity that we do not in this country still have a 'British System' with which to compare the approach you have in your own country, but there it is." For his colleagues dominating the new English approach to addiction treatment, he had words of censure: "It is so much easier to be repressive and reactive than put effort into understanding the realities of the problem and dealing with them appropriately."

Although some important similarities exist between current English and American treatment methods, the differences remain substantial. The official statistics do show clearly that English doctors are moving toward methadone. As of December 31, 1970, 51 percent of all addicts being prescribed drugs in treatment were receiving methadone alone. By 1978 the figure was 70 percent. On that same date in 1970, 30 percent of all addicts in treatment (430 patients) were receiving heroin alone or in combination with other drugs; by 1978 it was 9 percent (211 patients).[36]

This trend away from heroin is unmistakable, but other statistics demonstrate that the English are a long way from abandoning injectables in addiction treatment. An informal survey of London clinics by some of their staff showed that injectables were still the predominant mode of prescribing. Of 997 patients recorded at the fourteen clinics in February 1978, only 35 percent received oral methadone exclusively; 48 percent received injectable methadone; and 17 percent, injectable heroin. Thus, fully 65 percent of the addict-patients in London were receiving injectable drugs. This survey offers some evidence that the clinics are moving toward a patient society of two unequal classes: the established injectors, who get their prescriptions regularly, though in reduced dosages, and stay in regular attendance; and the new patients, who are refused heroin and are offered oral methadone or mental health therapy, with some coming off drugs entirely and many others simply disappearing from the clinic rolls and returning to the streets.[37]

This situation also underlines a curious perception of the pharmacological qualities of methadone. The British have never accepted the American pharmacological concept of the methadone blockade. Neither British addicts nor doctors understand what the Americans are talking about, and their addicts have told me of their enjoyment in using both drugs at once, in various combinations, and in huge dosages.

The official British compilations of the amounts of licit heroin and methadone prescribed for addicts throughout England and Wales show trends similar to the informal London survey. In 1970, 17.4 kilograms of heroin were provided to addicts; by 1978 this figure had dropped to 8.5 kilograms. In 1970, 3.5 kilograms of methadone were prescribed to addicts in forms suitable for oral use while 11.3 kilograms were provided in the form of ampules for injection. The corresponding figures for 1978 were 17.5 and 14. Thus, in 1978, of the total of 40 kilograms of heroin and methadone prescribed throughout most of the country for addicts, 22.5 kilograms, or 56 percent, were in injectable form. Despite rumors to the contrary, then, it is clear that injectables have not disappeared from the British scene, although they have not been so used in America since the closing of the Shreveport outpatient clinic in 1923.[38]

Another important difference is reflected in the fact that the Home Office Statistical Bulletin describing the treatment of drug addicts from 1970 through 1978 lists thirteen different drugs used in treatment during those years.[39] The international discussion on the use of drugs in addiction treatment seems to assume that there are only two choices, heroin or methadone, the latter having a much nicer reputation. But, as I argued in regard to the Shreveport situation, the choice of treatment drugs by doctors is important only in relation to the choice of drugs by addicts in the community. That parallel choice was not determined by the chemistry or pharmacology of any single drug.

British doctors can and do prescribe methadone if they wish, but they also have the flexible legal authority to change their choice of treatment drugs in response to the unpredictable and changing choices made by addicts. I would wager that few American drug-abuse experts could guess the second most popular drug used by British doctors to treat addiction. Methadone is first, as we have seen, but heroin is not second; nor is morphine, pethidine, dextromoramide, cocaine, hydrocodone, phenadoxone, oxycodone, levorphanol, phenazocine, or medicinal opium,[40] although all those drugs were used by British doctors to treat addiction at some point between 1970 and 1978. That second-place drug is dipipanone, a synthetic morphinelike drug, often known by its trade name, Diconal. Its choice by doctors has nothing to do with its pharmacological properties, which in fact some English doctors mistrust. It is selected so often by physicians because many British addicts in the mid-1970s suddenly started to use it, for reasons nobody can explain. By the end of 1978, 296 English addicts were being prescribed that drug alone. Any British doctor, not necessarily one in the clinics, has the right to dispense the drug in addiction treatment and for long-term maintenance if he believes it necessary. Because of socialized medicine, the cost to the addict is pennies, in most cases, and doctors would normally receive no additional income. By contrast, no drug but methadone may be used in long-term addiction maintenance in America. To complicate matters more, dipipanone is prohibited even in ordinary American medicine, because it has been lodged in Schedule I of the Controlled Substances Act along with heroin. As far as I can tell, few American recreational users or addicts have discovered this drug. But if the usual pattern of imitation got reversed, and if Diconal were to start flying to America from Britain in the pockets of jet travelers, and if widespread abuse or addiction developed, it would, for all practical purposes, take an act of Congress to make it available to doctors for the treatment of addicts. The odds on the timely enactment of such a statute are somewhere between slim and none.

But the British Parliament would not have to enact a single cultured syllable in order for major changes to be made in the current dominant philosophy in English addiction treatment. No law-enforcement action intruded into British medicine and mandated the change away from injectables and toward psychiatry. The doctors and their staffs made that change as a matter of independent professional judgment—often in spite of government opposition. The medical professionals made the policy. They can unmake it tomorrow morning, at the start of business.

I suspect that the sensible English medical profession will not persist long in its current path. A compromise must evolve soon. Indeed, a countermovement has already started.

IV

The new movement prominently features a searching reassessment of the drug heroin itself. Just as vehemently as the clinic staffs suddenly rejected injectable drugs, especially heroin, because they allegedly carried special problems when used to treat addiction, so have some of the counterrevolutionaries been saying that, on balance, heroin is really quite advantageous as a treatment drug in part because it helps control certain forms of aberrant behavior.

Such ideas have existed for years in English medicine but have received scant attention. The Rolleston committee, for example, paid no attention to the unique qualities of heroin as a medicine for disturbed people and for addicts; it simply was investigating the circumstances when it might or might not be used to treat addicts. One of the most persuasive cases for its use in treating emotional distress was made by the celebrated British psychiatrist R. D. Laing, who argued in his classic *The Divided Self* in 1960 that many disturbed people who turned to heroin, and indeed became addicted, were making a fairly sensible decision. For them the choice may well have been between suffering from an acute psychosis, on the one hand, and using heroin, on the other. The medicine forestalled psychosis, allowing the person to build his emotional resources, to hold his life together, until such time as he could control his sense of inadequacy and emotional pain without drugs. Following this logic further, premature withdrawal from heroin could, in some cases, leave open the danger of the psychosis returning. Dr. Laing wrote, "From my own clinical practice, I have had the impression on a number of occasions that the use of heroin might be forestalling a schizophrenic-like psychosis. For some people heroin seems to enable them to step from the whirling periphery of the gyroscope, as it were, nearer to the still centre within themselves." In the ethereal world of the mind and the emotions, the choice of heroin versus psychosis seems an easy one.[41]

Laing is not completely alone in British psychiatry in regarding regular heroin use, even addiction, not as the ultimate human degradation but as a potentially remediable condition that serves to block the progression of a sometimes even more destructive condition. One might, I submit, compare it to the setting of a controlled forest fire so as to block the spread of one not under control. In 1972 Alexander R. K. Mitchell, consultant psychiatrist and clinical tutor at Fulbourn and Addenbrooke's Hospitals in Cambridge, wrote a book to advise parents on how to approach drug taking by their children. He provided some guidance which could perhaps have come only from an English physician: "Certain young people 'mature' on the use of heroin. Provided it is obtained regularly and in clean supplies, these people are often better in that they can work and cope with their problems. They can also mature out of the habit after a time. Using heroin is a way of going into 'cold storage' until they are ready to cope, but the method has its dangers." Moreover, Dr. Mitchell suggested, "It is believed that taking drugs may protect certain predisposed young people from breakdown into serious mental illness. Many of the backgrounds and root causes are similar. It is as though working at being an addict provides an identity without which the young person could slide into a psychosis of the schizophrenic type. Here the choice lies between taking drugs for a number of years with all the known dangers, or having to go into a psychiatric hospital with the risk of becoming a longterm psychiatric patient."[42]

Compared with the usual run of medical opinion on the crushing harmfulness of using heroin, the Laing-Mitchell position is jarring, which is what makes it so important. More recent medical pronouncements deal directly with the move away from heroin on the part of the clinics.

Dr. Beckett pushed the debate in Britain to a new and unprecedented level when he wrote in the July 26, 1979, issue of the magazine *New Society*: "I started treating heroin addicts in 1965, stuffed full of the current newspaper myths. It took years for it to dawn on me that heroin is very gentle. If proper care is taken in self-injecting, it is extraordinarily safe." This pronouncement came in the context of an article describing the painful journey Beckett had taken in ten years of treating addicts. He now sees a difference between treatment and maintenance, although the two may sometimes overlap. Treatment is helping the addict to change; once he is better able to handle emotional pain, he does not need the heroin, and at that point, "a sensitively designed withdrawal from heroin is easy for the addict to handle." Thus, some addicts benefit from both psychiatric treatment and the provision of heroin, with psychiatry predominating in those cases where a reasonably rapid withdrawal seems feasible.

But a large number of addicts cannot respond for years to normal psychiatric treatment and therefore cannot tolerate withdrawal. "For these unfortunate addicts," the former clinic director cautioned, "a 'treatment centre' . . . should be a 'maintenance centre.' There they can be prescribed an appropriate steady dose of heroin, plus sterile syringes and needles. Sheltered in a drug cocoon, they can slowly learn how to handle life until they have gained sufficient wisdom to leave the cocoon." In actual clinical situations many doctors are tempted to forcibly "treat" their patients by pushing them off heroin "without adequate attempts at personality integration beforehand." The result is that the addicts go back to their drugs with a vengeance, usually in greater torment and emotional pain from the frustrating experience of the forced treatment.

Dr. Beckett worked his way out of this terrible dilemma a few years ago by gradually recognizing the gentle nature of heroin. Before, when he was maintaining addicts on heroin, he felt almost like a fascist, sacrificing the few, the addicts in his care, for the many, the good people of society. Now, he sees only two dangers in heroin addiction: first, because heroin, like alcohol, tends to cause psychological depression, and because many heroin addicts are already chronically depressed, continual use could lead in some people to more depression and suicide; second, once injecting starts, many addicts might be tempted to try other, more destructive drugs, such as barbiturates or Diconal. But when he weighed these unwanted effects against the new benefits he saw, he concluded, "There is really no valid argument to be raised against maintaining addicts on heroin, not only for the good of society, but to reduce their death and mutilation from barbiturates and Diconal and to allow a gradual personality growth which otherwise would be impossible."

With these words Dr. Beckett, a member of the Royal College of Psychiatrists, challenged the clinical preconceptions of many addiction experts around the world. This humane philosophy, I believe, contains the essential refutation of the currently dominant English treatment philosophy. The Beckett ideology is the latter-day essence of Rolleston. It cautions against mass diagnoses of individual problems, against black and white solutions, when the only sensible ones are gray. To say, as the clinics now do, that *no* new patients should get injectables makes as much sense as a policy that *all* new addicts must accept injectables. Some addicts need therapy and heroin, but therapy and confrontation more than the drug; some need both therapy and drugs; others need heroin or other drugs only, until they are ready for therapy; and when they gain the internal "wisdom," it is hoped that most will drop all drugs. It's all quite "dicey," as the British say, and not at all subject to mechanistic mass policies. This approach graphically demonstrates that the emphasis should be on care rather than cure until the addict matures enough to cure himself. Moreover, Dr. Beckett's position does not depend solely on heroin; other drugs and nondrug psychiatric therapy still play major roles in his approaches.

An even more outspoken critic of the clinics is a middle-aged Catholic priest, the Reverend Terence E. Tanner, director of the ROMA Housing Association Limited of London, on whose board of directors Dr. Beckett once sat. As soon as I met Terry Tanner, in July 1979, I understood why certain leading figures in the drug-abuse establishment considered him a difficult person to get along with. His attitude toward the clinic directors and their staffs, always explicit and never implied, was that of an Old Testament prophet surrounded by unrepentant sinners.[43]

In 1971 Reverend Tanner led in the creation of a caring institution whose mission and eventual fate should provide an enduring lesson for anyone concerned about coping with drug abuse. Even in Britain ROMA was unique. Indeed, there may have been nothing quite like it anywhere in the world.

To understand ROMA, it is necessary to understand Tanner's ideology. His view of drugs starts roughly where mine does: he is against the use of drugs and believes in psychiatric therapy for those times in a person's life when help is needed. As he wrote in 1979, "I am a disciple of Jung and had depth analysis in Switzerland in the 1930's and in England in the 1940's. I hold that in an ideal society people should be able to live without drugs and other crutches, that their lives should be full and free, independent and inter-dependent." He then added the qualification of reality: "By definition, however, the ideal society does not exist. We all live on the thin edge of compromise."[44]

Thus, he wishes that no one used drugs but accepts the fact that many people do. Sometimes these substances come from doctors in the form of the pill to prevent conception—or heroin to feed an addiction. In each case there may be emotional, ethical, and even medical reasons for the patient *not* to take that particular drug, but in the end the patient should have the right to decide, after the doctor has fully explained all the risks and negative arguments against the drug. "It is his life, not mine. He decides, not me." Most people can accept that argument regarding most medicines, but, Tanner argues, such tolerance does not apply to the use of even licit narcotic drugs by addicts, "because addicts are the scapegoats of our age." In ancient times the priest chose a goat upon whom all the people's sins were recited; the goat was set free to wander in the forest and to take away those sins. "If anyone fed him or touched him, he was contaminated and the sins the goat carried were transferred to him," Tanner explained. As for today, "It is an apt description of what society does to the addict and to anyone who pleads the addict's cause." This cantankerous cleric thus sees himself dealing with society's scapegoats and, in a defiant fashion, his chin up like a bulldog, he accepts the contamination that comes with the territory.[45]

Tanner's views on the scapegoat heroin addict echo those of Dr. Beckett, whom he frequently quotes. But he goes beyond Beckett and talks about the wonderfully *euphoric* qualities of heroin when used in treating the organically ill. It was perhaps because he delights in shocking his listeners that he looked at me rather impishly on that July day in 1979 at ROMA and asked if I had ever tried it. When I stammered, "No," he volunteered, "It's rather good, you know. Heroin. Several years ago, I was severely burned in an accident; a third of my body was burned. It was given to me in the hospital. I felt no pain. I thought it was a gorgeous drug. It gave me a euphoric feeling. As the burns healed, I was taken off it slowly and felt no withdrawal pains." Tanner urged that doctors "give cancer patients a drug that will control both their physical pain and also their mental pain. Heroin can make them feel euphoric. Why can't we make [cancer patients] feel happy?" Tanner has a positive view of heroin as a medicine, which, as I have suggested, tends to affect one's viewpoint about its potential use in treating the addicted.[46]

All this, however, provides only background for understanding the creation of ROMA (Rehabilitation of Metropolitan Addicts), which was established in response to the 1968 *Report of the Advisory Committee on Drug Dependence* calling for the creation of hostels to assist in the rehabilitation of homeless addicts. The report dutifully urged that the aim of rehabilitation should be to get the addict free of drugs. Tanner and the initial organizing group accepted the challenge because they had seen the despair and human waste in the rootlessness of so many impoverished addicts living and sleeping in the streets, alleys, and Underground tunnels of London. But they broadened and deepened the recommendation, and in the process changed one vital part of it. They determined to provide housing in which addicts and their families could live like normal people but without seeking to force them off their drugs. Decent housing, a normal life, and legal drugs—a trilogy that made ROMA unique.

Because of the notorious instability and infantile behavior of so many addicts, especially injectors, many knowledgeable people believed that this fundamental trilogy would be impossible to implement. The behavioral traits of many addicts make most responsible people—such as landlords, social service workers, teachers, and physicians—wary of getting involved with them except when forced. This causes addicts to feel more rejected, to rely more and more heavily on junkie friends for support and on junk to ease the pain of their unhappy social status as scapegoats and outcasts. "It is a vicious circle ROMA tries to break," wrote Tanner in the ROMA annual report of 1975. He then described the key elements of ROMA's expectations of its tenants: "We give a limited and conditional acceptance of their life-style, a chance for them to prove that they can live without being a burden or a threat to the rest of us. We insist that they get work, keep out of crime and establish stable relationships. . . . When they succeed (and any success is theirs) we have helped to restrict the contagion of drug addiction, have saved many lives and many thousands of pounds in social security payments, unemployment and supplementary benefits, hospital treatment, prison custody, police and court time."[47] Earlier, he had written: "The French have a proverb, 'By doing the work of a blacksmith you become a blacksmith.' We would adapt it to our work, 'By living a normal life, you become normal.'"

These are perceptive and humane sentiments. What Tanner and the staff of ROMA did was to put cash behind them. When addicts (and their spouses or stable companions) passed the initial screening which indicated that they wanted to live a relatively normal life, Tanner sometimes would hand these newcomers, virtual strangers, several hundred pounds in cash, as a loan, so that they could buy furniture for their new flats in one of the hostels—an act of faith that perhaps only one trained to believe in the fundamental goodness of human beings could carry out without wincing. The addicts and their families (often children were involved) were expected to use that money responsibly, to pay it back when promised, and to pay rent for their flats on time, in accordance with their leases. Of the hundreds of addicts who have inhabited the various accommodations provided by ROMA, very few have been financially irresponsible. In July 1979 Tanner explained that while total rental income normally approximates £12,000 per year, the full sum in arrears for that year, up to the day of our talk, was £12.[48]

In many practical ways, then, ROMA worked. People generally took care of themselves, were kind to their fellow addicts in the hostels, got along with their nonaddict neighbors, and paid their bills. There were crises and problems, overdoses and separations, even some violence on occasion, but these were dealt with as part of normal life and did not disrupt the overall peace of the association and the calm belief on the part of staff and tenants that they were involved in something good.

All this rested on a fundamental assumption that the authorities would see to it that, somehow, the addicts who continued to want or need drugs would be able to get them legally. Unlike the so-called concept houses—the Phoenixes, the Odysseys, the Synanons, the Raps, and so on—ROMA refused to get involved with its tenants in confrontations over the use of drugs, so long as they were legal. In a talk on February 5, 1976, Tanner enlarged on these points: "ROMA is not specifically concerned with educating its residents to live without drugs. We try to help them to live with them." It is important to understand just how revolutionary that thought is; it flies in the face of virtually all drug-abuse doctrine in Britain and America throughout this century; most specialists would consider it heresy. To reluctantly accept the use of drugs is the height of compassion, as reflected by Rolleston; to help people live with drugs is to go beyond compassion and, according to accepted doctrine, on toward license, even sin. But that is what ROMA did. Tanner continued, "We do not encourage them to use drugs but equally we do not discourage them. We re-act, we even re-act violently, to the use of illegal drugs but we do not re-act to the use of legal drugs. If residents use drugs it is their concern and the concern of their clinics. . . . We encourage them to responsibility in every department of life and, as they begin to acquire responsibility, they limit their use of drugs or give them up altogether."[49]

Reverend Tanner and ROMA applied this existentialist philosophy, emphasizing the uniqueness of every human being's perspective and needs, to individuals whom other people, including middle-class addicts, might call the dregs
of society. A typical case, he wrote in 1979,

> would be an addict [who] comes to us, referred by his Treatment Centre,
> from Subway 4 Piccadilly Circus. He has no home and, therefore, no social
> security*: neither does he have a job and, of course, no money. He needs
> drugs and food. He steals, in one way or another, for them. He comes to
> us. We house him. He has an address and can get social security. . . . If his
> consultant will prescribe a reasonable amount of the drugs of his choice
> for him, we can get him a job, take him off social security, put him on the
> tax roll, help him to establish stable relationships and find him a flat to
> settle down with his partner. . . . Now he is living his own life, paying his
> own way and is not a burden or a threat to anyone. If his consultant does
> not change his prescription, there is no reason why that situation should
> not go on forever.[50]

The expectations of legal drugs from the consultant psychiatrists were met in
the early days of ROMA. Virtually all the tenants were injecting addicts on the
rolls of one of the London clinics, and there was a sense of confidence that the
clinics would provide enough drugs to meet their needs. ROMA, of course,
could not provide those drugs, but it could provide something else. Because its
staff was in constant contact with the addicts, whereas the clinic staff saw them
for perhaps half an hour every fortnight, ROMA could and did give information to the clinics when an addict was using illegal drugs. This relationship was
informal but important, at least in the eyes of the ROMA people. "In the old
days, I could call up Tom Bewley and say, 'Give old Gus an extra three amps,
please. He's buying them on the black market, you know.' Tom would say, 'O.K.
I'll give him a three-month trial [with a larger prescription]. Let's see if he keeps
his job.'" Thus, ROMA's staff served as a broker between the addicts and their
source of legal supply, and to some extent as an agent of control.[51]

The collapse of that balanced system, along with ROMA itself, was triggered
by the decisions of the London clinics to restrict prescribing. In July
1979 Tanner fumed, "Those *wretched* doctors! . . . even though they're my

---

*In the United Kingdom "social security" does not mean retirement payments, as in America, but
rather a whole range of welfare, unemployment, and disability benefits available to residents whose
income and health fall below certain minimum levels. A person must have a fixed address in order
to receive payments.

friends. . . . About 1972 they started moving off heroin to physeptone [metha-done]. Then off i.v. to oral. The result: the addicts go back on the black market, lose their jobs, and stop paying taxes. The cost is £500 per week. All this because the clinic doctors believe the addicts shouldn't have drugs!" In many clinics, Tanner said, notices were simply posted saying that from such-and-such a date prescriptions would be reduced by half and no new addicts would receive injectables.[52]

Some doctors, of course, tried to comfort their patients, which might have resulted, according to Tanner, in scenarios such as this:

> The consultant may take time and use reassuring statements like, "You can do as well on oral physeptone as on [an] injectable" or "You can do as well on physeptone as on heroin" but the addict is and remains a person. He says, "I can't or I won't." The last word is with the consultant. He says, "You can or you will." In most cases the result is that the addict goes back to the black market for the drugs he wants. The black market demands a lot of time and a lot of money. He loses his job and returns to social security and crime. . . . He becomes once more a burden and a threat to society. He returns to Subway 4 Piccadilly Circus. The police pick him up and he goes back to prison. I cannot see that any good has been done by his consultant's decision to refuse him his usual prescription.[53]

ROMA could not continue to exist, Tanner related, in this atmosphere. The association had to adhere to its basic rule of no illegal drugs, and the director believes that current clinic policy is to assure that virtually every addict in treatment is also using illegal drugs. ROMA had staff, money, and housing accommodations in July of 1979 but could find only eleven addicts to accept the 100 available places.

Reverend Tanner told me disconsolately, "We had achieved a balance. Now that balance has been destroyed." Earlier in 1979, as the demise of ROMA loomed closer, Tanner pleaded in an article that doctors apply the psychiatric method only to some patients, only to those ready for it. In cases not involving addiction, he said, other doctors "often use sedatives and tranquillisers because they do not have the time to 'talk through' their patients' problems or because their patients are too old or their IQ is too low for talking through to be a viable solution. I do not see (and again I rely on Doctor Dale Beckett's thesis and my own experience) why drug addicts should not be put in this class of people whose problems cannot be talked through. . . . As a priest with a lot of experience of drug addicts, I plead that they should be maintained on their drugs rather than treated for their addiction." Tanner put that bold message in an article titled provocatively, "More Heroin All Round."[54]

Phrases that get attention, however, often get misunderstood. ROMA's essential message was not simply the need for drugs but rather the need for balanced judgment, not mass policy declarations, and for finely honed clinical perception about the needs of individual cases. Moona ffrench-Hodges, deputy director of the association, wrote in 1977:

> I visit twenty or so addicts in their homes every week. The improvement I see in some who have been withdrawn from drugs (often against their will) is very considerable and every responsible person should applaud it. I see, unfortunately, the other side too. . . . It makes me angry and frustrated when I see a family in which parents and children are living happily, securely and responsibly (with one or both parents in regular work) broken-up because, as a result of a policy decision by doctors, all addicts are withdrawn from injectable drugs. . . . Some addicts can be withdrawn but others cannot. The dividing line between the two groups cannot be accurately drawn but if clinicians accepted that this was not "an either . . . or" situation and if they invited all the responsible persons in the addict's life to take part in the decision, much personal suffering and a great deal of crime would be avoided.[55]

In May 1980 Tanner wrote, "ROMA has been forced to close down. Doctors have not liberalised their policies—just the opposite. Their restrictions are so great that any addict worthy of the name must deal on the black market and agencies reputably helping addicts cannot help them because they are illegal. A vicious circle no one will break."[56]

Such sentiments now abound among drug-abuse experts in Britain. The clinics have become villains or, even worse, vacuous; according to the Institute for the Study of Drug Dependence, they have become irrelevant, a "backwater of our social response to drug abuse" because the young polydrug users will take anything they can get their hands on, such as barbiturates and amphetamines, not necessarily heroin. Yet the ISDD also finds the threat of cheap Iranian heroin disturbing, perhaps bringing the unstable drug scene full circle to opiates in a decade or so.[57]

Other experts predict a massive influx of heroin from countries other than Iran. In 1968, coincident with the new controls on private doctors, the first so-called Chinese heroin had appeared; actually, it was Hong Kong heroin brought in by ethnic Chinese with family ties in Britain. In July of 1979 Philip

Connelly, a senior investigation officer with H.M. Customs and Excise, told of the great increase in heroin from all over the Middle and Far East. He predicted, "Britain is about to get smacked in the teeth by an influx of Pakistani heroin."[58] The amount of illegal heroin seized in Britain between 1973 and 1978 went up by a factor of twenty, from 3.3 kilograms in 1973 to 60.8 in 1978.[59] Perhaps 80 percent of it, according to Connelly, was passing through England on its way to other markets, but the increase was still dramatic and disturbing.

Moreover, when the news was released that 4,000 addicts had come to notice during 1978, there were anguished cries for new moves to combat the "heroin epidemic." The national Advisory Council on the Misuse of Drugs was called into session to consider what changes in the British approach might be mandated by the apparently critical situation.

Criticism of the clinics' restrictive treatment and prescribing policies has also come from the top of the Drugs Branch at the Home Office. H. B. Spear has made it clear that he sympathizes with much of what Beckett and Tanner have been saying. The chief inspector now openly accepts Beckett's view that "heroin is a benign drug." Moreover, he contrasts the situation that existed prior to the implementation of Brain II with the multidrug scene of the present. He observed, "In the old days it was a nice clean heroin and cocaine scene, but now we have the injection of a wide range of substances, many of which were not intended for that purpose. Many drug experts and commentators say that we in England have always had a multi-drug scene. But as far as injectables are concerned, this is simply not true. I do not believe it is a coincidence that this [widespread use of many drugs in injecting] appeared only after the tightening up which occurred as a result of Brain II." Spear sees Britain today as being at a crucial crossroads. "We are on the threshold of a problem. The doctors must decide what they want to do. Either they are solely treatment oriented or they do have a function in social control."

Again reflecting on what had happened in the fifteen years since Brain II, Spear opined: "We didn't need clinics. We needed a thousand doctors with one patient each!" He added: "In any event, we never asked for clinics. We simply wanted machinery to enable us to deal with the few grossly irresponsible prescribers."[60]

But since they now exist and tend to dominate policy, "I'd like to see the clinics go back to injectables. It's the street scene that is so much worse now that the clinics are nicer places to work," Spear said recently. The most potentially troublesome addicts, those in the first flush of addiction, the younger, more defiant ones, are not coming to the clinics because they know that there is little there for them. To most addicts, Spear says, "treatment usually means a prescription."[61]

V

Inevitably, any discussion of heroin leads into the field of crime. Like so much else in this inquiry, the relationship between crime and drugs in Britain is not entirely clear. The available evidence is decidedly contradictory.

Inspector Spear is convinced that the new crop of younger addicts, having been repelled in various ways by the clinics, is resorting to the street, to the black market, and to crime in order to obtain money to buy drugs. The Drugs Squad of Scotland Yard (these are London police with criminal investigation and arrest authority, while Spear works in a national agency which primarily oversees the licit use of drugs) agrees. Detective Chief Inspector Colin Coxall estimated in July 1979 that 3,700 heroin addicts were on the streets of London using illegal drugs and that these addicts were spending between £60 and £80 per day to satisfy their habit. Most were forced to resort to crime in order to find that much money. He calculated further that £147 million (approximately $382 million) worth of illegal heroin was being traded on the streets of London annually.[62]

Obviously, these claims are based on speculation and imperfect data, but they are generally consistent with claims made by still other English experts. They are also consistent with stories of rising crime across the board. In June 1978, for example, Metropolitan Police Commissioner David McNee reported that crime in London had soared to an all-time high during 1977, when 568,952 indictable crimes were recorded.[63] For the first time London surpassed New York City, which had only 517,544 felonies that year. But when one looks into these stories from highly reliable sources about increased crime in general and by addicts in particular, the available facts seem to provide a mixed picture.

Increased criminal activity by addicts should be reflected, in part, by increased recorded drug offenses. While England authorizes addicts who have been prescribed drugs such as heroin and methadone to possess them lawfully, it is still a violation of criminal law for nonpatients to possess those and other controlled drugs. During the mid-1970s, when the clinics were tightening up drastically on their prescribing policies, the tally on persons found guilty of all drug offenses throughout England and Wales was completely unremarkable in statistical terms, except that it was low: 14,446 in 1973; 11,603 in 1975; and 13,394 in 1978. Looked at in terms of the type of drug involved, the data are equally flat. Cannabis (by far the most popular drug involved in violations) figured in 11,113 convictions in 1973; 8,834 in 1975; and 11,389 in 1978. There were 427 convictions involving heroin in 1973; 392 in 1975; and 483 in 1978. The drug showing the most dramatic increase was Diconal, or dipipanone, which rose from 196 convictions in 1973 to 491 in 1978. It is to be emphasized that these figures, presented in the Home Office Statistical Bulletin of July 19, 1979, were the cause of the heroin epidemic stories in the press and of the anguished calls for a reexamination of the failing British system. In the eyes of a sometime American crime-data analyst, these figures seem more appropriate for a few urban neighborhoods than for an entire modern industrialized nation.[64]

Of course, drug offenses tell only part of the story. When addicts are in desperate need of money, they may commit all sorts of crimes, especially larcenies and robberies. There has been a dramatic increase in overall crime in Britain during the last several decades, but there simply is no comparison with the United States. Precise comparison, of course, is extremely difficult because the offense categories vary so much; "indictable offenses" in Britain simply cannot be equated with "felonies" in the United States. Both cover a wide variety of sins having no relation or comparability. It is more fruitful to compare individual types of offenses, an endeavor which Dr. Allison Morris, assistant director of Cambridge University's Institute of Criminology, has attempted for several annual sessions of the London drug institute. Perhaps the most reliable data in any set of crime statistics relate to homicide, the unlawful killing of another human being—a definition rather similar in both countries. It also tends to be the one offense that is almost always discovered or reported. During 1977 in England there were a total of 432 homicides, or 8.8 per 1,000,000 inhabitants; in America there were 19,120, or 8.8 per 100,000. Thus, Britons were killing each other at a rate precisely one-tenth the level of their American cousins.

But what about the comparisons between London and New York, the two big cities of roughly similar populations? Despite Commissioner McNee's alarm, London comes out a poor second when the data are analyzed on truly comparable items. During 1977 in London there were 142 homicides; in New York, 1,553, more than ten times as many. In most other reasonably comparable offense categories, there were also wide disparities: 187 rapes in London and 3,899 in New York; 12,415 robberies in London and 74,404 in New York; approximately 10,000 serious assaults in London and 42,056 aggravated assaults in New York. Only in the incidence of burglary was London even within hailing distance of New York—123,179 compared with 178,907.[65]

. While crime is getting worse in England, compared with Americans the British are third rate. Some Britons openly admit their happy failings in these endeavors. Criminologist Terence Morris said in 1976, "Crime in this country has hardly exceeded the stage of cottage industry—for which we are duly thankful."[66]

But it is of interest to compare British and American constitutional protections concerning search, seizure, and arrest because some of the most controversial issues related to drugs involve how people manage to conceal their possession and how the authorities find out about it. Many of the most difficult cases in the entire field of constitutional law have dealt with drugs; in California three Los Angeles deputy sheriffs enlisted the help of a doctor who dutifully "searched" a suspect's stomach through the use of a pump, thereby finding the two capsules of morphine which he had just swallowed and which subsequently led to his conviction. The Supreme Court found this action too much to swallow and later reversed the conviction. "This is conduct that shocks the conscience," declared Justice Frankfurter.[67] But such stories about the American police combined with the polite Sherlock Holmes image of the refined English bobby have created a misleading picture in the minds of many people, including legal experts.

American criminal procedure was derived from the mother country's common law, one of its greatest contributions to civilization. One fundamental rule was that the officers of the law had to have a rational basis to believe—"probable cause," as it came to be stated—that a particular individual had committed a specific offense before an arrest could be made. It could not be made on mere suspicion. The same rule applied to searches. A police constable in eighteenth-century England or colonial America could not wander into a home on a hunch and look around for contraband, nor could the officer arrest someone because he looked vaguely suspicious. It is from English common law that the Americans learned that "a man's home is his castle."

During the unpleasantness of the mid 1700s a most galling habit of the English overlords was their widespread use of writs of assistance, general search warrants issued in the name of the king which authorized customs and excise officers to search virtually any home or structure where there was the slightest suspicion that smuggled goods might be found. Under these circumstances, an American Englishman's home was definitely not his castle.[68]

As a result of this bitter experience, the newly freed colonies enacted stringent restrictions on the powers of their own police to search, seize, and arrest. In the United States today, arrests can be made only on probable cause; reasonable searches may be conducted only after a lawful arrest or on the authority of a search warrant issued by a judicial officer independent of the police, specifying the place to be searched and the person or things to be seized; in the event that evidence is seized in violation of these rules, the exclusionary rule, devised in relatively recent times by the Supreme Court, operates so as to prevent the government from using the illegally seized evidence in most cases. Many American lawyers believe that the English rules are as good or better; and as for the writ of assistance, they quietly assume that this symbol of foreign oppression probably disappeared with King George III. But they are wrong.

The writ of assistance is quietly alive and well in England and in other countries of the Commonwealth, such as Canada. The Customs and Excise Act of 1952 provides that the writs be issued by the High Court at the beginning of the reign of a monarch to the commissioners of customs and excise, who are executive and not judicial officials. Those police officials hold the writ and authorize one of their agents to use it when the officer satisfies the commissioners that he has "reasonable grounds for suspicion" that contraband is present in some building or vessel. The writ applies to any type of illegally imported material but it has particular relevance, of course, to drugs in today's international market. In practical fact, this means that in any situation where there is some indication that drugs *might* be in a structure and that the drugs *might* have been imported, customs and excise officers have the legal authority—without having to show probable cause and without the need for a fresh review of the facts by a representative of the independent judiciary—to enter, to break down doors and windows, and to seize contraband. I have met drug specialists of H.M. Customs and Excise, rather intelligent and decent chaps actually, who admit that they often walk around with such writs in their briefcases when they are working on an important case.

Local police are not granted such general writs. Moreover, in most cases they are restricted, as are American police, from stopping anyone on suspicion and searching him or her on the street. But that conventional and civilized restriction does not apply if the constable "has reasonable grounds to suspect" that the person has illegal drugs in his possession. During the drug panic of the 1960s Parliament authorized this huge exception to traditional civil rights protections in the Dangerous Drugs Act of 1967, and it has been continued in subsequent legislation. Thus, the ordinary bobby may stop citizens if they look as though they might be carrying drugs. I have seen American police officers gasp in awe—and, sometimes, admiration but never disgust—upon learning of the vastly greater legal authority that their British counterparts have to play their hunches in drugs cases.

In practice, the British police have stopped many thousands of people and searched them for no reason other than their hippie clothes, long hair, black skin, youth, or presence in an area of high drug use, none of which in the United States would amount to probable cause. Indeed, some British experts claim that the requirement of "reasonable grounds" provides no control whatsoever but rather gives carte blanche to the police. During the House of Lords debates on the 1971 law, Baroness Wootton noted that only one in six searches from a typical London police station resulted in an arrest and only one in three in Birmingham. The baroness observed, "Reasonable cause to believe is unfounded cause to believe."[69]

Solicitor Bernard Simons, of London, who specializes in drug cases, would agree with Baroness Wootton. He concluded in 1973 that "the English police are search-happy with little to show for it." Only 4.8 percent of the people stopped and searched by the police in Leicester and Rutland, a mixed agricultural and industrial Midlands area, were found to possess controlled drugs. During a four-week period in 1968, Simons said, only 30 arrests for drugs resulted from the 22,650 stops and searches reported by the London police.[70] Of course, in practice there is probably great similarity in the statistical frequency with which American and British officers conduct groundless stops and searches for drugs, although the British police have more legal support for their fishing expeditions.

Such stops and searches on the streets of the cities of both England and America often bring about resentment in those accosted by the police. One reason for the shocking summer riots of 1981 in England may have been the widespread belief of many nonwhite citizens that police racism accounted for the frequent random searches for cannabis and other drugs in black neighborhoods such as London's Brixton. The attacks by gangs of white youth on the police during those riots may also have been sparked in part by antagonisms generated during such official searches.

In all cases involving the use of police powers, whether drugs are involved or not, it would seem that the Judges Rules, promulgated by the judges of the High Court in 1912 and updated in 1964, still have some controlling impact. These are the famous "cautions" that English officers are supposed to offer, warning an arrested person that he has a right to silence, that anything he says may be held against him, and so on. American lawyers have been weaned, enviously so, on the polite dignity of these rules. In fact, however, they are only matters of courtesy and not of law, as distinguished from the American Miranda rules. Failure to follow them rarely brings any penalty to the police or prosecutors. If an English judge determines that the police have violated any of the rules on cautioning, reasonable grounds, and search and seizure, he is not required to exclude the illegally seized evidence from the case. This is a matter fully within the judge's discretion, and only when he believes "the interests of justice" require will he exclude illegally seized evidence, including drugs. English judges admit that such exclusions rarely occur. The fact that an illegal search turned up evidence of crime, a marijuana cigarette or a package of heroin, is normally sufficient—though completely perverse by American standards—to satisfy the interests of justice.[71]

Thus, while I have maintained that the world has much to learn from the British model of drug-abuse control and treatment, I specifically exclude from that endorsement the British rules of arrest, search, and seizure.

However, despite the superiority of the American procedural rules, the response of the English criminal justice system is, overall, more gentle toward drug users than the American. One measure of that greater restraint is the extent to which imprisonment is actually used. For a variety of reasons, now as in the past, the British *seem* to imprison a much smaller proportion of their drug deviants. This statement is made with caution because it is impossible to prove—for a variety of reasons, not least because there is no reliable count of the total number of illegal drug takers in any society and there is no reliable count of the number of such drug takers who are imprisoned. But we have already seen some evidence of the persistent American habit of incarcerating drug deviants as compared with England's moderation on this score, in part through the individual stories of Canadian and American addicts who had migrated to Britain. More systematic evidence was presented in a unique and startling cross-cultural report by James Zacune, an American sociologist working at the Addiction Research Unit of the London Institute of Psychiatry. Zacune studied the lives of Canadian addicts who had migrated to Britain, mainly in the 1960s, and who, upon arrival, had been provided legal opiates by individual doctors and then by the clinics. He found that the twenty-five addicts in his sample, while in Canada, had led lives dominated by criminality and the need to somehow find enough money to buy drugs on the black market. After they emigrated to England, however, their criminality was dramatically reduced. So was the rate of imprisonment. In Canada the group had committed a total of 182 criminal offenses and spent a total of 141 years in prison; in England, 25 offenses and two years, five months in prison. "Of the total number of years spent in Canada since becoming addicted, 24.6% of that time was spent in prison by the sample." But "the proportion of time spent in prison . . . [was] less than 2% of the total of addicted years spent in England."[72]

More documentation of the moderate nature of the overall British response in practice—as opposed to what I see as harsher formal rules—is provided by the comprehensive official records of drug law violations. These official compilations deal only with offenses under the laws primarily relating to drug possession, sale, and trafficking. The statistics show that during 1977, for example, in the entire country of 55 million people, only 12,704 individuals were convicted of drug offenses; only 1,450 of these received a sentence of imprisonment; and of these, only 35 received sentences of more than five years. Moreover, in June 1977, according to the official Advisory Council on the Misuse of Drugs, only 839 persons in the country were serving prison sentences for drug offenses, the great majority of less than five years.[73] This by no means establishes the number of addicts in prison but it provides some evidence in that direction. (Most people who are addicted and deal in drugs only to obtain their own supply receive, on both sides of the Atlantic, relatively low sentences.) During 1977 the average number of prison inmates in the country at any given time was 41,570; thus 2 percent of all prisoners were serving sentences for violations of the drug laws.[74] The official annual report of the Prison Department places the number of drug-dependent persons (regardless of the actual offense charged and drug used) received in custody during 1977 at 1,166. ("Drug dependent" persons are those "who, in the opinion of a prison medical officer, are dependent upon drugs [excluding alcohol] whether or not the drugs are controlled by the Misuse of Drugs Act 1971 or are drugs controlled by that Act to which the Notification of Addicts Regulations apply.") This appears to be a small fraction of the comparable drug-dependent population placed behind bars in America during recent years, as we shall see.

VI

"Perhaps there is in the American make-up a fundamental exuberance that leads to that very peculiar American condition known as 'overkill,'" observed Terence Morris, a sympathetic and understanding interpreter of events in the United States. On the evening of July 23, 1976, in the Hall of Christ's College, Cambridge, his task—like mine at this point in my inquiry—was to reflect on how the cultures of the two countries affect their respective approaches to drug abusers. He told the Americans listening that night, "I remember just after the war a Frenchman explaining to me how Rouen had been practically flattened by American bombs in an attempt to destroy the bridges over the Seine. Tons of H.E. fell from large American bombers but none on the bridges which were later destroyed with deadly accuracy by low-flying Mosquito planes of the RAF. It may be an unfair story, but it may make the point that draconian penalties combined with wide-ranging police powers are in some circumstances counter-productive. Legislation that places the opiate user automatically outside the pale of the law can only encourage crime, as does any imposition of outlaw status for that matter."

Treat large numbers of opiate users like criminals and they will act like criminals. Treat fewer of them like criminals and fewer of them will act like criminals. Can the whole problem be reduced to such absurdly simple generalities? Of course not. But if we forget what the targets of social policy are, we may miss them entirely—and in the process harm a great many innocent people. Any social action, whether by legislation or otherwise, that automatically places opiate users in an outlaw status is certain to hurt many people, some of whom will be the narcotics users themselves, and some, those harmed by their further acts of outlawry.

The United States has clearly been guilty of overkill in this regard. But as Professor Morris was speaking, the British themselves were fashioning a national response to opiate abuse that would push many users into an outlaw status. Even though the official statistics do not fully reflect increased addict outlawry, the British must reemphasize the essential target of their policy: to the greatest extent possible, drug users must be kept within the law. The converse of that proposition is that to the greatest extent possible, the criminal law and its agents must be kept at the perimeter of the problem of drug abuse. Unless the British adhere to these precepts, which they can claim much credit in creating, they will indeed have destroyed the British system and adopted the American, as many knowledgeable Britons claim they already have.

But they have not. British criminal law has not invaded the center of the drug-abuse field. The essential flexibility of the system remains. A group of well-intentioned doctors in the clinics, along with their staffs and with the support of the national medical leadership, have applied modern psychiatric principles to many drug abusers. A minority of the addict-patients were helped to develop lives free of drugs, a truly positive outcome. But even larger numbers of addicts, most of whom were dependent primarily on heroin, were repelled by these intellectual principles and soon found themselves purchasing drugs on the black market and intensifying their involvement in criminal subcultures. They went back to being street addicts in the worst sense. But this was not accomplished in the American style, whereby the police invaded the clinics and forced the doctors to stop prescribing drugs for their patients. Rather, it was done in a uniquely English style: the doctors drove the addicts into the arms of the police.

The clinic staffs bristle indignantly when they hear such charges, and well they should. They are, after all, gross generalities which deny that addicts have

any power of free will. In fact, addicts *do* have a choice. They are not powerless
to resist heroin, although in a functional sense many of them may feel that way.
It may be more accurate to say that many users choose heroin and crime over
psychiatry and obedience to the law—and thus the doctors have invited the
addicts into the arms of the police, and they have eagerly accepted.

Under either formulation, too many English opiate addicts are now automatically given outlaw status. That situation should not be tolerated. It would
be imprudent for the British to wait until the increase in addict crime inundated
the official statistics and did, in fact, create an American-style crime situation.
The alarm bell the British should listen to is the repelling of so many addicts by
the clinics.

One of my greatest fears is that as the British go about coping with a confusing situation that everyone now seems to find intolerable, they may partially
abandon their sense of balanced judgment. It is possible that there will be
exuberant overkill in all directions, starting with the clinics. But such action
would be a mistake. The clinics did what was asked of them by the country and
its medical leadership. They cut down on legal heroin and built up the use of
mental health therapy. But the country placed too much of a burden on the
clinics as institutions and on the staffs as human beings.

The clinics as institutions were instructed to stop the spread of heroin addiction in the general population. But no one—not the second Brain committee,
not the other experienced drug-abuse doctors, not the criminologists, not the
police, and certainly not the visiting American experts—knew then, and no one
knows now, how to perform that task. That the cause of widespread recreational and deviant heroin use lay in the nominally legitimate prescription of
heroin by doctors was believed in Britain of the 1960s as it had been in America
of the 1920s. However, heroin abuse intensified in both countries after legal
restrictions on the prescribing powers of doctors had been imposed. The clinics
failed to do what was expected of them, but what was expected of them was
impossible. The essential causes of widespread heroin use in a large population
remain hidden in the minds and emotions and intimate personal choices of
countless individuals. The clinics had about as much of a chance to affect a
significant number of those choices as the Anglican Church did on the matter
of adultery.

This situation was made intolerable for clinic staffs by the day-to-day realities
of dealing with new addicts, many of whom were difficult even before they
started pursuing the needle and heroin. The addition of that mechanical and
chemical dependence made many of them, in simple terms, absolutely horrible
people to deal with. Because neither medicine nor penology, nor the church for
that matter, has produced any appreciable number of cures, a high level of

failure was predictable. In effect, a group of highly motivated professional people were dispatched to a social front line to do hand-to-hand combat. Had their mission been viewed in those quasi-military terms, it might have dawned on somebody in power that soldiers cannot be kept in combat continuously lest their efficiency, judgment, and emotional stability suffer terribly.

Any member of the helping professions who tries, over a long period of time, to assist addicts faces the dangers of combat fatigue. The New York clinic doctors in 1920 threw up their hands at the damnable ingrates and turned to the police for eventual control. Doctors Frankau, Swan, Petro, and their brethren in Britain apparently were captured by the addicts of the 1960s and practically shoveled drugs out so as to keep their patients happily coming back within some form of doctor-patient relationship. Some of the new clinic doctors started out on similar seductive paths but soon changed dramatically.

The real reasons for the clinical decision against injectables and for psychiatry in the 1970s constitute another of those great mysteries, like the reasons for the rise in heroin taking by youth or for the Brain II report. But one may speculate. Like Gaul, those reasons seem to be divided into three parts. One: objective judgments about the organic harm caused by repeated injections. Two: the natural tendency of psychiatrists to assume control over the lives of their patients, and the related tendency of some of these doctors to diagnose as harmful, even crazy, behavior that they personally feel is ethically intolerable. Three: ordinary human emotions such as combat fatigue, staff burnout, and simple irritation. To this observer it appears that the third reason covers more territory than the highly professional group of clinic doctors and staffs would feel comfortable admitting.

An even wider range of human emotions has been evoked in response to a phenomenon produced largely, it would seem, by the restrictive prescribing policies of the clinics—the reentry of private doctors into the addiction field, commencing in the late 1970s. These private doctors do not have the power to prescribe heroin and cocaine for addicts, but they do have the power to prescribe all other drugs, including methadone, Diconal, and morphine, to name but three. Some Harley and Wimpole Street doctors, among the elite of the profession, now see addicts and charge £30 ($60) and more for a brief visit and a prescription once a week or so. Although some doctors severely criticize these new private prescribers, they claim that they are providing a much needed, legitimate, and helpful service.

Evidence of the rise, once again, of the private narcotic prescriber is found in a recent Home Office data analysis of the addict index. In 1970 only 111, or 15 percent, of all original addict notifications to the Home Office came from general practitioners; by 1980 that figure had risen to 49 percent (803 addicts), as compared with only 36 percent (584 addicts) for the clinics and 15 percent (250 addicts) for prison medical officers. Although these statistics may reflect some major problems to come, it could also be argued that they reflect the operation of an enlightened balancing process allowed by the civilized British system. Virtually all the new British private prescribers would face prison sentences if they were in America.

So much for the present and the past. What of the future in England? Of course, the future of English drug policy concerns more than just the English. If they fail or seem to founder, this gives more ammunition to the hard-liners who have been claiming all along that a gentle social response to drug deviance cannot be justified in terms of effectiveness in this cold, cruel world. If the British, on the other hand, can work their way out of their present morass, then those of us who see in their moderate ways the path for much of the world will be strengthened in our resolve and in our ideological and political armament. Thus, while the suggestions made here are pointed at England, the target is much broader. Because of its unique position, because of its history of flexibility and moderation, and because it has kept the policeman out of medical practice, Britain is now ready, although it may not think so, to produce a new generation of ideas and models about opiate use and abuse for the world.

Until the late 1970s the clinics had held, for a decade, a virtual monopoly of addiction treatment. The clinics still appear to be dominant in the field, and furthermore, most British physicians continue to avoid getting involved with the often difficult problems of addicts as patients. While the number of private doctors who treat addicts is unknown, they appear to be a distinct minority of the profession. As in the past, moreover, addicts tend to flock to the few physicians who will take them on—and the potential for abuse, exploitation, and emotional misunderstanding, on all sides, is reappearing again.

At this juncture it would be prudent to remember the advice Jeffrey and Spear gave in 1964—to involve more general practitioners in the addiction arena and to spread the addicts out among many doctors. They argued that it might be wise to limit the number of addicts any individual doctor could accept (in the neighborhood of 10 to 15) and also to mandate that, in the event the physician wanted to provide a regular prescription of drugs, a second opinion from a drug-abuse expert be required. The two doctors together would set the dosage and the other conditions of treatment. Legislation might be helpful but would be unnecessary to carry out this recommendation. It is conceivable that the home secretary could simply issue licenses to those physicians who wished to have the authority to prescribe heroin and cocaine to addicts. Unless the doctor was obviously qualified, the Home Office could require a special training course for a new applicant. In most other respects the uniquely open and trusting British legal-medical system would need no fundamental alteration to achieve these results. It is possible that many of the private physicians now treating addicts, who do not have the power to prescribe heroin and cocaine, would apply for the licenses allowing them to do so.

Somewhat different views were expressed in the *Times* of January 23, 1981, in a letter signed by Dr. Connell and twenty-two other London drug-treatment specialists. Noting with concern the reemergence of the heavily prescribing private doctor, which the creation of the clinics was supposed to curtail, the group called for the placing of even more narcotic drugs, such as methadone and Diconal, in the restricted category. This restrictive recommendation was quite different from the essence of the Jeffrey-Spear proposals, since under existing law only specially licensed doctors may prescribe restricted drugs to addicts. Yet that recommendation was balanced by another, calling on the home secretary to issue more of those licenses to general practitioners who would, however, be required to work in close consultation with a clinic. Thus, the crosscurrents of emotions and ideas continue to flow across the British addiction landscape.

At some point in the near future, the question of the place of the clinics in that changing landscape must be squarely faced and resolved. The drug-dependence clinics could be renamed; perhaps drug-dependence care centers would be more appropriate. The centers might have the mission of coordinating local community responses to the full range of problems of all people with any type of drug-dependence difficulty. In addition, they might provide education, research, and consultation, especially to the individual physicians who would have the primary responsibility for patient care. If a second opinion were needed by a GP regarding the setting of a dosage of an opiate prescription, the center doctors would be logical choices. Where local GPs refused to get involved, moreover, the center would have to step in and treat addicts directly.

In any case, each patient should get an individual diagnosis and an individually tailored regimen of treatment; at least that would be the clinical message the centers would promulgate to the GPs then taking primary responsibility. Alcohol and barbiturate users, for example, would never be prescribed regular dosages of the drugs on which they were dependent because these drugs, especially in combination, can be lethal. Opiate abusers, on the other hand, might get such prescriptions. How the details of the clinic mission are defined is less important, at this stage, than acceptance of the idea that the vital rethinking process must be started in Britain now; its drug-abuse professionals are, as a group, far ahead of any in the world in that process, and they should be capable of making new intellectual breakthroughs.

The British addiction experts also might well try to settle, for their country and for others, the conflict over treatment versus control. This debate, it is submitted, should be recognized as a snare and a delusion. It sets up a false dichotomy by assuming that "treatment" equals "psychiatric help" and "control" equals "giving the addicts drugs." But good professional psychiatric help can and often does involve massive doses of control if the psychiatrist happens to believe that it is required in a given case. For example, a patient who often drove while drunk was told by his psychiatrist that if ever there was further evidence of such behavior, both that doctor and the man's lawyer had agreed to immediately refuse any further assistance. Other psychiatrists demand that patients with histories of erratic employment stay at a job or face the withdrawal of assistance. If a patient is being patently self-destructive—swallowing old hypodermic needles, for example—most psychiatrists would hastily enact the legal-medical control of committing the patient to a mental hospital.

Moreover, doctors *are* agents of social control, and it would be best for all concerned if they carried out that function with an appreciation for all the ethical and social, as well as medical, issues involved. And always, there is pursuit of that impossible balance. If the bargains they drive in seeking control are too hard for addicts to live with, if too many are repelled, then adjustments must be made. It is an art, as I have said, like maintaining a relationship in marriage, and not a science, like building a dam or a bridge.

Some patients, in sum, desperately need structure, and if the helping professions are able to add a significant element of control to their lives, this can be an excellent form of treatment. Others need some relief from incredible and intractable psychic pain, at least for a while, and the giving of drugs may also be an excellent form of treatment. Many addicts simply want the drugs, do not consider themselves to be sick, and want to hear no talk about treatment.

The goals of the helping professions, however, must extend beyond the treatment-or-control controversy; they must include a definition of the type of behavior expected of patients. That definition must consist mainly of socially responsible behavior. The main test of the success of a drug abuse-control program, therefore, would be the number of addict-clients who ceased being social misfits or floaters and settled into some form of socially responsible life, with a regular job, residence, and family relationships. In some circumstances this might be brought about by using the ROMA approach, dispensing adequate supplies of drugs so long as they were legal; in other cases, depending on the needs of the client, by using individual and group therapy without drugs. In still others, again depending on the initial diagnoses, a combination of drugs with therapy might be attempted. The social stew, then, must contain ingredients of both treatment and control.

Unless it does, new addicts, often the most troublesome and the most deviant, will not be attracted to seek help. Once in the care of a doctor, moreover, most will continue to be repelled by middle-class, puritanical psychiatric concepts. The litmus test for the future, then, as to whether the British system has adjusted to the new challenges will be found in reports that private doctors' surgeries and drug clinics have again become difficult and somewhat chaotic places in which to work.

8: MODERN AMERICA: SOMETHING IS WRONG

"Something is wrong when the junkies and the pushers are so confident on the streets of our City . . . that they will . . . out of shopping bags, in the sight of all, pull out and sell packages or 'decks' of heroin by their brand names of 'Tru-Blue,' 'Bingo,' 'Di-gel' . . . 'Dynamite,' and 'Foolish Pleasure.' . . . We saw . . . youngsters, forced to grow up in this vicious drug cycle, learning to count by knowing that a packet of 'Tru-Blue' sold for $5, thus 2 packets were $10 and 3 packets were $15."—Percy E. Sutton, President, Borough of Manhattan, 1976[1]

I

Something *is* wrong, as Mr. Sutton observed, when heroin is sold openly on the streets of American cities. We have managed to move from an era in which American citizens could read rather prosaic labels on boxes of a legal medicine (such as "Heroin: The Sedative for Coughs") to one in which more colorful labels (such as "Dynamite" and "Foolish Pleasure") may be read only on illegal heroin sold by criminals.[2] It would be the height of romanticism to seek to turn back the clock to those good old days of completely free and legal traffic in drugs. But it would be equally foolish to ignore the historical perspective when we formulate balanced policies for the future, as we look at the modern American drug era, which started in the early 1960s.

Despite that Harlem heroin market, this era has witnessed many enlightened events. During the 1960s the centrist tendencies of the American political system finally began to work again in the drug-abuse field. Numerous events signaled the historical divide that was being formed. Two of the most important were the resignation of Harry Jacob Anslinger as commissioner of narcotics in 1962, which had been accomplished with the active encouragement of the Kennedy brothers, and the commencement of methadone maintenance therapy by Drs. Vincent P. Dole and Marie Nyswander in

1964. Viewed in historical perspective, the acceptance of methadone as a treatment drug for heroin addicts represents the greatest theoretical and practical departure in American rehabilitation strategies and clinical attitudes since the early 1920s.

No single official in the drug-abuse field was ever again to wield the fearsome power that Anslinger did for over three decades. After he left the FBN, many other ideas for humane approaches to addicts, in addition to methadone, were rejuvenated and began to take on new form. Federal and state governments in the 1960s and 1970s developed innovative programs for the diversion of arrested addicts into treatment and for vastly expanded rehabilitation efforts in all spheres.

But although much has changed in recent years, law enforcement and the criminal sanction have continued to dominate the official response of American government and society toward drug abuse. To many government leaders, methadone was allowed for heroin addicts not as medical treatment but only as a device to control crime. In fact, with the exception of methadone—and this is a large exception in terms of the number of addicts it reached—America has fiercely guarded the legal-medical ramparts against the use of drugs in the treatment of addiction. Thousands of addicts continued to appear in jail, having been convicted of a whole catalog of serious crimes, usually committed in order to obtain money to buy heroin on the black market.

In addition to heroin, the use of all types of illegal drugs, especially marijuana and cocaine, seems to be on the increase in all strata of society. In some middle and upper-class circles it is considered acceptable for a good host to offer his dinner guests their choice of a rare unblended malt Scotch, a tried and true selection of Acapulco Gold marijuana cigarettes, or a new variety of Colombian cocaine, highly recommended by the supplier who, you will remember, has never been wrong in the past. Allegations of such high-toned use of illegal drugs, mainly marijuana and cocaine, have even gone as high as the born-again Carter White House, although they have been hotly denied. Reports persist that marijuana and cocaine are extensively used throughout the federal government, including in drug-control and treatment agencies. Again, these reports are consistently denied. But no one in authority doubts that the business of filling the vast and varied illicit drugs shopping list of modern America has taken on the dimensions of a major industry, dwarfing many legitimate ones in terms of gross sales and net profits and leaving a destructive trail of crime, violence, and official corruption wherever it appears.

It would be fortunate indeed if somebody could formulate a comprehensive overall strategy for dealing with the multifaceted drug situation in this country.

However, such an undertaking, which is attempted annually by agencies of the federal government, is impractical because the drugs and their effects are so different. My focus remains on heroin abuse, which still seems to be associated with the greatest harm to society and to individuals.

It should be obvious by now that I think American efforts to control heroin abuse are simply not on the right track. The position of most leading government officials and drug experts is quite the contrary. It is important that this difference of opinion be recognized in order to understand why my reading of modern American drug-abuse history leads me to recommend fundamental changes in American approaches—and why the conventional American expert catechism is to plead for improvement, more money, and fine tuning of the existing model.

II

On July 5, 1962, President John F. Kennedy accepted "with regret" Harry J. Anslinger's resignation as commissioner of narcotics.[3] The imminent departure, allegedly a retirement because of age, was announced to the press but no precise date was given. On August 17 Anslinger was formally replaced when his long-time deputy, Henry L. Giordano, was sworn in as the new commissioner. In September the White House called a national conference on drug abuse. At the same time, the White House released a progress report from its new ad hoc panel on drug abuse laying out some old and some new thoughts on the subject. The professional panel, composed of eight M.D.'s and Ph.D.'s, stuck to the existent medical philosophy that nearly all compulsive drug abusers could be rehabilitated and restored to normal social functioning, because, the experts said, drug misuse was a symptom of an underlying psychological or physiological disorder; also, they rejected the notion of supplying maintenance doses of drugs to addicts. But they also rejected the accepted practice of long prison terms as a kind of social quarantine and cure for addicts. Instead, the panel recommended long and intensive parole supervision, as had been implemented in California.

The report was not strongly liberal, but it did chart some new directions and showed an openness to new ideas. It was also, according to Rufus King, highly political. King's persuasive interpretation of this watershed period was that the Kennedy brothers simply could not tolerate a rival power center like that created by Harry Anslinger. Their interest in the drug-abuse field grew as their archenemy, Richard Nixon, seeking the California governor's office, attacked incumbent Governor Edmund Brown for being soft on dope peddlers; the Kennedys wanted to come to the aid of their Democratic friend and supporter. This, according to King, accounted for the hasty manner in which Anslinger was forced to depart and the sudden interest of the Kennedys in the field of drug abuse. Whether or not King's interpretation is correct, there is no doubt that from that date on, the issue of drug abuse was never far removed from White House politics. It was consistently tied into the emerging issue of domestic crime, and no president could ever again afford to ignore these twin agonizing concerns. This fact meant greater presidential involvement but not always greater rationality in policy.

In January 1963 President Kennedy appointed a new Advisory Commission on Narcotic and Drug Abuse. On November 1, 1963, a few weeks before the president was shot, the commission recommended "that Federal regulations be amended to reflect the general principle that the definition of . . . legitimate medical treatment of a narcotic addict [is] primarily to be determined by the medical profession." This important recommendation was virtually ignored by the Johnson administration and by subsequent ones.[4]

Instead, the drug-abuse record of the Johnson tenure in Washington revealed a series of themes that were to be seen throughout the modern era. First, the drug issue had become so highly visible that it was now rich with political capital; no tenant of the Oval Office could allow it to be the fiefdom of an underling in the Treasury or any other department. Second, the incumbent president had to show periodic leadership on the drug issue, but since it evoked such contradictory emotions in the electorate—some wanted to lock up all users, some wanted to treat them, and most had a favorite drug they wanted untouched by government hands—the actions proposed had to be varied so as to please various constituencies. Third, in order to show that action was being taken, new laws and regulations were enacted; more often than not, these imposed greater restraints on the use of drugs by doctors and, in particular, on their use in the treatment of addicts, thus flying in the face of the 1963 presidential commission recommendation and a similar one by the Nixon administration's National Commission on Marihuana and Drug Abuse ten years later.[5] Fourth, the enactments usually carried criminal penalties, which meant that whole new areas of drug activity were criminalized. This, plus the inbuilt tendency of bureaucracies to expand, led to a steady rise in the number of federal narcotics policemen, far beyond the few hundred supposedly elite officers that were the pride of Anslinger. As late as 1959, official records indicated that the number of agents in the Federal Bureau of Narcotics was 294; in 1980 the Drug Enforcement Administration carried 1,926 agents on its rolls.[6] Fifth, in

recognition of the growing power of the "treatment and rehabilitation" constituencies, however, all modern presidents have made extensive investments in
programs that would help addicts and drug abusers. All five presidents of the
1960s and 1970s followed these diverse trends, each in his own way and with
his own emphasis.

On July 31, 1965, President Johnson signed into law the most far-reaching
of the drug laws enacted during his tenure, the Drug Abuse Control Amendments of 1965. Based upon the expanded view of the constitutional Commerce
Clause rather than on the taxing power, the law nevertheless had many of the
features of the old Harrison Act. In one important respect it was different,
however. It extended federal controls much further into the drug field by placing Harrison-like controls on barbiturates and amphetamines. Harry Anslinger
had testified in 1956, when a similar proposal was before Congress: "Right
now we are getting from various facets of the medical profession this statement
that the narcotics traffic is too much of a police problem and it should now
become a medical problem. I would prefer to see the barbiturates problem
remain a medical problem and see if the doctors cannot keep this stuff in the
bottle and control it in that way, rather than to suddenly make it a police
problem. I think we would probably be as popular as the Prohibition Bureau if
this thing went into effect." But the "thing" did go into effect in 1965. The new
law even made it a crime to counterfeit drugs. As Rufus King has pointed out,
"Nowhere else had criminal sanctions ever been attached directly to mere trade
infringements." Normally, if one manufacturer puts out a product that takes
advantage of another's name or trademark, the remedy is civil litigation; now,
even this aspect of the drug field was criminalized.[7]

On the other hand, the Johnson administration did make a contribution to
the treatment side of the field. The 1963 commission had recommended a
federal civil commitment program. Three years later, after extensive political
negotiations and maneuvering, President Johnson signed the Narcotic Addict
Rehabilitation Act (NARA). It was the first concrete sign that a powerful
political consensus had developed regarding the need for nonpunitive approaches to drug addicts. The law was full of exceptions, excluding repeat
offenders and those who had committed acts of violence, but it did provide for
the treatment rather than imprisonment of some federal offenders, and also
allowed for voluntary commitment by addicts to federal health facilities. While
it represented a major ideological departure, in practice NARA ran into many
of the difficulties experienced by state civil commitment programs. Addicts
committed under its provisions tended to view themselves, and were often
viewed by staff, simply as prisoners. The program served a relatively small

number of people—only 1,723 between 1968 and 1979. And there were conflicts and ambiguities about what type of treatment was best for an addict in
that twilight status of part-patient, part-prisoner. Nevertheless, even the symbolic positive impact of NARA on the evolution of the drug-abuse field should
not be minimized.[8]

Richard Nixon was the first person to be elected to the presidency on a
platform whose main plank was an attack on crime in the streets and the failure
of the incumbent administration to bring about law and order. Nixon's campaign against Vice-President Hubert Humphrey was carefully calculated to
play on fears in the electorate and to personify the crime issue by promising to
force liberal Attorney General Ramsey Clark to vacate his position. On October
30, 1968, for example, Nixon said to a Marion, Illinois, audience, "I tell you,
my friends, that when 43 percent of the American people in this great country
are afraid to walk in the streets of their cities, it's time for a housecleaning, a
new Attorney General and a new policy to establish freedom from fear in this
country. . . . Let me tell you, I am an expert in this field. I pledge you I'll take
personal charge." Some idea on how this expert would take charge was revealed
in an earlier speech, on September 13: "I say that doubling the conviction rate
in this country would do far more to cure crime in America than quadrupling
the funds for Mr. Humphrey's war on poverty." Candidate Nixon also spoke
out for job training and rehabilitation for convicts, but he never became very
specific about the details of his anticrime program. He said even less about
drugs, declaring in another September speech: "Narcotics are a modern curse
of American youth. . . . I will take the executive steps necessary to make our
borders more secure against the pestilence of narcotics."[9]

His campaign pronouncements led many observers to expect a repressive
regime in the field of crime and drug-abuse control once Richard Nixon took
office. Some critics, such as many of the fellows of the Drug Abuse Council and
especially Edward Jay Epstein, say that is precisely what he delivered as president. Indeed, as we have seen, Epstein devoted a whole book to an attempt to
prove that through the various drug-abuse law-enforcement agencies Nixon
created—most notably the now-discarded Office of Drug Abuse Law Enforcement and the Drug Enforcement Administration (DEA), the currently dominant federal narcotics police agency—he sought to subvert the entire democratic process. It is not known how many readers Epstein has convinced of his
main theory. He did convince at least one, the prestigious writer Charles Silberman, of a subsidiary theory, as we have also seen, that Nixon and his cohorts
invented the heroin epidemic of the late 1960s.

In fact, a number of repressive actions by federal drug enforcement agents were taken and a number of illiberal legislative proposals were made during the Nixon administration—but none of this was markedly different from the administration before or after. If Epstein has made any point well in his general critique of Nixon, it is that the new president had no idea about how the national government was going to deliver on his repeated promises to reduce crime in the streets.

The new administration finally focused on the idea that there was room for a major initiative in regard to the crime committed by heroin addicts. One new technique, offering much promise but raising many questions, involved that curious drug methadone. By the late 1960s it had spread far beyond the experimental stage and was being used in a number of major cities, including New York and Chicago, on a large scale. After extensive review of the available facts, a presidential briefing paper in early 1971 concluded: "Although controversial on moral, social, and medical grounds, and although not the answer to heroin addiction, methadone is the most effective technique now available for reducing heroin and criminal recidivism and increasing the employment of drug dependent persons."[10]

Allegedly, therefore, President Nixon decided to push the expansion of methadone maintenance, not because he believed it would help addicts but only because it would control their crimes and would, in the end, win votes. His hope, supposedly, was that methadone would produce measurable results in time for the 1972 reelection campaign. Nixon's new Special Action Office for Drug Abuse Prevention (SAODAP) was the presidential spearhead for all federal treatment and prevention activities, but it was generally understood that the main target was heroin addiction, and the main weapon, methadone.

The apparent cynicism of the Nixon administration's war on heroin and the arrogance of some of the international initiatives—such as Operation Intercept in 1969, sealing off the Mexican border for a time, and the 1972 arrangement to pay the Turks for not raising opium poppies—led some people to conclude that the Nixon "war" accomplished nothing of significance in the drug-abuse field, that it was mainly media hype and not substance. Yet an analysis of federal budget documents in the early 1970s showed, to my surprise, that more than rhetoric was then going into the drug-abuse field. Under Nixon, the federal role in drug abuse was expanded as never before or since, and it was not simply in the area of publicity-gathering events to impress the media and the electorate or tough law enforcement. The last Johnson administration budget, for fiscal 1969, allocated $86 million for all federal drug-abuse activities. The fiscal 1971 budget, the first to be completely prepared by Nixon officials, was for $212.4 million, most of it ($146.5 million) for treatment and prevention, and the rest

($65.9 million) for law enforcement. This emphasis was to continue. The last Nixon budget, for fiscal 1975, allocated a total of $767.6 million for all federal drug-abuse programs, $446.8 million (52 percent) for treatment and prevention, and $320.8 million (48 percent) for law enforcement.[11]

Although Nixon talked tough and openly supported law enforcement, the criminal sanction, and potentially repressive new laws, at the same time he appointed a group of liberal, nominally Democratic drug-abuse specialists, such as psychiatrists Jerome Jaffe (the first director of SAODAP) and Robert DuPont (the second director of SAODAP and, later, the first director of NIDA), to lead a relatively humane treatment effort. In this respect Nixon was not an American aberration—he was reflecting the mainstream of modern American thought which, as we have seen, has worked both sides of the street on the drug problem. Indeed, the current era of American drug policy is one of combined tough law enforcement and expanding medical treatment. In the language of the federal bureaucracy, it is a balanced program, with law enforcement attacking the problem from the standpoint of supply, and treatment, from that of demand.

The laws and regulations enacted during Nixon's tenure increased the scope and power of the criminal sanction and of government control over the use of drugs by doctors and their treatment of addicts; at the same time, more funds were made available for treatment. The most far-reaching piece of legislation was the Comprehensive Drug Abuse Prevention and Control Act of 1970. This may well have been the most comprehensive single enactment affecting drugs ever passed by Congress. It sought to codify and simplify almost every one of the numerous federal laws and amendments that had been passed since the first controls on opium smoking of 1887.[12]

Virtually all drugs were placed within the classification system of Title II, the so-called Controlled Substances Act. In order to place a drug in one of the five schedules, the attorney general, upon the advice of the secretary of health and human services (actually FDA and NIDA), must determine if the substance "has a currently accepted medical use in treatment in the United States." This, combined with other language, makes it clear that the federal government had determined that it had the legal power to delimit the boundaries of proper medical practice, a power no British government body or official has authoritatively exercised. At the same time, Title I of the law contains provisions for expansion of treatment facilities for drug abusers.

The criminal provisions—covering possession, sale, and trafficking—are infinitely more complex, having both liberal and repressive features. Mandatory minimums, for the most part, have been done away with. For some first offenders there are provisions for probation and expungement of records upon good behavior during probation. But new features were added that provide potential threats to the rights of defendants and, in all probability, a rich living for lawyers for years to come, unless they are revoked. There are vague and confusing provisions for fines, forfeitures, and long sentences, up to and including life for offenders who have been engaged in a "continuing criminal enterprise" or who are determined to qualify as a "dangerous special drug offender." Federal narcotics policemen could, moreover, seek "no-knock" warrants from judges, empowering them to dispense with the hallowed democratic requirement of giving notice of their "authority and purpose" before breaking into private homes and structures. (DEA's "no-knock" authority was taken away by Congress in 1974, apparently because that body felt this special power had been abused.)[13] In other respects, the law succeeded in taking from the Treasury Department and giving to the Department of Justice (then led by Attorney General John Mitchell) an incredible array of powers to supervise and police licit and illicit drugs in every nook and cranny of American society and, indeed, throughout much of the world. Because Nixon has managed to evoke such raw hatred from so many people, a facile explanation for this law would be that it was pure Nixonian repression. I see it as part and parcel of the split-personality modern era in American drug policy.

In another respect Nixon fit securely, and not aberrationally, into the modern American drug-abuse picture. He claimed clear progress in controlling the problem as a result of his efforts. On September 11, 1973, he proclaimed, "We have turned the corner on drug addiction in the United States."[14]

Political creature though he was, Richard Nixon did not invent this victory posture. Drug-abuse specialists were assuming it and sometimes explaining it in highly idealistic terms. Psychiatrist Robert DuPont, for example, had made a similar claim in his speech to the Fifth National Conference on Methadone Treatment, of which he was chairman, in March 1973. At that time DuPont was administrator of the District of Columbia Narcotics Treatment Administration, perhaps the showcase agency for Nixon's heroin-treatment effort. DuPont explained that for four years he had "participated in an effort to end the heroin addiction epidemic in the District of Columbia" and asserted that now that "effort appears to be drawing to a successful conclusion." Why had this occurred? For a host of reasons, including a balanced national policy of increased law enforcement and increased alternatives for the addict—education, jobs, and methadone.

DuPont then reflected on the plight of a whole generation of southern blacks who had gone to northern cities during World War II looking for a decent life;

instead, many had found nothing but agony—and incredible numbers of their children, heroin. One of those children, Claude Brown, wrote a book about their quest, *Manchild in the Promised Land*, in which he said, "The children of these disillusioned colored pioneers inherited the total lot of their parents—the disappointments, the anger. For where does one run to when he's already in the promised land?" To the assembled delegates, Robert DuPont concluded, "Many of the people Claude Brown wrote about are at this Conference today and many of them, through their work developing themselves and their communities, are answering Claude Brown's haunting question. . . . They stopped *running* to the promised land. They are creating it." DuPont thus announced the near-arrival of the drug-abuse promised land.[15]

The programs created by Nixon's war on heroin involved not only politics, or methadone. These were there in good measure but there were also hope and idealism and dreams of a better day to come for the poor and the deprived, who were so often the victims of drug addiction. But the dreams were not soon to be realized and the victory statements were soon seen to have been premature.

Gerald Ford carried on most of Nixon's drug-abuse policies and practices. The underlying level of idealism of some officials remained as did the officials themselves. But at the top the tone and tenor were different, and victory statements were hard to find. This new top-level posture was reflected in a 1975 White House report entitled *White Paper on Drug Abuse*. Coming as it did in the aftermath of Watergate, the document seemed to experts on crime and drug abuse like a breath of fresh and liberating air. Even the name "White Paper," borrowed from British officialese, suggested restraint and moderation. Remarkably, it did contain elements of humility, balance, and restraint.

The *White Paper* stated in the preface that the "cautious" statements about turning the corner on drug abuse made by the former president in 1973 were not quite accurate. "By the summer of 1974, Federal drug abuse program administrators began to realize that conditions were worsening and that the gains of prior years were being eroded." The report made it clear that the federal government was admitting that it had not beaten heroin addiction and was not even close to victory. On the other hand, the report also refuted those who would claim that Nixon invented the modern heroin problem for base political ends. It stated, "In 1965, an epidemic of heroin use began in the United States. New use (or incidence) increased by a factor of 10 in less than seven years." Then there was a drop in incidence and prevalence (the total number of all users) during 1972 and 1973, which the authors of the report attributed primarily to the work of the Nixon administration—the new, vast treatment network combined with aggressive law-enforcement efforts in America and Europe as well as the Turkish opium ban. (It therefore seems that the habit of attributing progress in controlling the total number of heroin addicts in society to the impact of planned and specific government programs is to be found on both sides of the Atlantic and among officials of varying political plumage.)

But as the Turkish connection, the report stated, dropped its share of the illicit American heroin market from approximately 53 percent in 1972 to 9 percent in 1974, Mexico's share went from 38 percent to 77. (This fact illustrates what might be called the "iron law of the opium trade," which for centuries has been that wherever there is a persistent demand for an illicit opiate, in time a supply appears; and when one source of supply is cut off, another soon replaces it in sufficient volume to satisfy the demand.)

The *White Paper* cautioned, "We should stop raising unrealistic expectations of total elimination of drug abuse from our society. At the same time, we should in no way signal tacit acceptance of drug abuse or a lessened commitment to continue aggressive efforts aimed at eliminating it entirely. The sobering fact is that some members of any society will seek escape from the stresses of life through drug use."[16]

The tone, therefore, was different, but as it worked out, the programs were not. President Ford did not seek to pull the federal government away from excessive involvement in the drug field, to lessen the criminal penalties of the 1970 act, or to give doctors more legal room, more options in the treatment of addicts. In the one brief message he issued dealing with drug abuse, on April 27, 1976, he spoke primarily of the need for increased law enforcement and criminal penalties and devoted only a few paragraphs to treatment.

When Jimmy Carter became president in 1977 there was speculation that major, even revolutionary, drug-abuse policy changes were afoot. To many, it seemed that the humane treatment-oriented philosophy of the liberal reformers, so long held in check by the Anslingers of the country, was finally going to triumph. The liberals had, by some standards, a sophisticated lobby in the Drug Abuse Council, founded in 1972 with foundation funds. Its regular staff, fellows, and consultants included some of the leading thinkers and writers in the field. They provided independent criticism of the excesses—some real, some imagined—of the Nixon administration. In time, the council became a virtual drug-abuse government-in-waiting. Several of the leading council figures were also members of the so-called Georgia Mafia. For example, Thomas E. Bryant, the president of the council, holds both law and medical degrees from Emory University in Atlanta. (During 1977–78, in addition to his DAC post he was chairman of the President's Commission on Mental Health.) Peter Bourne was another member of the group. This brilliant, literate, soft-spoken psychiatrist was born in England but educated in the United States. As it happened, he had settled in Georgia and become the governor's friend, mental health advisor, and head of that state's Narcotics Treatment Program. Another one of those happenstances that make history occurred in July 1971. Governor Carter and Dr. Bourne flew to Washington, where the governor testified before Congress on drug abuse, visited the District of Columbia Narcotic Treatment Administration, and met for the first time many of the national leaders of the Democratic Party. The Director of NTA at the time was Dr. DuPont, who related some years later, "As they were flying back to Georgia . . . Bourne suggested that Carter was at least the equal of any of the current national Democratic leaders and, therefore, he should consider running for the presidency in 1976. It appears that this was the first time anyone had suggested the idea to Carter. Bourne told me that Carter's reaction indicated that this was not the first time he had thought of the idea." However, it may well have been the first time that drug abuse and a drug-abuse advisor figured so importantly in moving a politician along the road to the highest office in the land.[17]

Although this incident was not widely known at the time, the obvious rapport between the two men was. In early 1977 the story around Washington was, "Peter Bourne has complete access to Jimmy Carter." It was also known that Dr. Bourne was familiar with the workings of the federal drug-abuse effort, having worked for a period of time with his friend Robert DuPont in SAODAP as his assistant director. To add to all this, Peter Bourne had what appeared to be a sound sense of national strategy.

Bourne's analytical talent was displayed in an article released at an important point in the 1976 campaign when he was serving as candidate Carter's chief advisor on health and drugs. The article appeared in a 1976 issue of the *Urban and Social Change Review* and was entitled, "It Is Time to Reexamine Our National Narcotics Policy." Bourne wrote that the three basic premises of the Nixon war on drugs—which he viewed with some sympathy, since he had helped formulate the policy—started with the belief that "opium cultivation throughout the world could be curtailed and gradually eliminated. Substantial money was appropriated to develop synthetic substitutes for morphine and codeine so that there would eventually be no need for opium poppies to provide medically required narcotics." Second, it was thought that the heroin epidemic of the late 1960s could be curbed rather handily by the pressure of law enforcement and the availability of treatment for large numbers of addicts. Third, "We were led to believe that intensive law enforcement programs with heavy funding could choke off heroin trafficking so that the drug would become scarce throughout the country."

What had happened as a result of policies based on those premises? "Four years after these policies were established, we have probably more addicts in the country than ever before, heroin is more available and of better quality than at any time previously, and the problem seems to be growing worse rather than improving," declared Dr. Bourne.

"What," he wondered, "went wrong with our national strategy which appeared at the time to be reasonable and realistic?" To start with, he observed that it would be wrong to call it a total failure. Many addicts had been helped by the new treatment system (150,000 were actually in treatment at that time), and huge amounts of heroin had been removed from the illicit market by the energetic efforts of law-enforcement agents.

However, Dr. Bourne concluded, "all of the basic hypotheses on which the old strategy was based are wrong." First, a synthetic substitute for codeine for moderate pain was not found, "and it appears unlikely in the foreseeable future. This means that there will be a continuing need for legitimate opium cultivation." Agreements with countries to stop growing opium and crop-substitution programs simply had not accomplished the American goal of drying up opium cultivation—which was established on the theory that the less opium in the world, the less would be diverted to illicit dealers who would convert it into heroin. "The fundamental fallacy has been the assumption that opium would only be grown in those places where it has traditionally been cultivated, and that by controlling it in those areas we could control the world heroin supply. It is now clear that opium has only been grown in a tiny fraction of the places in the world where it could grow, and that as long as there is a market in the world and immense profits to be made, traffickers will always be able to find sites for cultivation despite our most vigorous efforts to suppress it."

Second, the heroin epidemic slowed down but did not die. Even with the availability of a historically high number of treatment slots in programs throughout the country, most heroin users were not attracted to them. "The third misconception was that law enforcement could have a strategic impact on heroin availability. The magnitude of the flow of heroin into the United States, the relatively small volume of the drug required by addicts, and the immense profits to be made have insured that despite an avalanche of new narcotic agents at both the federal and local level, heroin is still as available as it ever was."

What about a national strategy for the future? "Perhaps the most important change that is needed in our national strategy is to accept that *there can be no victory in the war on heroin addiction with the weapons we now have*." And although a massive treatment effort had not delivered the promised solution, the main emphasis in the future had to be on better and more innovative treatment policies. "Perhaps also it is time to at least look at some completely new strate-gies," Dr. Bourne suggested; but while this general suggestion was made in the plural, there followed but a single concrete example: "Much of our problem with heroin comes from it being illegal. This is what creates the immense profits, the police corruption and the soaring crime rates. We may also rapidly be reaching a point where legalized heroin could hardly result in much higher incidence of the problem. The legalization or decriminalization of heroin is a politically unthinkable notion at the present time, but it is an option that may well gain increasing attention in the next few years."[18]

During the next four years President Carter made drug-abuse history on a number of counts, some of which we have already seen. One was his decision in late 1977 to start a review of the therapeutic potential of heroin and mari-juana. He was thus the first president in our history, as far as the public record shows, who openly entertained the possibility of relaxing prohibition on the use of these substances in ordinary medicine, that is, for treating the organically ill. Research on the medical value of these drugs has been conducted for years by scientists operating under special research licenses. Tetrahydrocannabinol, or THC, the active ingredient in marijuana, has been seen as helpful to cancer patients suffering the nausea that often results from chemotherapy. The drug also apparently helps relieve the pressure on the eye of glaucoma sufferers. Working in cooperation with state authorities, the Carter administration openly encouraged these experiments. On September 10, 1980, it announced that it had arranged to have THC pills made available to approximately 4,000 cancer specialists for dispensation through hospital pharmacies to their pa-tients. In terms of legal status, marijuana remained an investigational or experi-mental drug still lodged in the prohibitory Schedule I of the Controlled Sub-stances Act, but the practical availability of the medicine meant that a major historical bridge had been crossed.[19]

In a special message in August 1977 President Carter advocated the de-criminalization in federal law of the simple possession of up to one ounce of marijuana. This too was a historic step—however modest it may seem to some observers—because it was the first presidential recommendation for a relaxation of criminal penalties on the *nonmedical* use of any of the drugs that carry such negative emotional freight among many members of the electorate.

In many other respects the Carter forces made strenuous efforts to create and implement rational federal drug policies. Efforts were also made to provide greater coordination of the vast network of federal drug-abuse programs through the activation in March 1977 of the Office of Drug Abuse Policy (ODAP) in the White House and the naming of Dr. Bourne as its director. (By this time, SAODAP had disappeared and NIDA had been swallowed as a third-rank agency into the maw of HEW.)

But in the arena of drug abuse, as in so many others, the efforts of the Carter administration contained a mixture of brilliance, courage, humanity, inconsistency, strange gaps in planning, diffidence, and plain hard luck. For example, ODAP barely had the opportunity to start its herculean task when the office was abolished as part of the president's own Reorganization Plan No. 1 of 1977. After ODAP ceased to exist in April 1978, Bourne stayed on to advise the president on drug policy as a special assistant. Because so much of the progress during the Carter administration emanated from his leadership and from his close association with the president, there was still hope for further enlightened breakthroughs.[20]

A few months later, however, Dr. Bourne wrote a prescription for his assistant, Ellen Metsky, because she had complained of trouble sleeping. As a qualified doctor, with a valid DEA license under federal law, Bourne had a legal right to do so, even though the drug was methaqualone (Quaalude), often abused by street users. To protect his aide's privacy in the "fishbowl" situation of the White House, however, Bourne put a fictitious patient's name on the prescription, an illegal act on his part; the aide asked a friend to fill it at a suburban Virginia drugstore, a state narcotics inspector was called and arrested the friend, and the whole story appeared in the press. When interviewed by reporters, Bourne said he did not want to go through the agony of months of congressional hearings—and then, in a somewhat bizarre twist, remarked that there was a "high incidence" of marijuana use and occasional sniffing of cocaine among White House staff. On July 20, 1978, Bourne resigned. A few days later a presidential memo directed all White House staff to obey the drug laws irrespective of their personal attitudes about those laws: "You will obey [the drug statutes] or you will seek employment elsewhere."[21]

These embarrassments caused by individuals should have nothing to do with national policy, but of course they always do, especially in such an emotional and conflicted field. The harm done to the evolution of more rational laws and practices may have been great; we shall never really know. With Bourne's departure went any real sense of progress toward major breakthroughs in policy, although the announcement of the wider medical availability of THC came after he resigned.

In most respects the Carter drug-abuse program followed that of Presidents Nixon and Ford. The federal drug-abuse budget remained huge, with a rough balance maintained between treatment-prevention and law enforcement. There was one mild surprise in these figures: despite his liberal human rights pronouncements, especially in contrast with those of Nixon, the proportion of federal drug-abuse dollars budgeted to law enforcement rose significantly during Carter's incumbency. For example, in the last budget prepared by the Carter administration—that for fiscal year 1981, which started on October 1, 1980—the total requested for all federal drug-abuse programs was $902.16 million. Law enforcement's share was $537.71 million, amounting to 60 percent of the total, while treatment and prevention were allocated $364.45 million. The last Nixon budget called for comparable allocations, as we have seen, of 48 and 52 percent.

The only "completely new" strategy that Bourne had suggested in 1976 did indeed receive increasing attention in some quarters, but it soon faded far into the background of federal policy discussions. Bourne took a 180-degree turn on the matter, perhaps reflecting the harsh realities of political life in Washington. At his Senate confirmation hearing as director of ODAP, on May 13, 1977, he maintained his previous position on the decriminalization of marijuana use, but as for the harder drugs like heroin and cocaine, "I don't see any reason at this time to consider legalizing the other drugs." Then in September 1977 he told a reporter for the *Seattle Times*, "The idea of heroin maintenance is defeatist."[22]

The generally liberal Washington press, reflecting enlightened American public leadership opinion, supported the Carter-Bourne approach to heroin. In an editorial in March 1977, for example, the *Washington Post* reflected on the emerging Carter drug policy by observing that while previous administrations, including that of Nixon, had tried to interdict the heroin supply, without great success, a continuing and perhaps more sophisticated attack on international supply sources, as proposed by Dr. Bourne, still seemed the wisest course. The *Post* dismissed, as had Bourne, the "talk of heroin maintenance programs, some in imitation of the British system." The editorial said that, instead, "Dr. Bourne's approach is to go forward on supply interdiction rather than surrender on one front in the fight against heroin, as a maintenance program would appear to do."[23] The editorial did not point out that the presidential advisor's policy position in 1977 contrasted sharply with the one he enunciated in 1976. After four years of the Carter administration, however, it would seem a fair assessment to say that, with a few changes in names and dates, Bourne's critique of national *narcotic* (as distinguished from marijuana) policy in the summer of 1976 could have been reprinted virtually verbatim in the summer of 1980.

III

Where, then, does the American nation find itself 67 years after the Harrison Act and 83 after Dr. Heinrich Dreser's speech in Dusseldorf? Approximately $6.5 billion were spent by the federal government on drug abuse during the 1970s. This treasure, along with vast additional amounts from the states and localities, has created a whole new industry and a whole new cluster of careers. It is likely that several hundred thousand Americans now work in this burgeoning business, many making attractive incomes. In 1978 Dr. DuPont estimated that over 150,000 people worked, full- or part-time, in some aspect of drug-abuse prevention, treatment, research, and administration, not including those in law enforcement. Since the role of the police in American drug-abuse control is so great, it is conceivable that the number involved in law enforcement would equal or surpass those involved in so-called demand reduction. This is reflected somewhat in the staffing of the two leading federal agencies; on November 30, 1980, the dominant treatment agency, NIDA, employed 363 full-time people; on the same date, DEA had 4,004 staff members, of whom 1,926 were agents.[24]

These drug-abuse professionals are not old-fashioned bull-necked cops or narrow-minded moralistic fundamentalist preachers, although such are to be found in their ranks. More often they are intelligent, reasonably well-educated, and idealistic individuals. Many, especially those new to the field, believe they are involved in a crusade to save society. (Walking back to the office after lunch in Washington recently, a supervisory federal narcotics police official said, "See that building. [It seemed to have ten or twelve stories.] The new agents are so intent on getting their quarry that if I told them to go to the top and jump off after him, they would all do it if they thought they could catch a dealer . . . without question!") At the top levels of the drug-abuse professional hierarchy in modern federal government, no matter who was president, the qualifications have been virtually unbeatable: often Ivy League educations, all the right connections in the Eastern Establishment or in the Georgia Mafia or both, and generally enlightened attitudes on race and social issues. The American drug-abuse leadership unquestionably contains some of our best and brightest people.

But what of the bottom line in this accounting process—the current extent of heroin addiction and the level of social agony imposed by addicts? Whatever the differences between the Carter and Nixon administrations, they both claimed a reduction in the prevalence of heroin addiction due to their efforts. In 1978 Dr. Bourne gave most of the credit for a claimed 40 percent drop in heroin-related deaths to the Mexican program to stop illicit poppy growth, an effort supported by the Carter forces. In 1978 similar claims of success were made by Mathea Falco (former special assistant to the president of the Drug Abuse Council), the State Department's director for international narcotic control matters. These claims were most consistently made, however, by Peter Bensinger, the administrator of DEA. Bensinger's claims were based upon statistical reports from a system operated by his agency and by NIDA that measured price and purity of heroin in the illicit market, as well as heroin overdose deaths. Rising price and decreased purity were taken by government experts to mean that the federal effort was working; and in 1977, 1978, and 1979 the indicators generally were moving in the right direction.[25]

These claims of documented and measurable progress eventually found their way into a presidential statement. On January 21, 1980, President Carter informed the Congress and the country in his State of the Union message: "At the beginning of my administration there were over a half million heroin addicts in the United States. Our continued emphasis on reducing the supply of heroin, as well as providing treatment and rehabilitation to its victims, has reduced the heroin addict population to 380,000, reduced the number of heroin overdose deaths by 80 percent, and reduced the number of heroin related injuries by 50 percent."[26]

The difficulty with such statements is that they sound so precise and scientific when in fact they flow from a series of guesses and conjectures. This is necessary in part because the United States does not have a national system of legally mandated reporting of drug addiction cases as does Britain. The conjectures are that the sampling process for determining illicit price and purity is accurate and that the higher price and lower purity of illegal heroin are good signs, not bad ones. (It would be hard to argue, on the other hand, that a lower heroin-related death count was bad.) However debatable the price and purity indicators may be to some analysts, the figures are often used not simply as bloodless entries in an inconsequential accounting scheme but as prime pieces of evidence about the overall impact of major national policies, as seen by Carter's declaration. Moreover, a NIDA pamphlet, *The British Narcotics System* (1978), explained how that system had failed to destroy the black market and how, in fact, the British street drug scene was moving in the American direction, toward crime. The linchpin of the argument was, "Today (1978), the price of illegal heroin on the streets of London is about the same as the price on the streets of New York City."[27]

For years I have read such pronouncements and have been quite impressed with their scientific-sounding validity. But that favorable impression has been replaced by overwhelming suspicion because of numerous encounters such as the following. In July 1978 I had a discussion with one of the leading British customs experts on heroin smuggling and the commander of the narcotics unit of a major American metropolitan police force. I told them of NIDA's claim regarding similar prices and mentioned that the pamphlet had also said that ten milligrams of pure heroin could be purchased on the London black market for £5 ($9.00 at the 1978 exchange rate). Asked their opinions of these claims, both experts doubted the veracity of the London price and of the whole comparative exercise because they felt it was simply impossible to find comparable samples on the street in terms of weight, composition, form, or level of purity, except in those limited cases where diverted pure English medicinal heroin was involved. It was (and is) not, as official American announcements on price would have us believe, like comparing the cost of a gallon of a precisely defined type of fuel oil in London and the same substance in New York. It is rather like comparing some random packages of a powder of varying purity and composition, purchased furtively by undercover agents under chaotic conditions with no real documentation of the price actually offered or paid. Those were my general impressions based upon limited inquiries.

However, on July 30, 1980, the General Accounting Office released a comprehensive report presenting a serious indictment of the reliability of *all* the heroin indicators used by the federal government, including those the president had mentioned in his State of the Union message progress report. This study by the comptroller general, who reports to the Congress and not to the president, was entitled, pointedly, *Heroin Statistics Can Be Made More Reliable*. It observed that the DEA data base of purchases had shrunk below acceptable levels as the agency had shifted its focus to higher level dealers: "the number of retail heroin purchases in the data base fell from about 400 each quarter in 1972 to about 100 each quarter in 1978"—simply not enough, the GAO felt, to provide a reliable foundation for national illicit price estimates. The report also stated that although declining death and injury statistics—obtained through DEA and NIDA data systems—are the most important basis for all the claims of decreasing heroin addiction in the United States, in visits to emergency rooms and medical examiners' offices GAO investigators found that many injuries and deaths are not reported or inaccurately reported. One investigation found that 45 percent of drug-abuse cases treated in emergency rooms were not reported at all. The GAO cautioned about the confident use of heroin indicators by government officials: "So cited, they give the impression that they are precise measures; however, they are not."[28]

The GAO did not claim that heroin addiction was getting worse; it simply cast doubt on the Carter administration's claims that it was getting better. In other words, after the monumental and largely well-intentioned drug-abuse control programs of the 1960s and, especially of the 1970s, it is impossible to demonstrate that the problems associated with heroin abuse have lessened. It is conceivable, of course, that real progress has been made, but there are no reliable indicators of that progress. Even if heroin abuse has actually declined somewhat, the indicators that *are* available continue to show that the present level of heroin addiction and the crime associated with it are causing great harm to American society.

But how does one convince a society and its leaders that a condition which they are tolerating is intolerable? That may be our greatest challenge. American society may be tolerating the present excessive burden created by heroin addiction because it believes there is no option, no alternative approach—that the condition is intolerable but that, like death and taxes, it simply *must* be tolerated.

However, there *is* an option. It is based on both the British and the Shreveport models and does not involve only the simplistic notion of giving addicts all the heroin they want. We will return later to how these models might apply to modern America, but for now let us deal with the question whether we in America should continue to tolerate the heroin affliction. That question can be dealt with only by a subjective evaluation. The facts can support almost any point of view. I am proceeding on the basis of a subjective judgment that is deeply affected by the situation I have seen with my own eyes in the clinics and on the streets of England, which is much gentler than the fear and crime I have seen with those same eyes in the clinics and on the streets of America.

Although the core of my judgment process is subjective, some statistics do support it. In this regard, some persuasive pieces of data would be indicators of, first, the total number of untreated heroin addicts in the society, and second, the amount of crime they commit.

The *White Paper on Drug Abuse* stated in 1975, "There are several hundred thousand daily chronic users of heroin not currently in treatment." The report admitted that the number was imprecise (200,000–900,000) but that it was the most reasonable it could produce given the restraints of rationality and reality.[29] In its only annual report (for 1978) the Carter White House Office of Drug Abuse Policy stated, "It is estimated that at any one time [in the year 1976] there are 500,000 daily heroin users." Daily users are considered addicts. The White House group estimated that 170,000 heroin users were in treatment; therefore, an estimated 330,000 daily users were not in treatment.[30] If we were to accept, for the purposes of argument, the later Carter administration claim that the total number of American heroin addicts had been reduced to

380,000, and also to accept the number of 170,000 in treatment (the highest such estimate encountered), then the number of untreated heroin addicts drops to 210,000. Federal agencies questioned in late 1980 about the latest data said that the statistics were not available because they were being reworked; when pressed, they officially responded that the number 200,000 untreated heroin addicts was "not unreasonable." This number was the lowest I encountered in my research, and therefore I estimate that there are *at least* 200,000 daily users of heroin who are not in treatment.

Do these 200,000 citizens pose a serious problem of crime and violence to the other citizens of America? Remember, we are not talking about less-than-daily heroin users (ODAP said that in 1976 there might have been 3,500,000 of them). We are asking if there is evidence that 200,000 heroin addicts, not in treatment or under control, represent a criminal danger. The answer of most people would be wide-eyed wonder that the question was asked at all. Some proof of public attitudes was found in 1973 in a random survey of 3,291 citizens by the National Commission on Marihuana and Drug Abuse; it found that over 90 percent believed that heroin users often commit crimes in order to obtain money to buy drugs and that addicts commit many crimes they would not commit if they were not addicted. Those seeming truisms are also accepted by many professionals and commentators in the field.[31]

Accordingly, it is surprising to realize how fashionable it has become in some intellectual circles to question the relationship between heroin addiction and crime. There is no doubt that heroin use in and of itself should by now be recognized as a neutral act in terms of its potential criminogenic effect upon an individual's behavior. That is, there is nothing in the pharmacology, or physical and psychological impact, of the drug that would propel a user to crime. (Some other drugs, of course, do seem to have a negative impact on users, such as alcohol, barbiturates, and PCP.) Moreover, many heroin users are "chippers"—they can take the drug irregularly and not become addicted; others can take it regularly, function relatively normally, and pay for it from their personal wealth. The revisionists of recent years, however, raise doubts about the general belief that many heroin addicts cause a great deal of crime and violence in America, and that their status as addicts has an important connection to crime. For example, in September 1974 Mathea Falco and John Pekkanen—then both associated with the Drug Abuse Council—observed in a critical review of Nixon policy in the *Washington Post* that "there is no solid evidence linking [heroin] addiction to increased crime."[32]

Criminologists often speak in terms of preaddiction criminality. As the National Commission on Marihuana and Drug Abuse declared in 1973, "criminal

behavior is not a by-product of dependence but results, as does the drug dependence itself, from psychological and social deviance which predates dependence. . . . This conclusion challenges the theory that drugs cause crime and
stresses that drug dependence and criminality are two forms of social deviance,
neither producing the other."[33] These words were quoted by Charles Silberman
in *Criminal Violence, Criminal Justice* to strike the final blow, as it were, in his
critique of the Nixon war on heroin. Silberman observed, "It would be fatuous
to suggest that the growth in heroin use has contributed nothing to the increase
in crime; but we simply do not know how large that contribution is, or what
the processes are through which drug abuse contributes to crime."[34]

There are elements of truth in all these doubting commentaries on the relationship between heroin and crime, but they create, I suggest, a perverted view
of the overall truth. The doubts are usually raised, as they were by Silberman,
in the context of a criticism of the practice of giving methadone to American
addicts, which is analyzed in detail later. For now we will continue to look at
the simple relationship, the obvious connections—not the ultimate or root
causation—between heroin use and crime.

There is enough evidence, if only one wants to look at it, to indicate a
compelling relationship between the taking of heroin *daily* and the commission
of a great many crimes. Does the use of heroin cause, in an ultimate sense, the
person to commit those crimes? We shall never know, no matter how much
time or money we spend on research, even as medieval monks could never
ultimately calculate how many angels could dance on the head of a pin. We do
know that large numbers of daily heroin users are walking crime waves. Virtually every such addict I have spoken to confirms this statement.

The research of Dr. William McGlothlin in 1977 found that people who used
heroin on a less than daily basis were, for the most part, only marginally involved in crime; but all this changed for those who escalated to daily heroin use
and who were thereby classified as addicts. The amount of crime they committed increased greatly. Addicts were arrested five times as often as those who
used heroin but not every day. Such research reports provide impressive support for the widely held belief that heroin addicts are major criminal threats.

Reflecting on the McGlothlin studies, Dr. DuPont said in 1977, "Our latest
data at NIDA suggest that, during the time an addict is involved in crime . . .
annual income exceeds $24,000—58 percent of which (or $14,000) is required
to cover the cost of drugs. Of course, the actual value of goods stolen is generally estimated to be 3–4 times the amount obtained through fences. So we
estimate that a single heroin addict may cost society up to $100,000 a year in
property loss."[35]

A 1974 study placed the annual property loss due to all thefts by heroin addicts at $6.3 billion.[36] If, however, DuPont's $100,000 loss figure were to be multiplied by 200,000, our minimum estimated number of addicts not in treatment, annual property loss would amount to $20 billion, an improbable figure. Since, however, it has been arrived at by multiplying one unknown number by another, as is so often done in such efforts, it would seem the better part of wisdom to project cautiously that such losses could well amount to multiple billions.

By the beginning of the 1980s a whole universe of new and unanticipated problems seemed to be developing in connection with heroin abuse. Some were linked with events that in the past were not even considered by drug-abuse experts and criminologists, such as the inflation in the prices of precious metals. For example, a burglary detective in the affluent Virginia suburbs of Washington, D.C., tells me that almost all his suspects now are heroin or Dilaudid addicts; almost all are white and from middle-class backgrounds; and many are inseparable man-woman teams. They specialize in gold and silver robberies from homes, frequently laying the prospective loot out on a table in the victims' homes and then expertly selecting only the genuine articles for removal. The burglar-addicts often sell the items on the same day to legitimate dealers in gold and silver who now promise immediate cash in high-pressure advertising campaigns. That cash fuels the black market for imported Iranian and Pakistani heroin. Habits of $300 to $500 per day are usual for these suburban addicts, with the result that the national annual cost of heroin-related thefts may soon exceed all previous high estimates, much like the cost of imported oil.[37]

But whatever the real value of the property lost to criminal heroin addicts, none of the estimates can truly reflect the much more terrible cost of heroin addiction in terms of the personal violence committed by addicts to obtain money for drugs and the violence associated with the black market. In the days of Harry Anslinger, even marijuana users were portrayed as depraved murderers because of the allegedly irresistible impact of the drug. In recent years, however, many public officials have seemed to recognize that it is not heroin itself that causes violent crime but rather the driving compulsion to obtain money in order to buy the illegal substance. For example, when Governor Rockefeller introduced his stringent new law to the state legislature on January 30, 1973, he testified that addicts were "robbing, mugging, murdering day in and day out for their money to fix their habit." In its 1980 final report the Drug Abuse Council cited this testimony as typical of the type of emotional exaggeration that has marred public policy debate on drug abuse. The council admitted only that regular heroin use seems to be associated with "a higher rate of revenue-producing crime by the addict" but not with *violent* crime.[38]

In the same vein was a 1980 report by the Institute for Law and Social Research of Washington, D.C., that brought headlines in the public and professional press, one of which stated, "Drug Users Unlikely to Commit Violent Crime." The facts behind those headlines were: in a major study of 17,745 arrestees in the District of Columbia in the years 1973 and 1974, Dr. Eric Wish and his colleagues found that only 22 percent of those charged with robbery tested positively for drugs (probably heroin) in their urine, as did 18 percent of those charged with homicide and 10 percent of those charged with aggravated assault. This would suggest that the great majority of those charged with these violent offenses were not drug users. These results, which were consistent, in broad outline, with those of many other studies, should provide comfort to those who fear that America is being completely inundated by the violent crime of heroin addicts. But not too much comfort.[39]

While most of those arrested for violent crime such as robbery may not be addicts, the addict-robbers have a constant need to commit crime in order to buy their drugs—and thus they may commit a whole string of them before being apprehended. Criminologists James Inciardi and Carl Chambers estimated in 1972 that among a sample of addicts they studied, only one crime was cleared by arrest for every 120 offenses committed.[40]

One of the most comprehensive studies ever carried out on the relationship between drug use and crime was directed in the 1970s by William I. Barton, a sober-minded, hard-to-convince DEA statistical expert. This massive study, conducted under the auspices of the Law Enforcement Assistance Administration and the Bureau of the Census, surveyed the inmates of state correctional facilities in January 1974. The staff conducted detailed interviews of 10,400 inmates, which provided information applicable to all 191,400 state prison inmates as of that date. A total of 18,700 were serving their sentences because they had violated state drug laws. (This was 28 times the closest comparable British number of 671 on June 30, 1974.) Sixty-one percent of all prisoners had used illegal drugs at some point in their lives. Of more significance, 51,700, or 27 percent, said they were using illegal drugs daily—were addicted—at the time of the offense for which they were imprisoned. A slight majority of those addicts were dependent primarily on one drug, heroin. Thus, 14 percent, or 26,100, of the prisoners admitted that they were daily users at the time of their most serious crimes. The greatest correlation between heroin addiction and an individual crime category (apart from drug offenses) was with robbery; 18

percent of all the incarcerated robbers admitted that they used heroin daily at the time of the offense.

One might look at these data and declare that *only* 18 percent of the imprisoned robbers were heroin addicts—as were only 14 percent of those imprisoned for burglaries and only 16 percent, for larcenies. However, Barton observed, "this in *no* way means that narcotic addicts committed this proportion of these offenses when they were previously in the community. A heroin addict may commit any number of offenses while at large; however, when arrested he may be charged with only one or several offenses resulting in that 'unknown and unreported' amount of criminality that Inciardi and Chambers speak of among narcotic addicts." Each of the 7,614 addict-robbers imprisoned in January 1974, therefore, might have committed scores of holdups before being apprehended.[41]

A relatively small number of violent crimes, moreover, may create inordinate fear and intolerable social conditions. Robbery—the taking of property by force or by the threat of force—is often the most fear-producing type of crime for a community in terms of its effect on others than the immediate victim. It must also be recognized that many so-called property crimes, such as burglary and larceny, are often considered nonviolent because the element of stealth is present; but if a personal confrontation happens by accident, then the burglar or thief may be instantly transformed into a robber or worse. It is disturbing that as of the early 1980s many if not most of those identified 7,614 addict-robber prisoners of 1974 have been released from prison. Even if only a minority have continued in their violent ways, it is as if a brigade of armed terrorists have been set loose to rejoin their even more numerous fellows on the streets.

While the 1978 NIDA pamphlet on the British system, and thus the official American view, suggests that the streets of London are getting to be like the streets of New York, nothing could be further from the truth. One can wander the streets of London night and day and find nothing remotely resembling the American criminal street scenes. The 'Dilly scene is sad, pathetic, disturbing— with addicts of all types lolling about—but it does not, at least to this American and to many others of my acquaintance, seem threatening. The official English statistics seem to support this impressionistic notion. Of course, impression can be another word for fear. To the British the fear of street heroin addicts would be a rather uncommon emotion. To an American that is an astounding thought.[42]

To an American living in a big city today, heroin addicts and the crime they commit are so pervasive as to be almost taken for granted. Stories of heroin trafficking, heroin street markets, heroin addict burglaries, heroin addict robbers, and heroin addict arrests are standard grist for the daily newspaper mill. Did heroin use cause the crimes? That is, as I have said, never clear, but the heroin presence seems to be almost everywhere there is trouble and disruption. While social scientists may debate the precise statistical *causal* relationships between heroin abuse and crime, the view from American streets continues to demonstrate a side-by-side phenomenon of compelling and appalling dimensions: a high level of heroin addiction in many poor, minority neighborhoods, and a high level of crime, violence, and social pathology in those same neighborhoods. To those sophisticated experts who suggest—as did, for example, the Drug Abuse Council in its 1980 final report—that a reduction in the scope or virulence of the first phenomenon might have little observable effect on the second, one is moved to reply that it would be worth almost any cost to see what those communities would be like with heroin addiction under some form of civilized social control.

Let us glance briefly at the situation in two American cities, New York and Washington. The state of New York enacted perhaps the toughest of the archetypical American drug control laws on September 1, 1973. Although it was passed during the Nixon era, Governor Rockefeller's law went much further than any drug statute ever supported by that president or any other, as far as I can determine. The New York law was designed to provide draconian sanctions for all sellers, big and small, especially those who operated in the flourishing drug supermarkets of New York City. A person who sold at least one ounce or possessed more than two ounces of heroin, for example, was subject to a mandatory minimum sentence of fifteen years up to a maximum of life, with no possibility of plea bargaining. The law has had little effect on heroin use and crime in New York City. A 1977 study by the New York City bar association observed, "Heroin use was as widespread in mid-1976 as it had been when the 1973 revision took effect, and ample supplies of the drug were available."[43]

The day-to-day human dimensions of this continuing social agony were explained in a statement on November 19, 1976, by Percy E. Sutton, president of the borough of Manhattan. Sutton had arranged a tour of the city's street drug markets with U.S. Congressman Charles B. Rangel, who represents a Harlem district; he then testified before the House of Representatives Select Committee on Narcotics Abuse and Control hearing, which was then chaired by Rangel:

Today, too many of the streets of Harlem and many of our neighborhoods in Manhattan, Brooklyn, Queens, and the Bronx have been taken over by users and pushers of heroin and cocaine. This, as though our streets have been abandoned to the drug users and the drug pushers. . . .

Something is wrong when the junkies and the pushers are so confident on the streets of our City; so confident that they will not be arrested that they will come to the corners of our streets and onto the sidewalks, and there, out of shopping bags, in the sight of all, pull out and sell packages or "decks" of heroin by their brand names of "Tru-Blue," "Bingo," "Di-gel" . . . "Dynamite," and "Foolish Pleasure." And all of this, Mr. Congressman, with an absolute feeling of confidence that no police will interfere.

Gentlemen, I know that we are a City in trouble. No one knows it better than I. But . . . not everyone knows that it appears today New York is a City being abandoned to the users and pushers of drugs. And for drug users to get drug buying money for a "fix," many New York residents and business people are being subjected to robbings, vicious beatings, muggings and various other outrages, including murder. . . .

I will . . . always remember how cruel was the scene of that thoroughly drugged mother standing there, deep into her "high," at the corner of 117th Street and 8th Avenue, selling packets of drugs over the heads of her 2 children, neither of which could have been more than 5 years old.

We saw it, that sight, and we wondered what kind of life was ahead for these youngsters, forced to grow up in this vicious drug cycle, learning to count by knowing that a packet of "Tru-Blue" sold for $5, thus 2 packets were $10 and 3 packets were $15.[44]

It would probably be difficult to convince Sutton and Rangel and many of their constituents that no significant connection exists between heroin addiction and crime. At the same time, it is important to note that the reactions of both men to these scenes of crime and human despair are typical of those of many prominent black leaders: even tougher law enforcement should be the predominant method of coping with heroin abuse and related criminality. (Rangel has been an especially outspoken opponent of proposals to provide legal heroin to addicts through doctors.) Their expressed sense of frustration concerning the powerlessness of the police was based upon an accurately perceived reality: the city police department had made a deliberate policy decision not to enforce the tough new law in the manner intended by the Albany legislators. Indeed, Police Commissioner Patrick Murphy had made that decision in 1971 under the old law, when he saw that mass arrests of street dealers seemed only to clog up the courts with little impact on the overall heroin traffic. The police chose to enforce the new law primarily as they had the old one: against middle and upper-level dealers. But, again, even that policy seemed to have no observable impact on crime in the streets.[45]

Stories about Washington heroin addicts appear routinely in the daily newspapers, relating their names, the size of their habits, and their crimes. Even one of the addict-burglars, who supported a $300-per-day habit by working every morning at his "business," admitted it was all becoming rather routine; Winston McKutchin told a reporter, after his arrest: "It ain't no big job. . . . By 12 o'clock I'm through with it." The general public seemed to accept the destructive activities of Mr. McKutchin, and thousands like him, almost as part of the landscape.[46]

A few events did seem rather unusual even in a city becoming almost numbed to them. On December 20, 1978, international heroin smuggler Linwood Gray shot the federal prosecutor who was investigating him. Assistant U.S. Attorney Barry L. Leibowitz was only slightly injured in the attack, which took place in the parking lot of the federal courthouse, virtually within sight of the Capitol building. Neither the lawyer nor any official nor the press suggested that such an attack might signal the need to reevaluate national drug policies.[47]

On May 23, 1980, in the early morning hours, four or five men engaged in the Washington heroin trade broke *into*—not out of—a lightly guarded District of Columbia prison facility located in rural Virginia. The men had been selling heroin, not only on Washington streets but also within the prison system. Some harsh disagreement had occurred in a complex web of criminal relationships, and the breakers-in were on a deliberate murder mission. Of the two inmates they were seeking, they found one, Douglas Boney, a heroin addict with an extensive record as a dealer, robber, and perpetrator of assorted other violent criminal acts. Boney, serving a sentence for selling heroin, was shot and killed at point-blank range by Edward Ford, a convicted robber and narcotics trafficker—and later a convicted murderer as a result of this incident. The event was considered unique—no one could remember a similar assassination foray into a prison—but not one that should cause a rethinking of overall narcotics-abuse strategy.[48]

However, such heroin-related crimes are events which, combined with the comparative history related herein, should compel Americans to conclude that the present national situation is intolerable. That conclusion should lead us to ask what might be done differently in the future.

IV

Before that question is answered, the treatment programs that were available during the modern era in America must be reassessed. The 1960s and 1970s saw an enormous growth in the nationwide drug-treatment capability.[49] But not all these developments have been positive, since the "treatment" placements for many addicts have been traditional prison cells. Many others spent time behind bars in coerced or voluntary civil-commitment status, some finding release from the talons of addiction but most merely marking time. Addicts with funds, however, often found help in individual or group therapy.

Every treatment method had its passionate advocates, usually armed with data from scientific evaluations to prove how well it was working; and there seems no doubt that every method has helped some addicts. But all these treatment modalities had low measurable success rates—often less than one in ten. Only two modalities appealed to many people and created new enthusiasm on a broad scale. These two were the therapeutic community and methadone maintenance.

The therapeutic communities, sometimes called TC's or concept houses, have roots in modern mental health theory and are consistent with the works of psychiatric thinkers from many nations. But the advent of the TC for drug addicts seems to have been a peculiarly American happening. The first one, called Synanon, was founded in 1959 as a treatment program for alcoholics by Charles Dederich, who had an alcoholic past. Synanon was originally modeled after Alcoholics Anonymous and seemed to simply drift into the treatment of heroin addicts. As James V. DeLong wrote in *Dealing with Drug Abuse* (1972), "Many of the TC's retain some of the basic AA characteristics—the concept that there is no such thing as an ex-addict, only an addict who is not using at the moment; the emphasis on mutual support and aid; the distrust of mental health professionals; and the concept of continual confession and catharsis. However, the TC has extended these notions to include the concept of a live-in community with a rigid structure of day-to-day behavior and a complex system of punishment and rewards."[50] The TCs also have developed the confrontation-attack model of treatment, which is antithetical to the warm, supportive ambience of AA.

Many of the leaders of TCs have a rough-and-ready air of frontier independence, a distaste for treating drug addicts as poor unfortunates or as romantic figures, and an abhorrence of professionals who treat addicts with methadone. Obviously, they are staunch opponents of those who advocate opening the drug gates any wider to include a substance such as heroin. Even if one disagrees with some of their positions, one must admire their style and their belief in the willpower of addicts. It is possible to see how some addicts, many of whom suffer from extremely low self-esteem, can be lifted from the pit of despair only by a "priest" who preaches sermons of self-reliance or by a strong father figure, for whom, as Dr. Beckett reminds us, many heroin addicts are searching desperately.

John Maher founded the Delancey Street project in San Francisco in the early 1970s. He had been a heroin addict for twelve years, as well as, almost inevitably, a burglar, pickpocket, and prison inmate. He was able to stop using heroin and to start a socially more useful life through the help of Synanon. Many of the Synanon group-encounter techniques were adopted by Maher in Delancey Street. As many TC leaders have done, Maher has added a dose of political activism to his philosophy. He believes that addicts need most of all a chance to earn back their dignity and self-respect. In order to do that they must work, and work hard, at a job and at improving their communities. In April 1976 he told a reporter:

> You know the cure for drugs in this country? It's organizing the people to get them working for things that are worthwhile. The question isn't how many addicts you cure. The question is how you trend the society. If you create one Malcolm X, you save 100,000 black kids. If you get 10,000 sniveling nobodies standing in line drinking dope out of orange juice bottles, what have you cured? Is that the way you'd like to spend your life?
>
> Let me tell you something. . . . The Black Muslims have cured more addicts in this country, and the Catholic Church and the Southern Baptists have cured more alcoholics than all the treatment programs combined. You know what I tell these people? If I get a black addict in here, I tell him the truth. He's a friend of the slum lords and the racists. . . .
>
> You know where all free heroin talk comes from? A bunch of well-meaning liberal punks at cocktail parties, that's where. . . . I don't know about you, but I don't want my tax dollars going to support somebody else's vices. And I don't want my kid brother getting onto free heroin when he's 17 and staying on it for life.
>
> That's not a solution. It would be the same thing as taking all the drunks and lining them up at Clancy's saloon every morning for a free slug of booze.
>
> The hell with all that liberal, groovy jazz. We've got serious problems in this country. This business is like the fashion business. Do you realize that? First it was federal hospitals. Then detoxification. Then therapeutic com-

munities. Then methadone. Now it's heroin. Whatever's in. Whatever sounds groovy. Everybody in this business is looking for grant money, that's all. It's Fords one week, Chevrolets the next. Whatever sells.[51]

Although Maher apparently rejects the label *therapeutic community* in regard to the Delancey Street project, he seems to be, in many respects, typical of the politically active TC leaders. They strike many responsive American chords in their condemnations of those who do not see the light as they do. Unfortunately, it is virtually impossible to ascertain the success rate of the TC movement. Few objective evaluations have been accomplished, since attempts at such ventures seem to be resented by TCs. Many addicts never pass the initial, sometimes offensive, screening tests, and many others are repelled by the often humiliating experience of staying in the residential houses. A few stay and while they are in residence lead drug-free lives; many of them relapse soon after reentering regular society.

What James DeLong wrote in 1972 may still be true today: "Looking at all the available evidence, and the impressions of experts in the field, it is hard to escape the conclusion that TC's are, at best, good for a very limited number of drug addicts. As a rough guess, considering the initial reject rates, the split rates, and the relapse rate, it would be surprising if careful evaluation showed that more than 5 per cent of those who come into contact with the program are enabled to lead a reasonably drug-free, socially productive life." I take no pleasure in reporting that assessment because there is a need for TCs in virtually every community—for those addicts who are ready for them. But the relative numbers of such people will always be low and most addicts would as soon enroll in a TC as they would in the priesthood or the marine corps; all three are, for better or worse, elitist organizations.[52]

Methadone maintenance provides quite another story, which starts, like so many of those that have a chemical beginning, with German scientists. Cut off from the natural supply of opium by Allied armies during World War II, chemists in I. G. Farbenindustrie created a wholly synthetic painkiller. It is said that out of respect for the Christian name of their esteemed national leader, the loyal chemists called the new medicine Dolophine, although it had a number of other scientific names. A team of American investigators then found the secret of the drug in the files of the huge chemical cartel and it came to the United States as part of the spoils of war. In a program coordinated by Dr. Nathan B. Eddy, the U.S. Public Health Service tested the drug throughout the country, primarily to determine its analgesic impact on the organically ill. But it was also tested as a treatment drug for addicts at the Narcotics Farm in Lexington,

Kentucky. For reasons surrounded by the mystery which so often envelops the birth and early life of psychoactive compounds, this one soon became crowned with a medical halo. On October 19, 1947, the press reported that methadone "does not produce the euphoria, the feeling of exaltation which comes to the addict from . . . other narcotics" and, moreover, that "it is the safest narcotic drug yet produced."[53] Nothing in its brief German chemical history would suggest that it differed from other opiates in these respects, but the stories persisted. On August 9, 1948, *Life* magazine ran a dramatic story about what was then called Methadon with the sub-headline "A Synthetic Drug Relieves Pain and Dope Addiction." The article pointed out that even though the new substance was habit forming like other narcotics, "because it created far less physical dependence than morphine it could be used to treat addiction." Photographs of addicts at Lexington showed how morphine brought ecstasy, deprival of that drug brought hideous suffering, and then: "An injection of methadon ends the addict's suffering. . . . In time this patient will transfer his addiction from morphine to methadon. He will then be able to give up drugs without intense suffering, for abstinence from methadon causes no violent reactions."[54]

Even Harry Anslinger had good things to say about this medicine, which he perceived as an aid to withdrawal, not as a maintenance drug, a point on which many of the early reports were ambiguous; witness the tale in *Life*. Even some doctors treated this narcotic drug as something other than what it was and is— almost as a vitamin, a vaccine, or some other nonpsychoactive medicine. George M. Belk, New York district supervisor of the Federal Bureau of Narcotics, was moved to write the *Bulletin of the Medical Society of the County of Kings and . . . Brooklyn* in December 1965. "I feel it is my duty to inform the various physicians in this area of its true status. Methadone is a narcotic, an opiate. . . . We have received several inquiries from physicians stating they did not know methadone was a narcotic drug."[55]

It is likely that Belk was reacting to a series of clinical experiments that seemed to run counter to the accepted dogma, so long promulgated by the FBN and the AMA, that providing nondiminishing doses of any narcotic to addicts had a destructive impact. In October 1963 Dr. Vincent P. Dole, an expert in metabolic diseases, arranged a series of meetings with Dr. Marie Nyswander, a psychiatrist with extensive experience in the treatment of opiate addicts. Soon the two formed an experimental addict-treatment program at the Rockefeller Institute in New York City. In January 1964 they began to test the impact of various drugs on two confirmed heroin addicts who had been through a typically full route: many years of addiction, several in prison, stays at Lexington, and courses of psychotherapy. Nothing had worked for them.[56]

"We started the addicts on morphine, a quarter of a grain four times a day. In three weeks, in order to keep them comfortable, we had to go up to eight shots a day of an increased dosage, a total of ten grains a day. Obviously, it was going to be impractical to devise a maintenance program on morphine. Also, on morphine the patients were rendered practically immobile," Dr. Nyswander explained. "I was confronted with an abysmal lack of knowledge of what to do next. And then there was an accidental circumstance. We switched them to methadone. . . . From that point, my life changed and the addicts' lives changed."[57]

Nyswander explained the epiphany that she and her partner in medicine (later in marriage) experienced: "I was still staggering back from my failure with morphine, and it was Dr. Dole who realized what was happening in front of us. Striking alterations in behavior and appearance were taking place in the two patients. The older addict began to paint industriously and his paintings were good. The younger started urging us to let him get his high-school-equivalency diploma. We sent them both off to school, outside the hospital grounds, and they continued to live at the hospital. Neither of them—although both of them had every opportunity—copped heroin on the outside. From two slugabeds they turned into dynamos of activity."[58]

Dole and Nyswander observed that when the addicts in this and in subsequent larger experiments had taken large doses of methadone, they did not obtain any euphoria from heroin or other narcotics. Thus was born the theory of the methadone blockade. The doctors found that by taking methadone orally—they started to put it in orange juice and simply continued the practice, as did others—once a day in gradually increasing but eventually stabilized doses, addicts who injected heroin simply got no euphoric kick and thus had no reason to keep taking heroin. As they explained in the *Archives of Internal Medicine* in October 1966, "With a blockade produced by a maintenance dose of 100 mg methadone, patients become refractory to the euphoric action of 80 mg or more of heroin—an amount equivalent to the drug contained in several illegal 'bags' in New York." Thus, while an addict might need to inject heroin three or four times a day because the drug has such a short duration of action, methadone could be taken once through the more normal oral route. When the addicts became stabilized, on 80 to 100 milligrams of methadone per day, they did not have to stay in the hospital but could live out in society and come back to take their medicine with orange juice as outpatients. Thus, ambulatory maintenance came back to America. In some stabilized cases take-home doses were allowed for self-administration, again a radical departure from traditional dogma.[59]

Articles and speeches poured from the medical team at Rockefeller University and later at Beth Israel Hospital (to which the experiments were soon extended). To a city and a country deeply concerned about the spread of heroin addiction and related crime, their pronouncements came as blessed relief. By 1973 approximately 73,000 people were listed as participating in a methadone-maintenance program. In 1980 the figure was roughly the same, according to federal statistics.

Related to the theory of the narcotic blockade was the concept that heroin addiction is not only a sickness but a precisely defined kind of sickness, a metabolic disease. Heroin ingestion, it was explained, apparently alters the chemical balance in the bodies of addicts so that in order to function normally, in a physical sense, they need an opiate. Dr. Dole explained that "methadone, when properly prescribed, acts as a normalizer rather than as a narcotic. In this respect the treatment is similar to other maintenance therapies used in medical practice for treatment of patients with chronic metabolic disorders. The medical analogies are numerous—insulin for the diabetic, digitalis for the cardiac patient, cortisone for the arthritic. . . . The methadone patient, who is also dependent on the daily dose of his medication for his normal functioning, is in the same medical status."[60]

The practical implications of those words were revolutionary. A respected medical practitioner was saying that the dominant medical theory in America regarding drug addiction was demonstrably false. These patients were organically ill and needed medicine, Dole declared. They were not necessarily psychologically disturbed and did not need psychiatric treatment simply because they were addicts. "No specific psychiatric treatment was provided in the routine, but counseling was available to any patient with a psychiatric problem. There has, however, been very little need for psychotherapy. . . . The lack of formal psychotherapy in the treatment program thus reflected the experience of the professional staff that routine psychotherapy was not needed for rehabilitation of the patients that we had stabilized on methadone." Thus, great doubt was cast on the validity of the hallowed notion of an addictive personality and of the psychopathological basis for addiction.[61]

Did methadone maintenance reduce crime among addicts and thus improve their normal social functioning? This was perhaps the most important and one of the most controversial questions raised about the method. Dole and Nyswander were convinced that their approach created vast improvements in these areas. In an article in the *Journal of the American Medical Association* in December 1968, entitled "Successful Treatment of 750 Criminal Addicts," they claimed that after four years of experience with the program, "the number of criminal addicts who have been rehabilitated with methadone treatment is large enough to empty a moderate-sized jail. . . . Prior to treatment 91% of the patients had been in jail, and all of them had been more or less continuously involved in criminal activities. . . . Since entering the treatment program, 88% of the patients show arrest-free records." Only 5.6 percent of their patients had been actually convicted of a crime. Putting together all their arrest and conviction data, they concluded, "The reduction in crime, therefore, is at least 90%."[62] Such claims by respected physicians, supported by modern research methodology, have no rivals in the annals of drug-abuse treatment. Further, the two doctors told the opening session of the Fifth National Conference on Methadone Treatment in 1973, "As a conservative estimate, methadone programs in the New York area . . . are saving the community $1,000,000 per day in prevented crime."[63]

An independent evaluation unit created at the Columbia University School of Public Health and directed by Dr. Frances Rowe Gearing also came to positive conclusions about the impact of methadone maintenance on crime. Employment went up dramatically; crime, just as dramatically, went down. Some of her findings were even more favorable than those of Dole and Nyswander. In a 1969 report Dr. Gearing concluded that arrest records for one group of addicts in their third year of treatment had fallen to two per 100 man-years, a rate lower than that of the general population.[64]

But soon major questions began to be raised about the validity of the Dole, Nyswander, and Gearing claims. By 1973, for example, James Vorenberg and Irving Lukoff, of the Harvard Center for Criminal Justice, published the results of a study suggesting that the levels of crime reduction were inflated and that, in any event, the impact of methadone was unclear. While 94 percent of the addicts allegedly did not get arrested during their first year of treatment, according to one of the favorable studies, 80 percent had not been arrested during the year *before* they entered treatment. This amounted to a drop of "only" 14 percent—but the Harvard researchers admitted that even this was a significant indicator of a reduction in criminal activity.[65]

There are dozens, perhaps hundreds, of studies dealing with the impact of methadone maintenance on crime by addicts. The issue of preaddiction criminality is often raised in such studies: does it make any difference if we give narcotic drugs to a criminal when it is probable that the onset of drug addiction had no substantial impact on his criminal behavior? One can cite multiple studies supporting any point of view. What is required, as in the case of the equally ambiguous British data on heroin versus methadone, is an almost impossible balancing act. There simply are no definitive answers in the "scientific" studies. It all seems to depend on the manner in which you approach the data and how you read them. In 1975 Edward Jay Epstein wrote an influential article titled "Methadone: The Forlorn Hope," in which he ridiculed favorable evaluation studies and derided the beguiling notion that "most crime was the product not of 'criminals' but of 'sick' individuals who could be cured by the distribution of an inexpensive medicine." Charles Silberman agreed with Epstein on many counts, including the preaddiction criminality argument, and described the methadone maintenance program as a prime example of a simplistic solution to a complex problem. "There is no evidence," Silberman concluded, "that methadone treatment programs have contributed to a reduction in crime."[66]

When I read the same data I come to different conclusions. Doubtless many addicts were criminals before they became addicts, but the evidence is also strong that the level of criminal activity increased significantly after the onset of addiction. Still others started committing major crimes only after they became addicted. After they underwent methadone maintenance, not all were reformed but many changed significantly. One of the most enlightening studies I have seen was reported in 1974 by Dr. Paul Cushman, director of the Methadone Maintenance Clinic at St. Luke's Hospital in New York. Dr. Cushman reviewed the frequency of arrest of 269 addicts over time. Before narcotic addiction the rate of arrest was 3.1 per 100 person-years. In other words, many of these individuals committed crimes before they became addicted. But with addiction, the rate of arrest among the group rose more than ten times, to 35.1 arrests per 100 person-years during the period of addiction without treatment. After the addicts began methadone maintenance, arrests went down almost but not quite to the previous level, to a rate of 5.9. After they were discharged, arrests went up again, to a rate of 9.0, still only 25 percent of the previous high. It is my suspicion that the Cushman rates reflect a wider reality applicable to many groups of addicts throughout the country.[67]

Many of those addicts did not look upon the medicine with kindness even though it helped them control their criminal proclivities. Tens of thousands were introduced to methadone through a whole new generation of criminal diversion programs inaugurated by federal, state, and local governments. After arrest, addicts were often given a choice that virtually amounted to methadone or jail; few chose the latter. Some of those who chose methadone have told me of the bitterness they felt at having to take "that junk."

A large number of the methadone clientele, whether diverted from the criminal justice system or entering directly from the street, were black. While many black leaders recognized the benefits of methadone maintenance for those of their people with heroin habits, the drug was severely criticized by others who saw in the programs a white plot to control minority aspirations. Also, the use of any drug for almost any purpose offends a strain of abstinent fundamentalism in the religious philosophy of many black clergy, who put alcohol in the corner with the devil, and consider such substances as methadone and heroin to be totally beyond the pale of civilized discussion.

On the whole, the advent of methadone maintenance in America did not bring a cure to either heroin addiction or crime, even for those addicts who took part fully in all aspects of the richest programs, some of which included extensive therapy, vocational placement, and other supportive elements beyond that single medicine. But the trinity of the 1960s—Dole, Nyswander, and methadone—deserve every bit of adoration bestowed on them; they were the best America had, they reduced crime, and they helped a great many human beings achieve a decent life. As James V. DeLong wrote in 1972, "The basic consistency of results is quite impressive. Although we may not yet know exactly how good methadone maintenance is, its essential efficacy is as well established as anything in this field can be. It is now generally acknowledged that methadone is medically safe, acceptable to many heroin addicts, effective, and administratively feasible for large scale programs." In 1975 DeLong looked at the issues regarding methadone again and concluded, "No matter how the issues are resolved, the existence of methadone maintenance changes the situation in a fundamental way. Before, an addict had few alternatives, given the difficulties of remaining abstinent. He had no real choice except to continue his addiction. The existence of methadone provides at least the possibility of a way out that did not exist before. This means a lot to someone on the street, and to the future of society's efforts to deal with the problem."[68]

If, then, methadone achieves such a high rating, why not accept it and leave the American system where it is? Granted the imperfection of human institutions, this may be the best of all possible (real) worlds. To come to grips with these issues is to realize that while methadone has done much good, and while it should remain as a major treatment drug, America and other countries can approach it and addicts on a much more realistic basis than the present American system allows.

The legal status of both methadone and narcotics maintenance in general has improved in the modern era, but it can be made infinitely more rational. The Narcotic Addict Treatment Act of 1974 was passed because officials in DEA and FDA believed there was a need to control the mushrooming growth of methadone maintenance programs, especially the few run by private doctors who saw the power to write methadone prescriptions as the equivalent of a license to print money. The new law provided a series of interlocking controls on the whole arena of addict treatment with narcotic drugs. It has not been generally appreciated, however, that for the first time in history a federal statute has actually acknowledged that providing drugs to addicts for either detoxification or maintenance was within the scope of "the lawful course of . . . professional practice." The purpose of the law was restriction, not liberalization, of the powers of doctors, but as of May 17, 1974, American physicians could claim a broad power based upon statute to provide any legal narcotic drugs to addicts. But what American law gave with one hand it sharply limited with the other.[69]

The statute put precise legal parameters on the two types of medical treatment it had authorized. "The term 'maintenance treatment' means the dispensing, for a period in excess of twenty-one days, of a narcotic drug in the treatment of an individual for dependence upon heroin or other morphine-like drugs," stated the first section of the law. It continued: "The term 'detoxification treatment' means the dispensing, for a period not in excess of twenty-one days, of a narcotic drug in decreasing doses in order to alleviate adverse physiological or psychological effects incident to withdrawal from the continuous or sustained use of a narcotic drug and as a method of bringing the individual to a narcotic drug-free state within such a period." Within the context of American history, these legal restrictions on medical practice, these intrusions into the doctor-patient relationship, may seem quite appropriate, even necessary. How else can society control the venality of doctors and the evil habits of so many citizens?[70]

In addition to the registration of those who wish to prescribe controlled substances, already required by existing law, the new act provided that any practitioner who wished to dispense narcotic drugs to individuals for maintenance or detoxification treatment had to obtain a "separate registration for that purpose." This registration was to be provided by the attorney general (in effect, DEA) if he determined that the applicant was qualified and that the applicant would follow the federal regulations regarding the security of stocks of the drugs, the maintenance of records, and the quantities of drugs to be provided addicts for unsupervised use, primarily meaning take-home privileges.[71]

These legislated controls were supplemented with an extensive series of detailed executive regulations from DEA and FDA prescribing the methods for operating and controlling narcotic addict treatment centers. One of the most important and intrusive of these regulations was the one from the FDA which selected only one drug as "safe and effective" in the treatment of narcotic addiction. That drug was methadone. It remains the only narcotic drug that may be used by American doctors in the care of narcotic addicts, and it must be provided only in a form suitable for oral use, not for injection. Even methadone, however, has not received the full legal blessing of the federal bureaucracy for the treatment of addicts. It remains in a status of legal-medical limbo as a new drug still under investigation through large-scale research projects, namely the vast number of methadone programs now under way throughout the country. Therefore, *no* drug has received final legal approval in the United States for the treatment of addicts.[72]

What if a physician makes a clinical judgment that an addict-patient might be helped by a weaker narcotic drug, such as codeine? If the doctor used it, he would be in virtually the same category, technically speaking, as any criminal trafficker who violated the statute. During recent years some physicians have used Darvon, a relatively weak synthetic opiate, to treat narcotic addicts. This practice was either ignored or allowed for a number of reasons, not least that the substance had not been listed as a narcotic drug under the 1970 comprehensive law. This loophole was closed on June 24, 1980, when DEA placed Darvon in Schedule IV, thus classifying it as a narcotic drug and making it off limits for the treatment of addicts.[73]

In an anguished communication to the *Journal of the American Medical Association* on May 10, 1976, Drs. Dole and Nyswander bemoaned the web that had been spun over methadone maintenance programs by federal and state agencies:

> With rigid rules mandating every detail of treatment and teams of inspectors from five or more separate agencies combing the records of clinics for technical violations, the physician is made to feel as defensive as the addicts and is left with no real authority in his clinic. He is told what addicts he is permitted to treat, the dosage limits and the permitted dose forms, the required frequency of clinic visits, what laboratory tests are mandated, the numbers and kinds of paraprofessional staff required for licensing of the clinic, and he must justify a decision to continue treatment of any patient after an arbitrary period of time. . . . As a result, most of the maintenance clinics are now essentially paraprofessional operations, with a part-time physician hired to sign prescriptions.[74]

In January 1977 Dr. Cushman wrote: "Paperwork reached such levels that a New York clinic doctor with 300 patients should spend 100% of his time solely in filling out mandated forms; just seeing a patient would place him in violation of some rule, since he would have to leave some paperwork task unperformed."[75]

The federal regulations controlling the operation of methadone treatment programs, promulgated by DEA and FDA to implement the statutes enacted in the 1970s, must be seen in historical context as the direct descendants of the early Treasury Department directives, especially the Roper pronouncement of 1919. The new rules are infinitely more comprehensive and intrusive into medical practice. Failure to observe them might be treated as a clinical misjudgment, as it would often be in Britain, or, on the other hand, the full force of the following section might be applied: "If the program sponsor or the person responsible for a particular program fails to abide by all of the requirements set forth in these regulations, or fails to adequately monitor the activities of those employed in the program, he may have the approval of his application [to operate the program] revoked, his methadone supply seized, an injunction granted precluding operation of his program, and criminal prosecution instituted against him." After reviewing the latest version of these regulations, it would be my legal judgment that they virtually create a rebuttable presumption that a doctor who treats addicts with drugs is going to violate some provision and thus commit a crime. Others may see less intimidation in the regulations, but, I claim, their intrusiveness explains why many doctors would never accept employment in a methadone program and why private doctors have practically no legally acceptable role in the treatment of addicts.

American medicine, in general, now seems to accept such intrusions as normal, although it is assumed that government dictation of how to treat, say, heart disease or diphtheria would be greeted by organized medical resistance. That, of course, is another matter. The transcending difference between the British and American approaches to narcotic addiction is not heroin or any other drug but the widespread intrusion of the government into what should be a delicately and intensely private relationship between a patient and his or her doctor. Heroin is important, but government intrusion is more so. The scope of that intrusion can best be understood by viewing it against the backdrop of the British experience, as we have been doing. In more personal terms, I remember the disbelief that came over the face of a British clinic doctor when he was told by the American doctors and treatment officials in my 1979 London Institute about these regulations. He had just described how he had treated a fifteen-year-old heroin addict by maintaining him on methadone, which provided a level of stability to the boy's life and enabled the doctor to proceed with an allied program of psychiatric therapy. This doctor was one of those who had decided, on the basis of his own clinical judgment and not because of governmental fiat, to use methadone rather than heroin to treat addicts. There was nothing remarkable about the case in the British context. However, the Americans in the seminar room pointed out to him that FDA regulations forbid the maintenance of any addict under sixteen on methadone; that when such an addict appears for treatment, he may be given methadone only in the process of detoxification; and that the period of detoxification is limited, not only by regulation but also by statute, to twenty-one days. The British doctor was speechless.[76]

In the same vein, I remember the annoyance of an American methadone clinic administrator who asked her counterpart in an English drug dependence clinic for copies of official patient admission forms and was told somewhat vaguely, "Oh yes, I am sure we have some in the back of the office somewhere; let me look." Even though there is now a system of addict notification to the Home Office, and a form for the purpose, the form is not required, and such notification would be accepted by Her Majesty's ministers even if, in the words of Mr. Spear, it was sent in on the "back of a cigarette package."[77]

Even if it could be shown that methadone had all the unique qualities originally attributed to it, explicitly or implicitly, by Dole and Nyswander, the American reliance on it as the sole legal narcotic in addiction treatment would be irrational in light of British experience and, it is hoped, American common sense. *But methadone does not have all those qualities.* When Dr. Nyswander said in 1964 that she could not maintain those two original addicts on morphine but that methadone did wonders for them, the important fact was that those patients were helped by methadone and not by another drug at that point in their lives. These helping medicines, however, do not work on all addicts in the same way. Forty years earlier, even larger doses of morphine had worked for Dr. Butler's patients in Shreveport, and mixed large doses of heroin, morphine, and cocaine have worked for years for some British addicts. Thus, clinical diagnoses of what good doctors see with their own eyes should properly be balanced by a reflective sense of medical history and comparative sociology.

9: A PRACTICAL VISION FOR THE FUTURE

"If there is no take-home heroin, then there is little attraction for the addict. . . . The idea of hundreds of addicts fixing in a clinic every day is appalling to me. Imagine the mess and confusion! Take-home heroin—the only alternative—is a completely crazy idea. . . . Heroin maintenance for the United States fails for purely practical reasons."—Robert L. DuPont, 1977[1]

"If you want to talk about heroin, it might help some addicts. If our purpose is to lure the social delinquent into a social contract of some sort, then I'm willing to do it. Then if he can be further seduced into conformity, fine. Who cares if it's methadone or heroin? If he wants oranges or cottage cheese, what do I care?"—Richard Blum, 1976[2]

"Drugs are with us to stay. Fight them and they will grow ever more destructive. Accept them and they can be turned into nonharmful, even beneficial forces."—Andrew Weil, 1972[3]

I

The only way we will be able to ameliorate the heroin situation in America is to encourage our Andrew Weils to try their hand at repairing the damage wrought by our Harry Anslingers. That is the major part of my vision for the future. This does not mean that we should permit doctors to use any drug they like under any circumstance, but it does mean that the law should pull back and encourage them to evolve new ways of using drugs in medical practice—especially as part of clinical techniques to help the addicted stabilize their lives.

From a practical point of view, that vision also assumes that if we can make room for medical mavericks like Weil, this will automatically authorize the Willis P. Butlers of the healing profession to reemerge and to try again. Dr. Butler had no theories in 1919 (and did not, when I last spoke to him, in May 1980) about altered states of consciousness or how to teach people to use drugs beneficially, as does Weil. Butler saw himself as a conservative physician treating patients with ordinary medicines in an effort to bring a measure of comfort and freedom from pain to their lives. He never prescribed heroin but relied mainly on morphine, and he sought to control the entire life-styles of many of his addict patients. The Shreveport doctor combined that focused professional mission with a superb sense of medical and community politics and managed to create a calm belief in his city that the drug problem, on balance, was under control. It appears, moreover, that within tolerable limits it was. If a disciple of Dr. Butler could re-create that community balance in Shreveport or any other city today, using the same tactics and the same drug, he should be encouraged to do so, and the police should be prohibited from interfering in this phase of the newly legitimate practice of medicine.

Similar thoughts apply to Reverend Terence Tanner, who had no prescribing power but viewed drug taking as neutral. He simply asked that adequate doses of all kinds of drugs be supplied to the residents of his hostels in London by the English drug dependence clinics. In return, he demanded of the addicts, as did Willis Butler, socially responsible living. England must provide room for organizations like Tanner's ROMA to be reinvigorated, and the United States and other countries must provide the legal and medical space for them to be created.

The essence of future policy must be flexibility and trust in individual physicians and individual communities. To a large extent the English system retains those attributes, but the establishment of the clinics and the restriction of the power to prescribe heroin and cocaine to clinic doctors has limited the involvement of general practitioners. Some private doctors have reentered the addiction arena, but even more must be brought in. This may be comparatively easy for the English to accomplish, at least in terms of the needed legal and administrative actions.

The removal of decades of accumulated legal restrictions will be more difficult in America, but it is feasible. In the same way that we have shed the oppressive and corrupting burden of alcohol prohibition, we could move the federal government away from its dominant role in policing the consumption and medical use of narcotics by allowing states to design their own systems of narcotic use and control. Next, we could encourage the states to allow flexibility in their own communities. The states should be urged to authorize many private physicians, perhaps *all* licensed physicians, to treat addicts—with drugs when the physicians decide to do so. But each state should be free to set up virtually any scheme of control appropriate to its circumstances. The practical result could be, at least in the early years under this approach, that in some states addicts would be treated only by clinics in large cities, in others only by private doctors, and in still others by a combination of modalities involving private physicians and public clinics. Among the results should be a monumental increase in the number of addicts who would be attracted to at least one element of the new array of treatment resources and in the number who would stay in one form of treatment or another over the years until they were cured. Concomitant decreases in crime should be even more dramatic.

It is probable that federal drug-abuse executives and private physicians would be the ones most horrified by these proposals. Federal officials tend to distrust the ethics of American doctors when the scent of financial gain is in the air. On the other hand, in regard to the treatment of heroin addicts the dominant emotions I have discovered among American doctors are apathy and fear. It is likely that with the removal of restrictions some American doctors would jump eagerly into the addiction field and proceed to amass quick fortunes by prescribing legal heroin, and nothing more in the way of treatment, to large numbers of addicts. Many other doctors would refuse to have addicts in their waiting rooms at all, much less to prescribe narcotics for them. Are not these potential problems serious enough to stop any further consideration of the approaches recommended here?

My answer is no, primarily because they fit within the notion of middle-level expectations. But by extending to many doctors the power to prescribe narcotics, including heroin, for addicts, we would be taking addicts off the streets, out of police lockups, and out of prisons, and placing them in doctors' offices. When doctors violate medical ethics, it should first be the concern of the medical disciplinary committees to deal with them. Only when these efforts have failed should we call in the police and the criminal law. We would consciously be trading off the large number of existing criminal addicts for the future possibility of a smaller number of unethical, even criminal doctors and, on the other hand, the probability of a large number of ethical and effective physicians who would actually provide comprehensive care to addicts. In our unending pursuit of the impossible balance this would actually represent progress and a good social bargain.

This vision combines the best elements of the old American narcotic clinic system with elements of the traditional British approach to drug dispensation. It does not call for more research before any action is taken on the legal dispensation of heroin, as did the National Commission on Marijuana and Drug Abuse. It does not call for experimental and limited use of heroin maintenance, as did Edward Brecher and the Drug Abuse Council. It does not call for the use of heroin as a lure, as is sometimes said of the Vera Institute proposal in New York City, whereby the heroin would be phased out after addicts entered treatment. The vision goes beyond all these proposals, but it does not go as far as the drugstore model of Philip C. Baridon, who advocated that heroin be available over the counter to anyone above the age of eighteen. It does maintain that addiction treatment could be undertaken by virtually any licensed physician, state and local law permitting, and that these physicians could control the nature of that treatment, including the periodic dispensation of any narcotic drug. The model should go into effect rapidly throughout America and in as many other countries as possible, so that both comprehensive medical care and medical control of heroin could become commonplace.[4]

Before rushing in with a new model, what about better organization and direction of the existing one? While it is possible to carp at details, it is difficult to see how, in any strategic sense, the current American model could have been funded more lavishly or managed more effectively than it has been. Its major shortcoming is that the host of talented people involved have not recognized that the American system of drug-abuse control was designed to fail at the task assigned to it.

Like their modern British counterparts, the American drug-abuse experts, in and out of government, have let the nation believe that they know how to control heroin addiction in the general population. However, there is not a single documented example in modern times of a successful governmental attempt to control heroin addiction on a large scale in a democratic Western society—and thus there is no rational support for the idea that the knowledge exists to undertake such a mass intervention. The most that the American experts should have promised was the design of a system that would attract many addicts into treatment; that would protect the rights of all addicts, including those who did not want to change but merely wanted legal drugs; that would provide mental health support for those who wanted to change when they were ready; and that would treat all drug users humanely without necessarily endorsing their life-style. The American drug experts should have stated flatly that they did not know how to cut down the total number of addicts. They should have expressed the hope that if many were brought into a caring treatment situation, the drug scene might get somewhat stabilized, and at some point in the future the total amount of heroin addiction in the society might drop—but for reasons unknown to any expert. That would have been an honest appraisal of the state of the art of drug-abuse control, then and now, but such an appraisal was not offered, perhaps because it would have been politically impossible.

This position is both humble and visionary. It admits only limited knowledge and promises only limited results. Yet those results seem achievable because the model is based upon a practical assessment of the past.

II

The past in America and in Britain shows that no single drug has magical qualities and that drugs vary in impact, depending in part on their chemistry and pharmacology and in part on the perceptions of the users. Because, how-

ever, the opiates do not cause significant organic harm when used in appropri- ←
ate dosages, virtually any of those drugs is suitable for maintenance. To restrict
the range of treatment drugs to methadone alone has no rational basis. My
earlier mention of codeine, for example, was based on the fact that it is a
relatively weak opiate, receiving little public attention. Nevertheless, at least 30
people died in America during 1978 from using that drug alone, while 750
died from using codeine in combination with other psychoactive substances.[5]
An unknown but substantial number of addicts to the drug must exist, therefore, but if one of them comes to the medical profession for assistance, the best
that can now be offered is a variety of drug-free modalities—detoxification,
psychotherapy, a TC, which will help some but not others—or maintenance on
a much stronger narcotic, methadone. It would be legal, then, for a specially
licensed doctor to provide regular doses of a strong opiate, methadone, but not
of a much weaker one, codeine, to which the addict was addicted. This condition is perverse.

Apart from the matter of relative strength, some physicians claim that the
more natural drugs are better for treatment than semisynthetics, such as heroin,
or synthetics, such as methadone. For example, Dr. Andrew Weil argues that
the more natural the drug and the more natural the route of ingestion, the more
natural the impact on the human body and psyche. Of the opiates, therefore,
the most natural would be the parent drug, opium. While it may seem out of
geographical and chronological step, there are some addicted opium smokers
in America, most of Oriental background. When their illegal supply dries up
and they cannot stay abstinent, they are often put on oral methadone maintenance in accordance with the unique rules of the American system.[6] It could be
argued that we should be experimenting with new ways to use the most natural
of the opiates, the parent drug itself, to treat opium addicts.

What about using opium to treat *heroin* addicts? When Dr. Weil was asked if
he advocated the decriminalization of heroin, the physician-writer responded
in 1978 that he did (as well as of "all other controlled drugs"), but that he had
some problems with heroin maintenance because "I am not in favor of intravenous use of potent narcotics, and I would like to see some effort made at
getting addicts to change their drug behavior. My suggestion would be to try
opium maintenance. Tincture of opium is an accepted medical drug, provides
a high that many addicts would like, and has a built-in deterrent to overuse: it
causes very uncomfortable nausea if you take too much. I would prefer oral
opium maintenance to either heroin or methadone maintenance and would like
to see it given a try. To my knowledge no one has done it. If some addicts could
shift from intravenous heroin to oral opium, that would be a major accomplish-

ment. Opium by mouth is long acting, easy to stabilize over time and much less liable to abuse."[7]

Whether or not the implementation of Weil's suggestion would help stabilize the lives of addicts, his novel idea is precisely the type of thinking that should be encouraged. The vast debate about narcotic maintenance generally is conducted on the assumption that only two drugs are involved in the controversy: the wholly synthetic methadone, in this corner, versus the semisynthetic heroin, in that one. An open medical mind and an open legal structure, however, should produce a wide range of narcotic options. Any licensed British doctor could experiment immediately with Weil's idea. But if Dr. Weil himself tried it in Arizona, where he resides, without going through the laborious process of obtaining special experimental permits from the authorities, he would risk federal and state prosecution for numerous crimes. Yet there is no way of knowing how any of the drugs might affect addicts and their life-styles unless physicians are allowed to experiment with the full range of opiates.

The future, moreover, involves coming to grips with the imponderables of the human will. The most important "will" involved is not that of physicians but that of addicts. The most powerful argument against exclusive reliance on methadone is that not enough addicts are willing to take it under medical supervision. It is considered sinful, of course, for policymakers to take into account the tastes of drug users, but those tastes must be recognized as among the most important elements in the rational design of future policies. It must be recognized, moreover, that when policymakers start to take the wishes of addicts into account, they touch a quivering nerve in the body of respectable society. One would really rather not talk about it, any more than one openly discusses masturbation. But that is, if we are frank about it, the type of activity involved: the private, purposeful creation of pleasure in one's own body without the help of another. If others, though, do help—lawmakers and doctors, for example—then they have joined forces in the unmentionable activity. The embarrassing chords struck are, for the most part, irrational and ideological, not scientific or legal. The emotions involved must be coped with in some way, however, before rational progress is possible. When Dole and Nyswander said that methadone did not give pleasure and indeed blocked it, they calmed these emotions; but Weil was more realistic when he said that oral opium provided a high that addicts would like. At this point we have reached the same sensitive question we faced in regard to heroin and cocaine for cancer patients: Is it ethical for doctors to deliberately provide euphoria for patients? Few doctors would answer yes, but if we are to attract addicts to treatment that must be society's answer. Yes to chemical highs. Addicts will answer yes even when receiving methadone, which according to some medical experts is a virtually inert medicine that blocks euphoria from heroin.

Although the methadone blockade may have occurred in many cases, for reasons that can only be guessed, the blockade theory has few adherents in Britain. And English addicts happily use heroin and methadone in combination from legal prescriptions quite frequently. Numerous reports from America, moreover, have stated that American addicts often take oral methadone at a clinic and then inject illegal heroin as a supplement. One study released in 1970 told of a Philadelphia maintenance program in which, on the basis of urinalysis, it appeared that fully 92.3 percent of the methadone patients used illegal heroin.[8]

Why? Perhaps they wanted to feel better than the methadone made them feel. In 1976 reporter William Overend wrote of one San Francisco criminal heroin addict named Bob, who was thirty, on the drug for ten years, in a methadone program for one year, and seriously wanted to get off heroin. Bob was taking 80 milligrams of oral methadone at the clinic daily—supplemented by a huge amount of heroin, $1,100 worth during the previous week. Asked why, he responded, "It's really crazy. I don't even get a rush any more. I've been using it so long I just feel normal when I take it. I'd like to leave it alone, period. But I doubt that I will. It's a habit. . . . I like doing it."[9]

Like Bob, hundreds of thousands of users simply like taking it. I think that fact, unpalatable as it may be, must be taken into account in view of the undisputed need to attract more addicts into treatment. My support of the medical use of heroin has been further influenced by the experience of those British experts who see heroin as a benign drug, and by the fact that no evidence exists that it is any worse or better for the health of the user than methadone. It would seem that the time has now arrived to view heroin as one legitimate component in the future treatment options of American doctors and addicts. If we have succeeded in demystifying the substance, it may be possible to view its use in treatment unemotionally—and to evaluate it by determining the extent to which it might help to bring criminal addicts into normal social functioning.

"You have to realize that we've already given heroin more drama than it deserves," cautioned Dr. Richard Blum, director of the Program in Drug, Crime, and Community Studies at Stanford University. He went on, "But if you want to talk about heroin, it might help some addicts. If our purpose is to lure the social delinquent into a social contract of some sort, then I'm willing to do it. Then if he can be further seduced into conformity, fine. Who cares if it's methadone or heroin? If he wants oranges or cottage cheese, what do I care?"[10]

Blum's rationale for allowing legal heroin in addiction treatment has a ring of eloquent simplicity in an arena often characterized by confusion, embarrassment, and irrationality. Despite all the criticisms of methadone maintenance, there seems no doubt that it attracted a great many addicts into a caring relationship with some members of the helping professions, that it helped to start many addicts on the road to a normal life, and that it also helped to reduce the crime committed by those addicts. It was not so much the special qualities of methadone as the fact that for addicts seeking some form of legal narcotic, this one happened to be available, along with a supportive treatment situation, often dealing with many aspects of life beyond drugs. Everything I have seen and read in England leads me to believe that heroin would improve the American medical menu, that it would encourage more addicts to seek out caring relationships, to start on the road to a normal life, and to reduce their criminal life-styles.

There are both English and American experts who disagree with those conclusions. Several years ago, when the public waters in America were being stirred up with talk of heroin maintenance, Dr. DuPont offered a comprehensive rebuttal at the National Drug Abuse Conference in May 1977:

> Arguments for heroin maintenance generally start from two false premises. The first is that our antiheroin efforts have failed. While I would not claim that we have been completely successful or that our efforts could not be improved upon, our national heroin problem is relatively small—involving less than .2 percent of our population—and by our best indicators it is no longer growing. The second false assumption is that making heroin available in clinics, as we now make methadone available, would "eliminate the profit" from the illegal heroin market. Such clinics in Britain have not taken the profit out of the illegal heroin traffic, and they would not do so here. In order to make heroin unattractive to criminal suppliers, we would have to make heroin as available as we now make aspirin or antihistamines. The idea of heroin for sale in our supermarkets boggles the mind of even the most enthusiastic supporter of heroin maintenance. Nothing less, however, will take the profit out of illegal heroin. On the other hand, I do not think the use of heroin as part of an American drug abuse treatment program would drive patients out of current treatment programs anymore than methadone maintenance has eliminated the demand for drug-free treatment. Neither do I think heroin as a treatment drug has much to offer. Heroin is a short-acting drug which must be taken intravenously several times a day to avoid painful withdrawal symptoms. I will be willing to

think more about heroin maintenance when its proponents—who rarely have any experience with drug abusers or drug abuse treatment—can answer four simple questions:

1. Who is eligible to receive heroin?
2. How much heroin will the treated person be given?
3. How long will the person be permitted to take heroin before he is forced to switch to methadone and/or detoxify?
4. How will take-home heroin be handled?

Of these four questions, the last is the most critical. If there is no take-home heroin, then there is little attraction for the addict and little danger to the community from the use of heroin. The idea of hundreds of addicts fixing in a clinic every day is appalling to me. Imagine the mess and confusion! Take-home heroin—the only alternative—is a completely crazy idea. Try to picture addicts—or for that matter any of us—walking out of a clinic every day with $100 to $200 worth of heroin! How much would be sold? How many overdoses would result from diverted heroin? My point is this: heroin maintenance for the United States fails for purely practical reasons.[11]

The independent and respected *U.S. Journal of Drug and Alcohol Dependence* reported that speech in its June 1977 issue and expressed its agreement in an editorial entitled "Heroin Clinics No Answer." Coeditors Milan Korcok and Gary Seidler observed that the renewed American interest in heroin maintenance had come just "at a time when authorities in the U.K. are acknowledging that governmental clinics are rapidly switching from dispensation of intravenous heroin to oral methadone." As for the United States, "In the rush toward developing a more humane approach to drug use and abuse in society, let's not be too hasty to embrace decriminalization of heroin." Then, significantly and typically: "It's quite possible that the present system of dealing with heroin addicts, as imperfect as it is, may be the best possible." That sentence represents the distilled essence of the dominant thinking of American experts on the overall worth of our system of controlling heroin abuse.[12]

Such opinions dominate practically the full political spectrum of American drug-abuse leadership, from right to centrist to left, from presidents to psychiatrists to policemen to editors. The fact that so many humane and enlightened professionals sincerely believe them explains why proposals for fundamentally new approaches to national narcotics policy face a virtual stone wall of united opposition.

A summary of the answers that might be offered to DuPont and to the *U.S.*

Journal would start with the assertion that while antiheroin efforts have not totally failed, the American heroin situation should be viewed as intolerable and the American system as in need of fundamental change; the British have not abandoned injectable drugs in favor of oral methadone; although the black market is building up there, it is minuscule by American standards, and the growth has been due in part to the adoption of some methods that have a distinctly American tone to them; the idea of heroin for sale in the supermarkets should boggle everybody's mind. While a few responsible scholars and practicing professionals periodically throw up their hands and fairly shout that the only solution is to sell the miserable stuff in stores over the counter, most of them calm down within a short time. There is no serious support for this idea, even though the Drug Abuse Council in its final publication in 1980 listed it, without endorsement, as a possible policy option for the future.

The most sensible approach is to recognize that the much maligned Harrison Act was right on the basic position that narcotics should be restricted to medical uses—and that the venerable liberal interpretations of the ambiguities in the act should finally be adopted in America as they have been in Britain. This would mean that doctors could prescribe any of the legal opiates, including heroin, to addicts within the course of legitimate medical practice.

The definition of legitimate medical practice would include the provision of maintenance doses to addicts. A fuller exposition of that definition would involve coming to grips with the specific questions posed by DuPont. The answers to the four questions he asks require no futuristic schemes or new vast research projects. But the very fact that the director of the National Institute of Drug Abuse, an enlightened psychiatrist, felt compelled to ask them shows the hammerlock that the puritanical approach to narcotic control still has on America's sense of reality. The answers come primarily out of the British experience and would, of course, require amendment of American law.

1. Any person should be eligible to receive heroin by prescription if a doctor has determined that the person is addicted and that the person, now his patient, might be helped by the drug. This answer purposely leaves out the chippers and the occasional heavy users. Accordingly, there will always be a black market, but this limitation is consistent with British practice and with the notion that an addict is a person worthy of receiving medical assistance. Someone someday may figure out how to provide occasional users with legal drugs, but the British have not, and *for now* we should be content to live with this rational and balanced restriction on prescribing.

American doctors, like their British counterparts, will have difficulty determining who is addicted, but that difficulty is nothing new. They have the same problem within existing systems. Before providing methadone for mainte-nance, American doctors must now determine that the person has been an addict *for the previous two years*.[13] I would dispense with the intrusive legal requirement, and with most others like it, and allow the doctors to determine the state of addiction according to medical judgment, as in Britain.

While doctors would gain power, and addicts a great deal of pleasure and comfort, it is important that no addict should be allowed to think he has gained any additional legal rights. If British rules were adopted, American doctors in the future could decide to provide any one of a range of opiates and cocaine to addicts, or none at all. Any addict would be eligible, but none could demand heroin.

How about minors? This seems to be a terribly sensitive issue for Americans. If the medical analogy is followed, the test is not age but a status of addiction. Addicts would be eligible to receive any drug, including heroin, if they were addicted to it. There should be no reason—in a new scheme of logic and law— why a doctor should not prescribe heroin to a ten- or fourteen-year-old if he thought it would help. Remember that some respected English doctors see heroin use as an alternative to schizophrenia.

But would this not open up the possibility that large numbers of impression-able youth would flock to doctors seeking heroin to treat all forms of illnesses, real, imagined, or feigned? Yes, without a doubt; but this would actually rep-resent an advance and an acceptable social trade-off. As I have argued, there are no complete solutions to any major social problem, only the trading off of one group of difficulties for another that might cost less in terms of personal agony and social pathology. Acceptance of the solution that costs less does not mean we should warmly embrace it. Those young people interested in obtaining heroin now may purchase it on the street from vendors who function at the end of a widespread and relatively efficient illegal trade network. Under the pro-posed system, young heroin seekers would have to convince a doctor, as in Britain, of at least two facts: that they were addicted to heroin and that their condition would be helped by having the doctor provide it legally. That would represent a great advance because now they simply have to convince a pusher that they have the funds; that is the only eligibility test on the street.

2. "How much heroin will the treated person be given?" That is a purely American question, with little relevance to British law or medicine. American regulations attempt to define every aspect of drug-abuse treatment. Indeed, any time an American doctor gives out a large quantity of drugs to any patient, addicted or not, he faces the possibility of criminal prosecution for violation of some law. The basic rule should be that the addict will be given enough drugs

to meet his needs for one day. On weekends or on holidays, more may be given to trusted patients.

Almost total responsibility should be placed on attending physicians to administer these basic rules; lawyers, policemen, and government administrators should be kept out of the picture as much as feasible. The response of many doctors will be that it is almost impossible to tell not only if a person is truly addicted but also how much the needed dosage truly is. However, experience on both sides of the Atlantic shows that while the setting of dosages is difficult, it is not impossible. Often patients have to be placed in hospitals and observed for some days under varying dosages before the appropriate dose is discovered, a process called titration. The greatest hurdle will be for American physicians to get their underlying philosophy straight—and to accept the fact that they are not partners in sin or unethical if they prescribe enough of a particular drug to allow a patient to get high.

There may, of course, be a greater danger—that patients will lie about their needs in order to obtain enough heroin both to use and to sell on the black market. Consistent with the philosophy of middle-level expectations espoused here, there is no doubt that a black market will continue and that some heroin patients will obtain extra supplies to sell on that market. It is often the denial of those unpleasant expectations that makes proposals for using heroin to treat addiction sound so unrealistic. But, on balance, the social trade-offs here would be favorable by most measures. As in Britain, American medicinal heroin sold on the illegal market from excess addict supplies would usually be kept in cleaner form and be healthier for users. It would often be cheaper since the original owner had only modest acquisition costs. (Legal heroin should cost only pennies for an average dose.) This purer and cheaper compound would tend to depress the prices on the regular black market. The illicit sale of British medicinal heroin by addicts is often referred to as the "gray" market.

Some English doctors argue that in cases of doubt a bit more rather than a bit less is ethically indicated. The exact needs of a particular patient can never be precisely calibrated, and he may need more than the physician is prepared to believe. If the physician has been deceived, the extra supply does not represent a calamity, but rather a pure and perhaps lower-priced entry in the competitive gray market.

3. "How long will the person be permitted to take heroin before he is forced to switch to methadone and/or detoxify?" In the United States today the answer would be found in a combination of governmental rules and bureaucratic interpretations. After two years, an American doctor must justify keeping an

addict on methadone maintenance. In Britain the length of treatment on any one modality depends on the decision of the doctor in charge of the patient. There is no need, and there may even be great danger, in changing that situation, either in England or in the American system proposed here. In both countries the doctors should be flexible enough to view the ingestion of drugs as presumptively neutral as long as the ingestor is living responsibly. This might mean that a patient could be on heroin for years, and in some cases for life.

Any decision to force an addict off legal heroin should be made on the basis of a clinical judgment by a doctor, not a legal judgment by a lawyer or a law-enforcement judgment by a policeman or prosecutor. This is not to say that medical judgments are always correct. We have seen the criticism that has been made of the collective English medical decision to reduce the use of heroin in addiction treatment. Giving the power to doctors produces not infallibility but rather appropriate accountability and flexibility. English doctors have the power to try a new clinical tack at any time. That power should be given to American doctors: to act on clinical hunches and to adjust them in light of rational criticism and experience.

4. The last and most critical question raised by Dr. DuPont focused on take-home heroin. How would legal heroin be dispensed in actual practice? Now, methadone is usually given out once a day under rigid supervision in a clinic. Nurses are even advised to make the addict talk after ingesting it so that he will have to swallow the medicine and will not be able to walk out with it in his mouth.

DuPont saw two major options for dispensation, as we saw, one "appalling" (allowing hundreds of addicts to fix in a clinic every day) and the other "completely crazy" (take-home heroin). Both British and American medical professionals want, quite understandably, decent working conditions with orderly offices and clinics. We have seen how the British drug dependence clinics were at one time messy and confused and how they are now much neater. But, of course, the streets of some English cities are a bit less orderly these days.

Disorder arises in a clinic not simply because addicts are there to inject drugs, although that is part of the problem. From what I have seen in English and American clinics, the simple concentrated presence of large numbers of addicts, in and of itself, seems to generate disorder. Addicts tend to be immature in their needs and impatient about having them met; at the clinics they are in the presence of the authority figures who both meet those needs and put limits on their gratification. A certain level of disorder is inevitable in such situations.

At the present time in America, there are no injecting addicts in clinics

because federal regulations prohibit the dispensation of methadone in inject-
→ able form, and heroin is illegal. Addicts who inject drugs now do so in their
homes, in streets and alleys, or in establishments known as shooting galleries.
The idea of several hundred thousand addicts fixing every day with illegal
heroin in those circumstances should be appalling to the entire society.

The realistic trade-off that must be sought is to get as many injecting addicts
as possible into doctors' offices and clinics, so that they can enter into some
form of caring relationship with a physician and with other treatment professionals. If heroin is to be prescribed legally, there is no doubt that it will be
more practical for addicts to have take-home privileges than to come in to the
clinic several times a day to inject their medicine. In any event, the presence of
large numbers of addicts, even if they visit the doctor only once every two
weeks, will create a great deal of tension and disorder.

That is precisely the result we should be seeking. We will have traded off
some of the tension and disorder on our streets and in our homes for more of
the same in clinics and doctors' offices. There might also be less in police
stations and jails. Many American doctors will consider this unfair. However,
along with more social and clinical responsibility, the proposed system would
give the medical profession even more power, more freedom, and perhaps more
money. While some aspects of the new responsibility might well involve tense
and difficult problems in the work place, no group is better equipped to handle
such problems than the medical profession. In time, moreover, with patience
and with the application of new approaches, it is quite possible that the disorder
created by the initial onslaught of new addicts will be brought under control.
But in the first few years the litmus test of the success of the new American
system, as with the reinvigoration of the British system, will be the increased
presence of large numbers of demanding, troublesome fixing addicts in doctors'
offices and drug treatment clinics.

And now directly to the answer on take-home heroin—as in England, the
law should allow doctors to determine who should get take-home heroin,
when, and how much. In most other respects, too, the English practices might
→ be followed. Usually, as we have seen, fourteen prescriptions are mailed to a
chemist's shop; the addict must appear once a day to get his drugs. He sees the
doctor every fourteen days. Any doctor can vary that procedure to meet the
perceived needs of the situation. Of course, any medical professional who encounters a new addict, as we have seen, is required to inform the national
government Home Office of the name and address of the person along with full
details of his condition and the drugs prescribed. Such a report by name and

address is not now required in the United States but it should be, so as to control the tendency of some addict-patients to seek drugs from several doctors. Even if probable strong opposition—based primarily on the confidentiality of the doctor-patient relationship—were overcome and such a system of national notification were established, there is no doubt that some addicts would still manage to patronize more than one doctor, that many would obtain excess supplies through one ruse or another, that some of this "legal" pure heroin would be sold illegally on the streets, and that some overdoses would occur.

But, on balance, how would the social trade-offs here work out? If at the time this system is put into operation we have adopted the major elements of the British approach, then we would have rejected the numerous appeals for experimental, limited programs in America. This would mean that within a short time, many thousands of addicts would be obtaining a whole range of narcotics legally from pharmacies all over the country. At that point, take-home heroin and other narcotics would have become legal in the United States. Some advocates of the move will hail this as the ultimate solution to the heroin problem, the black market, and related crime. Opponents will see it as the ultimate surrender, the arrival of the modern apocalypse. In fact, it would signal neither.

Take-home heroin would be a conservative, middle-level policy step creating middle-level advances in reducing the destructiveness of the heroin problem; but those advances might make a difference to a great many ordinary people. Most of the many addicts receiving adequate doses of heroin legally from doctors would no longer be purchasing drugs in the black market, nor would they be committing crimes in order to obtain money to buy illegal drugs. Three categories of people, however, would continue to purchase drugs on the illicit market: first, chippers; second, addicts in treatment who are not receiving the type or quantity of drugs they want legally from doctors; and third, addicts who, for one reason or another, do not want to enter a treatment program. To them, the "legal" addicts' excess supplies of heroin would continue to have market value. Therefore, those advocates of legalized drugs for addicts who believe this proposal will cause the illegal market to disappear are mistaken.

But many legal drugs of all varieties would now be in the gray market. The demand would be soft, in economic terms, and the price moderate. It is highly likely, therefore, that we would be trading a virulent and violent black market for a gray market of middling proportions. Crime by addicts might well drop because heroin and other drugs would cost less on the street, and each purchase might be cleaner and more potent. If pushed to the wall because of a temporary downturn in illicit supply, addicts could turn to the doctor rather than the gun. Take-home heroin admittedly would not provide a complete solution to the problem of heroin abuse, but is it a "completely crazy" idea?

III

In the more relaxed legal-medical atmosphere of the future, innovative members of the helping professions, especially physicians, will be encouraged to rethink other fundamental clinical concepts. That atmosphere may even allow the strong of heart and mind to reexamine the meaning of such terms as "addiction-as-a-disease" and "heroin maintenance."

The disease concept of addiction has been, in its season, a wonderfully humane idea. In practical terms, it often meant that in a choice between letting doctors or policemen handle addicts, society voted for the helping profession. But although that civilized concept was expressed—that addiction was a disease rather than a crime—it has provided absolutely no guidance to the helpers, to the doctors, nurses, and social workers, or to involved clergymen and families of addicts. As Dr. Connell said in London, there simply is no specific treatment for drug abuse. And reflecting on her early years in St. Clement's clinic, Dr. Margaret Tripp observed to Judson, "When we started, we were calling them sick. . . . But after a time, when I knew them, I wasn't calling them anything. I gave up being a headshrinker with these guys almost immediately. . . . The addicts themselves are against being labeled sick. . . . The main reason I finally left . . . was that to perpetuate my job I'd have had to create work, to go on labeling people sick who had not yet perceived themselves that way."[14]

Nevertheless, for decades the rallying cry of those who believed in humane treatment for addicts was that the condition was a disease. Even the Supreme Court has given it that kindly label. But what kind of disease? Ah, there's the rub! The central part of the latest World Health Organization definition of drug *dependence* (no longer *addiction*) is that it is a "state . . . characterized by . . . a compulsion to take the drug on a continuous or periodic basis in order to experience its psychic effects." In other words, the disease of drug dependence is defined by the leading experts in the world as, essentially, an irresistible urge to take drugs continually. This does not seem to offer much help to a clinician seeking to provide a specific treatment based on that general definition or to a policymaker attempting to formulate a better overall societal response.

In the 1960s Dole and Nyswander fleshed out their definition of this disease by calling it a metabolic disorder, like diabetes; this was understandable, and it provided the basis for a specific medical treatment and for a broader social policy. But, as some American doctors soon pointed out, the Dole-Nyswander analogy did not seem to be based on reality. Diabetes is a recognizable organic condition, characterized by insufficient production of the natural chemical insulin by the pancreas. There is no known cure for this disease although medical science has made a great deal of progress in dealing with the related medical problems of diabetics and thus prolonging their life expectancy. One method, not the only one, of dealing with the disease is to provide regular injections— maintenance doses—of insulin. A diabetic's emotions and mood, however, have no impact on how the insulin works in his body. This nonpsychoactive drug works in the same way in almost all cases, no matter what the recipient thinks about it. If the patient is one of those whose treatment depends on the drug, failure to take it in the regular prescribed dosage could, and often does, result in a coma and eventually death.

Opiates, as we well know, are psychoactive drugs. Such drugs affect both the mind and the body. And the way in which such drugs work may be affected by "set" and "setting"—by the mood of the taker and the expectations of those around him. Some addicts believe they cannot live without the drugs; their doctors believe they may be right; and the diabetes-insulin analogy seems to apply in those cases. But there have been numerous instances in which addicts took heroin for years and then matured to the point where they became fed up with the whole addiction game and simply stopped taking the drug. Such cases of the maturing-out of an addiction have been well documented for all narcotics. When the addicts stopped taking the drug, there was probably acute discomfort, but no coma and no death. In short, the addicts' minds and emotions controlled their use of the drug; when they became strong, or mature, enough to do so, they "cured" themselves. No diabetic can make his pancreas produce more insulin and cure himself. Thus, the diabetic-insulin analogy is humane but does not help us to understand the convoluted course of heroin addiction or its treatment.[15]

Experts will want to work out a more useful definition of drug addiction within the context of the more open system envisioned here. One possibility would be: "a chronic condition of unknown causation and treatment, characterized by compulsive drug taking and often accompanied by a wide variety of psychiatric and organic diseases." Such a definition, or one close to it, would have the advantage of honesty, humility, and utility. It would make clear that doctors do not really know what the causes of the core condition (repeated drug taking) are or how to cure it, but that they are uniquely qualified to treat many of its attendant ills, which are clearly recognizable as diseases, some of them treatable.[16] Recreational addicts, for example, have a high incidence of serum hepatitis from dirty needles. The death rate among nontherapeutic addicts in Britain due to this disease and to overdoses and suicides, Dr. Bewley reported in 1968, was twenty-eight times that of the general population.[17] Dr. Beckett reported a high incidence of depression among his addict-patients, a difficult condition to treat but nevertheless a recognizable mental illness. While there is no such thing as an addictive personality, addicts often suffer from a whole catalog of mental diseases. Keeping addicts physically and mentally healthy is a formidable task, therefore, but one for which doctors are qualified. In many cases doctors would seek to surround the taking of narcotics—the only universally accepted symptom of this "disease"—with a human body otherwise upgraded significantly in physical and mental health.

When a doctor turns from the more traditional treatment of relatively clearly defined diseases in addicts and commences to prescribe steady doses of drugs, his action can no longer be viewed, if the above arguments are accepted, as intended to stabilize a metabolic condition due to organic disease. Rather, it must now be seen as a method that combines relieving anxiety, reducing pain, providing emotional stability (for some patients), creating a chemical high, and directing attention away from the procurement of drugs so that the patient can focus his energies on creating a socially useful life. Drugs fit, therefore, into a system of comprehensive care for those addicts presenting themselves for treatment.

In order to facilitate communication, I have allowed the conventional phrase "heroin maintenance" to be used to describe the giving of drugs in such treatment, but at this point I would like to argue that it is a terribly misleading formulation and that we might give some consideration to a more accurate replacement, such as "heroin therapy," "appropriate heroin therapy," or "temporary heroin therapy." My reasons for suggesting these changes are in part symbolic and in part substantive. The term "heroin maintenance" suggests a system under which a person might walk into a clinic, ask for heroin, and upon being determined to be addicted, be given heroin virtually forever—which might imply a condition of almost complete surrender on the part of the doctor. Except in a small number of cases, this has not occurred in England. Even where it has, I suspect that the doctors involved had simply been worn down by the persistent demands of addicts and had forgotten the still valid clinical guidance given by the Rolleston Committee in 1926: "It should not . . . be too lightly assumed in any case, however unpromising it may appear to be at first sight, that an irreducible minimum of the drug has been reached which cannot be withdrawn and which, therefore, must be continued indefinitely. Though the first attempt entirely to free a patient from his drug may be a failure, a subsequent one may be successful."

Therefore, even in those cases in which the prolonged administration of a drug, including heroin, was necessary to allow the patient to function in a relatively normal fashion, the posture of the physician was not abject surrender; it was rather one of providing the medicine as a temporary crutch while at the same time encouraging the patient to throw the crutch away as soon as he was emotionally strong enough. Viewing prescribed heroin as temporary provides the symbolic hope that the addict himself might decide to drop his habit.

It is to be expected that under such a program of comprehensive care many addicts will go off drugs and then go on again. Such recurrences should not be viewed as failures but rather as expected behavior in a chronic condition for which there is no known cure. Addicts should be both reassured that they can come back to the doctor for their drugs and told—again and again—that they do not have to take drugs at all but may instead go into a detoxification program and psychotherapy or group counseling for support while they review their habits. They must also be advised that they have a right not to be treated, a right not to take any drugs from a doctor, a right not to go into psychotherapy, and thus a right to risk whatever social penalties may result. But the ideal for any modern society should be the availability of a complete range of treatment services for those addicts who want to take advantage of them—temporary heroin therapy, temporary methadone therapy, therapy with any drug that has a low risk of causing organic damage, psychiatric treatment, therapeutic community, detoxification, religious guidance, and meditation, as well as any other types of assistance and support that might be devised in the future. Lacking the availability of legal heroin, however, at least at the start of the treatment process, most heroin addicts will not seek medical assistance at all.

The feasibility of temporary heroin therapy runs counter to the current conventional wisdom about the permanent nature of drug taking among heroin addicts, but it does square with the habits of many users. Addicts change drugs and treatments. Heroin addiction occurs primarily in males in their twenties and early thirties. If they are given heroin by doctors during those periods of their lives, if they are given support in other aspects of their existence, more of them will come into treatment, more will stay over the years, and many if not most will mature out of their habits by age thirty-five. Even in a worst-case scenario, in which hundreds of thousands of heroin addicts stubbornly persist in demanding legal heroin from doctors, decade after decade, they would be healthier addicts because they would be under medical and mental health care—however much doctors might be repelled by their habits.

IV

The habits of much of this future medical caseload are now often dealt with by the police, in America as in many other countries. The police, however, have received relatively little attention in this book, because I believe the future lies in building up the treatment and prevention sides of the social equation. But the police have a vital role to play in the drug arena. After all, the nonmedical use of drugs remains outside the pale of the law. I have advocated expanding these boundaries, but however broad they become, there will always be some who will violate them. For the present, the police are the hapless people in the middle, caught between a vast worldwide hunger for drugs, on the one hand, and a worldwide pattern of prohibition laws, on the other.

While nations are groping toward more enlightened national legal and medical policies regarding drug abuse, their police officers must enforce existing laws. Some middle ground must be found that recognizes current realities and at the same time reduces the high risk of personal harm frequently created by existing tough law-enforcement practices—for the citizenry in general and also for the officers who must carry them out. Law-enforcement agencies must review those practices that cause the most difficulty, with particular attention to undercover work, to the use of police officers or paid informers to purchase drugs, and to excessive use of search-and-arrest powers in the pursuit of drug offenses. (It is to be noted that I have taken neither the ultraliberal position that law enforcement is to blame for all of society's drug-abuse problems nor the utopian view that law enforcement should simply depart the field and all will be well.)

The idea of reducing undercover work, especially the classic "buy and bust" (the use of police officers to buy drugs and then arrest the seller), must seem to many police leaders to signal the end of effective police work in narcotics. But the use of such entrapment practices is prohibited by law in England, where the effectiveness of the police seems reasonable. In America the buy-and-bust routine is at the very center of police narcotics work and, along with the related use of informers, has been the subject of a vast amount of litigation and judicial criticism. It may be an understatement to say that American police narcotics work is the most intrusive into individual liberty and the most dangerous of any aspect of law enforcement. And yet not a single law must be changed to allow the police to drastically limit these practices at once. The result may well be a vast reduction in drug-law arrests and convictions—balanced by a concomitant reduction in injuries to officers and intrusions into the lives and rights of citizens.

As the vision of the future medical model of drug-abuse control comes into being, innovative police leaders and researchers will have to work out new concepts of drug-law enforcement. I offer the following thoughts, in an attempt to ease the burden of those who work in law enforcement:

1. Remember the ancient maxim that was evolved to guide physicians: *nihil nocere*—do no harm. This means that police leaders should use their discretion to keep subordinate officers out of dangerous situations except where some major social good or the saving of life might result. Line officers should remember the same maxim when dealing with citizens. All police should be made aware that drugs are not the devil and that drug-law enforcement is not a crusade.

2. The definition of the boundaries of law enforcement should vary from community to community, from nation to nation, from culture to culture. Police often follow this guideline now but do not like to admit it. In countries with a past history of opium smoking, for example, it is to be hoped that the police will work out some compromise with addicted smokers—a compromise that might not be acceptable in a Western nation. The English police have evolved some approaches worthy of study in this context—such as the practice of assuming that if an addict on the rolls of a clinic is found on the street with heroin in his possession, the drugs are probably legal.

3. Police everywhere should stop taking on the drug problem as if it were its exclusive province. Police organizations should call for the active involvement of other professions, especially medicine. In America and other countries many doctors have managed to develop almost exclusively middle- and upper-class practices in part by shuffling off to other agencies and professions matters that might well be handled within their jurisdiction. The police and the entire criminal-justice network must become aware that they are playing into this game, which allows the medical profession to reap great rewards without paying its full social dues. The police should learn a new maxim: in case of drug abuse, call a doctor, not a policeman.

V

This vision for the future, indeed this entire work, may be criticized because it does not deal with all the hidden politics of heroin or with root causes of addiction. After almost a decade of study, however, I have found none of the conspiracy theories, none of the grand theories of causation, and none of the related utopian solutions to be adequately borne out by the facts.

There is no convincing support for the Epstein-Silberman theory that the

Nixon administration invented the heroin epidemic of the late 1960s. Although Alfred McCoy's book *The Politics of Heroin in Southeast Asia* (1972) made a major impact on the liberal community, it failed to prove its major thesis: that American foreign policy must bear a major part of the blame for the international heroin trade and also for the creation of so many American addicts.[18] In the same vein are books that put the blame on something indigenous to American society. *The Second Opium War*, for example, by the French writers Catherine Lamour and Michel R. Lamberti, also published in 1972, claimed that "the cause of the evil is essentially indigenous, . . . the inevitable by-product of a decadent capitalist system which must be called in question in its entirety." The capitalists are portrayed as racists who use their power to keep nonwhites subjugated and so miserable that even the small amount of money they have will be squandered on drugs to help them endure their oppressed status.[19] Some American writers, black and white, say virtually the same thing.

The summer 1979 newsletter of the Institute for the Study of Drug Dependence in London, a politically middle-of-the-road organization, reviewed, with apparent favor, studies of the Republic of China's social-revolutionary methods to eradicate opiate addiction: denouncing addiction as "anti-social and unhealthy," declaring that "the enemy in the antiopium campaign is a class enemy," organizing small-group controls on addicts, and the "execution of small numbers of unreformed addicts and traffickers." Applied to the United States, the ISDD writes, studies of China suggest it is essential to recognize the political basis of addiction. The United States may have to decide whether it wants "to seek solutions through extending institutional supports available within a valued social structure, or to seek radical transformation of the social structure itself." In that atmosphere, talk of, for example, a medical approach to addiction control does not get at essential causes, at what may be "a permanent problem for U.S. society."[20]

There is a homey ring to these grand assertions, even though many of them come from foreign pens. There may even be some truth in them. The difficulty is in finding *practical* truth that might help us to deal rationally with current social problems. We can all support the need to transform society and to deal with fundamental inequities, but major social reform should be seen as something good in and of itself and not as the *only* answer to crime, harmful deviance, and drug abuse. As Norval Morris wrote in regard to prison reform, "the radical utopian position . . . damning all reformist efforts, and insisting that we concentrate only on the restructuring of society required for social equity, is the ultimate 'cop-out.' It is an abnegation of responsibility."[21] Moreover, none of the conspirational or grand social theorists can explain why any individual, or large group of people, takes heroin. None of the utopian solutions, including a revolutionary transformation of society, offers any demonstrable hope for large-scale cures—at least nothing acceptable within a humane society.

My major criticisms of present American policy are that it criminalized heroin, converted addicts into criminals, and proselytized this repressive policy to the world. This is a far cry from saying that the policy created addicts or somehow conspired to induce people to stick needles filled with heroin into their arms, as either an antiblack plot or a capitalist plot—or that the capitalist structure of American society created addicts. Such theories are for the most part fairy tales, in the same league as placing the blame for the creation of heroin addicts on original sin, the papacy, the All England Lawn Tennis and Croquet Club, or Henry Anslinger's *bête noire*, Red China.

My belief is that the reason people use drugs "recreationally" is that they like what the substances do to their minds, their moods, and their bodies. Any more sophisticated explanation is beyond the current capability of the assembled learned disciplines of the world. Our inability to ferret out root causes does not mean that we are functionally ignorant when it comes to formulating social, treatment, and legal responses to drug use and abuse. To the contrary, I hold that excessive concern with ultimate etiologics in matters of human conduct is wasteful for people concerned with formulating practical programs and should be left where it properly belongs, with the utopians and theologians.

The heroin solution proposed here is a democratic, realistic, humble solution. It starts from today. It admits that there is no explainable cause and no complete cure—only amelioration, moderation, and middle-level expectations. It says that we can reduce police intrusion into the lives of free citizens and into medical practice; we can bring addicts into a varied system of medical, caring treatment; we can approach drug use by anyone calmly. By these moderate measures, our hope, but not our guaranteed promise, would be that the virulence of the overall problem will be reduced to tolerable levels.

VI

While I have just roundly criticized the radical utopians, some critics will argue that much of what I have proposed here deserves that label. Even I am prepared to admit that my final proposal, which follows, fits into that category, but it may also help us to come to grips with a crucial fact: approximately nine out of ten heroin users are not addicts. Our current system of law, medicine, and ethics sets up the abstinent person as the ideal and is just evolving a humane approach to the addict. But our philosophy for the future must take into account the whole range of human approaches to drug use, states of being, consciousness, and altered states of consciousness.

The system envisioned here can be summed up in four principles: (1) Every person should use as few psychoactive substances as possible in normal daily life. (2) Doctors should be legally empowered to prescribe heroin and all other opiates to the organically ill and the addicted. (3) Any interested person should be helped to use drugs in socially beneficial ways. (4) A new science of higher consciousness should be created that would teach the accomplishment of highs without drugs.

On their face these recommendations may seem contradictory. But in their essential human meanings they are consistent. These notions are ancient and have their roots in mystical beliefs, in aspects of all major religions, and in many modern customs and seemingly new religions. The range of alternatives to the drug experience today is wide: transcendental meditation, Zen Buddhism, yoga, and even jogging. All these activities, and many more, offer the possibility of mood alteration and a high without drugs. Sometimes the activities blend together—there are runners who talk of getting into the Zen of jogging. These are ideal states, therefore, and are to be seen as the way of the future although they have secure and healthy roots in the past.

For many people, however, they remain simply unattainable dreams. Such people believe they need drugs either to stay "normal" or to obtain highs or both. Others believe that while using drugs they attain intellectual and spiritual insights that are impossible to attain without them. As Andrew Weil urges us, the essence of our approach to these claims must be one of tolerance and understanding. It must not be one of arrogance and absolutism, as dominant social policy is now. There must be room in all civilized societies for people who believe in the use of *no* drugs and for those who believe positively in the use of drugs. The rich, the powerful, and the deviant and criminal now use the drugs they want whether they are legal or not. A future, more ingenious legal and medical system will work out ways for such experiences to be more accepted and more open. But at all times, I submit, we must view drug use as an inferior way of achieving human ends, as usually temporary, and as an activity to be superseded whenever possible by the more natural power of the human soul.

Nevertheless, the deviants in any modern society, in statistical terms, are those who take no drugs. National laws and social policies, therefore, must recognize that millions of people throughout the world will continue to use licit and illicit psychoactive drugs and that millions will become dependent on them. Future laws and policies must also allow practices that help users create as little social harm as possible (one of the main subjects of this book) and obtain as much positive benefit as possible (the threshold of a vast new subject).

I am more concerned with the first of these goals—preventing social harm. The very idea of teaching a potential user the positive recreational (not medical) benefits of heroin or even caffeine is ethically repugnant to me. But that is a personal feeling. What is repugnant to me may rationally be tolerated by the law—and that act of toleration may well be good for the society as a whole and for many individual citizens.

The path to the future—beyond dealing with addicts—may have to involve teaching people how to use drugs, including heroin, under controlled circumstances. In 1976 Dr. Norman Zinberg, of the Harvard Medical School, and researcher Leon G. Hunt recommended such experiments with heroin. They recognized that this was a "revolutionary approach" but argued that it faced the reality that most people who used heroin were chippers, not addicts, and that many of these occasional users purposely developed rituals of heroin use so as to enjoy the drug without becoming addicted.[22] It is conceivable, therefore, that future clinics, under an even more liberal legal structure than is recommended here, may function along the lines of the once unthinkable Masters and Johnson sex-therapy clinics—teaching people not how to abstain from partaking of the forbidden fruit but rather how to enjoy it without being harmed.

VII

Finally, here are the ten major findings and recommendations of this study.

1. *The problem of heroin addiction has taken on the dimensions of a worldwide epidemic and is worsening.* The same is true of other forms of drug abuse. The entire scene is far worse than when I started this inquiry in the early 1970s; more countries are involved, and in the countries already involved, heroin abuse has spread to all classes of society.

2. *Despite the growth of the problem, social policy cannot regress to the antiopium stone age. We must distinguish, moreover, between the encouragement of drug-free personal life-styles and the imposition of a prohibitionist public policy.* Nothing is wrong and much is right about trying to ban all drugs, legal or illegal, from one's own life and from that of one's family; everything is wrong with trying to impose such a personal philosophy on the rest of society or the world. That has been the major mistake of American (indeed, Western) policy in this century. The nonmedical use of drugs has increased dramatically despite a worldwide pattern of legal prohibition on such use. The gap between the laws, on the one

hand, and the actual behavior of millions of people, on the other, must be bridged in a rational and compassionate fashion.

3. *Some of the most compassionate bridges ever built over the chasm between addiction control policy and individual human needs were those of the British system during the Rolleston era and American counterparts such as the Shreveport clinic.* Rolleston and Shreveport, both middle-level compromises, accepted the reality of laws restricting many drugs to medical uses and of the existence of multitudes of people who were quite eager to violate those laws. They provided a way for those who sought help to come in out of the criminal cold into the warmer arms of legitimate medical practice. This did not satisfy the ultraliberals, who wanted all drugs to continue to be freely available to anyone with the purchase price; nor did it satisfy the ultraconservatives, who viewed providing drugs to addicts purely to satisfy their cravings as beyond the bounds of legitimate medical practice. In the actual field of social and human conflict, Rolleston and Shreveport worked. Those who deny this powerful reality, and there are many who do, are simply mistaken.

4. *In this context, medical heroin for addicts makes eminent good sense.* And only in this context. Heroin is important in dealing with heroin addicts because it is their drug of choice, and many of them must have the drug in order to stay in treatment and out of agony. In and of itself, however, medical heroin is not *the* solution to the worldwide heroin addiction epidemic.

5. *There is no reliable scientific evidence that heroin propels its users to criminal activity or causes organic damage.* Putting aside the problem of addiction, the chemical heroin seems almost a neutral or benign substance. Taken in stable, moderate doses, it does not seem to cause organic injury, as does alcohol over time, nor does it seem to push people into crime by making them aggressive, as do alcohol and PCP and amphetamines. At the same time, the evidence seems compelling that once a person is addicted to heroin, he has a greater tendency to become involved in criminal activity of all kinds—more and more of it, these days, violent. This increased crime is caused mainly by the legal prohibition of the drug rather than by its pharmacological impact.

6. *There is no evidence that heroin is an ineffective medicine, nor unequivocal scientific proof that it is a better analgesic than, say, morphine.* Ever so slowly, the law enforcement and medical establishments are moving toward acceptance of heroin as a medicine. As this book was being brought to a close, their position had become this: that while heroin was certainly a medicine, it was no better than others currently available, and that its bad name and its possible use by addicts made it an undesirable substance to have in ordinary American medicine. Nevertheless, this position provided evidence that a historical process was

commencing: heroin was slowly being divested of its demonic qualities. At the same time, its heroic qualities could not be demonstrated by scientific means; those had to be found in the perceptions of patients who were provided with it in order to ease the agony of organic pain or the pressures of addiction. Because some patients believe they may be helped greatly by the medicine, and because there is no indication that, when properly administered, heroin causes harm, the current legal prohibition should be repealed.

7. *Heroin should be made available, by new laws or court decisions, to all patients under the care of a doctor, not only to the terminally ill.* That part of the heroin legalization movement in America which focuses only on the terminally ill is well intentioned but misguided. The Madigan Bill, for example, introduced into Congress in May 1980, would unwittingly produce both ghoulish and impractical results. This bill would require a certification that the patients were indeed dying; once so certified, they could get their heroin. Most terminal cancer patients need no powerful narcotics at all; many burn patients need them desperately. Is a lung cancer patient more worthy of help than a cardiac patient—especially when the evidence is strong that personal habits contributed to the onset of the disease in both instances? When is a cancer patient "terminal"? Such questions have no easy answers and show the ethical impossibility of proposals to make heroin available *only* to the terminally ill. The choice of this medicine or another must be made only by the patient (or the relatives, where necessary) and the doctor on the basis of intimate and private discussions.

8. *Federal and state laws should be pulled back to the perimeters of the addiction problem. Doctors and other members of the helping professions should be encouraged to move, en masse, back into the center arena, where one of the primary functions of the guardians of the law will be to protect the helpers, not harass them.* The legalization of drugs for addicts, where appropriate and necessary, is important. Even more important is the creation of a legal structure and related enforcement practices that, together, assure doctors and other treaters that the law will allow them to try every rational approach, from temporary heroin therapy to traditional psychotherapy, oral methadone, Zen Buddhism, transcendental meditation, and opium. In cases where there is some doubt as to the good intentions of the treaters, the issue of criminal intent should be resolved in their favor. Only where the most extreme behavior takes place, clearly violating the new boundaries of legitimate medical practice, should the powers of the law be invoked.

For America, and for other countries following its lead, these may be the most important set of reforms for the immediate future. This legal structure does not mandate the use of one drug as opposed to another, or one modality exclusively, to treat addiction. Rather, it recognizes the need for healers to be allowed to heal as the situation demands, to pursue that impossible balance of treatment that will vary from patient to patient, from community to community, from time to time. If the criminal law moves back, far back, then a humane sense of rational and flexible treatment should take its place.

9. *Social policy in the future should devise methods to help people both to use drugs in beneficial ways and to create a new ethos of higher consciousness that goes beyond drugs.* If the previous recommendation was the most important, then this one is the most difficult. The task of creating rational legal and medical policies toward *addicts* is herculean; to create such policies in regard to *recreational users* and in regard to the related beneficial use of potentially addicting drugs may be beyond even the powers of the gods. This task may not be accomplished within our lifetimes. But the basic conceptual groundwork should be laid. More immediate and practical efforts, however, should focus on policy toward the addicted.

10. *The major thrust toward reform must come from coordinated national, as well as multinational, legal and political action.* This is not to suggest that scientific research and academic conferences should cease. It is to say, rather, that the basic technical issues have changed very little in decades. The major practical impact, during those years, has been made by ideology, political action, and legal enactments. Most objective scientific research has had little practical effect. In the face of growing fears about drug use and abuse, it is time for concerted action. To those who agree, here are a few brief suggestions for such action.

In Britain
- Mount a campaign to widen the involvement of private doctors in addiction treatment and also to revive some of the clinical practices of the Rolleston era, especially the more liberal medical dispensation of heroin and cocaine to addicts. This may be accomplished by amending the Misuse of Drugs Act or simply by having the home secretary issue more licenses to physicians to dispense those "restricted drugs" to addicts.
- Launch organized political-medical efforts to reduce the dominance of the drug-dependence clinics.

In America
- Public-spirited lawyers should take the lead in developing a legal assault on the restrictive legal control of medical practice in regard to opiates and addiction treatment. Enlightened physicians and other healing professionals should provide technical support for this legal reform effort.

- In some cases, legislative reform proposals will make practical sense. But in most matters, especially in regard to heroin and addiction treatment, the legislative route to reform may fall victim to popular prejudices. As in the civil rights efforts of a generation ago, the only realistic route may be court action.
- Court action must be taken to free up heroin for widespread use in medicine, either by placing it in Schedule II of the Controlled Substances Act of 1970 or by having it placed, like methadone, in a special investigational category for widespread experimentation.
- Such lawsuits must also be instituted to make any narcotic and cocaine available for use in treatment, unless it has been shown that the drug is organically harmful.
- The detailed intrusion of federal laws and administrative regulations into the treatment of addiction must be fought at every turn by court action so as to open up working room for innovative physicians—and thus to expand along British lines the concept of legitimate medical practice.

In Other Countries
- Drug control systems must be developed—with the prodding of lawsuits, where necessary—that fit the cultural contours of each nation. If, however, foreign models are needed, they should be sought in the Shreveport clinic of 1919–23 in America, the Rolleston era up to 1968 in Britain, and the American system we here dream about.

NOTES

PREFACE

1. Edward M. Brecher and the Editors of *Consumer Reports, Licit and Illicit Drugs* (Boston: Little, Brown, 1972), p. xi; hereinafter cited as Brecher.

2. For a detailed exposition of the philosophy of Dr. Weil, a Harvard-trained physician, see Andrew Weil, *The Natural Mind: A New Way of Looking at Drugs and the Higher Consciousness* (Boston: Houghton Mifflin, 1972); hereinafter cited as Weil.

3. For an excellent review of significant events in the drug-abuse field from the late 1960s to the late 1970s, including funding trends, see Robert L. DuPont, "The Drug Abuse Decade," *Journal of Drug Issues* 8 (Spring 1978), p. 173. One of the most authoritative histories of events in American drug-abuse control from around the turn of the century to the 1930s is David F. Musto, M.D., *The American Disease: Origins of Narcotic Control* (New Haven: Yale University Press, 1973); hereinafter cited as Musto 1973.

4. Brecher has already been cited. The citations for the other books are as follows: Edwin M. Schur, *Narcotic Addiction in Britain and America: The Impact of Public Policy* (Bloomington: Indiana University Press, 1962); hereinafter cited as Schur. Alfred R. Lindesmith, *The Addict and the Law* (New York: Vintage Books, 1965); hereinafter cited as Lindesmith. Rufus King, *The Drug Hang-up* (New York: Norton, 1972); hereinafter cited as King. Horace Freeland Judson, *Heroin Addiction in Britain: What Americans Can Learn from the English Experience* (New York: Harcourt Brace Jovanovich, 1974); hereinafter cited as Judson.

CHAPTER 1

1. Peter G. Bourne, "The New International Heroin Trade," *Addictions* (Summer 1976), p. 32.

2. Fellows of the Drug Abuse Council, "A Statement of Concerns" (Washington, D.C., 1973); mimeographed. Seven of the nine fellows signed the statement; David Musto was one of those who did not.

3. Edward Jay Epstein, *Agency of Fear: Opiates and Political Power in America* (New York: Putnam's, 1977); hereinafter cited as Epstein 1977.

4. Charles E. Silberman, *Criminal Violence, Criminal Justice* (New York: Random House, 1978), pp. 175–76; hereinafter cited as Silberman.

5. Early in my research, I decided not to become heavily involved in seeking to evaluate methods for determining the size and growth of the American heroin addict population. Those who wish to pursue this line of inquiry might start with Leon Gibson Hunt, *Heroin Epidemics: A Quantitative Study of Current Empirical Data* (Washington, D.C.: The Drug Abuse Council, Inc., May, 1973). I have accepted the figure of 500,000 heroin addicts as a working compromise because (1) it did not seem outrageous on the basis of many studies and pieces of information I have encountered, and (2) several federal officials whose judgment I respect have told me in interviews that they guessed this *might* be close to the truth. In 1978, moveover, the Carter White House Office of Drug Abuse Policy, headed by Dr. Peter G. Bourne, stated, "It is estimated that at any one time there are 500,000 daily heroin users." The report added that "there may be as many as 4,000,000 who have used heroin during the preceding year." To be conservative, the White House study assumed that on any given day "there are 1,500,000 less-than-daily heroin users" (Office of Drug Abuse Policy, *1978 Annual Report* [Washington, D.C.: U.S. Government Printing Office, hereinafter referred to as GPO], 1978, p. 59).

A 1975 report from the Ford White House stated, "In 1965, an epidemic of heroin use began in the United States. New use (or incidence) increased by a factor of 10 in less than seven years" (The Domestic Council Drug Abuse Task Force, *White Paper on Drug Abuse* [GPO, 1975], p. 14, hereinafter cited as *White Paper*). This task force refused to make a precise estimate of the number of heroin addicts. Others have done so, however, as we have already seen. On the basis of estimates of the Federal Bureau of Narcotics and the National Institute of Mental Health, Brecher (p. 62) placed the number of "opiate addicts" in 1971 between 250,000 and 315,000. After consulting the successor agency to the FBN, the Bureau of Narcotics and Dangerous Drugs, Judson (p. 11) reported that in January 1973 there were an estimated 626,000 "heroin addicts" in the United States. After consulting the successor agency to BNDD, the Drug Enforcement Administration, I was told that there were an estimated 725,000 "narcotic addicts and abusers" in the United States in 1975 (Joseph A. Greenwood, "Estimates of U.S. Narcotics Abusers," unpublished memorandum [Washington, D.C.: Drug Enforcement Agency, 1975]).

In February 1977 a House Committee headed by Congressman Lester L. Wolff (D-NY) stated in a report that "we have more than 800,000 heroin addicts" (*Interim Report of the Select Committee on Narcotics Abuse and Control* [GPO, 1977], p. 52).

Another writer who studied the early years of the Nixon administration came to the opposite conclusion from Epstein but subjected the federal government to equally harsh criticism for *under-estimating* the problem: "In 1971 the government was still churning out great reams of material on the dangers of marijuana and LSD, while at the same time telling us that there were '100,000 to 200,000 heroin addicts in the country' . . . when the actual figure was probably close to 750,000" (Richard Ashley, *Heroin: The Myths and the Facts* [New York: St. Martin's, 1972], p. ix; hereinafter cited as Ashley).

All these estimates or none of them may be accurate, depending on who is being counted and the sources and methods of calculation. I gladly leave this briar patch to others.

6. U.S. Department of Justice, *FBI Uniform Crime Reports* (GPO, 1977), p. 7. U.S. Department of Transportation, "News," November 21, 1979, p. 2. Marvin Wolfgang and Rolf Strohm, "The Relationship between Alcohol and Criminal Homicide," *Quarterly Journal of Studies on Alcohol* 17:3 (September 1956), p. 411.

7. Dr. J. R. Black is quoted in Brecher, p. 8.

8. Judson, p. ix.

9. *White Paper*, p. 11.

10. National Institute on Drug Abuse, *Heroin Indicators Trend Report* (Washington, D.C.: Department of Health, Education and Welfare, 1976), p. iii.

11. The "International Survey" reports make up one entire issue of *Addictive Diseases, An International Journal* 3:1 (1977); hereinafter cited as *International Survey*. The estimates of addict populations and the editors' conclusions appear on pp. 130–31.

12. *Borneo Bulletin*, April 29, 1978, p. 10.

13. Kuala Lumpur, *New Straits Times*, December 6, 1979, p. 1.

14. *Wall Street Journal*, July 6, 1977, p. 1. Quotations from Hanam and Chua Sian in *Miami Herald*, June 22, 1977. Statistics on dramatic rise in opiate addiction in J. H. K. Leong, "The Present Status of Drug Dependence Treatment in Singapore," *International Survey*, pp. 94–95. On invocation of the death penalty, London, Reuters dispatch, February, 19, 1980. W. H. McGlothlin, "The Singapore Heroin Control Programme," *Bulletin on Narcotics* 32:1(1980), 1, 4, 13.

15. *Washington Post*, August 23, 1978, p. B8.

16. James M. N. Ch'ien, "Voluntary Treatment of Drug Abuse in Hong Kong," *International Survey*, p. 99. The Action Committee against Narcotics, *Hong Kong Narcotics Report 1978* (Hong Kong: The Government Printer, 1979), p. 25.

17. Statement of Peter Rieff, Resident Agent-In-Charge, Guam Resident Office, DEA, before

the Select Committee on Narcotics Abuse and Control, U.S. House of Representatives, July 4, 1978, Guam (mimeographed). *Drug Abuse and Trafficking in the State of Hawaii and the Trust Territory of Guam*, a report of the Select Committee on Narcotics Abuse and Control (GPO, 1978), p. 20.

18. Wellington, *Evening Post*, July 13, 1979, p. 1.

19. Quotations from book review of Bernard Delaney, *Narc!*, by Richard Battley in Brisbane, *Courier-Mail*, August 31, 1979, p. 5.

20. Melbourne, *The Age*, August 28, 1979, p. 28.

21. Brisbane, *Courier-Mail*, August 29, 1979, p. 9.

22. Western European and German drug data in *Sunday Times*, January 9, 1977. Excerpts from testimony of Mathea Falco, Senior Advisor to the Secretary of State and Director for International Narcotics Control Matters, before the Select Committee on Narcotics Abuse and Control, November 22, 1978, as reprinted in "Asian Narcotics: The Impact on Europe," *Drug Enforcement* 6 (February 1979), p. 2. William J. Stoessel, Jr., "U.S.–German Cooperation in Narcotics Control," *Drug Enforcement* 6 (February 1979), pp. 8–12. *New York Times*, January 9, 1978, p. A10. U.S. overdose deaths are reported in "Performance Measurement System, Statistics Compiled through December 1978," DEA, undated, probably mid-1979, p. 2.

23. Hartmut Palmer, "More Bad News in Fight against Drug Addiction," Munich, *Sueddeutsche Zeitung*, May 4, 1979, p. 4.

24. Manfred Schell, "The Fight against the Narcotic Trade Has the Same Priority as the Fight against Terrorism," Bonn, *Die Welt*, September 1, 1979, p. 2.

25. I had great difficulty with the German data and did not believe the heroin-overdose death figure. After calls to U.S. officials provided no clarification, I called the embassy of the Federal Republic of Germany. A helpful diplomat, Otto Wessell, confirmed my information of 600 deaths from heroin alone, not from all drugs; he even suggested the number 611 was more accurate. I replied that it seemed too high—the number must include *all* drug-overdose deaths. The diplomat countered that it was the best information he had. The next morning, June 18, 1980, I watched a presentation on heroin addiction in Germany by Fred Francis on the "Today" show. The camera showed heroin being openly bought and sold on the streets and addicts injecting the drug. Francis said that a whole generation of middle-class German youth seemed lost to heroin and that the number of addicts in the country was estimated by officials at 100,000. While I claim no direct knowledge of the German situation, I will look no further—at least for the purposes of this book— and will accept the sad accuracy of the heroin mortality figures mentioned above. Moreover, I think that the German officials who spoke on that television program were correct in forecasting that the epidemic had not yet peaked. And I also believe that I have probably understated in this book the agonizing virulence of the worldwide heroin epidemic. The preliminary U.S. figures for 1979 were provided by a NIDA statistical analyst on July 17, 1980.

26. Paris, *Le Figaro*, January 14, 1980, p. 11.

27. Copenhagen, *Berlingske Tidende*, January 6, 1980, p. 17.

28. Copenhagen, *Berlingske Tidende*, February 10, 1980, p. 10.

29. Brussels, *Le Soir*, January 25, 1980, p. 1. On their release, Paris, *Le Monde*, March 6, 1980, p. 11.

30. Zurich, *Neue Zuercher Zeitung*, February 15, 1980, p. 7; February 16, 1980, p. 22.

31. *New York Times*, April 28, 1978, p. 16. See also "Drug Abuse in the Armed Forces of the United States," A Report of the Select Committee on Narcotics Abuse and Control (GPO, 1978). Also Michael Satchell, "The Frightening G.I. Drug Boom," *Parade*, July 22, 1979, p. 4, which states, "casualties in the war with drugs in Europe are substantial. Last year, some 50 young GI's died of drug overdoses in West Germany—twice as many as in 1977. Another 40 soldiers also died last year in highway accidents blamed on drugs or alcohol."

32. *Time*, June 30, 1980, p. 39. *Washington Post*, July 9, 1980, p. A19.

33. *Al-Jumhuriah*, February 1, 1980, p. 9. Cairo, *Al-Ahram*, February 8, 1980, p. 10.

34. *Jerusalem Post*, March 20, 1980, p. 2.

35. Epstein (1977), p. 261.

36. *White Paper*, pp. ix, 14–21.

37. Carter administration testimony in "The Mexican Connection," *Hearings before the Subcommittee to Investigate Juvenile Delinquency of the Committee on the Judiciary, United States Senate* (GPO, 1978), pp. 1–44. *Drug Enforcement* 4 (December 1977), inside front cover. *Drug Enforcement* 5 (July 1978), inside front cover. Deaths for 1976 and 1977 in "Performance Measurement System, Statistics Compiled through December 1978," DEA, undated, probably mid-1979, p. 25.

38. *Washington Post*, June 24, 1979, p. A1.

39. "Doctors Warn of Heroin 'Epidemic,'" London, *Evening Standard*, July 19, 1979, p. 2. "Heroin Epidemic 'Out of Control,'" London, *Evening News*, July 19, 1979, p. 2. Home Office Statistical Bulletin, "Statistics of the Misuse of Drugs in the United Kingdom, 1978," 19 July 1979, Table 11; hereinafter cited as Home Office Statistical Bulletin for 1978.

40. *Washington Post*, August 26, 1979, p. A1.

CHAPTER 2

1. Cicely Saunders, "The Last Stages of Life," *American Journal of Nursing* 65:70–75 (March 1965), pp. 247, 249.

2. Eric Wilkes, quoted in Michael Satchell, "How to Enjoy Life—Up to the Last Moment," *Parade*, October 16, 1977, p. 23.

3. Victor and Rosemary Zorza, "The Death of a Daughter," *Washington Post*, January 22, 1978, p. C1.

4. Interview with Dr. Joseph Hanratty and tour of St. Joseph's Hospice, London, July 10, 1979.

5. Richard M. Marks and Edward J. Sachar, "Undertreatment of Medical Inpatients with Narcotic Analgesics," *Annals of Internal Medicine* 78:2 (February 1973), pp. 173–81.

6. Miller quoted in Judson, p. 9.

7. Stewart Alsop, "The Right to Die with Dignity," *Good Housekeeping*, August 1974, pp. 69, 130–32.

8. John H. Glick, "A Doctor's Prescription for Mercy," *Good Housekeeping*, August 1975, pp. 67, 132.

9. Comprehensive Drug Abuse Prevention and Control Act of 1970, P.L. 91–513, 84 Stat. 1236, 1970; hereinafter cited as 1970 Federal Act. Title II of this law lays out the various schedules and methods for controlling drugs. This title is sometimes referred to as the Controlled Substances Act, or CSA, leading some observers to believe that two laws, rather than one, are involved; e.g., Judson, p. 16. The so-called Controlled Substances Act is part of the comprehensive 1970 Federal Act. See sec. 201(a) of the CSA.

10. Letter from Arnold S. Trebach to Attorney General Griffin B. Bell, April 29, 1977.

11. Letter from Peter G. Bourne to Congressman Paul G. Rogers, June 10, 1977.

12. *Washington Star*, November 9, 1977, p. 1.

13. Office of Drug Abuse Policy, *1978 Annual Report*, p. 32.

14. American Society of Internal Medicine, 1978 House of Delegates, *Minutes*, May 4–7, 1978, Resolution 22.

15. American Medical Association, Report of the Council on Scientific Affairs. Report B (A–78), *Proceeding of the House of Delegates*, June 18–22, 1978, pp. 284–85.

16. *Washington Post*, October 6, 1978, p. A3.

17. *Health Care Week*, June 5, 1978, p. 8.

18. Judson, pp. 8–10. Quotation from Saunders in St. Christopher's Hospice, *Annual Report 1976–1977* (Sydenham, England, 1977), p. 17.

19. Judson, p. 8.

20. *Washington Star*, June 23, 1976, p. A–6.

21. Satchell, *Parade*, October 16, 1977.

22. Letter from Dr. Cicely Saunders, O.B.E., to author, October 21, 1977.

23. Myra Weinstein, interview with Dr. Eric Wilkes, St. Luke's Nursing Home, Sheffield, England, July 28, 1977. Satchell, *Parade*, October 16, 1977.

24. Myra Weinstein, interview with Dr. E. Wiltshaw, the Royal Marsden Hospital, London, July 21, 1977. Dr. Twycross is no medical Calvinist, but he has pronounced views on the extra euphoric qualities of heroin. In September 1980 he informed me in emphatic terms that "the controlled trial I did at St. Christopher's indicates that heroin is no more euphorigenic than morphine. . . . It would be lovely if heroin was euphorient in cancer patients. Life would be so much easier. . . . It is pain relief, rest, interest in them by the staff, general loving concern, etc. which allows the majority to feel good. . . . Please, in light of the controlled trial I did at St. Christopher's Hospice, and my own experience . . . do not continue the myth that heroin induces chemical happiness. I should emphasize that one of the apparent long-term effects of heroin, morphine, or any other narcotic analgesic appears to be depression, which requires the use of an anti-depressant. That seems to be a long way from euphoria!" Letter from Dr. Robert G. Twycross to author, September 16, 1980.

CHAPTER 3

1. This quotation appeared in the second of two important articles published in the same journal in 1898. The two articles are: Professor Dr. med. H. Dreser, "Pharmakologisches über einige Morphinderivate," *Therapeutische Monatshefte* 12 (September 1898), p. 509, and Dr. med. Floret, "Klinische Versuche über die Wirkung und Anwendung des Heroins," p. 512. I am deeply indebted to Lutz Kieso, M.D., Chairman, Department of Experimental Medicine, National Naval Medical Center, Bethesda, Maryland, for his translation of these articles.

2. This quotation is reproduced in written testimony that Hubbard submitted to Congress, which appears in *Hearings Before the Committee on Ways and Means, House of Representatives, on H.R. 7079, A Bill Prohibiting the Importation of Crude Opium for the Purpose of Manufacturing Heroin*, April 3, 1924 (GPO 1924), p. 32ff.; hereinafter cited as *1924 Heroin Hearings*.

3. Homer, *Odyssey*, trans. Walter Shewring (Oxford: Oxford University Press, 1980), p. 40.

4. Histories of various aspects of drug use abound, often differing from one another in facts and interpretations. A popularized historical summary on both marijuana and the opiates is Foster Farley, "Weeds and Seeds of Dreams: The History of Two Drugs," *International History Magazine* 14 (February 1974), p. 84. For the history of the opiates in America and Britain, see Brecher, part I, especially chapters 1, 2, and 3. See also David Musto's classic *The American Disease*. These books, like almost all studies in the drug-abuse field, give scant attention to the positive aspects of heroin as a medicine but emphasize addiction, deviance, and control. Judson is an exception to this rule.

5. C. R. A. Wright, "On the Action of Organic Acids and Their Anhydrides on the Natural Alkaloids," *Journal of the Chemical Society* 12 (July 1874), p. 1031.

6. Dreser and Floret, *Therapeutische Monatshefte*. The Musto quotation is from David F. Musto, "Early History of Heroin in the United States," in *Addiction*, ed. Peter G. Bourne (New York: Academic Press, 1974), p. 175; hereinafter cited as Musto 1974.

7. Charles E. Terry and Mildred Pellens, *The Opium Problem* (New York: The Committee on Drug Addictions, The Bureau of Social Hygiene, Inc., 1928), p. 76; hereinafter cited as Terry and Pellens. John B. Williams, *Narcotics and Drug Dependence* (Beverly Hills: Glencoe Press, 1974), p. 200.

8. John C. Kramer, "Heroin in the Treatment of Morphine Addiction," *Journal of Psychedelic Drugs* 9–3 (July-September 1977), p. 193.

9. *Journal of the American Medical Association* (hereinafter referred to as *JAMA*) 31 (November 12, 1898), p. 1176. *Lancet* 2 (December 3, 1898), p. 1511.

10. The Bayer advertisement originally appeared in a 1900 issue of *Medical Mirror*, an American medical journal.

11. The quotations from doctors appear in "History of Heroin," *Bulletin on Narcotics* 5 (April-June 1953), pp. 3, 6; hereinafter cited as "History of Heroin."

12. Musto 1974, p. 178.

13. The material on heroin in New York City and World War I is from Musto 1974, pp. 180–83.

14. An Act To prohibit the importation and use of opium for other than medicinal purposes, P.L. 60–22, 35 Stat. 614, 1909.

15. The various directives prohibiting the use of heroin in the medical services of federal agencies are reproduced in *1924 Heroin Hearings*, p. 2.

16. Committee on Traffic in Opium of the Foreign Policy Association, *The Case against Heroin* (New York 1924). The pamphlet is designated "Pamphlet No. 24 . . . Series of 1923–24." It seems probable that Representative Porter used this pamphlet in lining up expert testimony during the hearings on April 3, 1924.

17. *1924 Heroin Hearings*, p. 1.

18. Ibid., pp. 1–10.

19. Ibid., pp. 10–19.

20. Ibid., pp. 37–38.

21. Ibid., pp. 28–45.

22. Ibid., pp. 45–53.

23. Ibid., p. 33.

24. Ibid., pp. 32ff.

25. David F. Musto, "Dangerous Substance Abuse: An Uncommon History," *Trial Magazine* (November/December 1974), p. 59.

26. "The United States Bars the Manufacture of Heroin," *Bulletin on Narcotics* 5 (April-June 1953), pp. 20, 26.

27. Harry J. Anslinger, "Memorandum for the Secretary," September 3, 1936, unpublished, DEA Library.

28. *JAMA* 114–19 (May 11, 1940), p. 1188.

29. *JAMA* 114–26 (June 29, 1940), p. 2561.

30. As quoted in Musto 1973, p. 191.

31. Narcotic Control Act of 1956, P.L. 84–728, 70 Stat. 572, 1956.

32. "History of Heroin," p. 12.

33. Recent worldwide figures on legal use:

Table 2. Manufacture, Consumption, and Conversion of Licit Heroin
World: 1973–79 (in kilograms)

Country		1973	1974	1975	1976	1977	1978	1979
Manufacture								
United Kingdom		53	84	64	72	67	88	124
Netherlands		12	—	—	—	33	—	—
France		10	10	10	10	9	20	10
Belgium		—	—	—	—	2	2	—
	Total	75	94	74	82	111	110	134

Table 2 (*continued*)

Country		1973	1974	1975	1976	1977	1978	1979
Consumption								
United Kingdom		48	57	57	62	73	88	96
Belgium		4	2	1	1	1	1	1
United States of America		3	—	—	—	—	—	—
Finland		—	—	—	—	—	—	4
	Total	55	59	58	63	74	89	101
Conversion into nalorphine								
(a narcotic antagonist)								
Netherlands		—	9	—	—	31	—	—
France		5	11	8	14	14	8	14
United Kingdom		15	27	6	5	—	14	—
	Total	20	47	14	19	45	22	14

SOURCES: International Narcotics Control Board, *Statistics on Narcotic Drugs for 1977* (New York: United Nations, 1978), p. x; and *Statistics on Narcotic Drugs for 1979* (New York: United Nations, 1980), p. xiv.

34. Dan Waldorf, Martin Orlick, and Craig Reinarman, *The Shreveport Clinic 1919–1923* (Washington, D.C.: The Drug Abuse Council, Inc., 1974), p. 24; hereinafter cited as Waldorf. Dr. Willis P. Butler, director of the clinic, confirmed to me in interviews during 1979 and 1980 the widespread fear among local doctors of treating organically ill patients outside a hospital with narcotic drugs for any length of time.

CHAPTER 4

1. William B. Loan, James D. Morrison, John W. Dundee, Richard S. J. Clarke, Robert C. Hamilton, and Stuart S. Brown, "Studies of Drugs Given before Anaesthesia XVII: The Natural and Semi-Synthetic Opiates," *British Journal of Anaesthesia* 41 (January 1969), pp. 57, 63; hereinafter cited as Loan.

2. Unpublished memorandum from Dr. Twycross in July 1978 and 1979. Mimeographed. Hereinafter cited as Twycross 1978–79.

3. *U.S. Journal of Drug and Alcohol Dependence*, December 1977, p. 12.

4. Ellen Metsky, as quoted in Mark Shwartz, "Heroin as Medicine—Lead to Legalization?" *Synapse*, December 1, 1977.

5. *Washington Star*, May 13, 1978, p. F1.

6. National Clearinghouse for Drug Abuse Information, *Heroin*, series 33, no. 1, January 1975, p. 6.

7. Judson, p. 5.

8. Figure 2 from Jerome J. Platt and Christina Labate, *Heroin Addiction: Theory, Research, and Treatment* (New York: John Wiley and Sons, 1976), p. 48.

9. Judson, p. 7.

10. Claus W. Reichle, Gene M. Smith, Joachim S. Gravenstein, Spyros G. Macris, and Henry K. Beecher, "Comparative Analgesic Potency of Heroin and Morphine in Postoperative Patients," *Journal of Pharmacology and Experimental Therapeutics* 136, no. 1 (1962), p. 43.

11. Louis Lasagna, "The Clinical Evaluation of Morphine and Its Substitutes as Analgesics," *Pharmacological Reviews* 16:1 (March 1964), p. 47.

12. John W. Dundee, Richard S. J. Clarke, and William B. Loan, "Comparative Toxicity of Diamorphine, Morphine, and Methadone," *Lancet* (July 29, 1967), p. 221.

13. Loan, p. 63.

14. H. R. MacDonald, H. R. Rees, A. L. Muir, D. M. Lawrie, J. L. Burton, and K. W. Donald, "Circulatory Effects of Heroin in Patients with Myocardial Infarction," *Lancet* (May 20, 1967), p. 1070.

15. National Cancer Institute, "Fact Sheet—Advances in Cancer Treatment," n.d., p. 3.

16. Robert G. Twycross, "Clinical Experience with Diamorphine in Advanced Malignant Disease," *International Journal of Clinical Pharmacology, Therapy and Toxicology* 9:3 (1974), pp. 196–97; hereinafter cited as Twycross 1974.

17. Ibid., pp. 189, 195.

18. Ibid., pp. 195–98.

19. Robert G. Twycross, "Choice of Strong Analgesic in Terminal Cancer: Diamorphine or Morphine?" *Journal of the International Association for the Study of Pain* 3 (April 1977), p. 93; hereinafter cited as Twycross 1977.

20. Robert G. Twycross, *Studies on the Use of Diamorphine in Advanced Malignant Disease* (M.D. diss., University of Oxford, 1976), p. 88. Mimeographed. Eugene L. Shapiro, "The Right of Privacy and Heroin Use for Painkilling Purposes by the Terminally Ill Cancer Patient," *Arizona Law Review* 21 (1979), pp. 46–47; hereinafter cited as Shapiro.

21. Twycross 1978–79.

22. The bill was H.R. 7334, "To amend the Controlled Substances Act to authorize the use of heroin for terminally ill cancer patients," 96th Cong., 2d Sess.

23. "Statement by Jane E. Henney, M.D., National Cancer Institute, Before the Subcommittee on Health and the Environment, Committee on Interstate and Foreign Commerce, House of Representatives, September 4, 1980," p. 5. Morphine sulfate salt and morphine acetate salt are, in layman's terms, simply different preparations of the same basic ingredient for use in medicine, with the former being the more common mixture. When interviewed in November 1980, both Dr. Henney and research pharmacist J. Paul Davignon, of the NCI, said that they did not see the development, actually the resurrection, of freeze-dried morphine acetate as a great scientific breakthrough, although they viewed it as an important event. In a letter to the *Journal of the American Medical Association*, three NCI researchers explained: "Morphine acetate, a Schedule II substance, is extremely water soluble (1:2.5). This salt was described in the eighth revision of the *United States Pharmacopeia* but fell into disuse because of instability. A reexamination of some pharmaceutical properties of morphine acetate indicates that a soluble stable form of morphine can be prepared using freeze-drying technology. . . . The [new] data indicate adequate stability of the freeze-dried dosage form. The reconstituted solution is sufficiently stable for use as a multidose vial. In contrast to the available fixed-concentration solutions of morphine sulfate, a sterile freeze-dried dosage form of morphine acetate can be reconstituted to a wide range of concentrations, depending on individual patient requirements. An advantage of heroin over morphine in patients with terminal cancer is its greater water solubility. The acetate salt of morphine appears to meet this requirement and can be prepared in a suitable dosage form" (G. K. Poochikian, J. C. Cradock, and J. P. Davignon, "Morphine Acetate," *JAMA* 244 [September 26, 1980], p. 1434).

24. *JAMA*, October 6, 1978, pp. 1601–02.

25. The Sloan-Kettering and Georgetown studies are discussed in Shapiro, p. 47.

26. Robert F. Kaiko, Stanley L. Wallenstein, Ada G. Rogers, Patricia Y. Grabinski, and Raymond W. Houde, "Analgesic and Mood Effects of Heroin and Morphine in Cancer Patients with Postoperative Pain," *New England Journal of Medicine* 304:25 (June 18, 1981), p. 1501; hereinafter cited as Kaiko.

27. Kaiko, pp. 1501, 1505.

28. Louis Lasagna, "Heroin: A Medical 'Me Too,'" *New England Journal of Medicine* 304:25 (June 18, 1981), p. 1539.

29. Interview with Philip Schein, June 19, 1981. Also mentioned in Victor Cohn, "Cancer Team Finds Heroin, Morphine Pain-Killing Equals," *Washington Post*, June 18, 1981, p. A16.

30. See world figures in Table 2.

31. Legal heroin use in England:

Table 3. Consumption of Licit Heroin in England: 1969–78
(in kilograms)

	1969	1970	1971	1972	1973	1974	1975	1976	1977	1978
For addicts (through clinics)	23	17	14	14	14	15	15	13	11	9
For the organically ill	26	25	27	29	34	42	42	49	62	77
Total	49	42	41	43	48	57	57	62	73	88

SOURCES: Reports from Department of Health and Social Security, Home Office, Institute for the Study of Drug Dependence, and U.N. International Narcotics Control Board. (Figures rounded to nearest whole kilogram.)

32. Use of heroin and morphine in England:

Table 4. Consumption of Heroin and Morphine in England: 1971–79
(in kilograms)

	1971	1972	1973	1974	1975	1976	1977	1978	1979
Heroin	41	43	48	57	57	62	73	88	96
Morphine	364	318	363	322	313	286	295	289	266

SOURCES: International Narcotics Control Board, *Statistics on Narcotic Drugs for 1975* (New York: United Nations, 1976), pp. 10, 11, 58, 59; *Statistics on Narcotic Drugs for 1979* (New York: United Nations, 1980), pp. xiv, 54, 55.

33. Helen Keating Neal, "Why Can't the Dying Have Heroin?" *New York Magazine*, October 2, 1978, pp. 76, 88; hereinafter cited as Neal.

34. Shapiro, pp. 48–59. *Roe* v. *Wade*, 410 U.S. 113 (1973).

35. 1970 Federal Act, 21 USCA 812.

36. Neal, p. 87.

37. Judson, pp. 157–61. Also see statistical reports of various British ministries, including the Home Office and the Department of Health and Social Security. The Institute for the Study of Drug Dependence, 3 Blackburn Road, London NW6 1XA, is an excellent central reference source for all types of drug information, including statistics.

CHAPTER 5

1. Ministry of Health, Departmental Committee on Morphine and Heroin Addiction, *Report* (London: His Majesty's Stationery Office, 1926), p. 18; hereinafter cited as Rolleston Report.

2. Quoted in Walter R. Cuskey, Arnold William Klein, and William Krasner, *Drug-Trip Abroad: American Drug-Refugees in Amsterdam and London* (Philadelphia: University of Pennsylvania Press, 1972), p. 108; hereinafter cited as Cuskey.

3. Harney quoted in Schur, pp. 177–78.

4. Home Office official quoted in Schur, p. 178.

5. Schur, pp. 179–80.

6. Among numerous good accounts of the history of British laws controlling drug use, I have relied very much on H. B. Spear, "The British Experience," *The John Marshall Journal of Practice and Procedure* 9 (1975), p. 67; hereinafter cited as Spear 1975.

7. Ibid., pp. 68–70.

8. Ibid., pp. 77–78.

9. Elliot quoted in Judson, pp. 17–18.

10. Campbell's comments have often been quoted by American writers. This version appears in Brecher, p. 121.

11. Spear 1975, p. 75. In here reporting on the situation in the early 1920s, Spear was, of course, paraphrasing the Rolleston Report.

12. Delevingne quoted in Judson, p. 17.

13. Rolleston Report, pp. 6–7.

14. Ibid., p. 7.

15. Ibid., p. 9; the author himself attempts to improve on this definition—on p. 283.

16. The estimate of 100–500 is my own, based upon a variety of reports, most of which are mentioned in this book. The committee's comments on the prevalence of addiction appear ibid., p. 10.

17. Spear 1975, p. 76.

18. Rolleston Report, p. 10.

19. Ibid., p. 11.

20. Ibid., p. 17.

21. Ibid., pp. 17–19. The summary section, in which the phrase "regular allowance" was added, is on p. 32.

22. Ibid., pp. 24–25. The rule implementing the regulation may be found in *Dangerous Drugs Consolidation Regulations*, December 14, 1928.

23. Ibid., pp. 26–27.

24. Spear 1975, pp. 77–78.

25. Quoted in Philip Bean, *The Social Control of Drugs* (London: Martin Robertson and Company, Ltd., 1974), p. 68; hereinafter cited as Bean.

26. H. B. Spear, "The Growth of Heroin Addiction in the United Kingdom," *British Journal of Addiction* 64 (October 1969), p. 245; hereinafter cited as Spear 1969.

27. Ibid., pp. 249–50; 251–53.

28. Ibid., p. 254.

29. For accounts of the move to ban heroin in 1955, I relied heavily on Judson, pp. 29–34, and Bean, pp. 133–36.

30. Bean, pp. 133–35.

31. Ibid., p. 135.

32. Judson, p. 33.

33. Bean, p. 136.

34. Ministry of Health and Department of Health for Scotland, *Drug Addiction: Report of the Interdepartmental Committee* (London: Her Majesty's Stationery Office, 1961); hereinafter cited as Brain I.

35. Ibid., p. 3.

36. Bean, p. 74.

37. Spear 1975, p. 80.

38. Bean, p. 75; Judson, pp. 35–38.

39. Brain I, p. 9.

40. Ibid.; Ashley, p. 153.

41. Brain I, p. 11.

42. Ibid., pp. 22–23.

43. Ibid., pp. 11–12.

44. Bean, p. 75; Judson, p. 35.

45. Interviews, Home Office, August 6, 1980.

46. Ministry of Health and Scottish Home and Health Department, *Drug Addiction: The Second*

Report of the Interdepartmental Committee (London: Her Majesty's Stationery Office, 1971); hereinafter cited as Brain II.

47. Ibid., pp. 4–5.

48. Ibid., pp. 5–6.

49. Ibid., p. 6.

50. Ibid., p. 7.

51. Griffith Edwards, "Some Years On: Evolutions in the 'British System,'" in *Problems of Drug Abuse in Britain*, ed. D. J. West (Cambridge: Institute of Criminology, 1978), p. 4; hereinafter cited as Edwards. This volume contains papers presented to the Cropwood Round-Table Conference held in December 1977.

52. Brain II, pp. 7–11.

53. Judson, p. 59; Spear 1975, pp. 78–79, 81–84. For more details of this period see Richard V. Phillipson, "The Implementation of the Second Report of the Interdepartmental Committee on Drug Addiction," in *Modern Trends in Drug Dependence and Alcoholism*, ed. Richard V. Phillipson (London: Butterworths, 1970), p. 75.

54. Schur, pp. 158–64.

55. Ibid., p. 209.

56. Bewley's response quoted in Edwards, p. 5.

57. Ibid., pp. 5–6.

58. Cuskey, pp. 52–53.

59. Ibid., pp. 56–60.

60. Ibid., pp. 99–109.

61. Ibid., pp. 65–74.

CHAPTER 6

1. Daniel C. Roper, Commissioner of Internal Revenue, Treasury Department, "Enforcement of the Harrison Narcotic Law," M-Mim 212, July 21, 1919, copy on file in Drug Enforcement Administration Library, Washington, D.C., p. 3; hereinafter cited as Roper.

2. Remarks of Dr. Theodore G. Klumpp, December 2, 1954, Baltimore, Md., as quoted in the resume of Harry Jacob Anslinger, copy on file in DEA Library, Washington, D.C., pp. 3–4.

3. Harry J. Anslinger, *FBI Law Enforcement Bulletin*, January 1959, as quoted in Stanley Meisler, "Federal Narcotics Czar," *Nation*, February 20, 1960, p. 159.

4. Harrison Narcotic Act, P.L. 63–223, 38 Stat. 785, 1914.

5. Lindesmith, p. 4.

6. Brecher, p. 49. Ashley, p. 116. King, p. 21.

7. Troy Duster, *The Legislation of Morality* (New York: Free Press, 1970), p. 15.

8. An Act To prohibit the importation and use of opium for other than medicinal purposes, P.L. 60–221, 35 Stat. 614, 1909. An Act Regulating the manufacture of smoking opium within the United States, P.L. 63–47, 38 Stat. 277, 1914.

9. U.S. House of Representatives, "Registration of Producers and Importers of Opium, Etc.— "REPORT," June 24, 1913.

10. While the law was of great importance, at the time there was little public interest and no hearings were held. Discussions in the Senate, sitting as the Committee of the Whole, appeared in various editions of the *Congressional Record*; the quotations cited appeared in the editions of June 6, 1914 (p. 10779), and August 15, 1914 (pp. 15002–3).

11. Hon. John M. Coffee, "An Investigation of the Narcotic Evil," *Congressional Record*, June 14, 1938, as quoted in Henry Smith Williams, *Drug Addicts Are Human Beings* (Washington, D.C.: Shaw Publishing Company, 1938), pp. xiii, xix.

12. *United States* v. *Jin Fuey Moy*, 241 U.S. 394 (1916).

13. Lindesmith, p. 5. Treasury Department *Annual Report* quoted in Musto 1973, p. 130.

14. *United States* v. *Doremus*, 249 U.S. 86, 90, 94 (1918).

15. *Webb* v. *United States*, 249 U.S. 96, 98–99 (1919).

16. *Webb* v. *United States*, 249 U.S. 99–100 (1919). Musto 1973, p. 132.

17. *Jin Fuey Moy* v. *United States*, 254 U.S. 189, 193–94 (1920).

18. *United States* v. *Behrman*, 258 U.S. 280, 288–89, 290 (1922).

19. *Linder* v. *United States*, 268 U.S. 5, 18, 20 (1924). Lindesmith, pp. 8–11.

20. Lindesmith, especially chaps. 1–3. While Lindesmith was one of the chief intellectual pioneers, others have contributed, as we have seen, to our understanding of the federal assault on addicts, including Edward Brecher, Rufus King, and David Musto.

21. Musto 1973, p. 123.

22. TD 2200 quoted in Musto, ibid.

23. Arthur D. Greenfield, "Some Legal Aspects of the Narcotic Drug Problem," *New York Medical Journal* (July 19, 1919), p. 7.

24. Roper, pp. 1–2.

25. Ibid., pp. 2–3.

26. Ibid., p. 3.

27. Ibid., pp. 3–5.

28. AMA committee report quoted in King, pp. 34–35. A reflective assessment of the activities of the AMA during this period may be found in "Review of the Operation of 'Narcotic Clinics' between 1919 and 1923," a selection from a report by the Council on Mental Health, AMA, reproduced in John A. O'Donnell and John C. Ball, eds., *Narcotic Addiction* (New York: Harper and Row, 1966), p. 180.

29. The pamphlet bears this legend: "Revoking Pro-Mimeograph, Pro. No. 316, Dated May 21, 1923, and Outlining Treatment of Narcotic-Drug Addiction Permissible Under the Harrison Narcotic Law—Narcotic Pamphlet N–No. 56., Treasury Department, Bureau of Prohibition, Narcotic Unit, Washington, June 23, 1928."

30. "Pamphlet No. 56, Revised September 1963, Treasury Department, Bureau of Narcotics, Washington, D.C., Prescribing and Dispensing of Narcotics Under Harrison Narcotic Law." The exact language of the 1921 report is found on p. 8 of this pamphlet; the joint statement on pp. 9–10; and references to aged and infirm addicts on p. 23.

31. The O'Donnell study is discussed in Brecher, pp. 129–34. The full citation is John A. O'Donnell, *Narcotic Addicts in Kentucky* (GPO, 1969).

32. Lindesmith, pp. 88–90.

33. Maxine Cheshire, *Ladies Home Journal*, November 1978.

34. Dr. Ratigan's story is based on the account in King, pp. 47–58. The case citations are *Ratigan* v. *United States*, 88 F. 2d 919 (9th Cir., 1937), *cert. denied*, 301 U.S. 705, 1936; *rehearing denied*, 302 U.S. 774 (1937).

35. *Hawkins* v. *United States*, 90 F. 2d 551, 553 (5th Cir., 1937).

36. Ibid., p. 556.

37. Platt and Labate, *Heroin Addiction*, p. 205.

38. Lindesmith (chap. 5) provides a succinct analysis of the early American clinics and conflicting verbatim accounts about the Shreveport clinic from the Bureau of Narcotics, on the one hand, and from Terry and Pellens, on the other. Chapter 7 of Musto's book is devoted to "The Narcotic Clinic Era," but references to the clinics are found throughout *The American Disease*. Musto is unclear as to the exact number of clinics and at one point mentions "forty-odd" (p. 151), while Lindesmith (pp. 142–43) states that there were 44 clinics which registered fewer than 15,000 addicts. Official reports agree with Lindesmith, but a review of independent reports of the various clinics suggests that inadequate records were kept.

39. Musto 1973, pp. 151–52.

40. Ibid., pp. 156–63.

41. Terry quoted in Musto 1973, pp. 174–75. Lindesmith, p. 161.

42. On the Shreveport clinic see Terry and Pellens, pp. 864–72. See also Lindesmith; Musto 1973; and Waldorf. My own views have been shaped by these written reports and by my interviews with Dr. Butler on August 31, 1979, in New Orleans; on April 2, 1980, by telephone; and, for a total of approximately 12 hours, on May 17 and 18, 1980, in Hermitage, Tenn.

43. Interview with Butler, April 2, 1980.

44. Waldorf, p. 5.

45. Waldorf, pp. ix, x, 28–29.

46. Waldorf, pp. 33–40; and interviews with Butler, August 31, 1979, April 2, 1980, and May 17–18, 1980.

47. Interviews with Butler, April 2, and May 17–18, 1980.

48. Waldorf, pp. 21, 28–30.

49. Ibid. Information on the current situation in Washington, D.C., is based on reports from the Substance Abuse Administration and visits to its facilities during the fall of 1979 and the spring of 1980.

50. Waldorf, pp. 21–22; and interviews with Butler, August 31, 1979, and April 2, 1980.

51. Musto 1973, p. 168.

52. Willis P. Butler, "How One American City Is Meeting the Public Health Problems of Narcotic Drug Addiction," *American Medicine* 28 (March 1922), p. 154.

53. Waldorf, p. 39.

54. Interview with Butler, April 2, 1980.

55. Internal Revenue Annual Report as quoted in Lindesmith, p. 140.

56. Rolleston Report, p. 20.

57. *Robinson* v. *California*, 370 U.S. 660 (1962).

58. Musto 1973, p. 204.

59. The President's Commission on Law Enforcement and Administration of Justice, *Task Force Report: Narcotics and Drug Abuse* (GPO, 1967), p. 12.

60. Lt. Joseph Healy as quoted in Lindesmith, p. 95.

61. The Drug Abuse Survey Project, *Dealing with Drug Abuse* (New York: Praeger, 1972), pp. 184–85.

62. Brecher, p. 71.

63. The Drug Abuse Survey Project, *Dealing with Drug Abuse*, p. 183.

64. Nicholas N. Kittrie, *The Right to Be Different* (Baltimore: The Johns Hopkins University Press, 1971), p. 243.

65. Material on file in DEA library. Also, references to the FBN appear in many parts of Musto 1973, especially pp. 206–29.

66. Coffee quoted in King, p. 65.

67. Musto 1973, p. 235.

68. New York Academy of Medicine, Committee on Public Health, Subcommittee on Drug Addiction, *Bulletin of the New York Academy of Medicine* (August 1955), p. 592.

69. Published originally in limited editions, the work of the joint committee was eventually published by the Indiana University Press in 1961: *Drug Addiction: Crime or Disease? Interim and Final Reports of the Joint Committee of the American Bar Association and the American Medical Association on Narcotic Drugs* (Bloomington: Indiana University Press, 1961). Both Lindesmith and King, brothers in arms in the battle against the excesses of the Bureau of Narcotics and its director, give extensive accounts of the repressive drug laws of the 1950s in their books. Lindesmith, pp. 35ff. King, chaps. 13–18. The titles from the popular press articles are quoted in King, p. 120.

70. P.L. 82–255, 65 Stat. 767, 1951.

71. Narcotic Control Act of 1956, P.L. 84–728, 70 Stat. 767, 1956.

72. Report of the Daniel subcommittee as quoted in King, p. 145.

73. Lindesmith, pp. 246–48.

74. Anslinger testimony as quoted in King, pp. 134–35.

75. Waldorf, p. 42. During all three of my interviews with him, Butler reiterated the essential facts of this incident with the commissioner of public safety. The quotations commencing "You mean . . . " and "No, sir . . . " were tape-recorded in the May 1980 interview.

76. Lindesmith, chap. 7; King, chap. 21.

77. For an organized exposition of Anslinger's views, see Harry J. Anslinger and William F. Tompkins, *The Traffic in Narcotics* (New York: Funk and Wagnalls, 1953); and Harry J. Anslinger and Will Oursler, *The Murderers* (New York: Farrar, Straus and Cudahy, 1961).

CHAPTER 7

1. Robert Searchfield quoted in Alan Massam, "Doubt and Uncertainty Cloud Apparent Success of 'British System,'" *The Journal* (of the Addiction Research Foundation of Ontario), December 1, 1974, p. 9; hereinafter cited as Massam. Searchfield was coordinator, Standing Conference on Drug Abuse.

2. Jasper Woodcock, "The British Response to Heroin Addiction—Some Myths and Misconceptions," speech, First International Action Conference on Substance Abuse, Phoenix, Arizona, November 11, 1977.

3. Interview with Terence E. Tanner, July 23, 1979.

4. Massam.

5. Thomas Bewley, "Heroin and Cocaine Addiction," *Lancet* 1 (April 10, 1965), pp. 808–10.

6. One must, accordingly, express disagreement with such statements as the following from a respected American criminologist: "Most of what Lindesmith was so scathingly attacking in the United States was, under pressure of events, being recommended in the second Brain Committee Report" (Paul Jeffrey Brantingham, "The Medico-Penal Model of Drug Abuse Control: The English Experience," in *Drug Abuse Control*, ed. Richard L. Rachin and Eugene H. Czajkoski [Lexington, Mass.: D.C. Heath, 1975], p. 64).

7. Kenneth Leech, *Keep the Faith Baby: A Close-up of London's Drop-outs* (London: The Camelot Press, Ltd., 1973), p. 62; hereinafter cited as Leech. Further documentation of the impact of the American drug scene on British habits as well as the idealistic inspiration of many young drug takers is found in the source of Rev. Leech's book title—the Eucharistic Rite of the Free Church of Berkeley.

Go in peace and love,
Serve God, serve the people,
Keep the faith baby,
You are the Liberated Zone.

8. Jock Young, "Drug Use as Problem-Solving Behavior: A Subcultural Approach," speech, Anglo-American Conference on Drug Abuse, London, April 17, 1973.

9. Personal Communication, August 6, 1980, London.

10. The Jeffrey and Spear proposals are reported in Judson, pp. 54–55.

11. H. Dale Beckett, "Facts and Myths about Narcotic Drug Abuse," *Transactions of the Medical Society of London*, Ordinary Meeting, December 11, 1967, pp. 65, 70.

12. Leech, p. 45.

13. Leech, pp. 42–46. Since the erasure order, however, there have been reports, some as recent as July 1979 from my institute participants who went looking for him, that he was still ministering

to the abscesses, withdrawal pains, and assorted agonies of the addicts on the streets and in the Underground stations near Piccadilly. Thus, John Petro remained a junkie "doctor," even though he lost the formal title and the license that authorized him to prescribe drugs. He died in 1981.

14. Leech, p. 46; Judson, p. 58; *Daily Telegraph*, November 1, 1969; and interviews, Home Office, August 6, 1980. Swan served part of his sentence in an institution for the mentally disturbed, was released, is no longer involved with addicts as far as can be told, and recently has been seen at a new occupation—driving a taxi through London traffic.

15. Leech, p. 46.

16. Misuse of Drugs Act 1971, schedule 2.

17. Examples of such misstatements are found in P. W. H. Lydiate, *The Law Relating to the Misuse of Drugs* (London: Butterworths, 1977), p. 13, and in Brecher, p. 177. Lydiate, a barrister, assigns no medicinal value to heroin and declares flatly: "only used to treat addicts." Moreover, the American Edward Brecher, in his excellent 1972 book *Licit and Illicit Drugs*, made a common mistake about the treatment of addicts when he stated, referring to the many British addicts then being maintained on methadone, "any one of those . . . methadone patients can at any time decide to go back to heroin and have a legal right to get it."

18. The third of the 1973 regulations deals with notification requirements and exceptions thereto.

19. Sections 12 and 13 of the Misuse of Drugs Act, 1971, lay out the basic legal authority of the home secretary to issue a direction to withdraw the power of a doctor to prescribe, administer, and supply certain controlled drugs. The total of criminal prosecutions and tribunal proceedings was obtained from interviews, Home Office, August 6, 1980.

20. Philip Connell has stated this "no specific treatment" theory in several presentations before the Institute on Drugs, Crime and Justice in England, the latest on July 6, 1979, at the Imperial College of Science and Technology, University of London. He has also discussed frankly, in numerous papers, the difficulties in establishing the simple fact of real addiction and the proper dosage, once addiction is established; one among many examples is Ramon Gardner and P. H. Connell, "One Year's Experience in a Drug Dependence Clinic," *Lancet* 2 (1970), pp. 455–58, which contains the statement quoted here about the difficulty of establishing proper dosages.

21. Quoted in Edwards 1978, pp. 31–32.

22. P. H. Connell, "Treatment of Narcotic and Non-Narcotic Drug Dependence: The Need for Research," typed reprint from *Modern Trends in Drug Dependence and Alcoholism*, ed. Richard V. Phillipson (London: Butterworths, 1970), pp. 16–17 of reprint.

23. Connell presentation to institute, July 6, 1979.

24. Tripp as quoted in Judson, p. 91.

25. The data on addicts are from a variety of sources, including Spear 1969, pp. 247–48; Judson, pp. 158–59; Home Office Statistical Bulletin for 1978. These compilations from the Home Office, containing, as I have already suggested, perhaps the best and most revealing drug-use statistics in the world, are issued annually around mid-year from Home Office, Statistical Department, Room 1617, Tolworth Tower, Surbiton, Surrey, KT6 7DS. A new publication from the same source, started in July 1979, which attempts to provide even more information, is Home Office, *Statistics of the Misuse of Drugs United Kingdom 1977*.

26. Gerry V. Stimson, "Treatment or Control? Dilemmas for Staff in Drug Dependency Clinics," *Problems of Drug Abuse in Britain* (Cambridge: Institute of Criminology, 1978), p. 65.

27. Interview with Martin Mitcheson, March 1974.

28. The interchange took place during a visit of all the American University drug institute participants to the Maudsley Drug Dependence Clinical Research and Treatment Unit, London, July 18, 1977.

29. Dr. Mitcheson's talk to drug institute, London, July 21, 1978.

30. Richard L. Hartnoll; Martin C. Mitcheson; A. Battersby; Geoffry Brown; Margaret Ellis; Philip Fleming; Nicholas Hedley, "Evaluation of Heroin Maintenance in Controlled Trial," *Archives of General Psychiatry* 37 (August 1980), pp. 877–84.

31. From Mitcheson's speech text prepared for his 1977 visit to the U.S., "Maintenance Treatment of Heroin Addiction in Great Britain 1977." Mimeographed. Delivered, *inter alia*, to National Institute on Drug Abuse, Washington, D.C., May 24, 1977.

32. Visit to St. Clement's Clinic with institute participants on July 21, 1977; interviews with J. D. Denham, the consultant psychiatrist in charge; B. N. Saha, a psychiatrist and the clinical assistant to Dr. Denham; Rita Corbett, a social worker; Leslie Horan, a nursing sister; Ashley Sheldon, a social worker; and Pat Ellis, a nursing sister. The handbook title is Pat Ellis, "Assessment and Treatment Offered at St. Clements Hospital," Drug Dependency Unit, The London Hospital (St. Clements) Bow Road (London: March 1977). Mimeographed.

33. Interview notes of Thomas Fogle, July 1978.

34. McClure has appeared before six of the seven drug institutes between 1974 and 1981, and has consistently explained his clinical preference for using modalities other than heroin, such as oral methadone and psychotherapy. This has sometimes mystified visiting Americans, especially those who had come to Britain primarily to learn how to treat addicts with heroin.

35. McClean's presentation to drug institute, London, July 21, 1978.

36. Home Office Statistical Bulletin for 1978, table 11.

37. An unpublished, quasi-confidential report prepared by London clinic staffs and shared with the author by a clinic doctor; the copy I have is dated "vii 78."

38. The data in this paragraph come from two sources: *The Prevention and Treatment of Drug Misuse in Britain*, prepared by the Reference Division, Central Office of Information, London, October 1978, p. 23; and a letter from Jasper Woodcock, ISDD, to Randolph Wallace (my research assistant at the time), October 1, 1979. The first document is an excellent, brief, neutral summary of the overall situation in England.

39. Home Office Statistical Bulletin for 1978, table 11.

40. The drugs mentioned here that have not yet been described are as follows. Dextromoramide, sold under the trade name Palfium, is a synthetic opiate painkiller said to have a somewhat higher potency than morphine. Hydrocodone is a derivative of codeine and is said to be slightly more powerful but less constipating. It is manufactured in America under names such as Hycodan and Dicodid, and is used primarily as a cough suppressant. Oxycodone, an opiate derivative of morphine thought to have a dependence potential slightly lower than its parent, is manufactured under the trade name Percodan. Phenazocine is yet another synthetic opiate, apparently somewhat more potent than morphine; some reports indicate that three injected milligrams of this drug provide the equivalent analgesia of 10 milligrams of morphine. It is manufactured in America under the trade name Prinadol. The brief descriptions of drugs given here and elsewhere in the book have been taken from a variety of sources, including the *Physician's Desk Reference* (PDR), published annually by the Medical Economics Company of Oradell, New Jersey; Richard R. Lingeman, *Drugs from A to Z* (New York: McGraw-Hill, 1969); and *Jack S. Margolis' Complete Book of Recreational Drugs* (Los Angeles: Price/Stern/Sloan, 1978).

41. Laing's argument is discussed and quoted in Peter Laurie, *Drugs: Medical, Psychological, and Social Facts* (Harmondsworth: Penguin Books, Ltd., 1974), pp. 154–56. See also R. D. Laing, *The Divided Self* (London: Tavistock, 1960).

42. Alexander R. K. Mitchell, *Drugs: The Parents' Dilemma* (London: Priory Press, Ltd., 1972), p. 147.

43. Interview with Tanner, London, July 23, 1979.

44. Terence E. Tanner, "More Heroin All Round," *The Bart's Journal*, February 1979, pp. 72, 74.

45. Ibid., p. 75.

46. Interview with Tanner, July 23, 1979.

47. ROMA Housing Association Ltd., *Annual Report and Accounts 1975*, p. 3.

48. Interview with Tanner, July 23, 1979.

49. Terence Tanner, "The Philosophy of ROMA," February 5, 1976, typewritten manuscript of speech.

50. "More Heroin All Round," p. 76.

51. Interview with Tanner, July 23, 1979.

52. Ibid.

53. "More Heroin All Round," pp. 76–77.

54. Ibid., p. 77.

55. ROMA Housing Association Ltd., *Annual Report and Accounts 1977*, p. 25.

56. Letter to author from Tanner, May 9, 1980.

57. Institute for the Study of Drug Dependence, *Drug Link*, Information Letter, Spring 1980, no. 13, p. 6.

58. Philip Connelly, presentation to drug institute, London, July 12, 1979.

59. Home Office Statistical Bulletin for 1978, table 2.

60. Spear's remarks on heroin as a benign drug and his other comments about clinics were made primarily during a presentation to the drug institute, London, July 6, 1979.

61. Spear's presentation to the drug institute, July 28, 1978.

62. Field visit of the institute to New Scotland Yard, where a presentation was made by several members of the Drug Squad, including Detective Chief Inspector Colin Coxall, Detective Superintendent John Hoddinowt, Detective Superintendent Malcolm Campbell, Detective Sergeant Jim Driscoll, and Detective Sergeant Sam Kilner, July 12, 1979.

63. For example, see the Birmingham, N.Y., *Sun-Bulletin* of June 15, 1978.

64. Home Office Statistical Bulletin for 1978, tables 3, 5.

65. The comparisons between Britain and the U.S. are drawn primarily from statistical material gathered by Dr. Allison Morris for presentations to the drug institute on July 24, 1978, and July 16, 1979.

66. Terence Morris, speech, Third Institute on Drugs, Crime and Justice in England, Christ's College, Cambridge, July 23, 1976.

67. *Rochin* v. *California*, 342 U.S. 165 (1952).

68. Evidence of the hatred engendered by these general search warrants abounds in histories of the prerevolutionary period. When, for example, George II died in 1760 and the writs came up for renewal so that they might properly bear the name of the new sovereign, a group of Boston merchants banded together and hired an aggressive young lawyer to fight the case. Thus, James Otis achieved a certain degree of fame for his spirited legal resistance to the issuance of the new writs before the Superior Court in 1761; but to no avail. Alfred H. Kelley and Winfred A. Harbison, *The American Constitution* (New York: W. W. Norton, 1963), pp. 47–48.

69. Baroness Wootton as quoted in Bean, p. 163.

70. Bernard Simons, "A Drug Case in England: From Arrest to Sentence," *Contemporary Drug Problems* 2 (Spring 1973), pp. 105, 110–11.

71. For a scathing review of the differences between American and British criminal procedure in drug cases, see the article written by a participant in the first drug institute—Stephen Robert LaCheen, "First Impressions: A Philadelphia Lawyer's View of English Justice," *Shingle* 38:2 (February 1975), p. 29.

72. James Zacune, "A Comparison of Canadian Narcotic Addicts in Great Britain and in Canada," *Bulletin on Narcotics* 23 (October-December 1971), p. 41.

73. *Statistics of the Misuse of Drugs United Kingdom 1977*, p. 28. Advisory Council on the Misuse

of Drugs, *Report on Drug Dependants within the Prison System in England and Wales* (London: Home Office, 1979), pp. 1, 16.

74. Letter to author from H. B. Spear, Home Office, November 27, 1980.

CHAPTER 8

1. Percy E. Sutton, testimony as reported in *Hearings on New York City Narcotics Law Enforcement before the Select Committee on Narcotics Abuse and Control, House of Representatives*, November 19 and December 10, 1976 (GPO, 1977), p. 33; hereinafter cited as *1976 New York Hearings*.

2. The labels from the street heroin packages are reproduced in *1976 New York Hearings*, p. 61.

3. Kennedy's letter is on file in the DEA library.

4. The material on the Kennedy administration relies heavily on King, chap. 22.

5. As quoted in National Commission on Marihuana and Drug Abuse, *Drug Use in America: Problem in Perspective* (GOP, 1973), p. 329.

6. Information on the number of agents in 1959 and 1980 from Joseph Rainey, Manpower Management Staff, DEA, December 1980. The data appear in *Hearings before the Subcommittee of the Committee on Appropriations, House of Representatives*, January 27, 1958 (GPO, 1959), p. 111; and in an internal report—"DEA Ceiling Control System"—for November 30, 1980.

7. The material on the Johnson administration and the Drug Abuse Control Amendments of 1965 relies heavily on King, chaps. 25 and 26. The Anslinger quotation is on pp. 272–73.

8. A critical appraisal of NARA may be found in Ronald I. Weiner, "Shifting Perspectives in Drug Abuse Policy," *Crime and Delinquency* (July 1976), p. 347. Information on NARA inmate statistics based on telephone conversation with U.S. Bureau of Prisons official, Fall 1980. On August 19, 1980, there were 103 individuals in the entire NARA program.

9. The Nixon quotations appear in Arnold S. Trebach, "Nixon: Soft on Crime?" *Justice Magazine* (June/July 1972), p. 12; with the exception of the mention of narcotics, which appears in Epstein 1977, p. 61.

10. Epstein 1977, p. 132.

11. A good review of recent budgetary trends, including the cited figures, may be found in The Drug Abuse Council, *The Facts about "Drug Abuse"* (New York: Free Press, 1980), chap. 1; hereinafter cited as Drug Abuse Council 1980.

12. Rufus King's analysis of the 1970 act was thorough and harsh. He concluded that "passage of this comprehensive federal drug law in 1970 overreaches Commissioner Anslinger's furthest aspirations" (King, p. 319).

13. DEA's "no-knock" authority was granted by P.L. 91–513, 84 Stat. 1274, 1970, Sec. 509. It was repealed by P.L. 93–48, 88 Stat. 455, 1974, Sec. 3.

14. Nixon quoted in Drug Abuse Council 1980, p. 42.

15. Robert L. DuPont, "Where Does One Run When He's Already in the Promised Land?" speech, Fifth National Conference on Methadone Treatment, Washington, D.C., March 19, 1973.

16. The material referred to here appears on pp. ix, 5, 14, and 19 of the *White Paper*.

17. The Carter-Bourne anecdote appeared in DuPont, "The Drug Abuse Decade," *Journal of Drug Issues* 8 (Spring 1978), p. 181.

18. Peter G. Bourne, "It Is Time to Reexamine Our National Narcotics Policy," *The Urban and Social Change Review* 9 (Summer 1976), pp. 2–5.

19. Office of Drug Abuse Policy *1978 Annual Report*, p. 32. News release from U.S. Department of Health and Human Services, "FDA Approves Wider Use of THC for Aid to Cancer Patients," September 10, 1980; see also *Washington Post*, September 11, 1980.

20. ODAP is discussed along with SAODAP by Peter Goldberg in Drug Abuse Council 1980, chap. 1.

21. *Congressional Quarterly*, July 29, 1978, p. 1971. There were also charges at the time that

Bourne himself had used cocaine. According to Patrick Anderson, the revelation of those charges was the final blow in the Metsky affair. Anderson wrote that this event had occurred months earlier, during a 1977 Christmas party given by the National Organization for the Reform of Marijuana Laws and hosted by its director, Keith Stroup. Marijuana and cocaine were being openly used at the party. Anderson's account is: "Somewhat to Stroup's surprise, Dr. Peter Bourne showed up. . . . After a brief conversation, Stroup suggested they repair to a bedroom upstairs and have a little 'toot'—drug users' slang for cocaine use. Bourne smiled and said that sounded fine. They went upstairs. The cocaine was passed around. When it was his turn, Bourne took a 'hit' in each nostril, to the amazement of more than a dozen onlookers" (Patrick Anderson, "Pipe Dreams," *Washington Post Magazine*, December 14, 1980, p. 14).

22. Bourne is quoted in the *U.S. Journal of Drug and Alcohol Dependence*, June 1977, pp. 1, 2. *Seattle Times*, September 17, 1977, p. A10.

23. *Washington Post*, March 20, 1977, p. C6.

24. The figure of $6.5 billion spent by the federal government on drug abuse during the 1970s is, like so much in this field, an approximation. In Drug Abuse Council 1980, official statistics are cited to indicate that between Fiscal Year 1970 (which started in July of the previous year) and September 30, 1978 (the end of the fiscal year under the current system) the federal government spent $5,712.9 billion on drug abuse. However, statistics supplied by the U.S. Office of Management and Budget to the author in December 1980 do not fully jibe with the official statistics cited by the Drug Abuse Council. The discrepancy, however, is not great. Depending on the choice of data compilations, the total spent by the federal government between July 1969 and September 1979 was $6,369.3 or $6,579.9 billion; thus, an approximation of $6.5 billion seems reasonable. DuPont, "The Drug Abuse Decade," *Journal of Drug Issues* 8 (Spring 1978), p. 185. The NIDA staffing figures were supplied by Goldie Stoller of NIDA on December 16, 1980; the DEA figures, by Joseph Rainey of DEA on the same date.

25. These claims by the Carter administration were first mentioned in chap. 1, above. See citations for these statements in the notes to that chapter.

26. The quoted portion of the State of the Union message may be found on the back cover of the DEA magazine, *Drug Enforcement*, March 1980.

27. National Clearinghouse for Drug Abuse Information, *The British Narcotics System*, series 13, no. 2, April 1978, p. 11.

28. U.S. General Accounting Office, *Heroin Statistics Can Be Made More Reliable* (GPO, 1980), pp. 1–5.

29. *White Paper*, p. 20.

30. Office of Drug Abuse Policy, *1978 Annual Report*, p. 59.

31. National Commission on Marihuana and Drug Abuse, p. 154.

32. Mathea Falco and John Pekkanen, "The Abuse of Drug Abuse," *Washington Post*, September 8, 1974, pp. B1, B4.

33. National Commission on Marihuana and Drug Abuse, p. 172.

34. Silberman, p. 182.

35. McGlothlin's results and DuPont's observations are found in Robert L. DuPont, "Operation Trip-Wire: A New Proposal Focused on Criminal Heroin Addicts," speech, Federal Bar Association Convention, Washington, D.C., October 1, 1977, p. 11.

36. Special Action Office for Drug Abuse Prevention, "Social Costs of Drug Abuse," December 1974, p. 3.

37. Pers. comm. with burglary detective, Washington, D.C., 1980.

38. Rockefeller cited in Drug Abuse Council 1980, p. 84.

39. Eric D. Wish, Kandance A. Klumpp, Amy H. Moorer, Elizabeth Brady, and Kristen M. Williams, "*Executive Summary*—An Analysis of Drugs and Crime among Arrestees in the District of Columbia," Institute for Law and Social Research, Washington, D.C., 1980, p. 12.

40. James A. Inciardi and Carl D. Chambers, "Unreported Criminal Involvement of Narcotic Addicts," *Journal of Drug Issues* 2 (Spring 1972), pp. 57–64.

41. William I. Barton, "Drug Histories and Criminality: Survey of Inmates of State Correctional Facilities, January 1974," Drug Enforcement Administration, January 21, 1977. The statistical information mentioned in the text may be found in the summary starting on p. 1 of the report, and also on pp. 29–44 of the main body. The Barton quote, "this in *no* way . . . " is on p. 56. A briefer version of the report may be found in the *International Journal of the Addictions* 15(2), 1980, p. 233.

42. It is difficult to go beyond impressions and emotions to make more scientific comparisons of the addiction-crime situation in each country—in the same way that it is difficult to be precise about the relationship between addiction and crime within the borders of either nation. In America there is no single annual official compilation of all prisoners and their offenses, as there is in England. In the age of the American computer this may seem astounding, but it is a fact. Nevertheless, the bits and pieces of roughly comparable data tend to show a vastly larger American problem.

There *are* data on all federal prisoners. While they represent only a small proportion of the total in America, their numbers in the drug category exceed by far those for all of England. During the year that ended on June 30, 1977, 7,635 defendants were found guilty of violating the federal drug laws; and 1,466 of them received sentences of five years or more (*Annual Report of the Director of the Administrative Office of the United States Courts 1977*, p. 376).

Information received in August 1980 from the U.S. Bureau of Prisons (BOP), which is not completely congruent in statistical terms with the U.S. court data, shows that during the twelve months ending September 30, 1977, at least 3,671 prisoners were received who had been sentenced for violations of the federal drug laws. Of these, 1,164 had sentences of five years or more; 50, of twenty years and more. These 3,671 prisoners represented approximately 23 percent of the estimated 15,776 people received by the BOP on all offenses during that twelve-month period. Drug offenders, then, continue to represent a significant proportion of all federal prisoners.

During 1977 in England only 1,450 people received a sentence of imprisonment for violation of the drug laws; only 35 of these received sentences of five years or more. On June 30, 1977, a total of 839 prisoners were serving sentences for drug law violations; and for the entire year, 1,166 "drug dependent persons" were received in prison custody.

These data tend to support several possible hypotheses: (1) There is a greater connection between addiction and crime in America than in Britain. (2) The American approach to addicts and drugs causes more addicts and heavy users to become drawn into the criminal justice system than would occur in England. (3) Because of historical momentum, a vicious cycle has been created so that it is almost impossible now to tell if there are more American addicts in prison because there are so many addict-criminals here or if the American approach creates criminals out of addicts who, under other circumstances, would be addicts *but not criminals*. A reasonable person would have to admit that the resolution of these conflicting hypotheses is beyond the capability of existing knowledge, although one is entitled to make educated guesses.

43. The Rockefeller law is discussed on pp. 84–90 of Drug Abuse Council 1980. The quotation from *The Nation's Toughest Drug Law* is taken from p. 89 of the Drug Abuse Council book.

44. *1976 New York Hearings*, pp. 33–34.

45. Rangel's opposition to heroin maintenance is discussed in Cyril D. Robinson, "The Politics of a Heroin Maintenance Proposal in New York City," in *Drugs, Crime and Politics*, ed. Arnold S. Trebach, pp. 41ff. Police Commissioner Murphy's decision on arrests is analyzed in Drug Abuse Council 1980, p. 90.

In a study report issued as the manuscript of this book was almost completed, a group of experienced drug-abuse researchers admitted that even they were "shocked" at the amount of crime they encountered while conducting a detailed analysis of the activities of 243 male heroin addicts in Baltimore. These users committed over 500,000 crimes during an eleven-year period. John C. Ball, Lawrence Rosen, John A. Flueck, and David N. Nurco, "The Criminality of Heroin Addicts When

Addicted and When Off Opiates," Paper Presented to The International Congress on Alcoholism and Drug Dependence, ICAA, Medellín, Colombia, December 3–6, 1980, p. 21.

46. McKutchin is mentioned in the *Washington Post*, September 15, 1979, pp. 1, 5.

47. Regarding Linwood Gray see, among many other reports, *Washington Post*, June 6, 1980, p. 1.

48. On the prison break-in see *Washington Post*, May 24, 1980, p. 1, and August 21, 1980, p. C1.

49. While one may criticize the overall impact of American drug policies, as I have done, it is nevertheless awesome to contemplate the growth in the nation's treatment capability in recent years. "Fifteen years ago, our total treatment capacity consisted of two prison hospitals and a mere handful of outpatient clinics," wrote Lee I. Dogoloff, the top White House drug-abuse policy staff person, in 1980. He continued, "At the present time, in contrast, there are over 3,000 separate treatment units which have been identified throughout the country, treating over 750,000 patients each year. Of these, Federal funding for treatment services provides direct service to approximately 170,000 people annually" (*Annual Report on the Federal Drug Program, 1980* [Washington, D.C.: The White House, 1980], p. 14). All drug-abuse treatment organizations receiving federal funds are required to submit data on all clients admitted, regardless of whether a particular patient is actually supported by federal dollars, to NIDA's comprehensive Client Oriented Data Acquisition Process (CODAP). The CODAP reports provide a broad view of the prevalence of drug-abuse problems throughout the country. Although they do not provide a *complete* national picture and are not as reliable as England's data, the CODAP reports seem to provide a reasonably accurate image of the American drug-abuse scene. Summaries of 1979 CODAP data—as contained in National Institute on Drug Abuse, *Annual Summary Report*, 1979 (Rockville, Maryland: U.S. Department of Health and Human Services, 1980), pp. 4,6,7—revealed that during 1979 approximately 243,-000 people were admitted to treatment for drug-abuse problems in facilities that report to CODAP. Of this group, 48 percent stated that their primary drug of abuse was in the opiate category, with 40 percent claiming heroin and 8 percent other opiates. The next most frequently cited drugs of abuse were marijuana, 16 percent; alcohol, 8 percent; and amphetamines, 7 percent. The proportion of clients reporting heroin as their primary drug of abuse declined from 62 percent in 1976 to 40 percent in 1979.

50. *Dealing with Drug Abuse*, pp. 191–92.

51. Maher is quoted in William Overend, "Addiction: Will There Ever Be a Solution?" *Los Angeles Times*, April 11, 1976, pp. V 1, 15–16; hereinafter cited as Overend.

52. DeLong, *Dealing with Drug Abuse*, p. 195. For an example of much more favorable attitudes toward the outcome of TC treatment, see George De Leon and Mitchell S. Rosenthal, "Therapeutic Communities," in *Handbook on Drug Abuse*, ed. Robert L. DuPont et al. (National Institute on Drug Abuse [GPO, 1979]), p. 39.

53. As quoted in National Clearinghouse for Drug Abuse Information, *Methadone: The Drug and Its Therapeutic Uses in the Treatment of Addiction*, series 31, no. 1, July 1974, p. 1.

54. *Life* magazine, p. 87. It is to be noted that I have not discussed LAAM (L-alpha acetyl methadol), the longer-acting variety of methadone, in the text. While it need be taken only every two or three days, no facts I have encountered would lead me to believe that it is significantly different from the other opiates reviewed here—good for some addicts, at some times, under some circumstances. Certainly, its continued use should be encouraged for addicts who believe that it helps to stabilize their lives.

55. George M. Belk, letter to the editor, *Bulletin of the Medical Society of the County of Kings and Academy of Medicine of Brooklyn* 44:12 (December 1965), p. 509.

56. The early days of the Dole-Nyswander partnership are described in Nat Hentoff, *A Doctor among the Addicts* (New York: Rand McNally, 1968), chap. 9.

57. Ibid., p. 113.

58. Ibid., p. 114.

59. Vincent P. Dole, Marie E. Nyswander, and Mary Jean Kreek, "Narcotic Blockade," *Archives of Internal Medicine* 118 (October 1966), pp. 304, 309.

60. Dole is quoted in Edward Jay Epstein, "Methadone: The Forlorn Hope," *The Public Interest* 36 (Summer 1974), pp. 3, 13.

61. Vincent P. Dole and Marie E. Nyswander, "Heroin Addiction—A Metabolic Disease," *Archives of Internal Medicine* 120 (July 1967), pp. 19–20.

62. Vincent P. Dole, Marie E. Nyswander, and Alan Warner, "Successful Treatment of 750 Criminal Addicts," *JAMA* 206:12 (December 16, 1968), pp. 2708–11.

63. Dole and Nyswander quoted in Epstein, "Methadone: The Forlorn Hope," p. 11.

64. Gearing is quoted in Brecher, p. 143.

65. The Harvard studies are discussed in Epstein, "Methadone: The Forlorn Hope," p. 10.

66. Ibid., p. 22. Silberman, p. 180. In 1975 Dr. Bourne reviewed the same data, including the Epstein critique of methadone, and came out roughly, but not precisely, where I did: "Although much of the criticism of the data produced seems valid, particularly that of Epstein, it tends to dispute claims regarding the *magnitude* of crime reduction, rather than be a refutation of the basic hypothesis. There appears, to date, to be no persuasive argument against the belief that methadone maintenance reduces crime rates to some undetermined degree" (Peter G. Bourne, *Methadone: Benefits and Shortcomings* [Washington, D.C.: Drug Abuse Council, Inc., 1975], p. 8).

67. Paul Cushman, Jr., "Relationship between Narcotic Addiction and Crime," *Federal Probation* 38:5 (September 1974), pp. 38, 39.

68. DeLong, *Dealing with Drug Abuse*, p. 210. DeLong, "The Methadone Habit," *New York Times Magazine*, March 16, 1975, pp. 16, 93.

69. *Narcotic Addict Treatment Act of 1974*, P.L. 93–281, 84 Stat. 1242, 1974.

70. The 1974 law amended the 1970 comprehensive law by, among other things, adding to section 102 of the Controlled Substances Act a new paragraph 27, to define maintenance, and a new paragraph 28, to define detoxification.

71. Section 3 of the 1974 act.

72. The major part of the federal regulations affecting methadone appear in *Code of Federal Regulations*, title 21, secs. 291.501 and 291.505. Under the Federal Food, Drug, and Cosmetic Act, a new drug must be shown to be safe and effective before it can be introduced into interstate commerce. P.L. 75–717, 52 Stat. 1040, 1938. The "safe and effective" provision is now found in 21 U.S.C. 355, as amended, November 1977.

73. "Classification of Dextropropoxyphene as a Narcotic Drug in Schedule IV of the Controlled Substances Act," 21 Code of Federal Regulations, part 1308, *Federal Register*, June 24, 1980, p. 42264.

74. Vincent P. Dole and Marie E. Nyswander, "Methadone Maintenance Treatment," *JAMA* 235 (May 10, 1976), p. 2117.

75. Paul Cushman, *Wall Street Journal*, January 28, 1977, p. 12.

76. The incident occurred on July 18, 1979, during the Sixth Institute on Drugs, Crime and Justice in England. Dr. John McClure was the speaker for that session.

77. Spear's observation appears in an unpublished paper prepared by a student in the 1975 London drug institute—Ira Frazer, "Notification and the Official Statistics: Strictly British," June 22, 1975, p. 11.

CHAPTER 9

1. Robert L. DuPont, "New Directions for the National Institute on Drug Abuse," speech, National Drug Abuse Conference, San Francisco, May 6, 1977.

2. Richard Blum, as quoted in Overend, pp. V 1, 14.

3. Weil, p. 200.

4. National Commission on Marihuana and Drug Abuse, p. 337. Brecher, p. 530. Paul Dana-ceau, *What's Happening with Heroin Maintenance?* (Washington, D.C.: The Drug Abuse Council, Inc., 1977), p. 20. This study also provides a good review of the various proposals for heroin maintenance put forward in the United States during the 1970s, including a bill presented to the Michigan House of Representatives in December 1975. The support of experimental programs *only* in this 1977 study was echoed in the final council report—Drug Abuse Council 1980, p. 247. The Vera Institute proposal is discussed in Danaceau, *What's Happening with Heroin Maintenance?* p. 13; a full exposition of the emotions and politics behind it appear in Cyril D. Robinson, "The Politics of a Heroin Maintenance Proposal in New York City," in *Drugs, Crime, and Politics*, ed. Arnold S. Trebach, p. 31. Philip C. Baridon, *Addiction, Crime and Social Policy* (Lexington, Mass.: Lexington Books, 1976), p. 88.

5. According to information from the Drug Abuse Warning Network, 30 people were listed as having died from codeine abuse in 1978 when it appeared to be the only drug involved. That drug was involved, along with others, in an estimated 750 deaths. This information appears in a press release, "NIDA Capsules," from the National Institute on Drug Abuse, September 1979.

6. It has been alleged that because of American pressures, hundreds of thousands of opium addicts in the Third World have been forced to give up their habits, and many have switched to heroin.

7. Letter from Andrew T. Weil to Michael C. Elsner, September 9, 1978, which appeared in an unpublished paper prepared by Elsner, a participant in the 1978 London drug institute, "Zen and the Art of Heroin Maintenance: A Look at the Concept of Non-Harm," November 1, 1978. While Dr. Weil's observation about the nauseating effect of too much opium appears to be correct, this effect does not seem to be unique to opium; most opiates have this impact when taken orally in excessive amounts.

8. Epstein, "Methadone: The Forlorn Hope," p. 16.

9. Overend, p. V 1.

10. Blum, as quoted in Overend, pp. V 1, 14.

11. Robert L. DuPont, "New Directions."

12. *U.S. Journal of Drug and Alcohol Dependence*, June 1977, p. 6.

13. Sec. 291.505 of Title 21, *Code of Federal Regulations*, sets out the two-year requirement.

14. Judson, p 94.

15. A major nationwide study in 1976 by Dr. John O'Donnell and his associates indicated that as many as 96 percent of those who had been addicted to heroin (that is, who reported taking it daily in the past) had ceased to do so at the time of the interview. This might have been due to maturing out or to a host of other factors, such as family pressures, fear of hurting one's health, fear of arrest, the high expense of buying the drug on the black market, and difficulty obtaining a regular supply. The last two factors were the major reasons offered by Vietnam veterans who gave up the habit, according to the classic study by Dr. Lee N. Robbins, of the Washington University School of Medicine in St. Louis. She found that 88 percent of those who had been addicted in Vietnam were not addicted at any time in the three years following their return. This study is often cited to support enforcement policies, on the theory that if heroin is difficult to obtain and expensive, fewer people will use it. True, to an extent, especially for marginal users; but there is also evidence that more expensive heroin pushes determined users to commit more crimes in order to get money to keep their supply line open. In any event, the Robbins study would seem to contradict the diabetic-insulin analogy and lend support to my plea for a redefinition of the disease concept of addiction. The O'Donnell and Robbins studies are discussed in Lee N. Robbins, "Addict Careers," in *Hand-book on Drug Abuse*, pp. 332–33.

16. My suggestion of a new definition of drug addiction aims to challenge medical experts to come up with a better, more functional one than now exists. I recognize that the task is difficult and

that many physicians who may otherwise be sympathetic to most of my basic arguments will disagree with my attempt to cast doubt on the utility of the present definition. One of these has already raised questions about the wisdom of my recommendation. Dr. Beckett observed that the current World Health Organization definition has proved quite adequate in his practice, and in a letter of September 11, 1980, declared that "the definition you suggest of drug addiction is something so wide that many things other than drug addiction would fall within its ambit."

17. Thomas H. Bewley, Oved Ben-Arie, and I. Pierce James, "Morbidity and Mortality from Heroin Dependence," *British Medical Journal* (March 23, 1968), pp. 725, 729.

18. None of my work dealt with the actual heroin traffic in Southeast Asia. Accordingly, until I see contrary evidence, I accept as truth McCoy's statements about the corrupt involvement of local government officials, who were often supported by the CIA, in the heroin trade. But on most significant interpretations of facts within the areas covered by my research, McCoy was misleading or simply wrong. His grand assumption was, "American heroin addicts are victims of the most profitable criminal enterprise known to man—an enterprise that involves millions of peasant farmers in the mountains of Asia, thousands of corrupt government officials, disciplined criminal syndicates, and agencies of the United States government" (Alfred W. McCoy, *The Politics of Heroin in Southeast Asia* [New York: Harper and Row, 1972], p. 8). This is misleading because it contains many half-truths which have been converted into whole truths by those who have a need to blame almost any problem on the CIA and our Southeast Asian foreign policy. The grand assumption, moreover, ignores the fact that the opium trade has persisted for centuries, before either the United States or heroin existed. And it makes an even grander assumption: that foreign policy can explain why *anyone* would take *any* drug—why anyone would become a victim-addict. At one point in the book, McCoy offers an even more ingenious explanation for the "root of the problem" in America: "When heroin was introduced into the United States by the German pharmaceutical company, Bayer, in 1898, it was . . . declared nonaddictive, and was widely prescribed in hospitals and by private practitioners as a safe substitute for morphine. After opium smoking was outlawed in the United States ten years later, many opium addicts turned to heroin as a legal substitute, and America's heroin problem was born" (p. 17). The leaps of faith in this statement are mind-boggling. Sadly, many members of the liberal establishment believe McCoy's major arguments, especially about the CIA's creation of heroin addicts. Nothing encountered in my work supports them.

19. Catherine Lamour and Michel R. Lamberti, *The Second Opium War* (London: Allen Lane, 1974), pp. 261, 263. (The original French edition was published in 1972.) The French experts also inform us, "It is by no means fortuitous that, sooner than promote a policy of full employment, the American government should prefer to hand out the dole to the unemployed ghetto-dwellers, knowing full well that these underprivileged people will squander the better part of it on drugs." The familiar thesis affixing blame for heroin addiction to American foreign policy is, in addition to the capitalism argument, central to their book.

20. Institute for the Study of Drug Dependence, *Drug Link, Information Letter*, Summer 1979, pp. 4–6. The comments in the text were made as part of a review of a series of articles and books on China and on other countries.

21. Norval Morris, *The Future of Imprisonment* (Chicago: University of Chicago Press, 1974), p. 29.

22. Leon G. Hunt and Norman E. Zinberg, *Heroin Use: A New Look* (Washington, D.C.: Drug Abuse Council, Inc., 1976). Hunt and Zinberg concluded: "In order for such a revolutionary approach to be tried even experimentally, the myths and stereotypes about heroin, as an *inevitably* addicting drug, must be abandoned."

INDEX

Addiction, 25–26, 63, 85, 259; causes of, 26, 51, 54–58, 69–70, 83, 93, 147, 172, 288–89, 320nn18, 19; as crime, 157–58, 161 (*see also* Crime(s), drug-related; Crime/heroin relationship); danger of, 56, 99, 100; defined, 92, 283–84, 319n16; as depravity, 137, 148; as disease, 93, 103, 131, 139–40, 154, 163, 169, 187, 189, 282–84; maturing out of, 283, 285; through medical treatment, 55, 56, 94 (*see also* Addicts, therapeutic); as metabolic disease, 259, 282–83; not a disease, 135–36; statistics re, 82–83, 97, 103 (*see also* Addicts, numbers of); in terminal illness, 34. *See also* Heroin addiction; Treatment

Addiction control and treatment: in England, 102–03, 201–12; U.S./British comparison, 163, 168–70, 171, 172–73. *See also* British system; Drug policy

"Addictive personality," 25, 259, 284

Addicts, 83, 93, 151, 156, 174, 248; accepting/rejecting treatment, 219–20, 238, 256, 261–62, 272–73, 281; aged and infirm, 135, 140–41, 151; behavioral characteristics of, 178, 206, 255, 279; case studies (England), 105–06, 113–17; controlling deviance of, as goal of treatment, 189, 190; death rate of, 12, 13–15, 143, 284; diseased, 62, 283–84; drug of choice, 44, 57, 148, 151–52, 200–01, 292, 317n49; free will, 220, 272; living normal life with drugs, 94, 104–06, 206–07; medical care of, 169–70; minor, 277; new, deviant (England), 93, 97–99, 102, 173, 174–77, 178–79, 188–89, 198, 200, 211–12, 280; numbers of, 3, 6–7, 9–10, 12, 297n5; numbers of—England, 19–20, 89, 92–93, 102–03, 107–08, 111, 140, 178; numbers of—U.S., 44, 49, 140–41, 147, 175, 243, 245–46; opiate, 38–39; recreational, 284 (*see also* Chippers); registration of, 103–04, 280–81 (*see also* British system, notification of addicts in); requirements of responsible living for, 152–53, 187, 189, 206–07, 224–25, 268; rights of, 183, 277, 285; as scapegoats, 205–06; at Shreveport clinic, 150; stabilized, 104–

06, 140, 152, 174, 258–60; therapeutic, 55–56, 82–83, 97, 98; young, deviant, 113, 155. *See also* Crime(s), drug-related; Maintenance; Narcotic clinics; Treatment

Advisory Commission on Narcotic and Drug Abuse, 229

Advisory Council on the Misuse of Drugs (England), 211, 218

Alcohol, 3, 4–5, 88, 160, 162, 246, 292

Alcoholics Anonymous, 254

Alsop, Stewart, 27–28

American Bar Association, 163

"American disease." *See* Heroin addiction

American Medical Association, 30–31, 96, 100, 156, 162, 174, 257; condemned ambulatory treatment, 138–39; Council on Health and Public Instruction, 138–39; Council on Pharmacy and Chemistry, 53; Council on Scientific Affairs, 31; Department of Drugs, 76; House of Delegates, 47, 76, 139; joint committee with American Bar Association, 163; on method of treatment, 139–40; position on heroin as medicine, 49, 64, 65, 66, 76

American Society of Internal Medicine, House of Delegates, 30–31

Amphetamines, 15, 180, 181, 230, 292

Analgesic research, 30, 63–75, 239, 294

Anderson, Patrick, 314n21

Anslinger, Harry Jacob, 52, 174–75, 199, 230, 248; on methadone, 257; narcotics enforcement career of, 100, 113, 141, 160–68; resignation of, 226–27, 228, 229

Ashley, Richard, 103; *Heroin*, 119, 298n5

Australia, 6, 11–12

BNDD. *See* Bureau of Narcotics and Dangerous Drugs (BNDD) (U.S.)

Balance, impossible, 154, 155, 224, 294

Ball, John C., 7

Barbiturates, 4, 106, 204, 230, 246

Baridon, Philip C., 269

Barry, Marion, 19

Barton, William I., 249, 250

Baum, Gerhart, 13

Bayer company, 42

Bazell, Robert, 76–77
Bean, Philip, 102, 107; *The Social Control of Drugs*, 100
Beaver, William T., 76, 77, 80
Beckett, H. Dale, 178, 199, 203–04, 205, 211, 255, 284, 319n16
Behrman, Morris, 130
Belgium, 14
Belk, George M., 257
Bell, Griffin, 29
Bensinger, Peter B., 18, 243
Beth Israel Hospital (New York City), 259
Bevan, Aneurin, 100
Bewley, Thomas, 111–12, 173–75, 178, 284
bin Haji Ahmad, Encik Mohamed Noor, 8
Black, J. R., 4
Black market, 20, 57, 167, 248, 276; in England, 83, 97, 98–99, 208, 209, 212, 244; sale of legal drugs in, 278, 281
Blalock, J. C., 144, 145
Bloedorn, W. A., 44
Blue, Rupert, 47, 50
Blum, Richard, 273–74
Boggs Act: (1951), 163–64; (1956), 164
Borneo, 7–8, 167
Bourne, Peter G., 1, 15, 18, 32, 80, 236–39, 242; estimate of number of addicts, 297n5; "It Is Time to Reexamine Our National Narcotics Policy," 237–38; on methadone and crime, 317n66; special assistant to Carter on drug policy, 240, 241; supported idea of heroin as medicine, 30, 239, 241
Braaten, David, 34
Brain, Sir Russell, 101, 102, 184
Brain Committee, 173, 175
Brain Committee reports, 101–11, 117, 140, 152, 177, 178–79, 183, 199
Brandeis, Louis, 130
Brecher, Edward, 141, 159, 269, 298n5, 308n20; *Licit and Illicit Drugs*, 119
Brewster, Sidney W., 50–51
Brill, Henry, 59–60, 69; G. W. Larimore and, "The British Narcotic System," 96
British Medical Association, 100–01, 169
British Medical Journal, 96, 100, 187
British system, 17, 21, 85–86, 90, 109, 111–17, 124, 149, 150, 199, 213, 222; Anslinger on, 167; doubts re, 171–246; flexibility and trust in, 268; as model, 87, 217, 245, 276–80, 281, 292, 295; notification of addicts in, 95, 97–98, 99, 110, 175, 180, 182, 185,

266, 280–81 (*see also* Home Office [England], addict index); preventive aspects of, 111–12
Brompton Cocktail (Brompton's Mixture), 31, 35, 58, 71
Brown, Claude: *Manchild in the Promised Land*, 235
Brown, Edmund, 229
Bryant, Thomas E., 236
Bureau of Narcotics and Dangerous Drugs (BNDD) (U.S.), 2, 298n5
Butler, Willis P., 148–56, 157, 166, 174, 187, 266, 267–68, 303n34

Califano, Joseph A., Jr., 31
Campbell, Harry, 88–89, 122
Canada, 6, 215
Cancer, 22–24, 27–28, 33, 35–36, 239; heroin in treatment of, 63–65, 66, 67–75, 76–79, 293
Cannabis. *See* Marijuana
Caring institutions, 204–10
Caring relationships, 24–25, 96, 274, 280
Carter, Jimmy, 236–37, 239–43
Carter administration, 18, 29, 31–32, 60
Chambers, Carl, 249, 250
China, 288, 289
Chipp, Donald L., 12
Chippers, 4, 246, 276, 281, 291
Chua Sian, 9
Chupanya, Khachit, 9
Churches, Mal, 11
Civil rights, 153, 165
Clark, Ramsey, 231
Clarke, Richard, S. J., 64, 65–66
Clinic treatment system (England), 19–20. *See also* Drug-dependence clinics (England); Narcotics clinics
Cocaine, 4, 13, 81, 121, 122, 201, 227; control of, 29, 45, 87, 110, 181, 184, 185; as drug of choice, 148; effects of, 50–51; prohibition of, 123; recreational use of, 98, 99
Codeine, 39, 42, 62, 81, 181; as medical substitute for heroin, 50
Codeine addicts, 271
Coffee, John, 162, 163
"Cold turkey," 9, 115. *See also* Withdrawal
Columbia University School of Public Health, 260
Commitment, institutional, 156–60, 161, 170, 230–31, 254

Committee on the Treatment of Intractable Pain (U.S.), 29, 34

Comprehensive Drug Abuse Prevention and Control Act of 1970 (U.S.), 29, 31, 233–34; Title II: Controlled Substances Act, 31, 75, 81, 201, 233, 239, 300n9

Connell, Philip H., 186–87, 188, 191, 196–97, 223, 282

Connelly, Philip, 210–11

Consciousness, altered states of, 267, 290, 294

Controlled Substances Act. See Comprehensive Drug Abuse Prevention and Control Act of 1970

Copeland, Royal S., 44

Corruption, 11, 14, 227, 239

Counseling, 146, 169, 170. See also Psychiatric treatment; Psychotherapy

Court action, 295

Coxall, Colin, 212

Crime(s), alcohol-related, 4

Crime(s), drug-related, 9, 50–51, 139, 212–18, 232, 245–53; and legalization of narcotics, 280–81; and methadone maintenance, 259–62, 274; in Shreveport, La., 149, 153; U.S., 213, 229, 231, 232

Crime/heroin relationship, 2, 3, 4, 15, 239, 247–53, 292; in England, 20, 98–99. See also Heroin, criminogenic effects of

Criminal procedure: U.S./England compared, 214–17. See also Drug-law enforcement

Criminality, preaddictive, 3, 246–47, 260–61

Criminalization of drug activity, 167, 229, 230

Culture: community, and treatment method, 153–54, 155, 187–88, 268; and drug use, 6

Cure(s), 93, 96, 136, 139, 157, 168, 169; nonexistent, 159; prison as, 154

Cushman, Paul, 261, 264–65

Cuskey, Walter R., Arnold W. Klein, and William Krasner: Drug-Trip Abroad, 113–17

Customs and Excise Act (1952) (England), 215

DEA. See Drug Enforcement Administration (DEA) (U.S.)

Dangerous Drugs Act: (1920) (England), 87, 92, 93, 101, 124; (1951), 103; (1967), 110, 180–81, 215

Daniel, Price, 163, 164, 165–66

Darvon, 264

Davignon, J. Paul, 304n23

Day, William R., 127–28

Deaths, heroin-related, 12, 13–15, 243. See also Overdoses

Decriminalization, 239, 241, 271. See also Legalization

Dederich, Charles, 254

Defence of the Realm Act (England), 87

Delancey Street project (San Francisco), 255–56

Delaney, Bernard, 11–12

Delevingne, Malcolm, 91

Delianis, Paul, 12

DeLong, James V., 158–59, 256, 262; Dealing with Drug Abuse, 254

Demerol. See Meperidine

Denham, J., 197

Denmark, 14

Dependence. See Drug dependence

Depression, 204, 284, 301n24

Detoxification, 146, 157, 263, 271; at Shreveport clinic, 150–51

Dextromoramide (Palfium), 200–01, 312n40

Diacetylmorphine. See Heroin

Diamorphine. See Heroin

Dilaudid, 77

Dipipanone (Diconal), 201, 204, 213, 221, 223

District of Columbia Narcotics Treatment Administration, 234

Doctors, 56, 95, 108–09

Doctors, British, 89, 106; in clinics, 182–83, 186; disciplinary machinery for, 110, 183–85 (see also Medical tribunals); overprescribing, 107–10, 114n, 173, 175, 176, 177, 179, 183, 187, 221; power in prescription of drugs, 24, 36, 78, 95, 96, 97, 106, 108–10, 111, 175, 178, 180, 182, 185, 201, 220, 221–22; prosecution of, 182, 183–84, 185. See also Medical profession, England

Doctors, U.S.: abusing precription powers, 107, 125, 126, 128–30, 131, 133, 136, 144, 269; frightened away from legitimate use of drugs, 46, 57, 125, 134–35, 137, 151, 170; intimidated and harassed, 132; opposed ban on heroin, 52–53; prosecuted under Harrison Act, 125, 127–31, 133, 139, 141–45; right to prescribe drugs, 46, 119, 120, 122, 123, 124, 125, 263–64, 277, 279, 280; supported Treasury Department in drug-law enforcement, 132, 137–39, 140; treatment of addicts, 148, 268–69, 293–94. See also Medical profession, U.S.

Dole, Robert, 31
Dole, Vincent P., 226–27, 257–60, 262, 264, 266, 272, 282–83
Dolophine, 256. *See* Methadone
Doremus, Charles T., 127, 128. See also *United States* v. *Doremus*
Dosage(s), 148, 277–78; nondiminishing, 124, 125; reducing, 133, 134, 136, 169, 196–97; at Shreveport clinic, 152. *See also* Addicts, stabilized; Maintenance
Dowling, Oscar, 149
Dreser, Heinrich, 39, 40–41, 42, 56, 74
Drinamyl (Dexamyl), 180
Drug abuse, 5, 172; international patterns of, 6–16. *See also* Addiction; and specific drugs
Drug Abuse Council, 18, 231, 236, 246, 248–49, 251, 269, 276, 315*n*24; "A Statement of Concerns," 2
Drug-abuse programs, 254–66; employees in, 242; failure of, 270; federal, 239–41, 242, 244–45; funds spent for, 232–33, 241–42. *See also* Treatment
Drug control and treatment: models for, 295; U.S./British comparison, 198–99, 218–19, 265–66. *See also* Addiction control and treatment
Drug dependence, 43, 145–46, 290–91; causes of, 247; defined, 282; difference between U.S. and British approaches to, 106–07, 136, 140. *See also* Addiction
Drug-dependence clinics (England), 110, 117, 172, 179, 180–81, 186–201, 219–21, 222, 223, 268, 279, 294; criticism of, 210–12
Drug Enforcement Administration (DEA) (U.S.), 2, 17, 231, 234, 243; regulation of treatment by, 262, 263, 265
Drug-law enforcement, 7, 13, 89–90, 158, 227, 238; of Harrison Act, 125–31; international, 8–16, 167–68; intrusion of, into medical practice (U.S.), 57–58, 132–45, 233, 263–65; lack of intrusion in British medical practice, 183, 201; selectivity in, 141, 252–53; as treatment, 148. *See also* Prisons; Punishment
Drug laws: England, 87, 180–81; New York State, 251, 252–53; proposed (U.S.), 163, 293; regulating treatment (U.S.), 262–64; state, 121, 157; U.S., 29–30, 53–54, 163–64, 181, 230, 233–34. *See also* names of specific acts, e.g., Harrison Narcotic Act

Drug policy, England, 222–25. *See also* British system
Drug policy, U.S., 30–31, 45–54, 113, 161, 226–66, 281; future, 267–95. *See also* Balance, impossible; Social policy
Drug statistics. *See* Addicts, numbers of; Home Office (England), addict index
Drug trafficking, 9, 11, 12, 244; in England, 98–99, 181
Drug use: views of, 290–91
Drug users, 276, 290–91; pushed into criminality, 156, 219–20, 246, 248–49, 289, 292. *See also* Addicts; Chippers
Drugs: abuse potential of, 81; accessibility of, 176–77, 238; choice of, in treatment, 270–76 (*see also* Addicts, drug of choice); controlled (England), 181, 184, 185; diversion of, for nonmedical purposes, 82, 97–99, 278, 281 (*see also* Gray market); hysteria, irrationality toward, 168; illegal, 130, 133–34, 212, 227; legal prescription of, 163, 173–74; personal perception of, 78, 79; prohibition of, 88, 121, 291–92; recreational use of, 1–2, 98–99, 201, 289, 294; sold to addicts to gratify habit, 127–30, 136; synthetic, 102, 106–07, 201, 237, 238, 256, 271, 312*n*40; teaching beneficial use of, 207, 267, 290, 291; in treatment of organic illness, 46, 54–58, 122, 134–35, 137, 143–45, 151, 181–82, 239. *See also* Narcotics; Psychoactive drugs; and under specific drugs, e.g., Heroin
Dundee, John W., 64, 65–66
DuPont, Robert L., 5, 233, 234–35, 237, 242, 276, 279; on crime/drug relationship, 247–48; on heroin maintenance, 274–75
Duster, Troy: *The Legislation of Morality*, 120
Dymond, Geoffrey, 179
Dysphoria, drug-induced, 65

Eddy, Nathan B., 256
Edwards, Griffith, 109, 112
Egypt, 16
Elliot, Walter, 88, 89
Ellis, Pat, 197
England, 7, 216; addiction control and treatment in, 168–69, 294 (*see also* British system); conflict in, re treatment of addiction, 91, 92, 95, 100–01, 124, 171–225; consumption of licit heroin in, 108; deviant

subculture in, 108; licit use of heroin in, 20, 54, 78, 82–83, 103–04, 201–12; number of addicts in, 6, 19–20, 89, 92–93, 102–03, 107–08, 111, 140, 178; search, seizure, arrest in, 214–17; social policy re heroin in, 5, 87–117; spread of heroin addiction in, 97–99, 101–03, 107, 112, 168, 172; statistics on heroin use and abuse, 82–83; use of heroin as medicine in, 32–36, 74, 169, 181–82 (*see also* Cancer); youth unrest in, 176–77. *See also* Home Office (England)
England, Ministry of Health, 89, 91, 95–96, 110, 179; Departmental Committee on Morphine and Heroin Addiction, 89–90, 101
Epstein, Edward Jay, 18, 231–32, 287–88; *Agency of Fear*, 2, 3; "Methadone: The Forlorn Hope," 261
Euphoria, drug-induced, 26, 28, 36, 54–55, 65, 193, 272–73, 278, 301n24; lacking with methadone, 257, 258, 272; in organically ill, 205–06
Europe, impact of heroin on, 190, 191T

Falco, Mathea, 18, 243, 246
Fazey, Cindy, 199
Federal Comprehensive Drug Abuse Prevention and Control Act (1970), 54
ffrench-Hodges, Moona, 210
Floret, Dr., 39–41, 42, 74
Ford, Gerald, 235–36
Ford Foundation: *Dealing with Drug Abuse*, 158–59
Foreign Policy Association, 47–48, 49; *The Case against Heroin*, 48, 49; Committee on Traffic in Opium, 48
Foster, Rufus E., 144–45
France, 14
Francis, Fred, 299n25
François, Léon, 14
Frankau, Isabella (Lady Franco), 114, 115, 116, 179, 187, 221
Frankfurter, Felix, 214
Freud, Sigmund, 145

Gearing, Frances Rowe, 260
General Medical Council (England), 183, 184
Germany, 167, 299n25
Giordano, Henry L., 228
Glick, John H., 28

Goldstein, Avram, 62
"Good faith" practice of medicine, 46, 123, 125, 130, 131, 133, 134, 141–43. *See also* Medicine, legitimate practice of
Graff, Harold, 7
Gray market, 175, 278, 281
Guam, 10–11

Hague Opium Convention (1912), 45–46, 87
Hanam, John, 9
Hanratty, Joseph, 25
Hare, H. A., 49–50
Harney, M. L., 86
Harrison, Francis Burton, 113, 121
Harrison Narcotic Act (U.S.), 45, 57, 87, 88, 113–31, 146, 157, 160, 162, 175, 230, 276; amended by Boggs Act, 163; amendment re possession, 127n; constitutionality of, 127–28; intent of, 119–24, 126
Hartnoll, Richard, 193–96
Harvard Medical School, 63, 65
Hawkins, David B., 143–45, 182
Hawkins v. United States, 143–45
Healy, Joseph, 158
Heart disease, 67
Henney, Jane E., 75
Heroin (diacetylmorphine, diamorphine), 12, 61, 88, 210–11, 213, 238, 243–44; abuse potential of, 5–6, 7, 44–45, 59, 69–70, 81–82, 99–100, 161, 164; as addiction-treatment drug (England), 201–12; addictive potential of, 43, 55, 56, 60–61, 63, 65; as benign drug, 203–04, 211, 273, 292; control of (England), 181, 184, 185; and crime, 2, 3, 4, 15, 239, 242, 247–53; criminalization of, 53–54; criminogenic effect of, 246, 248–49, 251, 292; dangers of, 31–32, 46–54, 83; as demon, 37, 38, 41, 46–54; discovery of, 37, 39–41; as drug of choice, 148, 152; effects of, 4, 35, 48, 49–52, 61–63, 69–70, 79, 301n24; emotional reaction to, 30, 35, 248–49, 272, 274; impact of, on Europe, 190, 191T; legal manufacture, consumption and conversion of, 54, 302n33T; legal use of, 20, 54, 78, 82–83, 103–04, 201–12; legalization of, 12, 29, 31, 239, 293; as miracle medicine, 40–41; in morphine withdrawal, 40–42, 43, 59; misunderstanding of, 5–6; move away from, in treatment (England), 190–98; open sale

Heroin (*continued*)
of, 56–57; in prevention of psychosis, 202–03; prohibition of, 37, 52, 80–81, 99–101; recreational use of, 98, 99, 220 (*see also* Addicts, new, deviant [England]; Chippers); as restricted drug (England), 110; situation re, intolerable (U.S.), 276 (*see also* social problems caused by addicts); statistics re (U.S.), 243–45 (*see also* Addicts, numbers of); therapeutic potential of, 239

Heroin addiction: battle against (U.S.), 232, 234–35, 242–45; epidemic of, 1–21, 44, 291, 292; control and treatment of, 171–246; spread of (England), 97–99, 101–03, 107, 112, 168, 172. *See also* Addiction; Addicts

Heroin as medicine, 5–6, 22–36, 170, 206, 239, 274–75, 292–93; advocacy of, 27–28, 29–32; availability of substitutes for, 100; effects of, 54–55; experiments with, 63–75; history of, 37–58; legal issues in, 73, 75, 80–84; medical value of, 59–84; unique qualities of, 202–04; use of (England), 32–34, 74, 169, 181–82 (*see also* Cancer)

Heroin maintenance, 41, 271, 272, 273–85, 292; term, 284–85

Heroin solution, 2, 5, 289–95

Heroin trade, 16, 288. *See also* Black market; Drug trafficking

Herold, A. A., 52–53

Highs, nondrug, 290. *See also* Euphoria, drug-induced

Hobson, Richard P., 53

Holmes, Oliver Wendell, Jr., 126, 127, 130

Home Office (England), 177, 179; addict index, 82, 83, 97–98, 99, 103, 107, 178, 188, 221–22, 280–81; drug-use statistics, 311n25; Drugs Branch, 97; implementation of drug-control legislation, 89–92; Statistical Bulletin, 213

Hong Hoo Chong, 8

Hong Kong, 6, 10, 21, 167

Hospice movement (U.S.), 22, 24, 31, 73, 83–84

Hospices (England), 22–24, 33–35, 68–69, 73–74

Hostels, 206. *See also* ROMA

Houde, Raymond W., 76–77, 78

Hubbard, S. Dana, 48, 51, 55

Hunt, Leon G., 291

Hydrocodone (Hycodan, Dicodid), 201, 312n40

I. G. Farbenindustrie, 256

Illness, organic: drug-induced euphoria in, 205–06; drugs in treatment of, 46, 54–58, 122, 134–35, 143–45, 151, 181–82, 239; heroin in treatment of, 22–28, 29, 30, 41–42, 79–80. *See also* Cancer; Heroin as medicine

Illness, terminal, 33–35, 60, 80, 293

Inciardi, James, 249, 250

Injection(s), 38, 152, 271, 279–80; dangers of, 192–93, 221; effectiveness of, vs. oral, 70–74, 77; move away from, in treatment (England), 190–98, 199–201, 204, 208–09, 211–12, 221

Institute for Law and Social Research (Washington, D.C.), 249

Institute for the Study of Drug Dependence (London), 210, 288

Interdepartmental Committee on Drug Addiction (England), 107, 108. *See also* Brain Committee

Iran, 6, 15–16

Israel, 16

Italy, 6

Jaffe, Jerome, 233

Japan, 167

Jeffrey, Charles, 177–78, 222

Jin Fuey Moy, 129–30, 144

Johnson, Lyndon B., 229, 230, 232

Journal of the American Medical Association, 41, 52–53, 167, 259

Judges Rules (England), 216–17

Judson, Horace Freeland, 32–34, 39, 90, 101, 171–72, 188, 282; on Brain Committee report, 107; on clinics, 188–89; on effects of heroin, 61–62; estimate of number of addicts, 298n5; *Heroin Addiction in Britain*, 5

Kaiko, Robert F., 76–77, 78

Kennedy, Edward, 31

Kennedy, John F., 226, 228–29

Khalkhali, Sadegh (Ayatollah), 16

Kho, Vincent, 7–8

King, Rufus, 132, 142, 228–29, 230, 308n20; *The Drug Hang-Up*, 119–20

Kittrie, Nicholas N.: *The Right to Be Different*, 159

Klein, Arnold William, Walter R. Cuskey, and William Krasner: *Drug-Trip Abroad*, 113–17

Kolb, Lawrence, 162

Korcok, Milan, 275
Kramer, John C., 41
Krasner, William, Walter R. Cuskey, and Arnold William Klein: *Drug-Trip Abroad*, 113–17

LAAM (L-alpha acetyl methadol), 317*n*54
Labate, Christina, and Jerome J. Platt: *Heroin Addiction*, 146
Laing, R. D.: *The Divided Self*, 202, 203
Lambert, Alexander, 48
Lamberti, Michel R., and Catherine Lamour: *The Second Opium War*, 288
Lamour, Catherine, and Michel R. Lamberti: *The Second Opium War*, 288
Lancet, The, 41–42, 64, 173, 190
Larimore, G. W., and Henry Brill: "The British Narcotic System," 96
Lasagna, Louis, 64–65, 66, 69, 77, 78, 82
Laudanum, 38
League of Nations, 54, 100; Subcommittee on Health and Opium, 48
Leech, Kenneth, 179, 180; *Keep the Faith Baby*, 179
Legalization, 241, 280–81; of heroin, 12, 29, 31, 239, 293; of heroin as medicine, 73, 75
Leibowitz, Barry L., 253
Leo, H., 42
Levorphanol, 103, 181, 201
Linder, Charles O., 130–31, 137, 141, 143
Lindesmith, Alfred R., 111, 119, 126–27, 141, 159, 162, 167, 308*n*38; attempts to silence, 164–65; criticized enforcement efforts, 132, 137; on legality of maintenance, 131; on Shreveport clinic, 148–49
Loan, William B., 64, 65–66
London: drug-related crime in, 212, 213, 250; numbers of addicts in, 19; Piccadilly Circus, 108, 113, 186
Lukoff, Irving, 260

McCarthy, Joseph, 141
McClean, Phillip, 198
McClure, John, 198
McCoy, Alfred, 319*n*18; *The Politics of Heroin in Southeast Asia*, 288
McGlothlin, William, 247
McNee, David, 212
McReynolds, James C., 130, 131
Madigan, Edward, 75
Madigan Bill, 293
Maher, John, 255–56

Maintenance, 145–46, 155, 169, 241, 284; of aged and infirm addicts, 135; England, 174, 175, 183, 195; institutional, 138, 140 (*see also* Narcotics clinics); legality of, under Harrison Act (U.S.), 128–29, 130, 131, 133–34, 140, 141; at ROMA, 205–10; treatment different from, 203–04. *See also* Addicts, stabilized; Heroin maintenance; Methadone maintenance; Treatment
Malaysia, Federation of, 7–8
Marijuana (cannabis, hemp, hashish, pot), 4, 15, 181, 213, 227; as medicine, 30, 60; prohibition of, 168; recreational use of, 98, 99; therapeutic potential of, 239
Mark (British addict), 98–99, 100, 107
Marks, Richard M., 25–26
Maryland State Medical Society, 60
Massam, Alan, 171–72
Mayle, Francis, 60
Medical Calvinism, 26, 29, 36, 137, 276
Medical practice, legitimate, 46, 185, 292, 295; effect of ban on heroin on, 57–58; Harrison Act and, 123–24, 138; includes maintenance of addicts, 276; intrusion of law-enforcement efforts into, 57–58, 96, 132–45, 233, 263–65; legal use of opiates in, 276–80; proper boundaries of, 89–97; in treatment of addiction, 90–97
Medical profession, England: re addiction control and treatment, 173–75; in attempt to define legitimate practice, 89–97; support for heroin as medicine, 100–11
Medical profession, U.S., 31, 46, 53, 137; opposed heroin as medicine, 55, 76, 101
Medical tribunals, 95, 110, 177, 184–85
Memorial Sloan-Kettering Cancer Center (New York City), 76–77
Mental health therapy. *See* Therapy
Meperidine (Demerol), 26, 103*n*
Methadon. *See* Methadone
Methadone, 62, 81, 103, 152, 181; injectable, 190, 192–98; oral, 190, 193, 197, 198, 199, 258, 264, 293; in treatment of pain, 65–66; use of, in England, 19–20, 186, 190–201, 209, 221, 223
Methadone blockade, 200, 258, 259, 272–73
Methadone maintenance, 17, 131, 199, 271, 272, 274; length of, 278–79
Methadone-maintenance programs (U.S.), 168, 170, 226–27, 232, 254, 256–66
Methaqualone (Quaalude), 181, 240
Methedrine, 180

Metsky, Ellen, 240
Miller, Henry G., 26
Miranda rules, 216
Misuse of Drugs Act (1971) (England), 110, 181, 182, 185, 294
Misuse of Drugs Act (Singapore), 8
Misuse of Drugs Regulations (1973) (England), 182
Mitchell, R. K., 202–03
Mitcheson, Martin, 190, 192, 193–96
Montefiore Hospital and Medical Center (New York), 25–26, 58
Moral philosophy, 36, 54
Morel-Lavallé, Dr., 43
Morphine, 4, 29, 38–39, 44, 57, 58, 62, 81, 181, 200, 221, 266; as drug of choice, 7, 148, 151–52, 154–55; maintenance on, 131; as medical substitute for heroin, 31, 34, 50, 63–67, 71–74, 75–78, 79
Morphine acetate salt, 75, 79, 304n23
Morphine addiction, 103, 154; heroin in treatment of, 40–42, 43, 59; treatment of, 90–97
Morphine sulfate salt, 304n23
Morris, Allison, 213
Morris, Norval, 288
Morris, Terence, 214, 218, 219
Mount, Balfour, 73
Murphy, Patrick, 252–53
Musto, David, 39, 44, 51, 132, 157, 163, 308nn20, 38; on legality of maintenance, 128–29; on narcotics clinics, 146–47, 148
Myocardial infarction, 67

NIDA. See National Institute on Drug Abuse (NIDA)
Narcotic Addict Rehabilitation Act (NARA) (1966), 159, 230–31
Narcotic Addict Treatment Act (1974) (U.S.), 262–63
Narcotic Drugs Import and Export Act (1922), 49
Narcotics, 5, 42, 53; and cause/effect in addiction, 55–56; international control of, 48–49; in pain control, 24–28; restrictions on, 123, 124. See also Drugs; and specific drugs, e.g., Heroin
Narcotics agents, 46, 57, 88, 126, 229, 234; and narcotics clinics, 147, 148, 153, 155–56. See also U.S. Department of the Treasury
Narcotics clinics: private (England), 179–90

(see also Drug-dependence clinics [England]); U.S., 145, 146–56, 162, 187, 221
Narcotics hospitals (farms), federal, 158–59, 170; Lexington, Ky., 256–57
National Cancer Institute (U.S.), 68, 75, 76, 79
National Commission on Marihuana and Drug Abuse (U.S.), 59, 229, 246–47, 269
National Conference on Methadone Treatment (U.S.), 234
National Health Service (England), 174, 180
National Hospice Organization, 31
National Institute of Mental Health (U.S.), 298n5
National Institute on Drug Abuse (NIDA), 5, 10, 17, 60, 233, 240, 243, 247; The British Narcotics System, 243; Client Oriented Data Acquisition Process (CODAP), 317n49; employees in, 242; study of heroin as medicine, 76–77, 79
National Institutes of Health, 30
National Organization for the Reform of Marijuana Laws (U.S.), 314n21
National Research Council, 139–40, 174
Neal, Helen, 82
New Orleans, 147, 149
New York Academy of Medicine, 163
New York City: drug-related crime in, 212, 213, 251–53; heroin abuse in, 44; narcotics clinics in, 147–48, 152, 155, 221; police department, 51
New Zealand, 11, 12
Newman, Barry, 8–9
Nixon, Richard, 228, 236, 237, 241, 242, 298n5; drug-control efforts of, 2–3, 18, 231–36, 246, 288
Nutt, Levi G., 160
Nyswander, Marie, 226–27, 257–60, 262, 264, 266, 272, 282–83

ODAP. See Office of Drug Abuse Policy (ODAP) (U.S.)
O'Brien, William, 31–32
O'Donnell, John A., 140–41, 159, 319n15
Office of Drug Abuse Law Enforcement (U.S.), 231
Office of Drug Abuse Policy (ODAP) (U.S.), 30, 239–40, 245, 246, 297n5
O'Keefe, Charles, 32
Opiates, 4, 6–7, 37–38, 121, 172, 271; addictive danger of, 43; control of, 45–46, 181;

legal use of, 38–39, 42, 276–80; are psychoactive drugs, 283; research re, as medicine, 59–84; synthetic, 26, 103*n*
Opium, 5, 15, 16, 17, 42, 201, 293; control of
trade of, 52–54, 120–21, 122, 236, 238,
320*n*18; regulation of, 45, 87; use of, in
treatment, 271–72
Opium smoking, 6, 45, 167
Orlick, Martin, 150
Overdose(s), 152, 243, 281
Oxycodone (Percodan), 201, 312*n*40

PCP, 246, 292
Pain control, 22–28, 57, 84, 94, 95; morphine
in treatment of, 63–69; using heroin, 30,
31, 59. *See also* Heroin as medicine
Palmer, Hartmut, 12–13
Paregoric, 38
Patent medicines, 38–39
Pekkanen, 246
Pellens, Mildred, 150; Charles Terry and, *The
Opium Problem*, 40
Pelletier, Monique, 14
Penalties. *See* Punishment
Pethidine, 103, 200
Petro, John, 176, 179–80, 184, 187, 221,
310*n*13
Pettey, G. E.: "The Heroin Habit Another
Curse," 43
Phenadoxone (Heptalgin), 105–06, 201
Phenazocine (Prinadol), 201, 312*n*40
Phoenix [houses], 207
Physeptone (methadone), 209
Physicians' Protective Association (N.Y.C.),
147
Platt, Jerome J., and Christina Labate: *Heroin
Addiction*, 146
Police, 11, 46, 252–53; regulations of, 131,
132; role of, in drug area, 286–87. *See also*
Drug-law enforcement; Narcotics agents
Politics: of drug addiction, 2–3, 30, 288; and
drug policy, 229–34, 235
Porter, Stephen G., 49, 50, 51, 52, 101, 158
Porter Narcotic Farm Act, 158
Possession of controlled substances, 8, 126–
27, 164, 181, 239
Presidents (U.S.): involvement in drug policy,
229–41
Prisons: addicts confined in, 154, 157–59,
170, 217–18, 227; as treatment, 228, 254.
See also Punishment

Privacy, right to, 80–81
Psychiatric treatment, 188, 203, 209–10, 221,
224
Psychoactive drugs, 54, 283, 290–91; benefit/
harm ratio of, 99–100; legal controls on, 45;
varying impact of, 36
Psychosis: heroin in prevention of, 202–03
Psychotherapy, 145–46, 199, 259, 271, 293
Punishment, 7, 8–9, 158, 163–64, 181, 233–
34; England, 181, 217–18; New York State,
251
Pure Food and Drug Act of 1906, 45

ROMA (Rehabilitation of Metropolitan Ad-
dicts), 204–10, 224, 268
Rainey, Henry, 44
Raja Azlan Shah, 8
Rangel, Charles B., 251, 252
Rap [houses], 207
Ratigan, Thomas P., Jr., 141–43, 144
Rehabilitation, 159, 206–07, 227, 228;
through methadone maintenance, 259–60.
See also Cure; Treatment
Reinarman, Craig, 150
Relapse(s), 93, 148, 159, 256, 285; at Shreve-
port clinic, 155
Respiratory illness, 39–40, 42
Richardson, Charles, 49–50
Rieff, Peter, 10–11
Robbins, Lee N., 319*n*15
Robinson v. *California*, 157
Rockefeller, Nelson, 248, 251
Rockefeller Institute (N.Y.C.), 257
Roe v. *Wade*, 80
Rolleston, Humphrey, 90
Rolleston Committee, 124, 201
Rolleston Committee report, 90–97, 102,
103–04, 110, 113, 135*n*, 136, 154, 173,
182, 199, 292; favored institutional treat-
ment, 157; on length of treatment, 284–85;
on medical tribunals, 177, 184
Roper, Daniel C., 134–36, 137, 146, 147,
168
Rourke, James M., 184
Royal Marsden Hospital, London, 35–36

SAODAP. *See* Special Action Office for Drug
Abuse Prevention (SAODAP) (U.S.)
Sachar, Edward J., 25–26
St. Christopher's Hospice (London), 33–34,
35–36, 69, 73–74

St. Luke's Hospital (N.Y.C.), 26, 58
Sammons, James H., 63–64, 65, 66
Sarawak, 7–8
Satchell, Michael, 34, 35
Saunders, Cicely, 33–35, 66, 69, 73, 78
Saunders, Kevin Patrick (Mark), 98
Schein, Philip, 77–78
Schur, Edwin M., 111–12; *Narcotic Addiction in Britain and America*, 86, 111
Schur-Lindesmith thesis, 111–12, 113
Scotland Yard, 98; Drugs Squad, 212
Searchfield, Robert, 171–72, 310*n*1
Seidler, Gary, 275
Sentences. *See* Punishment
Serturner, F. W., 38
Shanghai Opium Commission, 45
Shapiro, Eugene L.: "The Right of Privacy and Heroin Use . . . ," 80
Shreveport (La.) clinic, 57, 147, 148–56, 187, 308*n*38; as model, 148–49, 245, 292, 295
Silberman, Charles, 18, 231, 261, 287–88; *Criminal Violence, Criminal Justice*, 2–3, 247
Singapore, 6, 8–9, 167
Single Convention on Narcotic Drugs, 102
Smith, Jean Paul, 7
Social control: vs. treatment, 125, 211, 224–25
Social policy, 9, 13, 111–12, 113, 162–68, 219; re benefit/danger of narcotics, 99–100; re heroin use, 4–6, 44–45; through taxing power (U.S.), 119–24. *See also* Balance, impossible
Social problems caused by addicts, 239, 242; tolerable/intolerable, 245–53, 276. *See also* Crime, drug-related
Social trade-offs, 189, 190, 196, 269, 277, 278, 280, 281, 291
Socialized medicine (England), 96, 201
Spear, H. B., 82, 89, 90, 93, 96, 99, 177–78, 183, 222, 266; on Brain committee, 102; critical of drug clinics, 211–12; "The Growth of Heroin Addiction in the United Kingdom," 98
Special Action Office for Drug Abuse Prevention (SAODAP) (U.S.), 232, 233, 237, 240
Standing Conference on Drug Abuse (England), 19
Stimson, Gerry, 189
Stroup, Keith, 314*n*21
Sunday Times (London), 12, 190
Sutton, Percy E., 226, 251–52

Swan, Christopher, 176, 180, 184, 187, 188, 197, 221
Switzerland, 15
Sydenham, Thomas, 38
Synanon, 207, 254, 255

Tanner, Terence E., 204–10, 211, 268
Terry, Charles E., 148; Mildred Pellens and, *The Opium Problem*, 40, 150
Tetrahydrocannabinol (THC), 239
Thailand, 6, 9–10, 167
Therapeutic communities (TC's; concept houses), 207, 254–56, 271
Therapy, 204, 225, 254; heroin, 284–85, 293. *See also* Psychotherapy
Thompson, Linwood, 18–19
Tolerance, concept of, 104, 152
Transcendental meditation, 290, 293
Trawick, J. D., 43–44
Treatment, 9, 12, 17, 85, 135–36, 238; ambulatory, 153, 161, 186, 258, 275, 279–82; ambulatory: illegal (U.S.), 128–29, 131, 138–39; approved methods of, 139–40, 145–60; choice of drugs in, 270–76; community culture and, 153–54, 155, 187–88, 268; vs. control, 224–25; different from maintenance, 203–04; in England, 103, 111–17, 182–83, 188–89; experiments with, 193–96; goals of, 189, 190, 224–25; humane approach to, 7, 91, 132, 135, 156, 159–60, 204, 227, 233, 236, 292; idealism in, 235, 242; individualized, 223–24; institutional, 139, 140, 145, 156–60 (*see also* Commitment; Narcotics clinics); length of, 278–79, 284–85; models of, 269–70; no specific, 187; modes of, 285, 293–94; nonpunitive, 230–31; options in, 267–95; reductive ambulatory system, 94, 133, 134, 136, 148; regulation of, 268; at Shreveport clinic, 149–55; success rates in, 254. *See also* Cure; Dosage; Maintenance; Relapse(s)
Tripp, Margaret, 188, 197, 282
Twycross, Robert, 58, 75, 77, 78, 79, 301*n*24; on heroin as medicine, 68–74

United Nations, 54; Commission on Narcotic Drugs, 100, 161
United States: attempts to stop international drug trafficking, 45–46, 232, 235, 237–38, 241, 242–43; battle against drugs, 17, 18, 37, 54, 100, 232 (*see also* U.S. Department

of the Treasury); as center of heroin abuse, 6, 7; centrist politics in, 161–65, 226; drug-control program in, 113–70, 226–66; drug-related crime in, 213, 229, 231, 232; future of heroin situation in, 267–95; heroin-related deaths in, 12, 13–14, 18; as model of drug control, 1–2, 7, 21, 96–97, 167–68, 289; numbers of addicts in, 9–10, 20, 44, 49, 140–41, 147, 175, 243, 245–46; operational principles of addiction control and treatment, 168, 169–70; police powers in, 120; prohibition of heroin, 89–90 (*see also* Harrison Narcotic Act [U.S.]); proposals for reform of drug control in, 294–95; search, seizure, arrest in, 214–17; social structure in, and addiction, 288–89; toleration of drug problem in, 245–53, 276; youth unrest in, 175–76

U.S. Army: addicts in, 44; heroin use in, 15, 17; prohibition of heroin in, 47

U.S. Bureau of Internal Revenue, 147, 160; agents enforcing Harrison Act, 125

U.S. Bureau of the Census, 249

U.S. Congress, House: Select Committee on Narcotic Abuse and Control, 11; Ways and Means Committee, 49–52, 121

U.S. Constitution, Fourteenth Amendment, 80

U.S. Department of Health, Education, and Welfare, 240

U.S. Department of Justice, 234

U.S. Department of the Treasury, 127, 234; destroyed Shreveport clinic, 155–56; enforcement of drug laws, 131, 162; Federal Bureau of Narcotics, 146, 160, 161, 162, 163, 164, 167–68, 175, 229, 233, 257, 298; regulations and directives, 132–45, 146

U.S. District Court (Pittsburgh), 126

U.S. Food and Drug Administration, 262, 263–64, 265–66

U.S. General Accounting Office: *Heroin Statistics Can Be Made More Reliable*, 244

U.S. *Journal of Drug and Alcohol Dependence*, 59, 275

U.S. Public Health Service, 49, 54, 147

U.S. Supreme Court, 46, 80, 141, 143, 157, 214, 282; decisions in violation of the Harrison Act, 125–31, 132, 133

United States v. *Behrman*, 130

United States v. *Doremus*, 127–28, 133, 134, 136, 146

United States v. *Jin Fuey Moy*, 126

University College Hospital Drug Dependency Clinic (England), 193, 196

Vera Institute (N.Y.C.), 269

Volk, Lester, 162

Vollmer, August, 162

Volstead Act, 160

Vorenberg, James, 260

Waldorf, Dan, 150

Walker-Smith, Derek, 101

Washington, D.C., 18–19, 20, 234, 253

Washington Post, 16, 19, 20, 22, 241, 246

Watson, Henry W., 49

Webb, Dr., 128–29, 144

Webb v. *United States*, 128–29, 133, 134, 136, 146

Weil, Andrew, 267, 271–72, 290

Wessell, Otto, 299n25

West Germany, 12–14

Western Europe, 12–15, 17

Wheatly, John, 89–90

White House Conference on Narcotic and Drug Abuse, Ad Hoc Panel, 65, 228

White Paper on Drug Abuse, 235–36, 245

Wilkes, Eric, 35, 74–75

Williams, John B.: *Narcotics and Drug Dependence*, 40

Wiltshaw, Eve, 35–36, 75

Wish, Eric, 249

Withdrawal, 94, 115, 135, 170; abrupt, 91; in institutional programs, 139, 140, 146, 148; tolerance for, 203. *See also* Methadone maintenance

Woodcock, Jasper, 198, 199

World Health Organization, 100, 282, 318n16

World Narcotics Research Foundation, 165

Wright, C. R. Alder, 39

Wright, Hamilton, 41

Yoga, 290

Young, Jock, 176–77

Zacune, James, 217

Zen Buddhism, 290, 293

Zinberg, Norman, 291

Zorza, Jane, 22–24